CHRISTIAN ETHICS

Sources of the Living Tradition

Edited with Introductions by

WALDO BEACH
DUKE UNIVERSITY

and

H. RICHARD NIEBUHR
YALE UNIVERSITY

SECOND EDITION

JOHN WILEY & SONS
New York • Chichester • Brisbane • Toronto

ISBN 0 471 07007-6

Library of Congress Catalog Card Number: 72–91122

PRINTED IN THE UNITED STATES OF AMERICA

10 9 8 7 6 5 4 3

PREFACE

Underlying the preparation of this book has been a belief that the essentials of Christian ethics can best be presented through the writings of great Christian thinkers of all ages. It is only through such writings that the full richness of the Christian tradition can be portrayed in its immediate applicability to present-day ethical questions. Yet the most important source materials are usually to be found only in out-of-the-way places, buried in unwieldy and expensive editions. To meet this problem we have tried in this volume to gather together a representative selection of these materials for use in college and seminary courses.

While the greater part of the book is devoted to original source materials, it is designed to be more than a mere collection of "readings." An introductory chapter summarizes the contribution of the Bible to Christian ethical thought and practice. Each subsequent chapter is provided with an extensive introduction which will help to place the selections in their historical context and to clarify their contribution to the Christian tradition as a whole. The final chapter surveys current trends and relates them to the main lines of earlier movements.

The historical organization of the source material is designed to make clear the development of the major themes of Christian ethical thought. At the same time, the selections from the work of each thinker were made with an eye to their universal and undated relevance. We have tried to let each major figure speak for himself and at sufficient length to warrant close study and independent reflection. The task of selection has been a hard one. There is an embarrassment of riches among the many Christian writings of the last two thousand years which could claim a rightful place in this volume. The rigid exclusion of personal favorites has been painful, and at times the final choice has necessarily been somewhat arbitrary. Yet the presentation of substantial blocks of material from relatively few representative thinkers seems preferable to the compilation of an anthology of brief selections from a larger number of writers.

The book may be used in a number of ways as a textbook for introductory courses in Christian ethics. The selections from each thinker could provide material for a comparative approach to the explication of the meaning of the Christian life. Alternatively, each chapter might be taken on its own as a point of departure for the discussion of one or more facets of Christian ethical theory, such as the Christian view of human nature, the problem of freedom and law, the concept of love, or the relation of the Christian to culture. Or again, the historical sequence of the chapters might serve as a guiding thread in a course traversing the development of the Christian ideal in Western culture. Though the book is mainly designed for the use of the undergraduate student, we hope that it will also be of value in theological seminaries as a general introduction to more detailed study. And we shall be pleased if individual readers outside the academic world can find in these pages a way to a richer appreciation of the Christian tradition in its contemporary context.

The planning and execution of this volume has been a process of mutual collaboration. Professor Niebuhr undertook the special responsibility for the selection of material and the introduction for Chapters 1, 8, 9, and 13. The remaining chapters were the responsibility of Professor Beach. A special word of gratitude is due to Professor Paul Holmer for selecting materials and writing the introduction for Chapter 14.

The editors would like to record their indebtedness for many kinds of assistance in the preparation of this book: to Professors Millar Burrows, W. D. Davies, Robert Cushman, Ray C. Petry, David Shipley, Shelton Smith, and Franklin Young for their counsel and critical suggestions in the preparation of many of these chapters; to the Duke University Research Council and the Carnegie Foundation for the Advancement of Teaching for financial assistance; to Miss Ruby Bailey and Mrs. Helen Hodges for clerical help as exact as indefatigable; and to numerous classes of students, on whom some of the ideas and interpretations herein have been tried out, and from whom the editors have learned much.

Durham, N. C. — Waldo Beach
New Haven, Conn. — H. Richard Niebuhr
February, 1955

PREFACE TO SECOND EDITION

Since the first publication of this source book in 1955, much has transpired in the field of Christian ethics. Though the death of Professor H. Richard Niebuhr in 1962 renders a collaborative revision in a sense no longer possible, it has seemed well nonetheless to bring this collection of major sources up to date. The substance of the changes consists in a thorough revision of the bibliographies of Further Readings at the end of each chapter. The dating indicates the latest editions available. Three chapters have been added: one on ecumenical ethics in its Protestant form, one on Roman Catholic ecumenical ethics, and a concluding overview of current trends.

W. B.

March, 1973

CONTENTS

CHRISTIAN ETHICS

INTRODUCTION

What does it mean to be a Christian? This question is asked anew by the seeker in each generation within the Christian tradition. Though he may have acquired certain "official" or automatic answers from his upbringing in a Christian environment, he may be puzzled by, or be restive with, the copybook formulae or the lecture notes. He may want to find out for himself the inward meaning of the old Christian terms learned from his parents and teachers. His search may lead him to the recovery of insights which his contemporaries have forgotten or perverted.

This volume is an attempt to gather together out of Christian history the most searching answers to the question of what it means to be a Christian, answers which by reason of their integrity and penetration have proved the most impressive to other Christians in their quest for a meaningful faith. For the most part, this is a source book of readings, where each Christian speaks for himself or confesses his faith about what he has found to be the essential Christian truth. This must of necessity range far beyond matters sometimes defined as "ethics," that is, particulars of right and wrong, into the more important concerns of theology, that is, faiths about the nature of God and man which lie behind human actions as their source and sanction. In its full sense, ethics deals not so much with the "whats" as with the "whys" of human behavior.

The One and the Many in Christian Ethics

One important preliminary matter to raise is whether these answers given in Christian history and found in these pages are one or many. It will not do to say, as is commonly done, that being a Christian means doing *one* particular thing or fulfilling one particular law, such as avoiding fleshly vices, or following the Golden Rule, or being kind, or believing in the brotherhood of man. As a matter of fact, to take one of these as the sum of the Christian life is quite to miss its point. If the Christian life could be defined in terms of some simple moral injunction out of the Bible or anywhere else, all subsequent Christian reflection would be unnecessary reiteration, closer or further away from the given answer. On the other hand, it will not do to say that the different beliefs of Christians are completely *plural* and unrelated, as though the ethical problems of each age were entirely novel, and the Christian approach in each case unprecedented. Such pluralism would require us to say that what it means to be a Christian in the twentieth century is something entirely different from what it meant in the first century. "Christian" then would be only a family name, and have no reference to an integrity which unites Christians in all ages.

Clearly, then, we are led to recognize that Christian ethics in history is both one and many. There is a certain unity in Christian writings, an inner resemblance shared even by the most apparently diverse thinkers. The Christian monk of the twelfth century is more akin to the Christian social reformer of the nineteenth century than may appear at first sight. This kindred spirit that unifies Christians in diverse centuries and places shows up more readily when we look at them in comparison with people whose behavior springs from non-Christian faiths, such as a faith that bodily enjoyments are ultimate or that the State is god. It must be granted, of course, that rarely is faith found in pure form; Christian and non-Christian faiths are usually found in complex mixture in most people whose "official" religion is Christianity.

What makes for the unity of Christian ethics is not, as with scientific knowledge, a continuity in the progressive accumulation of knowledge, whereby one generation adds to the fund of wisdom built up by its forebears. The latest book on Christian ethics is not necessarily the wisest one. For that matter, the earliest Christian book, the Bible, remains in a certain sense the main source book of Christian insight. Nor can we say that what makes for the one in the many Christian answers is a common body of rational philosophical premises, from which a variety of particulars are deduced.

The integrity of Christian ethics is better described as derived from a certain shared faith about the nature of God as Ultimate Reality and man's proper response to him. The unity of Christian ethics lies in its God-centered faith. By virtue of the kind of God it relies on as final, as being the Sovereign Power of the Universe, its Creator and Ruler and Redeemer, whose nature is made known in Jesus Christ, Christian ethics says in many different ways that the Christian life consists in the response of obedient love to God in whatever he wills. "This is the first commandment of all." And in the human sphere what God wills is the love of neighbor after the manner of God's love to man. Within the variables of Christian ethical theories, there is a constant *triadic* relation—the "vertical" relation of the believing and acting self to God, and the "horizontal" relation of the self to other selves—a relation in which God is, so to speak, the "middle term." How and why the neighbor is loved depends on how and why God is loved. Thus, in Jesus' summary of the law, the Second Commandment, to love the neighbor, is described as like or part of the First.

Some versions of the Christian ethic stress the vertical line, it would seem, almost to the exclusion of the horizontal, as with medieval mysticism (Chap. 6). Other versions, such as the movement within Protestantism known as the Social Gospel (Chap. 15), seem so preoccupied with the horizontal relationships that they lose sight of the vertical or else treat the triad so as to make God only a means to the surpassing end of social reform. Yet even in these divergent Christian viewpoints the triadic relationship is not wholly upset, and in a certain sense both parts of the great commandment are held normative.

The Sources of the Many

If the right love of God and man, after the great commandment, is the one theme integral to all types of Christian ethics, what accounts for its manyness? Why should there be such a wide range of particular answers to the meaning of the Christian life, whereby perennially the ethical formulations of one generation come in time to seem partial or distorted to those of a later generation, who then take on themselves the task of stating in a new way what the Christian life is?

There is neither space nor need here to go into the numerous explanations for the variations on the main theme of Christian ethics. There are, as a matter of fact, several cogent ways of accounting for its manyness. Approaching the problem philosophically, it may be said that there are two major types of Christian ethics: the ethics of obligation and the ethics of aspiration with subtypes under each head. The ethics of obligation or duty, the ethics of "the right," starts with the question: What is required by the great law or lawgiver? Different answers are then forthcoming, depending on which authority is taken to be final for the Christian as mediating the will of God: the Bible, the Holy Spirit, the conscience, the church. The ethics of aspiration, the ethics of "the good," starts with the Aristotelian question: What is the end-of-ends, to be hoped and striven for as the great and final goal? The subtypes under this heading vary with the notions of the Christian end: the vision of God, self-realization, the brotherhood of man on earth, and others.

Again—to take a different point of view—the diversity in Christian ethics may be seen as the result of a dialectic process, of a tension between polar opposites, within which one type of Christian swings towards one side and another moves, by reaction, in the counter direction. Some forms of Christian ethics, for instance, stress law and discipline, others "grace" and freedom. The triad discussed above affords another example: While one Christian, protesting the futility of externalism in works of charity, may look heavenward and claim the vision of God to be the essence of Christianity, another will regard such "mysticism" as socially irresponsible and find for himself the meaning of the Christian life in the amelioration of the social conditions of his day. Thus emerge "God-ward" and "man-ward" types of Christian ethics, with intricate combinations of the two.

A dialectic pattern may also be found in the various solutions to which Christians have resorted in order to resolve the tension between the demands of God-in-Christ, on the one side, and the demands of "the world" or culture on the other. Proceeding from this more or less sociological viewpoint, one finds both ancient and contemporary examples of those uncompromising Christians whose fidelity to Christ requires them outright to renounce culture as anti-Christ. Others, however, try to resolve the tension by conforming Christ to their culture, that is, by cutting down his demands to the size of the best their secular civilization offers. Still other Christians find their answer in some median position, which will be in one fashion or another a double response, affirming responsibility both to Christ and culture.[1]

The important thing to note about these explanations of the varieties of Christian ethics is that they all are of considerable help in the study of Christian thought in history, but no one of them turns out to be finally adequate by itself. No major Christian thinker fits quite neatly into the compartment made for him, and the complexity of influences on any one makes categorizing hazardous. One must take these theories, then, only as rough and ready ways of seeing particular contrasts, and more striking resemblances, among those whose common inheritance is stronger than their differences.

1 For the explication of this typology, the student is referred to H. Richard Niebuhr, *Christ and Culture* (New York: Harper and Row, 1951), where five main types are delineated. This volume might be treated valuably as interpretive parallel reading for the material in this source book.

Other major works interpreting the variety of historical types of Christian ethics are the following: Ernst Troeltsch, *The Social Teachings of the Christian Churches*, 2 vols. (New York: Macmillan, 1931. Republished, New York: Harper and Row, 1960); Anders Nygren, *Agape and Eros, a Study of the Christian Idea of Love* (1 vol. ed.; Philadelphia: Westminster, 1953);

It is even more important to stress the danger of taking any one among the variety of ethical viewpoints as *the* Christian way, to the exclusion of all others. It would be a mistaken approach to the chapters in this book to have decided ahead of time that the Roman or Lutheran or Baptist or Methodist distinction should constitute the only authorized version of the Christian Gospel. The materials here all convey authentically Christian insights. They represent the responsible reflections of Christians in a kind of historical conversation with each other, learning from each other even while protesting and correcting each other where they feel they must. Almost entirely, the great chapters of Christian ethical theory have been written in a confessional rather than a polemical mood. That is, they are written with the disposition of one who says, I have found this or this to be true of the Christian life, rather than as attempts to refute another's claim. Thus they find something new in the old, even where they are not conscious of the fact that there is also something old in the new.

The procedure used in this volume is a historical one. Not that this is the most arresting or profound way of presenting Christian answers. But it represents the method which, it is hoped, may prove the most useful for the teacher and student. It must be stated clearly at the outset, however, that this book is in no wise intended as a history of Christian ethics, tracing the main currents that make up the complex stream of Christian thinking about the good life. It is presented rather as a group of representative viewpoints, by no means exhaustive of all possible ones, taken out of the Christian past and addressed to the seeking Christian in the present.

The historical arrangement of materials is not intended to convey the impression that these are "period pieces" of possible antiquarian interest but quite remote from the urgent

---

James Gustafson, *Christ and the Moral Life* (New York: Harper and Row, 1968); Edward LeRoy Long, Jr., *A Survey of Christian Ethics* (New York: Oxford University Press, 1967). A useful sourcebook of historic readings is George W. Forell (ed.), *Christian Social Teachings* (Garden City, N.Y.: Doubleday, 1966).

dilemmas of present decision. The living situation of the university student is, if nothing else, a situation where he is under the necessity of making ethical choices. Whether they be choices about vocation, marriage, recreation, or political or economic matters, they always involve the hard options between right and wrong ways of dealing with the self and other persons. These foreground choices are made against a background of commitments, of which the student may be only dimly aware, about what is of supreme value and importance in the universe. These choices are always of a religious sort, using the word "religious" here much more broadly than to mean "church." This fact puts the seeking student, the "sober" man as Kierkegaard calls him, in essentially the same position with others of the past who shared similar dilemmas. In other words, the awareness of being a moral self makes the individual contemporaneous with those in the past who have wrestled with their problems and have come to their tentative conclusions. To be sure, there are certain peculiar circumstances of each age and place in these chapters which are remote and dated, just as the situation of the university student has its own uniqueness, which leads him to feel perhaps that no one has ever confronted *this* problem before. But if he will listen for the universal element *within* the transient and particular features of historical answers, he may discover not only that he is in straits that are perennial, but also that there may be wisdom and guidance for him in traditional answers.

Chapter 1

INTRODUCTION TO BIBLICAL ETHICS

The Bible has always been and will doubtless remain the chief source book for the study of Christian ethics. For one thing, it supplies the necessary historical introduction to the thought of the later theologians. Although it is difficult to understand Clement, Augustine, Thomas Aquinas, and other Christian thinkers about the moral life without reference to the grand line of classical, that is, Greek and Roman, ethical theory, it is impossible to think their thoughts with them if their Biblical heritage is ignored. When the Protestant thinkers are under consideration the need for knowledge of Scriptures becomes even more important; to try to read Luther or Calvin intelligibly without knowledge of Paul, the Gospels, the Law, and the Prophets, is like trying to understand Lincoln's speeches without knowledge of the Declaration of Independence and the Constitution of the United States. Since Christian ethics, by and large, is the moral reflection which goes on in the Christian community it is at least as necessary, if one would participate in it, to understand it in its early and most creative periods as it is to know the early and creative beginnings of a national or cultural society if one would understand its later development.

The Bible is not, however, only the book of Christian beginnings.[1] It is an authority for Christians in many and

[1] Since the present volume is devoted to Christian ethics the significance of the Old Testament for Jewish ethics need not be considered. It is as great, of course, as is the importance of both Testaments for Christians. See G. F. Moore, *Judaism* (Cambridge: Harvard University Press, 1932), I, 235 ff.; II, 79 ff.

unique ways. Its meaning for them may be compared with the meaning of a written constitution for a national community, or of sacred writings such as the Zend-Avesta and the Koran for certain religious communities. But though its authority for them is like these, yet it is unique; its significance is intimately connected with the Christian experience and concept of revelation. The Bible is the book in which the story of the self-disclosure of God, his nature and will, to Israel and to the world, is recorded. However Christians enumerate and relate to each other the various authorities through which God makes himself and his will known to men, they always include among them—along with reason, nature, spiritual illumination, the church, and religious experience—the historical revelation and therewith the Bible as its record. Sometimes it is for them the direct and only vehicle of revelation, quite apart from nature, reason, and so on. Then they call it simply "Word of God." Sometimes it is for them more the record of witnesses of divine revelation. Then it is a word of man about God, without which present revelation of God would be unintelligible and, indeed, unrecognized. One may think of it simply as the book of the great dialogue between man and God in which what God has said to men is recorded as well as their answers to him and his replies to their answers. From this point of view all later Christian life is but a continuation of that dialogue in which reference must always be made to what has gone before in the conversation and in which every generation needs to begin not where its predecessors left off but where the Bible ends.[2]

The question has often been raised whether there is enough unity in the thought of the Scriptures on any subject, including morality, to permit a summary statement of Biblical ideas. The diversity in the Bible is indeed very great. Its sixty-six books contain elements from a history of more than fifteen hundred years. The human actions which become in it the subject of moral criticism range from the barbaric feuds of primitive clans and the despotic acts of

[2] Further light will be cast on this meaning of the Scriptures for Christians by the ensuing chapters.

Oriental monarchs to the aberrations of imperial Roman justice and of sophisticated Hellenistic philosophy. Great also is the variety of standards employed in criticizing or commanding actions. In the Gospels, for instance, Jesus is quoted as setting into opposition what had been taught "to the men of old" with what he now requires. Then the law of vengeance prevailed, "an eye for an eye, a tooth for a tooth," but now the demand is, "Do not resist one who is evil." In the Old Testament, also, sharp antitheses occur, as when the writers of the books of Ezra and Ruth judge the marriage of Jews to non-Jewish women in opposite fashions and with the use of differing principles.[3] There is variety in fundamental ethical attitudes. The Book of Deuteronomy demands rigorous and full obedience to all the laws; but the writer of Ecclesiastes is a gentle cynic who counsels men not to take anything too seriously: "Be not righteous overmuch, and do not make yourself overwise; why should you destroy yourself? Be not wicked overmuch, neither be a fool; why should you die before your time?" (Eccles. 7:16-17.) There are also profound differences in the scales of value that are employed at different times or by different men. Prosperity, health, and longevity are the highly prized rewards of virtue according to the First Psalm; fellowship with God is the one great good desired by the writer of the Seventy-third.

Both uncritical worshippers of the Bible and equally uncritical detractors have made such uses of this variety that the impression of diversity in scriptural ethics has been exaggerated. The former have attached absolute authority to some single commandment and so have come into conflict with persons who made some other injunction absolute; as when, for instance, certain groups of Christians, basing their position on Jesus' statement about nonresistance, have been arrayed against those who accepted as fundamental Paul's statement about obedience to the state (Matt. 5:39; Rom.

[3] Ezra 9 and 10; cf. Neh. 13:23 ff.; cf. Ruth. All Biblical references and quotations hereinafter are to the Revised Standard Version (New York: Thomas Nelson & Sons, 1946, 1952) and used by the permission of the Division of Christian Education of the National Council of the Churches of Christ in the United States of America.

13:1-7). The uncritical detractors of the Bible have attempted to show its unreliability or even its deceptiveness as a moral guide by pointing out such conflicts and by calling attention to the primitive character of certain ethical standards reported in the book. Yet the unity of Scriptures in moral teaching, as well as in other respects, is more impressive and effective than its diversity. Understanding of that unity doubtless requires repeated and careful reading of these writings. It is at least as difficult to define once and for all exactly wherein that unity consists as it is to state in any final fashion what it is that gives unity to the democratic literature of America or to the philosophical writings of the Greeks, or, to take an example from another sphere, what it is that unifies the manifold artistic production of a Shakespeare, a Rembrandt, or a Beethoven.

A good beginning toward attaining understanding of this unity, as well as of the diversity in unity, may be made by discovering first of all what some of the main ideas and themes of Biblical ethics are and then by tracing their development in a few great documents representative of various periods of Biblical history.[4]

The discovery of these ideas and themes is made relatively easy by the fact that in the course of Hebrew-Jewish and Christian history, as portrayed in the Scriptures, repeated efforts were made by leaders of thought and action to summarize the ethical teaching they had inherited, appropriated, and sought to transmit. The early Christian church stated in one sentence what it had learned about man's duty from its Lord and from the prophets and law-givers who preceded him. That sentence read either, "Love your neighbor as yourself," or "Walk in love as Christ loved us."[5] Over and over again this is presented as the essence of right conduct. It is

[4] The following writings are recommended for reading and study in connection with this chapter: the Book of the Covenant, in Exod. 20:22-23:33; The Book of the Prophet Amos; the Sermon on the Mount in Matt. 5-7; the Epistle of Paul to the Romans.

[5] Rom. 13:8, 10; Eph. 5:2, 25; Gal. 5:14; John 13:34; 15:12, 17; I John 3:11 (see 2:7 ff.); 4:7, 11, 20, 21; II John 1:5, 6; Jas. 2:8. See also I Pet. 1:22; Heb. 13:1.

called the royal law; in it the whole law is fulfilled; it is a new commandment, as coming from Jesus Christ, but it is an old commandment, too, as representing the essence of all the words of God spoken through the prophets. In stating the principle of right conduct in this fashion it is evident that the church was dependent on Jesus' own summarization of the "law and the prophets," a summarization that the rabbis of Jesus' time were probably also making. According to the story in Mark, Jesus was asked by a scribe, "Which commandment is the first of all?" He answered, "The first is, 'Hear, O Israel, the Lord our God, the Lord is one: and you shall love the Lord your God with all your heart, and with all your soul, and with all your mind, and with all your strength.' The second is this, 'You shall love your neighbor as yourself.' There is no other commandment greater than these." In another version of the story he is recorded to have said, "On these two commandments depend all the law and the prophets," while in a third account the summary is ascribed to a Jewish lawyer and commended by Jesus.[6] The summary of ethical principles in the Gospels is closely related to earlier prophetic statements of the essence of God's requirements and of human duties. Micah's formulation of this essence is best known and most widely used: "He has showed you, O man, what is good; and what does the Lord require of you but to do justice, and to love kindness, and to walk humbly with your God?"[7] Finally, the Ten Commandments have served throughout centuries of Biblical and post-Biblical history as such a summary, whether or not they were first designed for this purpose. It is widely believed that they were all originally stated in terse manner, about as follows:

> I am the Lord your God, who brought you out of the
> land of Egypt, out of the house of bondage.

[6] Mark 12:28-31; Matt. 22:35-40; Luke 10:25-27. The first part of the double commandment is a quotation from Deut. 6:5, the second from Lev. 19:18.

[7] Mic. 6:8. Similar epitomes of the law occur frequently in the prophets though they are not stated as summaries. One of these is to be found in Hos. 12:6: "So you, by the help of your God, return, hold fast to love and justice, and wait continually for your God."

I. You shall have no other gods before me.
II. You shall not make yourself a graven image.
III. You shall not take the name of the Lord your God in vain.
IV. Remember the Sabbath day.
V. Honor your father and your mother.
VI. You shall not kill.
VII. You shall not commit adultery.
VIII. You shall not steal.
IX. You shall not bear false witness against your neighbor.
X. You shall not covet anything that is your neighbor's.[8]

Suggestive as are these summaries of Biblical ethics their significance does not appear until all the moral struggles in individuals and society of which they represent the outcome are taken into view and until all the detailed answers to special questions of "Why and How, When and Where" are considered. For in some respects Biblical ethics is less concerned with obedience to God and love of neighbor than with such questions as: "Who is this God who is to be obeyed? How can man obey him? Why be just? Who is my neighbor? What is love? What are murder, theft, and adultery?" Nevertheless the great themes of Biblical ethics are set forth in these summaries.

It is apparent from the last three of the summaries and it is implicit in the first that the initial and central reference of Biblical ethics is to God as the source of all moral requirements and as the highest value. Biblical ethics begins with God and ends with him. In this it is distinguished from those types of ethical thought which begin with the requirements of human nature or define human happiness or perfection as the final goal. Such interests are not absent from Biblical ethics but they are not primary; hence they scarcely appear in the summary statements.

Closely connected with this theme is the imperative tone of the ethics. All the summaries except Micah's are stated

[8] The Decalogue is reported in the Bible in complete form in two early documents, in Exod. 20:2-17 and Deut. 5:6-21. A comparison of these two editions is instructive especially in the case of the Fourth Commandment. Among many references to this summary attention may be called to the following: Matt. 19:16-19 and Rom. 13:8-10.

in sentences couched in the imperative mood, and Micah's emphasis on requirements indicates that his summary forms no real exception. Human moral reflection, it is often pointed out, tends generally to follow one of two procedures: It either begins by defining the end of action and seeks to relate specific conduct to the ultimate end, or it begins with the effort to state the primary laws or requirements that must be obeyed. Aristotle's ethics is a familiar example of the first type, Kant's of the second. In so far as this distinction is valid there is no doubt that Biblical ethics belongs to the second type. It is more concerned with the question, "What is right?" than with the question, "What is man's chief good?" It does not begin by setting ideals before men but by reminding them of their duties.

Another characteristic of Biblical morality which becomes evident in the summaries is its concentration on those acts which affect the "neighbor" or the companion. The apostolic summary of the whole law in love of neighbor, the close connection between love of neighbor and love of God in Jesus' summary, the prophetic demand for justice and mercy, and the concern of the Ten Commandments with conduct that affects the companion all underscore this point. Its significance appears further in the fact that none of these summaries indicates any interest in virtues apart from their place in one's relation to other persons. There is no demand in any of them for truthfulness as such but only for truthfulness toward the neighbor; there is not even a demand for love as such. No action is considered right simply on account of its effects on the self.

Finally, the close connection between attitudes and actions toward God with attitudes and actions toward the neighbor is noteworthy in all the summaries save the first, and there it is taken for granted, as the setting in which the summary is stated amply indicates. The fuller development of these themes in some great Biblical documents may now be traced.

The Book of the Covenant

Probably the oldest piece of Hebrew legislation preserved in Scriptures is the document recorded in Exodus 20:22-23:33, which is called the Book of the Covenant.[9] It is believed to date from the time of the early Hebrew monarchy, since it reflects the conditions of a relatively simple society, quite different from those which the great prophets of the eighth and seventh centuries B.C. assume. In content the document shows close relations to the Babylonian Code of Hammurabi on the one hand and, on the other, to the customary justice of Arab nomads.

Two distinct, familiar types of imperatives are united in the "Book": unconditional and conditional commandments. The former are directly addressed to the second person without qualifications; the latter are introduced by conditional clauses and represent directions to judges who need to make decisions about the moral conduct of their fellowmen. "You shall not make gods of silver to be with me" (Exod. 20:23); "You shall not afflict any widow or orphan" (Exod. 22:22); "You shall not follow a multitude to do evil" (Exod. 23:2); "You shall not oppress a stranger" (Exod. 23:9); these are commandments of the first type. "When a man strikes his slave, male or female, with a rod and the slave dies under his hand, he shall be punished" (Exod. 21:20); "When an ox gores a man or a woman to death, the ox shall be stoned" (Exod. 21:28); these are directions of the second sort. In accordance with the statement made in Exodus 24:3 that Moses "told the people all the words of the Lord and all the ordinances" these two types of laws are often designated as "The Words" and "The Ordinances." The two types have been so interwoven that in some instances the distinction is not clear, but, by and large, the beginning and end of the Book of the Covenant consist of the "Words" while the central section

[9] Exod. 34:10-26 duplicates part of Exod. 20:22-23:33 and is sometimes called "The Little Book of the Covenant." The name Book of the Covenant is derived from the reference in Exod. 24:7.

contains "Ordinances." It is significant that the similarities of the Book of the Covenant to Babylonian law are found almost exclusively in the "Ordinances" and that similarities, in content as well as in form between this code and prophetic utterances (as well as the Sermon on the Mount), are confined to the "Words." It is in the latter that what is distinctive of ancient and later Israelite morality appears most clearly.

Both sorts of laws are presented as divine declarations. They are the requirements of the one God of Israel, whose first demand is worship of and obedience to him alone. The whole setting of the ethics and the law is, in theological terms, "theocentric." While other types of morality assume as their starting point loyalty of the self to itself or to society, this ethics begins with the assumption that those to whom it is addressed are bound to God and that God has bound himself to them. Moreover, this God who is the ground of man's whole life is a personal God of complete integrity. He is not the object of magic practices whereby his power may be gained for the pursuit of human ends, as is the case in many religions. He is thought of rather in terms of a personal, constant will. And he is *one* God. The people to whom the commands are addressed are not dealing, and are not to think of themselves as dealing, with many different supernatural beings, so that they need to consult different wills in different departments of life, or so that different rules apply in different situations. They do not live in many separated provinces but in everything they do they are in the presence of one and the same will. Religious practices, such as building altars and offering sacrifices; economic actions, such as lending money and sowing and harvesting; political acts, such as administering justice, are all under the rule of the one Lord. The unity of life required here is distinguished from modern tendencies to discover different principles for the guidance of conduct in different spheres, as when art is carried on for art's sake, when politics and religion are separated, and economic life is thought to be under a separate and distinct set of demands.[10] It is distinguished also from the unity of primitive tribal morality, where all parts of action flow into each other but in which it is necessary to know the desires and vagaries of special gods who preside over various areas of life. In so far as rational ethics, as contrasted with customary morality, consists of an ordering of life in accordance with a single principle, the morality of the Book of the Covenant represents a strong movement toward rational ethics; though the rules and regulations which it brings together are derived from many sources, they are in process of being unified and criticized by being related to the one God with his consistent will and demand. How this movement toward rational coherence continues, an examination of later documents will partly illustrate.[11] Attention is also to be directed to the fact that the monotheism of the Book of the Covenant, like that of all other early documents of the Hebrews, is practical rather than speculative. Its point is that the individual and the group addressed are required to worship and obey only the one God whose will is made known through the law. It is not concerned with the questions whether there is only one God above all the world, or whether other groups are right in worshipping other gods.

The imperative nature of the ethics of the Book of the Covenant has been indicated above. It remains for us to attend briefly to its exposition of the other two themes of Biblical morality, the idea of the neighbor or companion and the interrelation of loyalty to God with loyalty to companion. The many references to social relations in the central part of the code are perhaps not particularly significant since legislation in all times and places must deal with such relations. It may be pointed out, however, that in comparison with the Code of Hammurabi, the Book of the Covenant shows a much

[10] See Walter Lippmann, *Preface to Morals* (New York: The Macmillan Co., 1929).

[11] On the process of rationalization in ethics as movement toward coherence see A. N. Whitehead, *Religion in the Making* (New York: The Macmillan Co., 1926).

greater equalitarianism in dealing with the various members of society. There is no such distinction here between the rights of rich and poor freeman as there is in the former code, and, while slavery is an accepted institution, the Hebrew law shows considerably greater concern for the human rights of slaves. They are not dealt with merely as chattels (cf. Exod. 21:2-6, 7-11, 20-21, 26-27, 32).

It is in the more definitely Hebraic elements of the book, however, in the "Words" or direct commandments, that the profoundest interest in the welfare of the neighbor comes to expression. Here it appears, for the most part, in the characteristic concern of God for the weak and the distressed. Foreigners, widows, orphans, the poor, and even animals in distress are to be the objects of a human care that is demanded in the name of justice rather than recommended as an act of charity (Exod. 22:21, 22-24, 25-27; 23:4-5, 6, 9). The seventh day of rest is to be observed not for reasons of ritual but "that your ox and your ass may have rest, and the son of your bondmaid, and the alien, may be refreshed (Exod. 23:12). The Sabbatical year is to be kept in order that "the poor of your people may eat; and what they leave the wild beasts may eat."[12] Though ancient ritual and even economic experiences may have influenced the original development of such Sabbatical observances, the Book of the Covenant, like much other Hebrew legislation and prophecy, seeks to direct the custom into humanitarian channels. These demands for justice are, on the whole, stated in simple imperatives; yet two motives are invoked to encourage obedience to them. On the one hand the Israelites are reminded of their former estate as strangers or slaves in Egypt (Exod. 22:21; 23:9); on the other hand God assures them that there is a

[12] Exod. 23:11. The same reason for observing the Sabbath is given in that version of the Ten Commandments which is recorded in Deut. 5:12-15; but elsewhere in Exod. 20:8-11; 31:15; 35:2, the day is dedicated to God rather than to the neighbor. The Deuteronomic Code sought to extend the humanitarian significance of the Sabbatical year and to make the custom effective under changed economic conditions (15:1-6), while in Leviticus a more ritual reason is given for its observance, though not to the exclusion of the humanitarian note.

justice in history and that oppression of orphans and widows will result in the destruction of the oppressors, in the widowing of their own wives, and the orphaning of their own children (Exod. 22:23-24). (This note, here merely indicated, prophetic ethics develops fully.)

Finally, the intricate interrelation of the service of God and the service of the neighbor, which is expressed in all the summaries quoted above, is quite explicit in the Book of the Covenant. Not all ritual commandments have a social reference, to be sure, though this is true of the Sabbath commandment. Some of the "Words" deal with religious ritual only, with the building of altars, the offering of sacrifices, and the keeping of religious feasts. But it is one and the same God who demands sacrifices, rites, and social justice; the holiness he demands is equally expressed in the observance of religious taboos and in concern for the neighbor. Ritual and justice in the courts, Sabbath observance, and economic practices are all parts of one common life in a community consisting of man, his neighbors, and the Deity, bound together in mutual duties and obligations; God rules over it with concern for every action and for every person.

The Prophet Amos

It seems a far cry from the Book of the Covenant to the prophecies of Amos. The simple conditions of a primitive agricultural society that are presupposed in the former document have given way by the time of Amos to much more complex economic conditions. The people the prophet addresses are not thinking about their oxen and harvests but about trade, speculation, and moneylending (Amos 8:4-6). Their religious practices are not centered around crude earthen altars but are concentrated in highly developed shrines with an established priesthood, elaborate ritual, and daily sacrifices (Amos 3:14; 4:4-5; 5:21-23; 7:10; 8:10). They possess private strongholds, summer houses, and winter houses (Amos 3:10-11, 15). Their society seems largely urban with a marked division between a leisure class and the poor

(Amos 6:4-6; 8:4-6). Moreover, this society is aware of foreign nations not through the presence of a few "strangers" but because it is involved in the wars, alliances, invasions, and cultural exchanges of an international movement (Chaps. 1 and 2). Whether one or two centuries have passed since the legislation of the Book of the Covenant, the culture and the customs of the people have changed radically.[13]

The remarkable figure of Amos was not a product of this society, for as his description of himself indicates (Amos 7:14-15; cf. 1:1), he was a simple shepherd from the village of Tekoa. Yet he cannot be understood as a product of nomad culture and a conservative defender of the old ways and customs. In outlook and interests this first, and perhaps greatest, representative of that prophetic movement which introduced one of the great revolutions in human history is like the princely Isaiah, the priestly Hosea, and Jeremiah. Two inseparably connected convictions dominate his prophecy: the conviction about God and the conviction about the supreme importance of justice.

As in the Book of the Covenant, though with an intensity and a breadth not there evident, Amos' ethics begins with consideration of God's nature and activity.[14] Man must decide what to do not by reference to his ideals or hopes but by reference to the requirements and the activity of the sovereign God. Just as the naturalist in ethics maintains that human life must be adjusted to the laws of nature first of all, or as the historical determinist requires men to conform their actions to the movement of history, so this divine determinist begins with "what is" rather than with "what ought to be" and derives his "ought" from his convictions about reality.

The essential point for Amos as for all the prophets is that God rules and that he is one, universal and intensely active. He is one, that is to say, is constant, unwavering, reliable; his

[13] The prophecies of Amos date from the days of Uzziah, king of Judah, and Jeroboam, king of Israel, i.e., from the middle of the eighth century B.C.

[14] For purposes of study the Book of Amos may be divided into three sections: I. The Oracle Against the Nations, chaps. 1 and 2; II. The Oracles Against Samaria, chaps. 3-6; III. The Visions, chaps. 7-9. The last section contains a historical interlude, chap. 7:10-17.

demands are not subject to change; he has no favorites. Though he is the God of Israel, yet he does not favor Israel above other nations (Amos 2:6; 3:1-2; 7:7 f.; 9:7). He cannot be bribed by sacrifices and worship (Amos 5:21-24). "The way of the Lord is equal"; this fundamental conviction lies back of Amos' method in attempting to persuade Israel that its conduct will lead to disaster unless it reforms. He gains the attention of his audience by pronouncing judgment on the crimes of neighboring nations, a judgment to which his hearers doubtless gladly assent. Thereupon he turns upon the Israelites, requiring them to judge themselves by the same standard that they use in judging others. This prophetic method, followed by Nathan in his encounter with David (II Sam. 11:1-12:15) and by Paul in the letter to the Romans (Rom. 1:18-2:25), is solidly based on the conviction of the unity, the steadfastness, and the incorruptibility of the Ruler of heaven and earth. The principle has a significance for the moral life of men comparable to the significance of the principle of the uniformity and constancy of nature for their scientific activities.

In Amos' thought the uniformity or unity of God's action is intimately connected with his universality. At an earlier stage, as perhaps in the Book of the Covenant, the essential feature of divine unity had been expressed in the narrower terms of Israelite life: Only one God rules over Israel and he is constant in his dealings with all Israelites; he has one and the same standard for all. Now in the prophetic literature, perhaps first of all in Amos, it is recognized that all the nations, all history, all creation are subject to one law and rule. God's rule is present in whatever happens, whether men think it good or evil. "Does evil befall a city, unless the Lord has done it?" (Amos 3:6.) His rule extends over nature (Amos 4:6 ff.), so that famine, drought, blight, and eclipse (Amos 8:9) are instruments he uses for his purposes. He is the Creator of the mountains, winds and rain, of the stars and the earth (Amos 4:13; 5:8; 9:5-6). This understanding that the God whose will is to be obeyed is the Creator and Ruler of nature is developed more extensively by Isaiah and by the authors of Genesis 1 and Psalm 8. For Amos, however, as for the Biblical writers in general, the emphasis falls more on God's rule over social than over natural events. Not only the emigration of Israel from Egypt but also the migrations of other nations are under his guidance (Amos 9:7). The catastrophes of history in invasions and wars are seen as divine judgments (Chaps. 1 and 2). This God is not a static constitution of the universe with which man must reckon in everything he does but an infinitely active deity, the executor of his laws. And he is wholly inescapable. In the ninth chapter Amos sounds the note that Psalm 139 develops:

> Whither shall I go from thy Spirit?
> Or whither shall I flee from thy presence?
> If I ascend to heaven, thou art there!
> If I make my bed in Sheol, thou art there!
> (Ps. 139:7-8.)

The ethical significance of this conception of God does not appear in Amos in the formulation of laws which men are required to keep. Like Micah in his great summary Amos assumes that man has been "shown what is good" and that he knows what the requirements are. Man's moral problem is not due to his ignorance of the right. It lies rather in his rebellion against the known requirements of God. It is not so much a purely moral problem about the good and the right as a problem of existence. The consequence of his rebellion and of his abuse of his knowledge of right and wrong is destruction and death, just as, conversely, seeking good and living belong together. The human problem, then, is the problem of salvation from sin and death. It is in this negative form, as a diagnosis of disease, rather than in the positive form of injunctions to perform specified right conduct, that the ethics of Amos is developed.

Two kinds of evil in particular call forth, according to Amos, the judgments of God in nature and in social history: injustice and oppression. Injustice appears in bribe-taking, in failing to give the poor the same treatment in courts that is accorded to the favored, in using false weights and measures

—in short, in all perversion of the principle of equitable treatment, which is the basis of any social life. Amos says little about the content of the social laws of Israel, nor are any of the other prophets much concerned with them. But like the others he is very certain that equal justice must prevail in economic as in political life if the nation is to live and that all the subterfuges by which men twist their laws to derive special benefits for themselves, for their class or their nation, lead, under the rule of God, to disaster and death. The justice that is demanded is "straightness"; it is "swearing to one's hurt and changing not"; it is using the same measure in selling that one uses in buying, judging oneself by the same standard that one uses in judging others; it is the rational ordering of all life by one standard rather than shifting about in the pursuit of desire after desire. The unity of God and the necessity of such justice are as inseparably connected for Amos and for the Biblical writers in general as the unity of nature and the necessity for disinterestedness in inquiry are connected for scientific inquiry. Justice, in this aspect, is moral "disinterestedness." To except oneself from the rule is rebellion.[15]

Rebellion against the rule of God appears also in oppression, which is the evident counterpart of inequity. The transgressions which are inviting disaster on Israel are, according to Amos, not only malpractices in the courts and in the market place, but the deeds of the apparently strong in taking advantage of the weak. They "sell the needy for a pair of shoes," "trample the head of the poor into the dust of the earth, and turn aside the way of the afflicted"; they "trample upon the poor and take from him exactions of wheat"; they enjoy their luxuries and are unconcerned about the miseries of the people. All this lack of concern for the neighbors is for Amos not simply a defect in charity but a crying injustice that is bound under God's rule to end in catastrophe. There are also other manifestations of rebellion against the rule of God, such as sexual immorality and drunkenness, but injus-

15 The Hebrew word translated by "transgression" in Amos 1 and 2 also means "rebellion."

tice and oppression are the primary ones that Amos regards as the source of impending doom.

Finally, attention must be called to an important feature of the prophetic understanding of the relation of obedience to God to justice. The prophetic understanding of life has no room in it for the distinction often made in modern times between religion and ethics. It distinguishes between God and man, not between religion and ethics, for the God of the prophets is not a being with whom men are concerned only so far as they are religious. Since he is Ruler of nature and history they are as close to him—or perhaps closer—in politics and economics as they are in worship. Amos, like Isaiah and Jeremiah, reserves his bitterest denunciation for those who seek to make up by means of religious rites the defects of their obedience in political and economic relations. Thus God speaks through Amos to the worshippers at Bethel and Gilgal with biting irony (Amos 4:4-5) and declares, "I hate, I despise your feasts, and I take no delight in your solemn assemblies. Even though you offer me your burnt offerings and cereal offerings, I will not accept them, and the peace offerings of your fatted beasts I will not look upon. Take away from me the noise of your songs; to the melody of your harps I will not listen. But let justice roll down like waters, and righteousness like an ever-flowing stream" (Amos 5:21-24). It is somewhat erroneous, therefore, to interpret the ethics of Amos, or prophetic ethics in general, as ethics based on religion. He is as much concerned with the reform of religion as with the reform of ethics. All life, all action takes place in the presence of the one God, is under his rule and judgment. God is not an idea in men's minds but the reality that confronts and challenges them in every moment, every place, in all nature and all history.

From Amos to the New Testament

Eight centuries of highly complex history lie between Amos' prophecy and Jesus' Sermon on the Mount. During that period the political history of the people to whom both were addressed included such decisive events as subjugation by the Assyrian and Babylonian empires, the exile, reconstruction under Persian rule, the Maccabean revolt against the Seleucids, a brief period of independence, and the imposition of that Roman rule which forms the political background of the New Testament. Internally, the history of the people was marked by the transformation of a political society or state, intent on self-determination, into a religious community, a church, which found the reason for its continued existence in its mission of obedience to the one God, who was increasingly recognized to be not only the God of Israel but the Creator of heaven and earth and the Lord of all history. Among the most important developments which took place in the ethical and religious thought of Israel during these eight hundred years four may be mentioned: the turn from a more social to a more individualized view of life, the wrestle with the problem of divine justice, the deepening of convictions about the reign of evil in the world, and the development of law.

Early law and prophecy among the Hebrews took for granted the social solidarity of the people. The nation as a whole was righteous or sinful; its life and death were what mattered; its unified loyalty to God was the important thing. Beginning with the prophets Jeremiah and Ezekiel, and under the influence of external events, the direct significance of the individual person's conduct and destiny came more prominently into view. The older thought had emphasized the unity of the generations as in the statement that the Lord was a jealous God, "visiting the iniquity of the fathers upon the children to the third and the fourth generation of those who hate me, but showing steadfast love to thousands of those who love me and keep my commandments" (Exod. 20:5-6; 34:7; Deut. 5:9-10). But Ezekiel expressed the principle of personal responsibility: "The soul that sins shall die. The son shall not suffer for the iniquity of the father, nor the father suffer for the iniquity of the son; the righteousness of the righteous shall be upon himself, and the wickedness of the wicked shall be upon himself" (Ezek. 18:20). In many

Psalms this turn toward the value of the person and toward concern for the responsibility of the individual was given poetic expression. A profoundly personal and inward religious life developed among the Jews (see Pss. 1, 15, 19, 22, 23, 27, etc.). Concern for the individual's fate also appeared in the doctrine of the resurrection of the dead which is taken for granted in the New Testament as the teaching of the orthodox Pharisees but which had scarcely been mentioned in Old Testament teaching. However, the concentration on the value and destiny of the individual never became so prominent that the value and destiny of society were left out of account.

Among all the struggles of the Jews their wrestling with the problem of divine justice is most moving and significant. The high points in this struggle are marked by such writings as the prophecies of Jeremiah and Second Isaiah, the Book of Job, Psalms Twenty-two, Forty-two, and Seventy-three. It comes to its final issue in the pages of the New Testament. The basis of all Biblical thought and conduct is the conviction that God rules and that he is just. This conviction was accompanied in the beginning by a second one, namely that justice consists in giving reward commensurate with good deeds and inflicting punishment commensurate with transgression. But experience did not wholly bear out this hypothesis about divine justice. It agreed with many of the facts but not with all. Hence the great questions arose: Why do the wicked prosper? (Jer. 12:1-4; Ps. 73:1-14; Ps. 94; Hab. 1:2-4, 13). Why do the innocent suffer? (Job 1-3, 29-31; Jer. 15:15-18). Is there any equality between the transgressions of Israel and its sufferings? (Isa. 40:2, 27; 49:4, 14). Is God just who requires so much of man who is so weak? (Job 9). Are victorious nations more righteous than their victims? (Isa. 10:5-19). It is in the struggle with such questions that the heart of Biblical religion and ethics is revealed. The answers which were given by the later prophets and the poets of Israel develop these main ideas: the ways of God are great and sublime, beyond man's present comprehension (Job 38:1-42:6; Isa. 55:8-9); faith in God's justice is sustained amid trials by the hope of its ultimate triumph and manifestation (Ps. 73:16-22; Isa. 40, 41); suffering cannot be interpreted as direct divine punishment of rebellion but is to be understood as part of the process by which souls are trained and tested (Deut. 8:2-5; Ps. 118:18; Prov. 3:11-12) and as the vicarious pain that the innocent suffer for the guilty (Isa. 52:13-53:12). But amidst all this questioning and these tentative answers the fundamental faith in the unity, universality, and justice of God was stated with ever greater power. What is even more significant is that God was understood ever more as acting in ways of mercy and forgiveness rather than of simple compensatory justice, for the undeserved blessings of sinners were seen as more abundant than the unmerited sufferings of the good.

This last development is connected with the growth and deepening of a sense of the radical evil present in the world and in human nature. Despite his vision of Israel's corruption Amos called for reform with some hope that the nation would turn to God, seek good, and live. A little later Isaiah understood that the moral and civic corruption of the people was so great that only a remnant could be saved. As the world view of the prophets widened they saw all nations as subject to the rule of God and yet all of them involved in injustice and oppression, that is, in rebellion against him. As psychological insight deepened it became apparent that moral evil was deeply rooted in the soul of man and not confined to external conduct. In the period just before Jesus Christ this conviction about the widespread and radical character of moral evil was expressed in the thought that not only human beings in their societies but superhuman forces shared in the rebellion against God and that history was being ruled by sinister powers. The author of the Letter to the Ephesians expressed an idea that had been prevalent long before his time when he wrote: "We are not contending against flesh and blood, but against the principalities, against the powers, against the world rulers of this present darkness, against the spiritual hosts of wickedness in the heavenly places" (Eph. 6:12). Associated with this vision of the power of evil, the old prophetic certainty of the actuality of God's reign came to expression in apocalyptic books that prophesied the revelation of his power, the defeat of wickedness, and the establishment of his kingdom. In highly symbolic and even mythological forms the prophets' view of Israel's history as one of rebellion, chastisement, and redemption was universalized and intensified. If evil was seen as more universal and more powerful than it had been for an Amos, then the power of God was also understood as greater and more mysterious and his design for the redeemed as more sublime and inclusive than earlier generations had thought.[16]

Finally, attention must be called to the development of the idea of the law of God and to the statement of that law in detailed fashion. The idea that God rules through the pronouncement of laws antedates, of course, even the Book of the Covenant. Most of the prophets had been less interested in this point than in the fact that God acts in history in accordance with his principles of justice, that is, more as executor of the laws than as legislator. Their work, however, had been accompanied by that of the lawgivers, and some of the later prophets, notably Ezekiel, were deeply interested in legal reform. The Deuteronomic Code (Deut. 12:1-26:15), developed on the basis of earlier legislation, was promulgated partly under the influence of the prophetic movement late in the seventh century B.C. Later the Holiness Code (mostly in Lev. 17-26) was developed and, finally, when the Jewish community was reconstructed under the leadership of Ezra and Nehemiah early in the fourth century, the so-called Priestly Code, which absorbed the earlier laws, was formulated.[17] In these successive formulations of the law the humanitarian element found in the Covenant Code was not lost; it was even developed and extended, but the ritual regulations which formed a small part of that early book were prominently developed so that the importance of such actions

[16] See especially the Book of Daniel and, in the Apocrypha, II Esdras.

[17] This Code is to be found for the most part in the present books of Leviticus and Numbers. See J. M. P. Smith, *Origin and History of Hebrew Law* (Chicago: University of Chicago Press, 1931), chap. vi.

as bringing sacrifices, tithing, abstaining from "unclean" food, and observing the festivals was greatly emphasized. This was in marked contrast to the early prophetic attitude toward ritual acts. The development of the law was connected with the rise of legalism in the attitude of the people, that is, with concern for keeping all the details of the written code, with concentration on external observance, and with the tendency to emphasize what God had done in the past in giving his law rather than his present action. This legalism had its good side, as such Psalms as One and One Hundred Nineteen show. Its morally dubious aspects were brought to light by Jesus and his disciples.

The Sermon on the Mount

The Sermon on the Mount, as reported in Matthew 5-7, represents in the briefest form available the essence of the ethical teaching of Jesus. It was probably designed by the writer of the First Gospel to be an incisive epitome of Christ's commandments to his disciples, for a comparison of the content of these three chapters with corresponding sections in the Gospel of Luke (especially 6:20-49) shows that it is a collection of Jesus' sayings uttered at various times and designed to be a guide to conduct, a kind of new law for Christians.[18]

The ethics of the Sermon, like that of the "Words" in the Book of the Covenant, is stated in direct imperatives. There are no "ordinances" introduced by conditional clauses, for this morality is not concerned with the question how to judge the conduct of other men but only with what is required of

18 For a brief history of the origin of the Sermon on the Mount, see Martin Dibelius, *The Sermon on the Mount* (New York: Charles Scribner's Sons, 1940), chaps. ii and iii; see also Hans Windisch, *The Meaning of the Sermon on the Mount* (Philadelphia: The Westminster Press, 1951).

While the sayings have been so grouped that it is difficult to discover a formal outline of the Sermon, certain bodies of material may be distinguished such as: The Beatitudes, 5:3-12; The New Law, 5:17-6:18; On Single-Mindedness, 6:19-24; On Anxiety, 6:25-34; On Judgment, 7:1-5; and the Conclusion, 7:21-27. Some individual sayings included in the collection, such as the Golden Rule, sound like proverbs and are not particularly characteristic of Jesus' teaching.

the active self. For the most part the imperatives are stated as simple demands without much reference to consequences. Such interpretations as that the enemy is to be loved in order that he may be made a friend, or that evil is not to be resisted in order that peace may be gained among men, are not supported by the Sermon itself. Even the interpretation that these sayings show men how they may achieve perfection or complete self-realization has little basis, for perfection itself is spoken of as something that is demanded, not as something men desire and for the sake of which they are to perform the various commanded actions. It is significant, also, that the imperatives of the Sermon on the Mount are stated as issuing from Jesus himself, rather than as words of God, the form in which similar imperatives were stated by lawgivers and prophets in the Old Testament. The formula, "You have heard that it was said to the men of old, . . . but I say to you," is characteristic of the Christian conviction that the authority of Jesus Christ is not wholly derived from a source other than himself.

Though this ethics is stated in terms of direct commandments it does not prescribe what men ought to do without reference to their actual situation. These apparently arbitrary commandments are the rational corollaries of a pronounced and definite conviction about the character of the human situation. The conviction may be briefly stated: God rules and his rule will soon become manifest. What Christ commands is what it is reasonable for men to do in a world in which God rules and in which the apparent rebellion against his rule is bound to come to an early end. The actuality of God's present rule in heaven and over nature is expressly asserted in the teachings on anxiety and on love of the enemy. It is the "little faith" of men which makes conduct other than obedience to that rule seem rational. Their "little faith" appears in their suspicion that the ultimate government of the world is indifferent to them and their needs, in their doubt that there is any reality beyond that which is now visible, in their consequent concern with tangible values. Nothing is said in the Sermon about the time when the rule, now discernible in nature, will be made evident in human affairs. It is taken for granted that it will become evident in crises such as the concluding parable indicates, but whether crisis occurs in individual life or in social history does not seem important; whether the pure in heart shall see God after their death or after some revolution in social history, whether those who hunger and thirst after justice will be satisfied when the kingdom of God will be manifest on earth or in a spiritual life beyond history is not the important matter. Jesus' fundamental conviction is not that the rule of God and the justice of that rule will be made evident at some early or late future date and that therefore it is now real in the sense that it can be anticipated. It is, rather, that God now rules and that the actuality of his rule and its justice will therefore be made quite evident. He does not argue so much from the future to the present as from the present to the future.

What gives the ethical teaching of Jesus its special character is not simply the strength of the conviction that God's rule will be made wholly manifest; it is even more his certainty that the God who rules nature and history is holy love. God, indeed, is just; he judges every man by his own standards: "With the judgment you pronounce you will be judged, and the measure you give will be the measure you get" (Matt. 7:2). He is just in that he makes up the unfair inequalities between men, granting to the poor, the meek, the hungry, the mourners what they have lacked (Matt. 5:3-11). His justice is the holy justice of one who demands complete, inner integrity (Matt. 5:17-6:6). But what the just God demands is what he gives before making any demands: love, mercy, forgiveness, kindness. He is the Father whose kindness appears in that indiscriminateness of nature which human despair regards as evidence of his nonexistence or of his injustice, for "he makes his sun rise on the evil and on the good, and sends rain on the just and on the unjust" (Matt. 5:45). Much more than human parents give good gifts to their children, he bestows his largess on those who turn to him (Matt. 7:7-11); on him men may depend for daily good, shelter, clothing, and the forgiveness of all their sins. This divine mercifulness is not for Jesus something added to God's justice; it is the very heart of the goodness with which God is good. This is what he is, mercy, and this is what he requires in the character of his children. The man who is merciless, unforgiving, and unloving is going against the grain of the universe, is trying to violate the inviolable law of nature, society, history, of God.

In the Sermon on the Mount, as in Jesus' summary of the law and in the documents previously studied, there are stressed the value of the human companion and the importance in conduct of those actions which affect him. But some significant differences in the treatment of this subject are to be observed. In distinction from the Book of Amos and from most of the other prophets Jesus does not address the strong and influential in the community, demanding of them that they do justice to the poor; he directs his address to the latter.[19] Hence there are no such injunctions to turn from oppression of the poor as we find in Amos. The situation with which Jesus deals is not that of the soldier who compels the citizen to carry a burden for a mile but that of the oppressed citizen, not that of the men who are "adding house to house and field to field" but that of men who are worried about the next day's food supply. A second point, which is of great importance not only in this Sermon but throughout the Gospels and which is especially underscored by the parable of the Good Samaritan (Luke 10:29-37), is the conception of the neighbor. Jesus goes beyond prophetic teaching particularly in his answer to the question, "Who is my neighbor?" Here, in the Sermon on the Mount, the enemy is counted among those to whom men have an obligation under the rule of God. The neighbor is no longer the member of a closed society

[19] In Luke's version of the Sermon on the Mount this direct address to the disinherited is made explicit. In Matthew the emphasis falls on the spiritual qualities rather than on economic and political status. Luke further adds a series of "Woes" against the Pharisees. In any case, as the whole of the Gospels makes clear, Jesus was concerned in all his work primarily with rescuing the poor, the sick, and the outcast and only secondarily with the reform of oppressors.

whose citizens support each other by rendering mutual services, but any member of that community of which the universal God is the head. A third and highly important difference lies in the emphasis which Jesus places on attitudes toward the neighbor. He discerns that the relations between men in the great community are matters not of obvious, external behavior but of psychological, internal attitudes. Not simply murder but anger, disrespect, and contempt are violations of the common life; not simply adultery but lust injures men's relations with one another and with God; not only false witness against the neighbor but every lack of candor and honesty is a breach of the community. Finally, it is evident that what Jesus sees to be required in this community by the character of the God who rules over the whole of it is no simple, compensatory justice whereby men receive from one another what they have merited. The action of man does not begin with the effort to merit a reward but with the reception of gifts from God through nature and fellow men. Though Jesus uses the common language of reward and punishment, it is clear that for him men live interpersonally by mercy and love. There is no suggestion in the Beatitudes that those who have the qualities praised there merit the rewards promised them. God gives to those who ask him and so man is to give to the beggar, without expectation of praise, and he is not to refuse the one who pleads for a loan. The image of the world economy that is in Jesus' mind is never that of the market place where men must pay for all they receive; it is that of the home where gifts are given before they are deserved and where the same spirit of graciousness is expected in the recipients. Hence both these things are true: "If you then, who are evil, know how to give good gifts to your children, how much more will your Father who is in heaven give good things to those who ask him?" (Matt. 7:11); and "If you forgive men their trespasses, your heavenly Father also will forgive you; but if you do not forgive men their trespasses, neither will your Father forgive your trespasses" (Matt. 6:14).

The intimate interconnections of man's relations to God and his relations to his companion is the final aspect of the

Sermon on the Mount to which we must attend. There is no such dispraise of religious rites in Jesus' statement as we found in Amos or Isaiah. But for him as for the prophets no sacrifice or religious rite can make good an interpersonal fault (Matt. 5:23-24) and what is demanded above all is sincerity in all man's directly religious conduct (Matt. 6:5-6, 16-18). The merely social religious practices in which men engage for the sake of public approval have, as he sees, no other consequence than just such approval (Matt. 6:1-6). This does not mean that communion with God is for Jesus a private affair, for it is communion with the God who is also the Father of the neighbor; but it is not to be sought for its social or other incidental results. The ethics of Jesus is the ethics of a single community, the community of which God, the Father, is author and ruler and in which relations to him are always of decisive importance. But these relations can never be severed from one's relations to the neighbor. The obligations and benefits of life in this actual, not ideal, community are the subjects of Jesus' ethical teaching as presented in the Sermon on the Mount as well as elsewhere.

Paul's Letter to the Romans

Next to the Sermon on the Mount no other Biblical document has had greater influence on the ethical reflection of the Christian church than the letter to the Romans. It was written about A.D. 59 by that great genius Paul, the zealous Pharisee and rabbinical scholar who after persecuting the Christians became a convert and then, more than any other apostle, helped to change the new faith from a Jewish sect into a world faith. His rich and paradoxical thought was found difficult even in the early days,[20] but it has also been the source of many important developments in later Christian reflection and action. Augustine was deeply influenced by it

[20] The author of the Second Epistle of Peter wrote, "So also our beloved brother Paul wrote to you according to the wisdom given him, speaking of this as he does in all his letters. There are some things in them hard to understand, which the ignorant and unstable twist to their own destruction, as they do the other scriptures." II Pet. 3:15-16.

and through Augustine the whole of Western Christendom. The Reformers, especially Luther and Calvin, understood Christian faith in dominantly Pauline terms.

Among all his writings the letter to the Romans is outstanding since it represents his ripest thought in most complete form. The difficulties that readers encounter in it are partly due to Paul's unfamiliar rabbinic habits of thought, partly to the fact that like his other writings it is a letter directed to a special group, alluding to circumstances with which the modern reader is not familiar. They are mostly due, however, to the profundity of Paul's understanding of the human situation and the depth of his religious insight. The letter to the Romans will remain obscure to those who have never thought deeply about God and the problem of human existence or have never faced and experienced the revolutionary meaning of the life and destiny of Jesus Christ.

Though popular prejudice regards Romans as dealing with speculative theology rather than with practical and ethical questions, even a cursory reading of the letter shows the prevalence and depth of its ethical interests. Its theme is "The Righteousness of God through Faith for Faith"; it opens, like Amos' prophecies, with a moral indictment of Gentile culture, which is turned into an indictment of the people who pride themselves on the possession of the Law; its main argument ends with a series of moral imperatives and counsels; its central portion is concerned with the significance of Jesus Christ for man's deliverance from the power and destructiveness of sin and death.[21] There are to be found in it some of the most frequently quoted statements about the moral life of man and Christian conduct: "I can will what is right, but I cannot do it; I do not do the good I want, but the evil I do not want is what I do"; "Anyone who does not have the Spirit of Christ does not belong to him";

[21] For purposes of study the following may serve as a convenient outline of the contents of the Epistle: Introduction, 1:1-15; Statement of the theme, 1:16-17; I. The universal reign of sin, 1:18-3:20; II. The manifestation of God's righteousness, 3:21-8:39; III. The problem of Israel and God's purpose in history, 9-11; IV. The ethics of the new life, 12-15:13; Conclusion 15:14-16:27.

"We know that in everything God works for good with those who love him"; "Do not be conformed to this world but be transformed by the renewal of your mind"; "Repay no one evil for evil"; "Do not be overcome by evil, but overcome evil with good"; "Nothing is unclean in itself, but it is unclean for anyone who thinks it unclean"; "Whatever does not proceed from faith is sin."

The great themes which we have found characteristic of Biblical ethics are present in Paul, but they are developed against a background which has been less evident in the previously studied documents than it is in this one. This background becomes the starting point of a great deal of later Christian ethical thought and practice. For Paul as for Micah the great moral problem is not one of knowledge but of will. He discerns, as others had before him, that the dilemma of the ethical man, who knows the good but lacks the will to perform it, is not merely his personal problem but universal among men. It is the problem of the Pharisees, that class of rigorous Jewish moralists to which he had belonged and which Jesus had severely castigated because they practiced the virtues for the sake of public approval, bound heavy burdens on men's backs by their detailed injunctions to right conduct in minor matters, and neglected the "weightier matters of the law, justice and mercy and faith." But it is not only the problem of the Jew; Paul notes that the disjunction between knowledge of the good and its performance is also the problem of the members of Hellenistic society, who know by reason what is right and wrong but practice every vice. His point of departure is, therefore, the situation of mankind in revolt against the moral law that it acknowledges, of man in revolt against himself.

Paul sees the whole human world as subject to the reign of sin, which has become almost an independent power holding men in slavery. His argument is not that Adam sinned and that therefore all men receive a tainted inheritance but that the universal reign of sin can be seen and experienced by looking at the world as a whole and by looking within one's self. Reference to the first man and his fall appear only in explanation of this fact, not as the fact itself. Acceptance of the fact had certainly been present in Amos who spoke against the background of the sinfulness of other nations and of Israel's own defection from its law. It was assumed by Jesus in many teachings, as when in the Sermon on the Mount he remarks, "If you then, who are evil, know how to give good gifts to your children, how much more will your Father who is in heaven give good things to those who ask him." But Paul develops the theme, and his development makes explicit the difference between Christian ethics and the ethics of many other communities. The former does not begin with the assumption that man is morally healthy and needs only knowledge in order to do the right thing. It begins rather with the understanding that man is morally ill and needs to be made well before he can act as a normal human being should and would act.

The Christian analysis of the human situation which is made very explicit in Romans is that man who is created as free citizen of the kingdom of God, or, better, as a child in the house of the Father, has fallen into slavery to a way of life and thought that runs contrary to his true nature and destiny and, above all, contrary to the actual constitution of the moral universe in which he lives. The evidence for this slavery is to be found, according to Paul, not only in the prevalence of that human conduct which is generally regarded as "unnatural"—injustice, crime, crude self-assertion, wickedness—but also in the ever-present antagonism, even in so-called good men, between their conscience and their desires ("the law in their mind and the law in their members") and in the inability of moral imperatives to secure obedience. This understanding of the universality and the inescapability of human slavery to the power of sin, of a bondage that extends into the innermost depths of the human soul, forms the background of all Paul's thought in Romans about the good life.

It does not, of course, form the whole background, for the fundamental fact with which man is concerned in his moral life is not human slavery to sin but the reign of God. Sin as rebellion against God's rule presupposes the actuality of that rule; it is rebellion within the realm of God, not attack by an alien power. Neither Paul nor any other theologian in the great line of Christian thinkers ever surrendered to a dualistic view, according to which the world is made up of two opposed realms, the kingdom of light and the kingdom of darkness, and according to which some things, such as the material world or the body, are inherently bad. Whatever evil powers are at work in the world, God is the author and ruler of all. The ethical thought of Paul rests on the double foundation of the convictions that God rules and that man is involved in a universal rebellion against that rule.

The God who rules is for Paul, as for the later prophets and Jesus, the Creator. He is the first and last reality; "from him and through him and to him are all things." He is the just executor of all his laws who "will render to every man according to his works" and who "shows no partiality." He is the God of Israel who made himself known to the fathers of that nation and chose it to be his people. He is the known but unacknowledged God of the heathen. But above all he is the Father of the Lord Jesus Christ, who has made himself known in a special way in Christ. For Paul, as for the great central tradition in Christianity, God the Father and Jesus Christ are so intimately related that faith in the Father and faith in Christ become almost synonymous. The reign of God and the reign of Christ, the love of God and the love of Christ, the spirit of God and the spirit of Christ are so closely associated that the problems of their distinction and their relations have occupied students of Paul and of Christian theology over and over again.

What is most significant for Paul's ethics in this connection is his conviction and experience that in and through Jesus Christ, not simply through his teachings but through his character and fate, God has made himself known to men in such a way that a new relation to him is possible. More than that, the coming of Jesus Christ marks the beginning of a new era in human history, an era characterized by the presence of a new spirit, which is the spirit of sonship to God, of hopefulness and love. For Paul, as for the prophets, God is active

Deity, the doer of mighty deeds in history. But the one great deed of God, which makes all other events intelligible and which is the decisive turning point in the relation of men to God and to one another, is the coming of Jesus Christ, his life, death, and resurrection. "God shows his love for us in that while we were yet sinners Christ died for us" (Rom. 5:8). Through Jesus Christ the internal rebellion of men against God is overcome, in principle if not yet universally, and they can live as those who are reconciled to God and who are at home in the house of the Father.

One consequence of this profound revolution in man's attitude toward God is, according to Paul, a change in his attitude toward the imperative moral laws. In a sense Paul's whole thought on the law may be interpreted as a development of Jesus' idea that a good tree brings forth good fruit and that no amount of external conduct can make men really good. In so far as the imperative moral law remains something external to man, an affair of "You ought" and "You ought not," it cannot make him good at the core; it cannot transform his motives. The imperative form of the law, not its content, is a relative thing which presupposes the presence in man of a desire contrary to the intention of the law. Moreover, the giving of injunctions to men is likely to arouse their self-will and so tempt them to transgress the law. Where there are imperatives, adults as well as children are tempted to see how close they can come to the edge of the forbidden. Again, imperative law cannot produce that innate, unforced graciousness of conduct evident in Jesus Christ which is so much more attractive and so much more fruitful than self-conscious goodness. The imperative law increases among men their fear of death and their sense of guilt, and because of this fear and guilt their actions are still further confused and directed into channels contrary to the spirit of the law. Law, sin, and death are all bound together for Paul. Because of sin there must be law; but law, increasing the sense of guilt and tempting men to rebellion, not only fails to eradicate the roots of sin but even tends to increase transgressions. This criticism of imperative moral law is one of Paul's great contributions to moral thought, though he makes explicit here only what was present in Jesus' teaching and conduct and what a Jeremiah had sensed.

Some of Paul's converts understood his criticism of the law to be so destructive of its claims that they felt under no obligation to obey the moral imperatives of society and conscience. It is evident that he countenanced no such destructive attitude, but continued to regard the law as relatively good though inadequate to achieve the necessary reorganization and renewal of human life (Rom. 7:7-25). His thought in this respect may be compared to that of a social revolutionary who, profoundly critical of the property system in a society, yet understands that so long as that system remains, the law against stealing must be fully enforced. Paul is concerned with the moral revolution whereby human motives will be radically changed. He calls this revolution a "dying and rising of the self," for it involves a complete inner transformation of the fundamental attitudes of men toward God, their world, themselves, and their neighbors. So long as the revolution is not complete there is for Paul always a place for the imperative law with its penalties and rewards. This becomes evident not only from his express statements about the goodness of the law but from his own use of imperatives in addressing those who have begun "the new life" but are not yet mature sons of God.

Paul's ethics with its interest in the internal transformation of man remains an ethics of concern for the neighbor: "Owe to no man anything except to love one another; for he who loves his neighbor has fulfilled the law." Three points are noteworthy in Paul's conception of the meaning of "love of neighbor"—his understanding of the internal, unforced, gracious character of true love; his practical application of the idea of the neighbor to all men; and his understanding of the interplay of social and individual factors in ethical life. His great hymn on love in I Corinthians 13 illustrates the first point more fully than any passage in Romans does, but the latter epistle abounds in statements which echo the eloquent strains of the former passage:

> Love is patient and kind; love is not jealous or boastful; it is not arrogant or rude. Love does not insist on its own way; it is not irritable or resentful; it does not rejoice at wrong, but rejoices in the right. Love bears all things, believes all things, hopes all things, endures all things. (I Cor. 13:4-7)

So far as the extension of the neighbor concept is concerned, it is noteworthy that the letter to the Romans is in one sense Paul's greatest defense of his life work as apostle to the "Gentiles" and his greatest statement of the truth he had learned from Jesus Christ that as God is universal Father so the Gospel of his love must be brought home to all men. What Paul emphasizes is not, however, the fact that because God is the Creator of all men therefore all are brothers but rather that since Christ died and rose again for all men he has made all of them neighbors both by showing their common sinfulness and by calling all to newness of life. To the conception of the universality of the human neighborhood and human brotherhood Paul gave classic expression in the statement in Galatians, "There is neither Jew nor Greek, there is neither slave nor free, there is neither male nor female; for you are all one in Christ Jesus" (Gal. 3:28). Less completely this formula is found in Romans 10:12. A certain duality of meaning appears at this point, however. In one sense Paul's ethics expresses the universality of human obligations and of human brotherhood; but in another it expresses the idea that a new society, the church, has been established. In this new society in which men acknowledge the one Lord, Jesus Christ, all men are brothers. The duality present here is connected again with Paul's thought of a revolution in human affairs, for the church is the germ of the new, inclusive society which will eventually do away with all the national, religious, and cultural distinctions that obtain among men.

Paul's understanding of the importance of both individual responsibility and social solidarity in the Christian life appears in his reflections that we are members of one another and that every man is subject to his own conscience. The Christian life is one of social solidarity. In history the interplay of the Jewish and the Christian communities forms one process in which there is no place for boasting on the part of Christians (Rom. 9-12). In the Christian community each person performs his special function as though he were the organ of a body relying on the other organs to perform their proper functions, all for the welfare of the whole (Rom. 12:3-8). It is contrary to the spirit of Christ for men to attach greater value to one kind of common service than to another. But on the other hand, every individual has a direct relation to the head of the body, that is, to Christ, and is to be ruled not by his brothers but by his own Christian conscience (Rom. 14). "Who are you to pass judgment on the servant of another? It is before his own master that he stands or falls."

How intimately the relations of the individual to God and his relations to his neighbor are intertwined and dependent on each other is indicated both in this figure of the body and its members that Paul employs and in his analysis of sin and the moral law. The roots of man's inhumanity to man and of all his wickedness are to be sought in his lack of confidence in God. It is man's suspicion and fear and hopelessness in the world that are at the root of his moral transgressions. On the other hand, the basis of love of the neighbor is trust and confidence in God and the spirit of sonship to him. Conversely, true service of God on the part of the converted man is the presentation of his whole life as a living sacrifice to God, and this offering of life in gratitude and love expresses itself in humility and mutual service among the neighbors (Rom. 12).

The Christian ethics of Paul is the ethics of life in the community of which God-in-Christ or Christ-with-God is the ever-present and ever-active source of all good, the constant director and inspirer, and in which men are members of one another. It is a community which is being reconstituted out of the rebellious nations and individuals which have lived in hopelessness, under the rule of law and death. It is the ethics of the community of the kingdom of God both as present fact and as promised reality, for it is the community of those who look back upon the great act of Jesus Christ in his declaration and demonstration of the reality of God's rule and love and who look forward to the time when all men shall acknowledge this kingdom and when righteousness and peace and joy in the Holy Spirit will prevail.

Further Readings

Anderson, Bernhard. *Understanding the Old Testament.* 2d ed. Englewood Cliffs, N. J.: Prentice-Hall, 1966.

Bornkamm, Gunther. *Jesus of Nazareth.* New York: Harper and Row, 1960.

Davies, W. D. *The Sermon on the Mount.* Cambridge (England) University Press, 1966.

———. *Invitation to the New Testament.* Garden City, N. Y.: Doubleday, 1966.

Furnish, Victor. *Theology and Ethics in Paul.* Nashville: Abingdon Press, 1968.

Perrin, Norman. *Rediscovering the Teaching of Jesus.* London: SCM Press, 1967.

Schnackenburg, Rudolf. *The Moral Teaching of the New Testament.* New York: Herder and Herder, 1967.

Scott, R. B. Y. *The Relevance of the Prophets.* Rev. ed. New York: Macmillan, 1968.

Spivey, Robert, and Smith, Moody. *Anatomy of the New Testament.* New York: Macmillan, 1969.

Wilder, Amos. *Eschatology and Ethics in the Teaching of Jesus.* Rev. ed. New York: Harper and Row, 1950.

Chapter 2

ETHICS OF THE EARLY CHRISTIAN CHURCH

In Western democratic culture of the twentieth century, Christian institutions have so deeply penetrated common life, and become so respectable, that it is difficult to imagine an age when the Christian church was an underground minority movement not only unrespectable but despised and persecuted.

This new, odd religion in the Graeco-Roman world had as its devotees simple people, for the most part poor and illiterate, who were on fire with a kindled affection to a crucified and risen Lord who brought new life to mankind, a new way of salvation, a new commandment. At the outset they were mostly Jews of Palestine. But as Paul and his followers took Christianity into Asia Minor, Greece, and Italy, it became increasingly a religion adopted by Gentiles. Scattered at far distance from each other, with little chance of communication, little cell churches lived constantly under the suspecting eye of the Roman state, which periodically tried to suppress them. Yet they were held together by a resolute and grateful confidence that God had revealed himself to a dark and decadent world in the figure of one Jesus, who had been a teacher and healer of men, had died a criminal's death, had been raised from the dead by the hand of God, and would come again at the end of time to express God's final purpose. The conviction that God had finally and fully spoken in this Christ, living, dying, and rising, meant that men henceforth to be saved must preserve his memory, in allegiance to him, and in belief and deed fulfill the requirements he laid upon them. Such was the radical and "foolish" faith that precipitated a new community and a new ethic.

Apart from Biblical material, discussed in the first chapter, we have relatively sparse record of the thought of the church of the first two centuries. In its early career the Christian movement was not interested in the development of a rationally ordered statement of Christian principles nor were there many among its members who could have undertaken the work of writing such statements. Paul and the writer of the Fourth Gospel were men of great intellectual stature, but for the most part Christians, as Tertullian described them in the second century, were "uneducated persons, and artisans, and old women, who, if they are unable in words to prove the benefit of our doctrine, yet by their deeds exhibit the benefit arising from their persuasion of its truth." Moreover, the Christian movement had not yet come into direct contact with Greek philosophy. Thus, the literature remaining from this period is the simple manual used for instruction in the faith, passing comments on this sect by pagan writers, and incidental letters from church officials dealing with some practical problem in the church's life. Yet, as one reads the lines and between the lines of this rather scanty material, one can catch a good deal of the spirit and actual content of the ethics itself.

The Church and the World

The first clear characteristic of the ethical spirit of the early church is its communal or "corporate" temper. The language is that of "we," not "I." The individual Christian thought and acted with a strong sense of being a member of a new, self-conscious community and fellowship of believers, over against "the world," with a common memory, a common mission, and a common destiny. This identification of "I" and "we" is a characteristic feature of the Jewish tradition from which Christianity sprung. In the Old Testament one normally finds the Jew speaking for himself and for the house of Israel synonymously. This Hebraic habit of mind is deepened in the consciousness of Christians by their separateness from "the world" and by the world's hostility to them. "The world," that is, the whole fabric of Graeco-Roman social, economic, political, and religious practices, was evil, under the domain of the devil. The Christians' real citizenship was a heavenly one. They had to live *in* the world, certainly, rubbing shoulders with the pagan soldier and merchant in the market place, but they must never be *of* the world, that is, accommodate to the practices of their secular neighbors. They must keep themselves "unspotted from the world."

The evil world headed up in the omnipresent and powerful Roman state. The early Christians were particularly insistent that those who would follow Christ must remain carefully separate from political activity. They refused to take their quarrels to the public courts, to hold public office, to bury their dead in public cemeteries, to attend gladiatorial combats, to serve in the Roman army. Most important of all, they refused to subscribe to emperor worship, the moderate form of state allegiance that was expected of every resident along with his adherence to whatever form of religion he espoused. It seemed to good law-abiding folk in the empire that this was hardly more exacting than saluting the flag would seem to a twentieth-century American. They could not fathom why the early Christians were adamant in refusal. For them it was idolatry, disloyalty to the God and Father of their Lord Jesus Christ. Whether or not the Christian would offer incense to Caesar was often used as the final test by which to judge his loyalty under persecution. He who refused under torture to perform this symbolic act was killed. In such straits many undoubtedly fell away from the faith, but many too were the martyrs, stubborn to the end, like Polycarp, the venerable bishop of Smyrna, who in the year 155, threatened with death in the flames, was urged by the Proconsul, "Swear, and I will release thee; curse the Christ." And Polycarp said, "Eighty and six years have I served Him, and He hath done me no wrong; how then can I blaspheme my King who saved me?"[1]

This is not to say that the Christians were anarchists intent

[1] Henry Bettenson (ed.), *Documents of the Christian Church* (London and New York: Oxford University Press, 1947), p. 15.

on undermining the government. While they refused participation in the state's life, especially at the points where pagan practices were a violation of their scruples, and while, in the first two centuries at least, they did not think of the Empire as good, on the other hand they felt themselves above the State, not against it. They were willing to submit to the state in many matters, to pay taxes, and to suffer arrests and penalties during persecution. They often protested their innocence of political sedition. There are some signs, indeed, of relative approval of the activities of the state, an approval which grows steadily along with the slackening of separatist rigor, down to the time of Constantine, when Christianity became first tolerated, then officially approved by the Empire. In general, however, the main attitude was mixed: passive submission to the State where necessary, indifference where possible, and nonviolent resistance where the State made demands that would compromise the Christian's prime allegiance to God.

What lay behind this high indifference to the world and all its external structures? In part, the answer is to be found in the authority of some of the "other-worldly" sayings attributed to Jesus and Paul, in part in the genuinely licentious practices of pagan life, in part in the plain fact of the social position of the Christians, who could hardly avoid thinking of the State as demonic when so frequently the only face the State presented to them was a hostile one. In larger part, however, the answer lies in the Christian's underlying world-view of history in its plan of beginning and end.

The Christian inherited from Judaism a conception of the scheme of history radically different from the classical Greek theory, which was the cyclical view that history moves in eternal recurrence, around and around, with no beginning or end. The Hebrew-Christian view, on the other hand, conceived of history as the fulfillment of a divine plan, a single line moving from a point in time when God's creation began, through the crisis or central point in time when God revealed himself in Christ, to the finis when God would ring the curtain down on history and end the present-world order in a mighty act of judgment. In the literature of the time, it was universally disbelieved that human history would stretch forever ahead in time; the final Judgment or the Day of Jehovah was sure, whether near or far. The Christian community felt that it lived in a crucial meanwhile, or interim, between the time when God had come in the form of man, as the climax of history, and the time when Christ would come again (the Parousia), as the agent of God "to judge the living and the dead." They looked back in gratitude and faith to the mighty act of God in the Incarnation and ahead in hope to the consummation of the world order.

This vivid eschatology of the early church, expressed in its first creeds, inevitably influenced Christian ethical thought. Just as in the nineteenth and twentieth centuries, men's ethical motivation has been sustained in great part by a unilinear and progressive theory of the scheme of history, in these first centuries Christian ethical thought and action were always carried on in the awareness of the cosmic power which had changed, was changing, and would change the world-order. The faith that the Christ had come and the hope that Christ would come again, closing the world order, account in part for the indifference of the Christian to the social structures of the world. Since the whole machinery of life, economic, racial, political, and domestic, was soon to be swept away, why put one's hope in them or struggle to change them?

Tightening the Lines

The fervor of expectation, the moral seriousness, and the freshness of the memory of Christ were not sustained automatically. Even before the first and second generation of Christians passed on, the spontaneous excitement of the Pentecostal church described in the Book of Acts began to wane. The very success of the church weakened its spirit. It began to prosper and draw into itself people who had no personal contact even with those who had known Jesus, who were still worldly and half-committed, "third-generation"

Christians. How to preserve the original genius which first sustained the movement? Within its own circle from the start, there were inevitable fallings out, the bickerings and murmurings that badger all human institutions, this one, established in the name of the humble and loving Christ, no less than any other. Then too the church wrestled with the problem of apostasy. What to do when some Christian had backslid from his ardent loyalty during a persecution and then had applied in genuine or pretended repentance for re-admission after the cloud had passed? Should the church be rigorous in its standards of membership or lenient to the penitent and the halfhearted? Furthermore, how should the church combat worldliness in its own midst, the compromises and laxity which were inevitable as the church made its way in a pagan culture, drawing into its fellowship those who still hankered after impious ways? Finally, there were many sincere souls who simply did not know the rules of the fraternity and who needed to be instructed in its ways. Just what *were* the qualities that marked the Christian life from the pagan?

The urgency of these problems shows up in the lines of the second-century literature. The church resolutely sought purity by emphasizing a sharp dualism between the way of the Christian and the way of the sinner, "the way of life and the way of death." Just as Stoic philosophy, a hardy rival to the Christian, tried at the outset to set up a sharp distinction between the "wise" and the "foolish," with no middle ground, so the Christian church, following a well-defined Jewish tradition, drew a firm line between those who were Christian and those who were not, between the good and the bad. This dualism had considerable significance for the development of subsequent Christian ethics into monasticism.

There were other ways in which the church tried to preserve itself against contamination: formulating the canon of Scripture and setting up an episcopal form of church government. But perhaps the readiest way was to try to codify the Christian ethic. For any group in danger of losing its original ethical inspiration, legalism becomes the strategy for preservation. This proves itself recurrently in the history of the

Christian church, when the followers of a reformer try to keep alive their acquired faith by setting forth specific requirements, whose fulfillment will lead to the possession of the faith. The same tendency can be clearly seen in the second-century church. The use of catalogs of virtues and vices and "household codes" of duties emphasized a view of the good life as constituted by obedience to a body of law. This was one of the very things that Jesus himself rebelled against in his protest against the misuse of the Law in Judaism. Certainly this legalism had its dangers—in the stultifying of the free spirit as well as in externalism in morality. But at the same time, even within its hardening lines, it served to insure the integrity of the Christian faith against loss by the fire of persecution and the flood of rival doctrines and practices.

The Qualities of the Christian's Life

In these writings of the early church, there are four ethical *motifs* that are fundamental, four habits of life that show forth in the man who would call himself a Christian. The first is faith. To believe in God, to trust him in all things, this virtue is the "mother" of all the virtues according to the Shepherd of Hermas, a second-century writer who lists it typically as the first of his commandments. Single-minded belief in the true God, the creator and judge of the universe, God the Father of our Lord Jesus Christ, is the great inward virtue that marks off the Christian. Thus, as with Biblical thought, morality and religion are never thought of as separate, but always one. The contrary to faith—doubt, unbelief, or "double-mindedness"—is the cardinal sin, the root of all others, leading to apostasy, the accommodation to pagan gods and pagan ways.

The second, the fruit of faith, and the central moral commandment, is love, or *agape*. Modern misunderstandings of the word "love" have made it a very weak and anemic translation of the Greek word *agape*, which meant for the early Christian a passionate, unself-centered, unqualified concern for the well-being of the neighbor, to be expressed in sacrificial care and support. As here understood, love was not an emotional sentiment of liking, nor romantic attraction, seeking love in return, nor yet an intellectual attitude, but an inward turning of the will of the self in devotion to the neighbor, as the reflection of the love of God to man and in imitation of Christ's love for his chosen disciples.

As to the question who should be the proper recipient of this love, whether it should apply to the circle of the Christian fellowship or to those outside the circle as well, the answer seems to be mixed. On the one hand, as Jesus commanded the love of the enemy, there are instances where Christians prayed for their persecutors and drew no line of distinction in their acts of mercy. But on the other hand, most evidence favors the idea that the second-century Christians conceived of the command of love as the rule of life almost exclusively for the Christian community itself. The most striking quality of the Christians was their *agape* in the care of their own group, as seen in their assistance to the bereft, to orphans and old people, in the care for prisoners and the sick and those condemned to the mines, and in their hospitality and the sharing of economic goods. "One in mind and soul, we do not hesitate to share our earthly goods with one another. All things are common among us but our wives," wrote Tertullian in his *Apology*. "See how they love one another," was the surprised and scornful comment of the pagan citizen, who saw only fanatic folly in the abandon with which Christians sacrificed for each other. The wealthy pagan Roman practiced charity too, but his did not arise out of any strong and personal sense of community such as prompted Christian action. Pagan charity generally had the character of a paternalistic dole system, a philanthropy of those who loved themselves more than those who received their gifts. Christian charity was of a very different order, since it sprang from a congregational feeling of mutuality in love. At another point, too, Christian love as well as the inheritance of Jewish ethics led to a standard markedly different from the Roman one: the absolute prohibition of infanticide and abortion, the common Roman practice of taking the life of unwanted infants.

The Christian's love for Christians no doubt tended toward exclusiveness and particularism of a sort not unlike the exclusive loves of a college fraternity man for his fraternity brothers. In this the universalism in the ethics of Jesus was in a measure neglected. But in defense of this practice of the church, it should be said that only by this intense particularism, this narrow fidelity to the interests of Christians, could the church strive for its separate integrity. Exclusiveness is almost inevitably the price one must pay for maintaining a vigorous and distinctive way of life in a hostile environment.

This tendency is to be understood as part of a tension, persistent in the whole history of Christian ethics, between the tendencies toward penetration of the world and purity from the world. The first-century church, in the mood of Paul's evangelical zeal, seemed to swing toward the first of these poles. The second-century church, in its heightened desire for separateness and uncontamination, seemed to swing toward the second.

The third moral quality of the Christian, the mark toward which all disciples should press, itself the fruit of *agape,* is humility or meekness. The true Christian was to be known among his fellows and to the world as one who when struck did not strike in return, who avoided slander and jealousy, who imitated his Lord in serving his neighbor in preference to himself. Like all radical groups, the Christians had no little difficulty keeping peace in their own circles. Ever and again there would be minor church spats or major breaches in the ranks as excessive zealots or die-hard conservatives or "false prophets" caused trouble. Many of the letters written to the early churches by Paul and later by the new bishops in Rome were addressed to this problem. The example of the meek and humble Christ was set before the quarreling offenders, and peace and order were urged as befitting the fellowship of his followers. The necessity of preserving the cohesion of the community was no doubt at work here.

Thus obedient submission to the rulers of the church, peaceable relationships, and forbearance of differences were the orders of the day. This particular moral stress had great significance, as we shall see, for the development of medieval Catholic ethics.

The fourth ethical *motif* to be noted is that which extolled personal purity. Christians must walk a wary way amid the temptations of a licentious pagan life, lest they profane the name of their God. The requirements of personal holiness in matters of sex practices, recreations and amusements, dress, and eating and drinking play a large part in the early church's writings. Drunkenness, gluttony, adultery, sensuality, the brazen display of finery—these are stepping stones on the way of death. There are several historical sources for this emphasis. For one thing, the Jewish tradition, from which Christianity consciously and unconsciously borrowed greatly, made much of the avoidance of fleshly sins. Many of its prohibitions and fasts were and still are measures against contamination by non-Jewish worldliness. Second, there was much in the Gospel material, in the remembered words of Jesus, which could be interpreted rightly or wrongly to imply a rejection of the pleasures of the flesh.

Even more, a foreign influence can be detected here, faintly at first, but more clearly when, in the second and third centuries, the church was trying to justify itself in a Hellenistic culture, namely, a dualism between man's "good" spirit and his "bad" flesh, characteristic of later Greek philosophy and Oriental mystery-religions in their understanding of man's nature.

There is beginning, then, a tendency toward moralism and asceticism in Christian ethics which, moderate in these first centuries, takes on more rigor and exactness in later Catholicism. There is more moralism in second-century writing than with Paul, who was primarily concerned with the internal reconstruction of man through the action of faith. In this period whatever negative ascetic elements are present in the Christian ideal are incidental expressions of the positive ideal of faith in God, love of neighbor, humility of bearing, and purity of life.

These four Christian virtues are the ways in which the

Christian believed that he might best fulfill the ultimate "form" of the good life: obedience to his Lord. The form of Christian life is more significant than the content.

Unless sustained by a constant inward moral mood of fidelity to God in Christ, these virtues are of no avail. When practiced out of obedience to God in Christ, they are the true fruits of the Spirit of God, who alone can redeem man's life from destruction. Thus, the new life in Christ was presented as demand, as requirement, but also it was known as a gift of the Spirit, as a free and glad response to God for what he had done for men in Christ.

The selections that follow are difficult to date accurately. Questions as to authorship cannot be answered with any final certainty. The *Didache*, or *Teaching of the Twelve Apostles* (pp. 58-61), is from a manuscript discovered in Constantinople in 1873. It was first thought to belong to the last part of the first century, but subsequent scholarship has dated it at about the middle of the second century. The so-called *First Epistle of Clement* probably antedates the *Didache*, but since the *Didache* illustrates so vividly the quality of a simple, unphilosophical manual of Christian morals, it is included here first.

Its first six chapters, describing the "two ways," are almost exactly paralleled in another Christian document, the *Epistle of Barnabas*, from the early second century. This suggests that the material of the "two ways" had currency among Christians not more than a generation or so after the death of Christ, about the time that Paul was writing his letters. At any rate, this unsophisticated handbook of moral rules, derived from Old Testament and New Testament quotations, undoubtedly represents the kind of instruction given to inquiring members of the struggling new church.

St. Clement of Rome, generally reputed to have been the third head of the church, from about A.D. 90 to 99, in succession from St. Peter, was one of the early bishops held in high veneration in Christian antiquity. His *Letter to the Co-*

rinthians (pp. 61-68) is the only surely authentic example of his writing that remains. It reveals the mind of a devoted and able administrator, deeply versed in scriptural writing, Paul especially, trying to contend with a disagreeable rift disturbing the distant church at Corinth. The Corinthian Christians, as Paul discovered earlier, seem to have been a quarrelsome lot. In Clement's time they had split themselves into divided camps, each contending for authority in the church. This was a scandal disturbing to all the other churches.

Clement, as leader of the Roman church, which had quickly come to be regarded as the central authority, sent them a lengthy and passionate entreaty in the interests of restoring unity. The whole purpose of the letter is a practical rather than theoretical one, but from his advice one may glean valuable insights into the ethical standards maintained by the leaders of the church, of which the dispute of the Corinthians was such a flagrant violation. The plea, of course, is for unity, submission, order, humility, and love. But these are set within a theological faith and within a full description of the Christian life, with its requirement of radical *agape*, separation from "the world" in personal purity, and the worship and imitation of God, who orders the world in peace and harmony. One may note also how Clement's apocalyptic world view adds a sense of urgency and warning to his message.

The most apt summary made by a contemporary of the quality of life of the Christian community is to be found in a curious anonymous letter addressed to one Diognetus (pp. 68-69). It is both a description and a eulogy, penned—possibly in the early second century, though any date is conjectural—by a man versed in Greek modes of thought and gifted with uncommon verve of style. He speaks of the Christians as "they," rather than "we," but it is quite apparent where his own persuasions lie.

SOURCES

From

The Didache or Teaching of the Twelve Apostles[2]

The Way of Life

There are two ways, one of life and one of death; and great is the difference between the two ways.

This is the way of life: "First, you shall love God who made you, secondly, your neighbor as yourself; and whatever you would not like done to you, do not do to another."

The teaching of these words is as follows: "Bless those who curse you, and pray for your enemies, and fast for those who persecute you." For what is the merit of loving those who love you? Do not even the pagans do this? But, "love those who hate you," and you will not have an enemy. "Abstain from carnal desires." "If anyone strikes you on the right cheek, turn the other to him," and you will be perfect. "If anyone force you to go one mile with him, go two." "If anyone takes your cloak, give him also your tunic." If anyone takes what is yours, do not demand it back, for you have no power.

Give to everyone who asks, and ask nothing in return; for the Father wishes that a share of His own gifts be given to all. Blessed is the man who gives according to the commandment, for he is without blame. Woe to the man who takes. However, if the one who takes is in need, he is without blame. But should he not be in need, he shall give an account of the why and the wherefore of his taking it. And he will be put in prison and examined strictly about what he did, and "shall not go out from there until he has paid the last cent." But in this matter the saying also holds: "Let your alms sweat in your hands until you know to whom you are giving."[3]

The second commandment of the Teaching is: You shall

[2] This and all subsequent sources in this chapter are from *The Apostolic Fathers (The Fathers of the Church,* ed. Ludwig Schopp, Vol. I [New York: Christian Heritage, Inc., 1947]). Copyright 1947 by Christian Heritage, Inc. Reprinted by permission.

[3] "The Didache or Teaching of the Twelve Apostles," chap. i.

not commit murder. You shall not commit adultery. You shall not corrupt boys. You shall not commit fornication. You shall not steal. You shall not practice magic. You shall not practice sorcery. You shall not kill an unborn child or murder a newborn infant. And you shall not desire the goods of your neighbor. You shall not swear falsely or bear false witness; nor shall you slander, or bring up past injuries. You shall not be double-minded or double-tongued, for duplicity is the snare of death. Let your speech not be false or vain, but carried out in action. You shall not be greedy or extortionate; nor shall you be a hypocrite, nor malicious, or proud. You shall not take evil counsel against your neighbor. You shall not hate any man; but some you shall admonish, and pray for others, and still others you shall love more than your own life.[4]

The Love of Neighbor

My son, flee from all wickedness and from everything like it. Do not become angry, for anger leads to murder. Do not become jealous, or quarrelsome, or irritable, for it leads to fornication. And do not use obscene language, or let your eye wander, for from all these come adulteries. My child, do not be an observer of omens, for this leads to idolatry; or engage in witchcraft, astrology, or ritual ablutions. Do not even desire to see these things (or hear them), for from all these idolatry is born. My child, do not be a liar, because a lie leads to theft; be not greedy of money or empty glory, for from all this come thefts. My child, do not be a grumbler, because it leads to blasphemy, do not be proud or malicious, for from all these arise blasphemies.

But be meek, for "the meek shall inherit the land." Be patient, merciful, guileless, and mild and gentle, and in every regard "fearful of the words," which you have heard. Do not exalt yourself or allow impudence in your soul. Your soul shall not cling to the proud, but associate with good and humble men. Accept the troubles that come to you as good, knowing that nothing happens without God.[5]

[4] *Ibid.*, chap. ii.
[5] *Ibid.*, chap. v.

My child, day and night keep in memory him who speaks the word of God to you, and you shall honor him as the Lord, for the Lord is there wherever the doctrine of the Lord is preached. And every day look for the company of holy men, that you may find comfort in their conversation. Do not desire any schism, but make peace among those who fight. Judge justly, and do not show any favor to any one in correcting offences. Do not waver whether a thing shall be or not be.

Do not hold your hands open for receiving and closed for giving. If you possess something by the labor of your hands, give it for the redemption of your sins. Do not be reluctant in giving, or murmur when you give, for you well know who He is who gives a good reward. Do not turn away from the needy, but share all with your brother and do not claim that it is your own. For, if you are sharers in immortal things, how much more in mortal.

Do not take your hand from your son or your daughter, but teach them the fear of God from their youth. Do not with bitterness command your servant or maid, who trust in the same God, lest they should cease to fear God who is above both of you, for, without respect of persons, He comes to call those whom the Spirit has prepared. And you who are servants, be subject to your masters, as being the representative of God, with modesty and reverence.

You shall hate all hypocrisy and everything that displeases the Lord. Do not abandon the commandments of the Lord, but keep what you have received, without adding or subtracting. You shall confess your offences in church, and shall not come forward to your prayer with a bad conscience. This is the way of life.[6]

The Way of Death

On the other hand, this is the way of death. First of all, it is evil and full of cursings, murders, adulteries, evil desires, fornications, thefts, idolatries, magical practices, sorceries, robberies, false witnessings, hypocrisies, double-mindedness,

6 *Ibid.*, chap. iv.

guile, pride, malice, arrogance, covetousness, filthy talk, envy, insolence, haughtiness, boastfulness [and lack of fear of God]. [Those who walk the way of death] persecute good people, hate the truth, love lies, do not acknowledge any reward of justice, do not follow goodness or just judgment, and are vigilant not for good but for evil, from whom meekness and patience are far removed, who love vanities, pursuing gain, without pity for the poor and without care for those who are oppressed. They do not acknowledge their Creator, they are murderers of children, corrupters of the image of God; they turn away from the needy, oppress the afflicted; they are flatterers of the rich, unjust judges of the poor, and are full of all sins. May you be saved, children, from all these.[7]

Beware lest anyone lead you astray from the way of the Teaching, since his teaching would be without God. If you are able to carry the full yoke of the Lord, you will be perfect; but if you are not able, do whatever you can. With regard to food, abstain as much as you can, and from whatever has been offered to idols abstain completely, for this is to worship dead gods.[8]

From

The Letter of St. Clement to the Corinthians

Humility in Obedience

Let us, therefore, be humble-minded, brothers, putting away all boasting and conceit and silliness and anger, and let us do what is written, for the Holy Spirit says: "Let not the wise man glory in his wisdom, nor let the strong man glory in his strength, nor the rich man in his riches, but let him that glories glory in the Lord, to seek Him and to do judgment and justice." Especially should we remember the words which the Lord Jesus spoke, when He taught clemency

[7] *Ibid.*, chap. v.
[8] *Ibid.*, chap. vi.

and long suffering. For He spoke thus; "Be merciful, that you may obtain mercy. Forgive, that you may be forgiven. As you do, so shall it be done to you. As you give, so shall it be given to you. As you judge, so shall you be judged. As you are kind, so shall you be treated kindly. With what measure you measure, with the same shall it be measured to you." In this commandment and in this counsel let us strengthen ourselves to walk obedient to His holy words, being humble-minded, for the Holy Writ says: "On whom shall I have regard except on the meek and gentle and him who trembles at My words."[9]

And so, brothers, it is right and holy for us to be obedient to God rather than to follow those who in arrogance and insubordination are the leaders in abominable jealousy. For we shall suffer no ordinary harm, but run a very great risk, if we rashly entrust ourselves to the designs of men who aim at strife and sedition, to alienate us from what is right. Let us be kind to one another after the model of the compassion and sweetness of Him who made us.[10]

The humility and obedient submissiveness of so many men of such proven reputation have made us better—and not only us, but likewise our fathers before us and all who have received His words in fear and truth. Sharing, then, in their many great and glorious deeds, let us run toward the goal of peace which from the beginning has been handed down to us, let us look steadfastly toward the Father and Creator of the whole world, and hold fast to His magnificent and surpassing gifts of peace and kindness to us. Let us look on His long-suffering purpose. Let us realize how peacefully He acts toward His whole creation.[11]

The Concord of Creation

The heavens move at His direction and are subject to Him in tranquility. Day and night complete the course assigned

[9] "The Letter of St. Clement to the Corinthians," chap. xiii.
[10] *Ibid.*, chap. xiv.
[11] *Ibid.*, chap. xix.

by Him without hindering each other. Sun and moon and the choir of stars revolve in harmony according to His command in the orbits assigned to them, without swerving the slightest. The earth, flowering at His bidding in due seasons, brings forth abundant food for men and beasts and all the living beings on its surface, without reluctance and without altering any of His arrangements. The unsearchable places of the bottomless pit and the indescribable regions of the lower world are subject to the same decrees. The mass of the boundless sea, gathered together in one place according to His plan, does not overrun the barriers appointed to it, but acts as He commanded it. For He said: "Thus far shalt thou come, and thy wave shall be broken within thee." The ocean, impassable by men, and the worlds beyond it are regulated by the same decrees of the Lord. The seasons of spring, summer, fall, and winter give way in turn, one to the other, in peace. The winds from the different quarters, each in its proper season, perform their service without hindrance. The ever-flowing springs, made for enjoyment and for health, unfailingly offer their breasts to sustain the life of man. The very smallest of the animals come together in harmony and in peace. The great Creator and Lord of the universe commanded all these things to be at peace and in harmony; He does good to all, and more than super-abundantly to us who have found refuge in His mercies through Our Lord Jesus Christ. To whom be glory and majesty forever and ever. Amen.[12]

Be on your guard, brothers, lest His many benefits turn into a judgment upon all of us. This will be so if we do not, by performing in concord virtuous deeds pleasing to Him, live lives worthy of Him. For He says in one place: "The Spirit of the Lord is a light, searching the inward parts." Let us see how near He is, and that not one of our thoughts or the plans we make escapes Him. It is right, then, that we should not be deserters from His will. If we must offend, let it be foolish and senseless men who exalt themselves and boast in the arrogance of their reason, rather than God. Let us fear the Lord Jesus, whose blood was given for us; let us re-

[12] *Ibid.*, chap. xx.

spect our leaders; let us honor the presbyters; let us teach the young in the school of the fear of God. Let us guide our women toward what is good. Let them reveal an exquisite disposition to purity, let them exhibit an unfaltering will to be meek. Let them show forth the control of their tongues by their silence. Let them show their affection, not with partiality but in holiness, equally to all who fear God. Let your children take part in the instruction which is in Christ, let them learn how powerful with God is humility, how strong is a pure love, how the fear of Him is beautiful and great and saves those who live in it in holiness with a pure mind. For He is a searcher of thoughts and desires; His breath is in us, and when He wills, He will take it away.[13]

The all-merciful and beneficent Father has compassion on them who fear Him, and with gentleness and kindness bestows His favors on those who approach Him with a simple mind. So, let us not be double-minded, nor let our soul form false ideas about His extra-ordinary and glorious gifts. Let that Scripture be far from us where He says: "Miserable are the double-minded who doubt in their soul and say, 'These things have we heard even in the days of our fathers, and behold, we are grown old, and none of these things has happened to us.' O senseless men, compare yourselves to a tree. Take a vine: First it sheds its leaves, then there comes a bud, then a leaf, then a flower, and after that the unripe grape, then the full bunch." You see how in a little time the fruit of the tree reaches its ripeness. Truly His will shall be fulfilled swiftly and suddenly, as the Scripture testifies: "He shall come quickly and not delay; and the Lord shall come suddenly to his temple, the Holy One whom you expect."[14]

The Works of Gratitude

Since we are a portion of the Holy One, let us do all that belongs to holiness, fleeing from evil speech, and abominable

[13] *Ibid.*, chap. xxi.
[14] *Ibid.*, chap. xxiii.

and impure embraces, from drunkenness and from rioting, and detestable lusts, foul adultery, and detestable pride. "For God," He says, "resisteth the proud but giveth grace to the Humble." Let us then join with those to whom grace is given from God; let us put on concord in meekness of spirit and in self control, keeping ourselves far from all gossip and evil speaking, being justified by works and not by words. For He says: "He that speaketh much shall also hear much; or does he that speaks fair think that he is just? Blessed is the man born of woman who has a short life. Be not full of words." Let our praise be with God, and not from ourselves, for God hates those who praise themselves. Let the testimony of our good deeds be given by others, as it was given to our fathers, who were righteous. Boldness and arrogance and presumption belong to those who are cursed by God; gentleness and humility and meekness belong to those who are blessed by God.[15]

And, if anyone will examine fairly each example, he will recognize the greatness of the gifts given by God. For from him [Jacob] come the priests and the Levites who minister at the altar of God; from him comes the Lord Jesus according to the flesh; from him come the kings and rulers and leaders in the line of Judah. And the other tribes are in no slight honor, since, as God promised: "Thy seed shall be as the stars of heaven." They were all glorified and magnified not through themselves or their own works or the good deeds which they did, but through His will. And we also, having been called through His will in Christ Jesus, are not justified by ourselves, or by our own wisdom or understanding or piety or the works we have done in holiness of heart, but through the faith by which the Almighty God has justified all men from the beginning; to whom be glory for all ages. Amen.[16]

What, then, shall we do, brothers? Shall we slacken from doing good and abandon charity? May the Lord never allow this to happen to us, but let us be diligent to accomplish every good work with earnestness and zeal. For the Creator and

[15] *Ibid.*, chap. xxx.
[16] *Ibid.*, chap. xxxii.

Lord of the universe Himself takes joy in His works. For in His overwhelming might He has set up the heavens, and by His unsearchable wisdom He has put them in order. He has separated the earth from the surrounding water and placed it on the solid foundation of His own will; and He has called into existence the animals that move in it by His own arrangement. Having prepared the sea and the living creatures that are in it, He enclosed them by His own power. Over all, with His holy and pure hands He formed man, the most excellent and greatest in intelligence, with the stamp of His own image. For God spoke thus: "Let us make man according to our image and likeness; and God made man, male and female He made them." Having finished all these things, he praised and blessed them and said: "Increase and multiply." Let us consider that all the saints have been adorned with good works; and the Lord Himself, adorning Himself with good works, rejoiced. Holding this pattern, then, let us follow out His will without hesitation; let us do the work of justice with all our strength.[17]

How blessed and wonderful are the gifts of God, beloved. Life in immortality, joyousness in justice, truth in confidence, faith in trustfulness, continence in holiness. And all these things fall within our understanding. And what shall we say of the things that are being prepared for those who persevere. Only the Creator and Father of the ages, the all-holy One, knows their greatness and beauty. Let us strive, therefore, to be found in the number of those who wait for Him, that we may share in the promised gifts. But how shall this be, beloved? If our mind be fixed by means of faith on God; if we perform what is proper to His faultless will and follow the path of truth, casting from us all injustice and wickedness, covetousness, strife, malice and deceit, gossiping and evil speaking, hatred of God, arrogance and boasting, vainglory and inhospitality. For they who do these things are detestable to God, and "not only those who do them, but also those who consent to them."[18]

[17] *Ibid.*, chap. xxiii.
[18] *Ibid.*, chap. xxxv.

Therefore, let our whole body be saved in Christ Jesus, and let each be subject to his neighbor, according to the position which grace bestowed on each. Let not the strong neglect the weak, and let the weak respect the strong. Let the rich man supply the wants of the poor, and let the poor man give thanks to God, because He has given him someone to supply his needs. Let the wise show his wisdom not in words, but in good works. Let the humble-minded not testify to his own humility, but allow others to bear him witness. Let him who is pure in the flesh be so without boasting, knowing that it is Another who grants him this continence. Let us consider, brother, of what matter we were made; who and what we are who have come into the world; from what a tomb and what darkness our Maker and Creator brought us into the world and prepared His benefits for us before we were born. We who have obtained all these things from Him ought to thank Him for all, to whom be glory forever and ever. Amen.[19]

Let him who had charity in Christ keep Christ's commandments. Who can explain the bond of the charity of God? Who can express the splendor of its beauty? The height to which charity lifts us is inexpressible. Charity unites us to God, "Charity covers a multitude of sins"; charity bears all things, is long-suffering in all things. There is nothing mean in charity, nothing arrogant. Charity knows no schism. Does not rebel, does all things in concord. In charity all the elect of God have been made perfect. Without charity nothing is pleasing to God. In charity the Lord received us; out of the charity which He had for us, Jesus Christ our Lord gave His blood for us by the will of God, and His flesh for our flesh, and His life for our lives.[20]

Brothers, we have written to you sufficiently concerning the things that befit our religion and are most helpful to the life of virtue for those who wish to direct their steps in piety and justice. For, in regard to faith and repentance and genuine charity and self-control and discretion and patience, we have treated every point. We have reminded you that you

[19] *Ibid.*, chap. xxxviii.
[20] *Ibid.*, chap. xlix.

must please Almighty God with holiness in justice and truth and long-suffering, in a life of concord. You should forget injuries in love and peace, and continue in gentleness, as our fathers aforementioned who, in their humility, were pleasing to God, the Father and Creator, and to all men. And we have reminded you of these things the more willingly because we knew well that we were writing to men who are faithful and well-reputed and had studied the words of God's instruction.[21]

From
The Letter to Diognetus

Christians are not different from the rest of men in nationality, speech, or customs; they do not live in states of their own, nor do they use a special language, nor adopt a peculiar way of life. Their teaching is not the kind of thing that could be discovered by the wisdom or reflection of mere active-minded men; indeed, they are not outstanding in human learning as others are. Whether fortune has given them a home in a Greek or foreign city, they follow local custom in the matter of dress, food, and way of life; yet the character of the culture they reveal is marvelous and, it must be admitted, unusual. They live, each in his native land—but as though they were not really at home there. They share in all duties like citizens and suffer all hardships like strangers. Every foreign land is for them a fatherland and every fatherland a foreign land. They marry like the rest of men and beget children, but they do not abandon the babies that are born. They share a common board, but not a common bed. In the flesh as they are, they do not live according to the flesh. They dwell on earth, but they are citizens of heaven. They obey the laws that men make, but their lives are better than the laws. They love all men, but are persecuted by all. They are unknown, and yet they are condemned. They are put to death, yet are more alive than ever. They are paupers, but they make many rich. They lack all things, and yet in all

[21] *Ibid.*, chap. lxii.

things they abound. They are dishonored, yet glory in their dishonor. They are maligned, and yet are vindicated. They are reviled, and yet they bless. They suffer insult, yet they pay respect. They do good, yet are punished with the wicked. When they are punished, they rejoice, as though they were getting more of life. They are attacked by the Jews as Gentiles and are persecuted by the Greeks, yet those who hate them can give no reason for their hatred.

In a word, what the soul is to the body Christians are to the world. The soul is distributed in every member of the body, and Christians are scattered in every city in the world. The soul dwells in the body, and yet it is not of the body. So, Christians live in the world, but they are not of the world. The soul which is guarded in the visible body is not itself visible. And so, Christians who are in the world are known, but their worship remains unseen. The flesh hates the soul and acts like an unjust aggressor, because it is forbidden to indulge in pleasures. The world hates Christians—not that they have done it wrong, but because they oppose its pleasures. The soul loves the body and its members in spite of the hatred. So Christians love those who hate them. The soul is locked up in the body, yet it holds the body together. And so Christians are held in the world as in a prison, yet it is they who hold the world together. The immortal soul dwells in a mortal tabernacle. So Christians sojourn among perishable things, but their souls are set on immortality in heaven. When the soul is ill-treated in the matter of food and drink, it is improved. So, when Christians are persecuted, their numbers daily increase. Such is the assignment to which God has called them, and they have no right to shirk it.

Further Readings

Primary Sources

Fremantle, Anne (ed.). *A Treasury of Early Christianity.* New York: Viking Press, 1953.

Grant, Robert, and Graham, Holt (eds.). *First and Second Clement.* (*Apostolic Fathers,* Vol. 2.) New York: Nelson, 1965.

RICHARDSON, C. C. (ed.). *Early Christian Fathers.* (*The Library of Christian Classics,* Vol. 1.) Philadelphia: Westminster Press, 1953.

SNYDER, GRAYDON F. (ed.). *The Shepherd of Hermas.* (*Apostolic Fathers,* Vol. 6.) New York: Nelson, 1965.

Secondary Sources

CADOUX, C. J. *The Early Church and the World.* Edinburgh: T. and T. Clark, 1925.

CHADWICK, HENRY. *The Early Church.* Baltimore: Penguin Books, 1967.

GRANT, ROBERT M. *The Apostolic Fathers: An Introduction.* New York: Nelson, 1964.

PHILLIPS, C. S. *The New Commandment.* New York: Macmillan, 1931.

Chapter 3

CLEMENT OF ALEXANDRIA

By the beginning of the third century, the Christian church had begun to make its impact fully felt in the Graeco-Roman world. It had now to be reckoned with as one of the powerful and permanent forces in the empire's life. Its growth in numbers and influence had been enormous. The state could not check its advance either by persecution or grudging toleration. Its relation to the world was not a one-way influence, however. As the church moved farther into the world, it was inevitable, as throughout Christian history, that the world would move into the church. The life of Christians was influenced by the thought forms of pagan culture, as pagan culture was influenced by Christianity. Christians of the third century were in the main more eager than those of the second to come to terms with the culture in which they lived. Although they believed that these terms should be Christian, it was inevitable that cultural interaction would make the terms both Christian and pagan. There is no more clear example of this development than in Clement of Alexandria (*ca.* 150–220).

In the third century, the Egyptian city of Alexandria was becoming the new Athens of the Roman world, the center of learning, culture, and wealth. In the autumn of the Roman empire's power, this city was at its zenith of spiritual and intellectual vitality. With its famous library housing all the lore of Greek and Roman philosophy, its proud tradition of philosophic achievement (Philo Judaeus, a century before Clement, had achieved there a highly influential synthesis of Hebrew and Hellenic thought), it was a busy place of trade in goods and ideas. The Christian church had made its way steadily amid the various philosophies and religions in this cosmopolitan center. By Clement's time, it was sufficiently well established to have a number of wealthy Alexandrians in its membership and a "catechetical" school of considerable size, a sort of "denominational college by the side of a secular university,"[1] where instruction was given in the Christian faith as well as in liberal arts. In this academic and urbane environment, the proponents of Christianity were faced with a relatively new task: that of justifying the Christian belief on intellectual grounds to the sceptical or receptive Hellene who had been brought up in the tradition of Greek philosophy and was probably a subscriber to one or another of the pagan religions that flourished in the city.

Clement's Intellectual Task

Clement was among the first of Christian thinkers who deliberately attempted to bring together the Christian religion and Hellenic philosophy. In so far as the presuppositions of Western culture are derived from these two sources, the significance of this first attempted synthesis is apparent. He was not the last nor the most successful in this effort. Figures of more classic proportions, notably Augustine and Thomas Aquinas, were to address themselves to the task in later centuries with greater success.

It was an enormous and baffling task. Many of the presuppositions of the Christian faith were poles apart from those of Greek philosophy. The world view of the Christian—his interpretation of the nature of God and the universe, of the nature of man, his destiny and ideal good—differed from, and at some points was irreconcilable with, the first principles of Plato, Aristotle, Seneca, Marcus Aurelius, and their spiritual descendants. Here on the one hand was the Greek ideal of the good life. Amid its numerous forms and variations—the Platonic pursuit of absolute values, the Aristotelian rational ethics of moderation, the Stoic principle of apathy,

[1] Charles Bigg, *The Christian Platonists of Alexandria* (Oxford: The Clarendon Press, 1886), p. 42.

the Epicurean enjoyment of refined pleasures—there was a single moral temper that warrants the use of the term "Greek." In the main, its ideal of the highest good was that of rational discipline, moderation, and self-restraint in a balanced and well-rounded life. The sprawling empire had become too vast and uncertain a unit to command a collective political loyalty in which the individual could lose himself. Hence there was a turn toward individualism, strongly marked in Stoicism and Epicureanism. The solitary man must find his own salvation through the valiant captaincy of his own soul, in a universe which at worst was hostile or indifferent to his fate and at best gave evidence of an impersonal natural law to which he must conform. In a stubborn and resolute fortitude against despair, and through a deliberate unconcern about the external fortunes of his life, the rational man could achieve in this life a relative peace of mind. This was the way of salvation offered by the later Greek tradition.

Set over against this ideal was the Hebrew-Christian pattern, with its theological orientation, its corporate spirit, its ethic of *agape* as a compassionate concern for the neighbor, and its voluntaristic way of stressing man's will as the mainspring of his nature. One can appreciate the difficulty of the task to which Clement addressed himself. His assignment was further complicated by the doctrinal confusion that prevailed in Christian thought itself. The church was wrestling with the problem of defining its central creeds. As might be expected in a religiously diverse culture, this brought about a great confusion of tongues. Novel and foreign elements were entering in, all claiming to be the true version of the Christian faith. One of the most appealing of these was Gnosticism, so popular in Clement's time as to bid fair to become the normative version of Christianity. The Gnostic theory, as set forth by Valentinus and Basilides, comes out of many sources, Babylonian, Egyptian, Persian, as well as Hellenic. Its world view was sharply dualistic, distinguishing between the good spirit and the bad flesh of man, and between the perfect realm of supernatural forces and the evil world. Salvation for man lay in escape from the world, not through moral discipline, but through a mysterious kind of knowledge (*gnosis*) that was granted to some and denied to others. In its Christianized form this *gnosis* was achieved for man through the activity of a saving God, Christ, a supernatural figure who bore no real relation, in the minds of Gnostics, to the Jesus of flesh and history. In time this sort of Gnosticism was ruled out of bounds by the church, but only after extended debate when clear thinking by men like Clement and others was necessary to expose the dangers of this heresy and its fundamental disparity with the spirit of orthodox Christianity, with its moral earnestness, its monistic world view, and its belief in an historical Jesus Christ, the Word made flesh. But the popularity of the Gnostic faith, even among Christians, is illustrated by the very fact, as will be seen in the selections below, that Clement uses the term "Gnostic" to describe the highest type of Christian man.

For the task of expressing Christianity to a Hellenistic culture Clement was well equipped. Born of pagan parents about the middle of the second century, possibly in Athens, he had received a thorough education in Greek and Hellenistic thought. In search of a satisfying philosophy of life, he seems to have sampled the studies at this and that "school," until he came to Alexandria to study under one Pantaenus, a Christian convert from Stoicism, head of the Christian catechetical school and a persuasive teacher. Clement was converted to Christianity, elected a presbyter in the church, and in time succeeded his teacher as head of the school. A man of scholarly inclinations and bookish, he was something of a recluse. Once, during the persecution of Septimus Severus in 202, he was forced to flee from Alexandria. He died about 220. From the voluminous pages of his writing one gets a mental picture of a gentle scholar, as thoroughly at home in Plato and the Greek poets as in Scripture, sweet-tempered and irenic, liberal in his desire to find worth in positions opposite to his own, and a man of piety and devotion to the practice of prayer.

Of his works left to posterity, one short treatise, "The Rich Man's Salvation," is of especial interest to students of Christian social ethics. It illustrates the problem of how to reckon with the original rigor of the Gospel command against wealth in an urbane and prosperous environment. His longer and major works are three. The "Exhortation to the Heathen" is an attack on the sordid practices and intellectually shoddy beliefs of current pagan faiths and an invitation to the Christian Gospel. The "Instructor," a guide to Christian behavior, sets forth his theory of the role of Christ, as the Divine Word, sent by God to be the tutor for men and their guide out of the darkness of ignorance. In this work Clement elaborates in great detail the manners and mores appropriate to the Christian. The "Stromata," or "Miscellanies," is an elaborate but quite unsystematic study of all the essentials of Christian belief. One of its central points is that the Christian should not scorn philosophy but should make use of its discipline, since he can find in the best of Greek thought, especially Plato, foreshadowings and "broken lights" of the truth revealed in Christ. "There is in philosophy . . . a slender spark, capable of being fanned into flame, a trace of wisdom and an impulse from God."[2] God gave philosophy to the Greeks, as he gave the Law to the Jews, to train them in righteousness and prepare them for the full truth. Clement's case for philosophy is a deliberate deviation in the history of Christian thought from the suspicion of philosophy, "the wisdom of the wise," which had characterized many earlier Christian apologists.

The Two Levels of the Christian Life

The ethical theory which Clement sets forth is a combination of Hellenic and Christian moral principles. He pictures the ideal Christian life as a graduated discipline of two stages. The lower preliminary way is the life of plain and simple faith, wherein the Christian follows the discipline of the church out of hope of reward and fear of punishment without

[2] "The Stromata," in *Fathers of the Second Century (The Ante-Nicene Fathers,* eds. Alexander Roberts and James Donaldson, Vol. II [Amer. ed., ar. by A. Cleveland Coxe; Buffalo: The Christian Literature Publishing Co., 1885; New York: Charles Scribner's Sons, 1926]), p. 320.

understanding the higher reasons for his actions. Here he is a good, docile, law-abiding believer. In a sense this is life under the Law, where the Christian carefully abstains from moral evils, and cultivates personal holiness. The higher way is the life which moves out of the negative discipline of the first stage to the higher plateau of the love and knowledge of God. This is the life of the true Gnostic. The Christian Gnostic no longer cultivates the virtues of the Christian life out of the ulterior motives of fear of punishment or hope of reward, but out of the love of the Good, which is God, for its own sake. The discipline of philosophy is now put to its true use. The love and contemplation of God is the supreme mark for which the Gnostic strives. "Ignorance of God is death; but the knowledge and appropriation of Him, and love and likeness to Him, are the only life."[3] Indeed, if the Christian had to choose between the love of God and his own personal salvation, he would choose the former, though fortunately Clement does not feel that this is an actual either-or. The higher *gnosis* consists in God-likeness. Clement means by this two things in particular: kindness and beneficence to all men after the pattern of the One who sends his rain on the just and the unjust, and passionlessness. In accord with Greek theology, Clement conceived of God as omnipotent, self-sufficient, and "destitute of all desire." Therefore the Godlike Christian will be freed from all passions and affections; the master of all circumstances and fortunes, he will remain serene and imperturbable amid the attractions of the world and the flesh. He will pass his days in quiet inward communion with God in prayer, in active out-going love to his fellows, Christian and non-Christian, and in the instruction of others in the beauties of the true way.

This two-leveled picture of the Christian life might seem to be too spiritually aristocratic, like the Stoic theory which maintained its class distinction between the "wise" and the "foolish." But note in Clement that simple faith is a *stage* on life's way, a discipline preliminary to reaching an advanced level of the Christian life. "Faith is the first move-

[3] *Ibid.*, "The Rich Man's Salvation," p. 593.

ment toward salvation; after which fear, hope, repentance, advancing in company with temperance and patience, lead us to love and knowledge."[4] He is realistic enough to recognize that few Christians will become true Gnostics. But he draws no predetermined line between those who would come to the highest fulfillment and those who traverse a lower way.

The Greek and the Christian in Clement

Even from the few source materials below, the student may readily discern the eclectic way in which Clement takes up both Hellenic and Christian strands in his thought. He is characteristically Hellenic, first, in his tendency toward individualism. Though allegiance to the Christian church has a real place in his ideal for the Christian man, the corporate sense in him is much more tenuous than in earlier Christians. Clement thinks of the single self, searching for a way of salvation in solitariness. His interest is much more in the individual than in the community. With the Greeks, too, he is inclined in his understanding of human nature to think of reason as the distinguishing quality of man. The true Gnostic can exercise this capacity to apprehend truth to the point where he becomes in a sense divine. Man is a responsible agent in his own salvation. As the bearer of reason, he is free to make his moral choices, choosing the life which leads toward *gnosis* or the death of ignorance. But sin is not a radical inherited corruption of man's nature; it is "missing the mark," to be ascribed fundamentally to an error of judgment rather than to a perversity of will. Clement has a high opinion of human capabilities, a trust in man's inherent rationality and good inclinations. Hence arise his appreciation of philosophy and his dislike of any religion that begins and ends in irrational credulity or in an affirmation of the depravity of man. Again, the moral principles of balance, moderation, and restraint, which Clement steadily repeats, sound much more

[4] *Ibid.*, "The Stromata," p. 354.

like Aristotle and the Stoics than the Gospels. Clement has the philosopher's disdain for excess. It is only in praise of the love of God that he almost lets go, but even here he is careful to give love a calm and intellectual cast. His proclivity for careful proportion in all things is seen in his attitude toward worldly pleasures. He is no ascetic who disparages the body. The body is an instrument of worth, to be treated with respect, neither dissipated nor unduly curbed. The fact that "the soul of man is confessedly the better part of man, and the body the inferior," is no reason to affirm that "the soul is good by nature, nor the body bad by nature." Here is a criticism not only of the pagan Gnostics, but of those Christian extremists who thought of their bodies as miserable carcasses to be punished in the cultivation of the spirit. No, says Clement. The wise Christian will treat his body and its pleasures with moderation, living simply, putting things of this world neither too high nor too low on his scale of values.

Finally, when Clement describes the Christian life as a progression toward the goal of the knowledge and love of God, or a sort of pilgrimage in gradual perfection through the discipline of moral training, he illustrates the teleological (or end-directed) character of Greek moral theory, which starts out by asking what is the greatest good to be striven for and what steps lead there. This teleological note is somewhat different from the Biblical way of ethical thinking, which deals more in terms of obedience to the present command of God than with aspiration toward a future goal.

On the other side, genuinely Christian factors are no less evident. Primary, of course, is Clement's belief that the life of the good man is one centered in God. It is by nothing on earth, but by the nature of the sovereign and transcendent God—his love, benevolence, and impartiality—that the Christian measures his own life. This makes Clement's ethics indubitably theonomous, or God-dependent, in contrast to the autonomous quality in much of Greek moral theory. Second, Clement belongs with the psalmists and Jesus in making moral purity both the precondition for and the fruit of the contemplation of God. It is only the pure in heart and those of clean hands who may ascend to the mount of vision.

Clement also has something of the Hebrew-Christian sense of the divine initiative and grace in the ordering of human life. Although at some points he gives the impression that man is to lift himself up by his own moral bootstraps in a process of self-salvation, he takes pains at other points, in truly Christian fashion, to show that the hand of God is present at every point of moral advance. After all, he says, "the ball-player cannot catch the ball unless it is thrown to him." The first commitments of faith and the later winning of knowledge are due as much to divine grace as to human response. Moreover, God's great gift to man is in Jesus Christ, the Word, who is the constant Instructor, the prompter and illuminer of men's minds as they seek their way out of darkness.

One of the abiding problems in Christian history is in economic ethics, in the clash between "God and Mammon," in reconciling the appeal of wealth with the suspicion or downright exclusion of riches in the Gospels. Evidently there were several well-to-do Christians in the Alexandrian church who were troubled by this contradiction and sought Clement's advice. His essay, *The Rich Man's Salvation* (pp. 94-98), a commentary on the story of the rich young ruler (Mark 10:17-31), is an effort to calm their fears and to suggest a way out of the dilemma. His answer is typical of his way of reconciling the demands of Christ with those of culture. What Jesus enjoined on the rich young ruler, Clement claims, is *inner* detachment from wealth, not literally an outer renunciation. This counsel is combined with the admonition to generosity and stewardship as expressions of the law of love. The rich man who is not possessed within by his possessions and who serves the needs of the poor may rest assured of his discipleship.

To what extent this realistic answer is more Stoic than Christian, to what extent it is an evasion of the Gospel and a compromise with the world, have been matters of continued debate among Christians. Radical monasticism, as we shall see, found such an answer false, whereas an American Protestant businessman might express his resolution of the problem in much the same terms as did Clement.

One can find readily many loose ends and inconsistencies in this attempt of Clement to bring together "Greek" and Christian elements. These are almost inevitable in any effort to reconcile philosophy and theology, reason and faith. Later attempts in Christian history may be more genuine syntheses, but to Clement of Alexandria should go the credit for an early and serious attempt to bring Christian ethics together with the ethics of the culture into which it moves. Whether Clement's composite ideal of the good life is more like that of a Greek gentleman or of a disciple of Christ is a question which deserves discussion, after the study is made of Clement's own words.

SOURCES

From

CLEMENT OF ALEXANDRIA: THE INSTRUCTOR[5]

Reason in the Christian Life

Everything that is contrary to right reason is sin. Accordingly, therefore, the philosophers think fit to define the most generic passions thus: lust, as desire disobedient to reason; fear, as weakness disobedient to reason; pleasure, as an elation of the spirit disobedient to reason. If, then, disobedience in reference to reason is the generating cause of sin, how shall we escape the conclusion, that obedience to reason—the Word —which we call faith, will of necessity be the efficacious cause

[5] This and all subsequent quotations in this chapter are from *The Ante-Nicene Fathers,* Vol. II. (Buffalo: The Christian Literature Publishing Co., 1885; New York: Charles Scribner's Sons, 1926).

of duty? For virtue itself is a state of the soul rendered harmonious by reason in respect to whole life. Nay, to crown all, philosophy itself is pronounced to be the cultivation of right reason; so that, necessarily, whatever is done through error of reason is transgression, and is rightly called sin.

But that which is done right, in obedience to reason, the followers of the Stoics call incumbent and fitting. What is fitting is incumbent. And obedience is founded on commands. And these being, as they are, the same as counsels—having truth for their aim, train up to the ultimate goal of aspiration, which is conceived of as the *end.* And the end of piety is eternal rest in God. And the beginning of eternity is our end. The right operation of piety perfects duty by works; whence, according to just reasoning, duties consist in actions, not in sayings. And Christian conduct is the operation of the rational soul in accordance with a correct judgment and aspiration after the truth, which attains its destined end through the body, the soul's consort and ally. Virtue is a will in conformity to God and Christ in life, rightly adjusted to life everlasting. For the life of Christians, in which we are now trained, is a system of reasonable actions—that is, of those things taught by the Word—an unfailing energy which we have called faith. The system is the commandments of the Lord, which, being divine statutes and spiritual counsels, have been written for ourselves, being adapted for ourselves and our neighbors. Moreover, they turn back on us, as the ball rebounds on him that throws it by the repercussion. Whence also duties are essential for divine discipline, as being enjoined by God, and furnished for our salvation. And since, of those things which are necessary, some relate only to life here, and others, which relate to the blessed life yonder, wing us for flight hence; so, in an analogous manner, of duties, some are ordained with reference to life, others for the blessed life. The commandments issued with respect to natural life are published to the multitude; but those that are suited for living well, and from which eternal life springs, we have to consider, as in a sketch, as we read them out of the Scriptures.[6] [There follows detailed guidance for the Christian's regulation of his life, in habits and manners.]

From

CLEMENT OF ALEXANDRIA: THE STROMATA

A Defense of Faith

Faith, which the Greeks disparage, deeming it futile and barbarous, is a voluntary preconception, the assent of piety—"the subject of things hoped for, the evidence of things not seen," according to the divine apostle. "For hereby," pre-eminently, "the elders obtained a good report. But without faith it is impossible to please God." Others have defined faith to be a uniting assent to an unseen object, as certainly the proof of an unknown thing is an evident assent. If then it be choice, being desirous of something, the desire is in this instance intellectual. And since choice is the beginning of action, faith is discovered to be the beginning of action, being the foundation of rational choice in the case of any one who exhibits to himself the previous demonstration through faith. Voluntarily to follow what is useful is the first principle of understanding. Unswerving choice, then, gives considerable momentum in the direction of knowledge. The exercise of faith directly becomes knowledge, reposing on a sure foundation. Knowledge, accordingly, is defined by the sons of the philosophers as a habit, which cannot be overthrown by reason. Is there any other true condition such as this, except piety, of which alone the Word is teacher? I think not. He who believeth then the divine Scriptures with sure judgment, receives in the voice of God, who bestowed the Scripture, a demonstration that cannot be impugned. Faith, then, is not established by demonstration. "Blessed therefore those who, not having seen, yet have believed."[7]

6 "The Instructor," Bk. I, chap. xiii.
7 "The Stromata," Bk. II, chap. ii.

Should one say that Knowledge is founded on demonstration by a process of reasoning, let him hear that first principles are incapable of demonstration; for they are known neither by art nor sagacity. For the latter is conversant about objects that are susceptible of change, while the former is practical solely, and not theoretical. Hence it is thought that the first cause of the universe can be apprehended by faith alone. For all knowledge is capable of being taught; and what is capable of being taught is founded on what is known before. But the first cause of the universe was not previously known to the Greeks; neither, accordingly, to Thales, who came to the conclusion that water was the first cause; nor to the other natural philosophers who succeeded him, since it was Anaxagoras who was the first who assigned to Mind the supremacy over material things. But not even he preserved the dignity suited to the efficient cause, describing as he did certain silly vortices, together with the inertia and even foolishness of Mind. Wherefore also the Word says, "Call no man master on earth." For knowledge is a state of mind that results from demonstration; but faith is a grace which from what is indemonstrable conducts to what is universal and simple, what is neither with matter, nor matter, nor under matter.

Now Aristotle says that the judgment which follows knowledge is in truth faith. Accordingly, faith is something superior to knowledge, and is its criterion. Conjecture, which is only a feeble supposition, counterfeits faith; as the flatterer counterfeits a friend, and the wolf the dog. And as the workman sees that by learning certain things he becomes an artificer, and the helmsman by being instructed in the art will be able to steer; he does not regard the mere wishing to become excellent and good enough, but he must learn it by the exercise of obedience. But to obey the Word, whom we call Instructor, is to believe Him, going against Him in nothing. For how can we take up a position of hostility to God? Knowledge, accordingly, is characterized by faith; and faith, by a kind of divine mutual and reciprocal correspondence, becomes characterized by knowledge.[8]

[8] *Ibid.*, Bk. II, chap. iv.

Accordingly, faith may not, any more, with reason, be disparaged in an offhand way, as simple and vulgar, appertaining to anybody. For, if it were a mere human habit, as the Greeks supposed, it would have been extinguished. But if it grow, and there be no place where it is not; then I affirm, that faith, whether founded in love, or in fear, as its disparagers assert, is something divine; which is neither rent asunder by other mundane friendship, nor dissolved by the presence of fear. For love, on account of its friendly alliance with faith, makes men believers; and faith, which is the foundation of love, in its turn introduces the doing of good. Such a change, then, from unbelief to faith—and to trust in hope and fear, is divine. And, in truth, faith is discovered, by us, to be the first movement towards salvation; after which fear, and hope, and repentance, advancing in company with temperance and patience, lead us to love and knowledge.[9]

The Gnostic's Likeness to God

He is the Gnostic, who is after the image and likeness of God, who imitates God as far as possible, deficient in none of the things which contribute to the likeness as far as compatible, practising self-restraint and endurance, living righteously, reigning over the passions, bestowing of what he has as far as possible, and doing good both by word and deed. "He is the greatest," it is said, "in the kingdom who shall do and teach"; imitating God in conferring like benefits. For God's gifts are for the common good. "Whoever shall attempt to do aught with presumption, provokes God," it is said. For haughtiness is a vice of the soul, of which, as of other sins, He commands us to repent; by adjusting our lives from their state of derangement to the change for the better in these three things—mouth, heart, hands. These are signs—the hands of action, the heart of volition, the mouth of speech. Beautifully, therefore, has this oracle been spoken with respect to penitents: "Thou hast chosen God this day to be thy God; and God hath chosen thee this day to be His people." For

[9] *Ibid.*, Bk. II, chap. vii.

him who hastes to serve the self-existent One, being a suppliant, God adopts to Himself; and though he be only one in number, he is honoured equally with the people. For being a part of the people, he becomes complementary of it, being restored from what he was; and the whole is named from a part.

Now Plato the philosopher, defining the end of happiness, says that it is likeness to God as far as possible; whether concurring with the precept of the law or whether instructed by certain oracles of the time, thirsting as he always was for instruction. For the law says, "Walk after the Lord your God, and keep my commandments." For the law calls assimilation following; and such a following to the utmost of its power assimilates. "Be," says the Lord, "merciful and pitiful, as your heavenly Father is pitiful." Thence also the Stoics have laid down the doctrine, that living agreeably to nature is the end, fitly altering the name of God into nature; since also nature extends to plants, to seeds, to trees, and to stones.[10]

The Christian Gnostic's Love and Its Motive

This is love, to love God and our neighbour. This conducts to the height which is unutterable. "Love covers a multitude of sins. Love beareth all things, suffereth all things." Love joins us to God, does all things in concord. In love, all the chosen of God were perfected. Apart from love, nothing is well pleasing to God. "Of its perfection there is no unfolding," it is said. "Who is fit to be found in it, except those whom God counts worthy?" To the point the Apostle Paul speaks, "If I give my body, and have not love, I am sounding brass, and a tinkling cymbal." If it is not from a disposition determined by Gnostic love that I shall testify, he means; but if through fear and expected reward, moving my lips in order to testify to the Lord that I shall confess the Lord, I am a common man, sounding the Lord's name, not knowing Him. "And if I give all my goods in alms," he says, not according

[10] *Ibid.*, Bk. II, chap. xix.

to the principle of loving communication, but on account of recompense, either from him who has received the benefit, or the Lord who has promised; "and if I have all faith so as to remove mountains," and cast away obscuring passions, and be not faithful to the Lord from love, "I am nothing," as in comparison of him who testifies as a Gnostic, and the crowd, and being reckoned nothing better.

"God," then, being good, "is love," it is said. Whose "love worketh no ill to his neighbour," neither injuring nor revenging ever, but, in a word, doing good to all according to the image of God. "Love is," then, "the fulfilling of the law"; like as Christ, that is the presence of the Lord who loves us; and our loving teaching of, and discipline according to Christ. By love, then, the commands not to commit adultery, and not to covet one's neighbour's wife, are fulfilled, [these sins being] formerly prohibited by fear.

The same work, then, presents a difference, according as it is done by fear, or accomplished by love, and is wrought by faith or by knowledge. Rightly, therefore, their rewards are different.[11]

The man of understanding and perspicacity is, then, a Gnostic. And his business is not abstinence from what is evil (for this is a step to the highest perfection), or the doing of good out of fear. Nor any more is he to do so from hope of promised recompense. But only the doing of good out of love, and for the sake of its own excellence, is to be the Gnostic's choice. To desire knowledge about God for any practical purpose, that this may be done, or that may not be done, is not proper to the Gnostic; but the knowledge itself suffices as the reason for contemplation. For I will dare aver that it is not because he wishes to be saved that he, who devotes himself to knowledge for the sake of the divine science itself, chooses knowledge. Could we, then, suppose any one proposing to the Gnostic whether he would choose the knowledge of God or everlasting salvation; and if these, which are entirely identical, were separable, he would without the least hesitation choose the knowledge of God, deeming that

[11] *Ibid.*, Bk. IV, chap. xviii.

property of faith, which from love ascends to knowledge, desirable, for its own sake. This, then, is the perfect man's first form of doing good, when it is done not for any advantage in what pertains to him, but because he judges it right to do good; and the energy being vigorously exerted in all things, in the very act becomes good; not, good in some things, and not good in others; but consisting in the habit of doing good, neither for glory, nor, as the philosophers say, for reputation, nor from reward either from men or God; but so as to pass life after the image and likeness of the Lord.

And if, in doing good, he be met with anything adverse, he will let the recompense pass without resentment as if it were good, he being just and good "to the just and the unjust." To such the Lord says, "Be ye, as your Father is perfect."

Such a one is no longer continent, but has reached a state of passionlessness, waiting to put on the divine image. "If thou doest alms," it is said, "let no one know it; and if thou fastest, anoint thyself, that God alone may know," and not a single human being. Not even he himself who shows mercy ought to know that he does show mercy; for in this way he will be sometimes merciful, sometimes not. And when he shall do good by habit, he will imitate the nature of good, and his disposition will be his nature and his practice.

But he who obeys the mere call, as he is called, neither for fear, nor for enjoyments, is on his way to knowledge. For he does not consider whether any extrinsic lucrative gain or enjoyment follows to him; but drawn by the love of Him who is the true object of love, and led to what is requisite, practices piety. So that not even were we to suppose him to receive from God leave to do things forbidden with impunity; not even if he were to get the promise that he would receive as a reward the good things of the blessed; but besides, not even if he could persuade himself that God would be hoodwinked with reference to what he does (which is impossible), would he ever wish to do aught contrary to right reason, having once made choice of what is truly good and worthy of choice on its own account, and therefore to be loved.[12]

[12] *Ibid.*, Bk. IV, chap. xxiv.

The Right Treatment of the World and the Flesh

Those who run down created existence and vilify the body are wrong; not considering that the frame of man was formed erect for the contemplation of heaven, and that the organization of the senses tends to knowledge; and that the members and parts are arranged for good, not for pleasure. Whence this abode becomes receptive of the soul which is most precious to God; and is dignified with the Holy Spirit through the sanctification of soul and body, perfected with the perfection of the Saviour. And the succession of the three virtues is found in the Gnostic, who morally, physically, and logically occupies himself with God. For wisdom is the knowledge of things divine and human; and righteousness is the concord of the parts of the soul; and holiness is the service of God.

The soul of man is confessedly the better part of man, and the body the inferior. But neither is the soul good by nature, nor, on the other hand, is the body bad by nature. Nor is that which is not good straightway bad. For there are things which occupy a middle place, and among them are things to be preferred, and things to be rejected. The constitution of man, then, which has its place among things of sense, was necessarily composed of things diverse, but not opposite—body and soul.

Always therefore the good actions, as better, attach to the better and ruling spirit; and voluptuous and sinful actions are attributed to the worse, the sinful one.

Now the soul of the wise man and Gnostic, as sojourning in the body, conducts itself toward it gravely and respectfully, not with inordinate affections, as about to leave the tabernacle if the time of departure summons. For all things are of one God. And no one is a stranger to the world by nature, their essence being one and God one. But the elect man dwells as a sojourner, knowing all things to be possessed and disposed of. The body, too, as one sent on a distant pilgrimage, uses inns and dwellings by the way, having care of the things of the world, of the places where he halts; but leaves his dwelling-place and property without excessive emotion;

readily following him that leads him away from life; by no means and on no occasion turning back; giving thanks for his sojourn, and blessing God for his departure, embracing the mansion that is in heaven.[13]

Freedom from All Passions and Desires

The Gnostic is such, that he is subject only to the affections that exist for the maintenance of the body, such as hunger, thirst, and the like.

The affections when produced rationally, are good, yet they are nevertheless inadmissible in the case of the perfect man, who is incapable of exercising courage; for neither does he meet what inspires fear, as he regards none of the things that occur in life as to be dreaded; nor can aught dislodge him from this—the love he has towards God. Nor does he need cheerfulness of mind; for he does not fall into pain, being persuaded that all things happen well. Nor is he angry; for there is nothing to move him to anger, seeing he ever loves God, and is entirely turned towards Him alone, and therefore hates none of God's creatures. Nor does he envy; for nothing is wanting to him, that is requisite to assimilation, in order that he may be excellent and good. Nor does he consequently love any one with this common affection, but loves the Creator in the creatures. Nor, consequently, does he fall into any desire and eagerness; nor does he want, as far as respects his soul, aught appertaining to others, now that he associates through love with the Beloved One, to whom he is allied by free choice, and by the habit which results from training, approaches closer to Him, and is blessed through the abundance of good things.

So that on these accounts he is compelled to become like his Teacher in impassibility. For the Word of God is intellectual, according as the image of mind is seen in man alone. Thus also the good man is godlike in form and semblance as respects his soul. And, on the other hand, God is like man. For the distinctive form of each one is the mind by which

[13] *Ibid.*, Bk. IV, chap. xxvi.

we are characterized. Consequently, also, those who sin against man are unholy and impious. For it were ridiculous to say that the gnostic and perfect man must not eradicate anger and courage, inasmuch as without these he will not struggle against circumstances, or abide what is terrible. But if we take from him desire, he will be quite overwhelmed by troubles, and therefore depart from this life very basely. Unless possessed of it, as some suppose, he will not conceive a desire for what is like the excellent and the good. If, then, all alliance with what is good is accompanied with desire, how, it is said, does he remain impassible who desires what is excellent?

But these people know not, as appears, the divinity of love. For love is not desire on the part of him who loves; but is a relation of affection, restoring the Gnostic to the unity of the faith—independent of time and place. But he who by love is already in the midst of that in which he is destined to be, and has anticipated hope by knowledge, does not desire anything, having, as far as possible, the very thing desired. Accordingly, as to be expected, he continues in the exercise of gnostic love, in the one unvarying state.[14]

The Gnostic's Perfection, in Summary

Respecting the universe, [the Gnostic] conceives truly and grandly in virtue of his reception of divine teaching. Beginning, then, with admiration of the Creation, and affording of himself a proof of his capability for receiving knowledge, he becomes a ready pupil of the Lord. Directly on hearing of God and Providence, he believed in consequence of the admiration he entertained. Through the power of impulse thence derived he devotes his energies in every way to learning, doing all those things by means of which he shall be able to acquire the knowledge of what he desires. And desire blended with inquiry arises as faith advances. And this is to become worthy of speculation, of such a character, and such importance. So shall the Gnostic taste of the will of

[14] *Ibid.*, Bk. VI, chap. ix.

God. For it is not his ears, but his soul, that he yields up to the things signified by what is spoken. Accordingly, apprehending essences and things through the words, he brings his soul, as is fit, to what is essential; apprehending (e.g.) in the peculiar way in which they are spoken to the Gnostic, the commands, "Do not commit adultery," "Do not kill"; and not as they are understood by other people. Training himself, then, in scientific speculation, he proceeds to exercise himself in larger generalizations and grander propositions; knowing right well that "He that teacheth man knowledge," according to the prophet, is the Lord, the Lord acting by man's mouth. So also He assumed flesh.

Consequently, therefore, though disease, and accident, and what is most terrible of all, death, come upon the Gnostic, he remains inflexible in soul—knowing that all such things are a necessity of creation, and that, also by the power of God, they become the medicine of salvation, benefiting by discipline those who are difficult to reform; allotted according to desert, by Providence, which is truly good.

Using the creatures, then, when the Word prescribes, and to the extent it prescribes, in the exercise of thankfulness to the Creator, he becomes master of the enjoyment of them.

He never cherishes resentment or harbors a grudge against any one, though deserving of hatred for his conduct. For he worships the Maker, and loves him, who shares life, pitying and praying for him on account of his ignorance. He indeed partakes of the affections of the body, to which, susceptible as it is of suffering by nature, he is bound. But in sensation he is not the primary subject of it.

Accordingly, then, in involuntary circumstances, by withdrawing himself from troubles to the things which really belong to him, he is not carried away with what is foreign to him. And it is only to things that are necessary for him that he accommodates himself, in so far as the soul is preserved unharmed. For it is not in supposition or seeming that he wishes to be faithful; but in knowledge and truth, that is, in sure deed and effectual word. Wherefore he not only praises what is noble, but endeavours himself to be noble; changing by love from a good and faithful servant into a friend, through the perfection of habit, which he has acquired in purity from true instruction and great discipline.

Striving, then, to attain to the summit of knowledge; decorous in character; composed in mien; possessing all those advantages which belong to the true Gnostic; fixing his eye on fair models, on the many patriarchs who have lived rightly, and on very many prophets and angels reckoned without number, and above all, on the Lord, who taught and showed it to be possible for him to attain that highest life of all—he therefore loves not all the good things of the world, which are within his grasp, that he may not remain on the ground, but the things hoped for, or rather already known, being hoped for so as to be apprehended.

So then he undergoes toils, and trials, and afflictions, not as those among the philosophers who are endowed with manliness, in the hope of present troubles ceasing, and of sharing again in what is pleasant; but knowledge has inspired him with the firmest persuasion of receiving the hopes of the future. Wherefore he contemns not alone the pains of this world, but all its pleasures.

In all circumstances, then, is the soul of the Gnostic strong, in a condition of extreme health and strength, like the body of an athlete.

For he is prudent in human affairs, in judging what ought to be done by the just man; having obtained the principles from God from above, and having acquired, in order to the divine resemblance, moderation in bodily pains and pleasures. And he struggles against fears boldly, trusting in God. Certainly, then, the gnostic soul, adorned with perfect virtue, is the earthly image of the divine power; its development being the joint result of nature, of training, of reason, all together. This beauty of the soul becomes a temple of the Holy Spirit, when it acquires a disposition in the whole of life corresponding to the Gospel. Such a one consequently withstands all fear of everything terrible, not only of death, but also poverty and disease, and ignominy, and things akin to these; being unconquered by pleasure, and lord over irrational desires. For he well knows what is and what is not to be done; being perfectly aware what things are really to be dreaded, and what not. Whence he bears intelligently what the Word intimates to him to be requisite and necessary; intelligently discriminating what is really safe (that is, good), from what appears so; and things to be dreaded from what seems so, such as death, disease, and poverty; which are rather so in opinion than in truth.

This is the really good man, who is without passions; having, through the habit or disposition of the soul endued with virtue, transcended the whole life of passion. He has everything dependent on himself for the attainment of the end. For those accidents which are called terrible are not formidable to the good man, because they are not evil. And those which are really to be dreaded are foreign to the gnostic Christian, being diametrically opposed to what is good, because evil; and it is impossible for contraries to meet in the same person at the same time. He, then, who faultlessly acts the drama of life which God has given him to play, knows both what is to be done and what is to be endured.

Accordingly, love makes its own athlete fearless and dauntless, and confident in the Lord, anointing and training him; as righteousness secures for him truthfulness in his whole life.

And the same holds with self-control. For it is neither for love of honour, as the athletes for the sake of crowns and fame; nor on the other hand, for love of money, as some pretend to exercise self-control, pursuing what is good with terrible suffering. Nor is it from love of the body for the sake of health. Nor any more is any man who is temperate from rusticity, who has not tasted pleasures, truly a man of self-control. Certainly those who have led a laborious life, on tasting pleasures, forthwith break down the inflexibility of temperance into pleasures. Such are they who are restrained by law and fear. For on finding a favourable opportunity they defraud the law, by giving what is good the slip. But self-control, desirable for its own sake, perfected through knowledge, abiding ever, makes the man lord and master of himself; so that the Gnostic is temperate and passionless, incapable of being dissolved by pleasures and pains.

The cause of these, then, is love, of all science the most sacred and most sovereign.[15]

From

Clement of Alexandria: The Rich Man's Salvation

Perhaps the reason of salvation appearing more difficult to the rich than to poor men, is not single but manifold. For some, merely hearing, and that in an off-hand way, the utterance of the Saviour, "that it is easier for a camel to go through the eye of a needle than for a rich man to enter into the kingdom of heaven," despair of themselves as not destined to live, surrender all to the world, cling to the present life as if it alone was left to them, and so diverge more from the way to the life to come, no longer inquiring either whom the Lord and Master calls rich, or how that which is impossible to man becomes possible to God. But others rightly and adequately comprehend this, but attaching slight importance to the works which tend to salvation, do not make the requisite preparation for attaining to the objects of their hope.[16]

What then was it which persuaded [the rich young ruler] to flight, and made him depart from the Master, from the entreaty, the hope, the life, previously pursued with ardour? —"Sell thy possessions." And what is this? He does not, as some conceive off-hand, bid him throw away the substance he possessed, and abandon his property; but bids him banish from his soul his notions about wealth, his excitement and morbid feeling about it, the anxieties, which are the thorns of existence, which choke the seed of life. For it is no great thing or desirable to be destitute of wealth, if without a special object,—not except on account of life. For thus those who have nothing at all, but are destitute, and beggars for

15 *Ibid.*, Bk. VII, chap. xi.

16 "The Rich Man's Salvation," par. 2.

their daily bread, the poor dispersed on the streets, who know not God and God's righteousness, simply on account of their extreme want and destitution of subsistence, and lack even of the smallest things, were most blessed and most dear to God, and sole possessors of everlasting life.[17]

What peculiar thing is it that the new creature the Son of God intimates and teaches? It is not the outward act which others have done, but something else indicated by it, greater, more godlike, more perfect, the stripping off of the passions from the soul itself and from the disposition, and the cutting up by the roots and casting out of what is alien to the mind. For this is the lesson peculiar to the believer, and the instruction worthy of the Saviour. For those who formerly despised external things relinquished and squandered their property, but the passions of the soul, I believe, they intensified. For they indulged in arrogance, pretension, and vainglory, and in contempt of the rest of mankind, as if they had done something superhuman. How then would the Saviour have enjoined on those destined to live forever what was injurious and hurtful with reference to the life which He promised? For although such is the case, one, after ridding himself of the burden of wealth, may none the less have still the lust and desire for money innate and living; and may have abandoned the use of it, but being at once destitute of and desiring what he spent, may doubly grieve both on account of the absence of attendance, and the presence of regret. For it is impossible and inconceivable that those in want of the necessaries of life should not be harassed in mind, and hindered from better things in the endeavour to provide them somehow, and from some source.[18]

And how much more beneficial the opposite case, for a man, through possessing a competency, both not himself to be in straits about money, and also to give assistance to those to whom it is requisite so to do! For if no one had anything, what room would be left among men for giving? And how can this dogma fail to be found plainly opposed to and con-

[17] *Ibid.*, par. 11.
[18] *Ibid.*, par. 12.

flicting with many other excellent teachings of the Lord? "Make to yourselves friends of the mammon of unrighteousness, that when ye fail, they may receive you into the everlasting habitations." "Acquire treasures in heaven, where neither moth nor rust destroys, nor thieves break through." How could one give food to the hungry, and drink to the thirsty, clothe the naked, and shelter the houseless, for not doing which He threatens with fire and the outer darkness, if each man first divested himself of all these things? Nay, He bids Zaccheus and Matthew, the rich tax-gatherers, entertain Him hospitably. And He does not bid them part with their property, but, applying the just and removing the unjust judgment, He subjoins, "To-day salvation has come to this house, forasmuch as he also is a son of Abraham." He so praises the use of property as to enjoin, along with this addition, the giving a share of it, to give drink to the thirsty, bread to the hungry, to take the houseless in, and clothe the naked. But if it is not possible to supply those needs without substance, and He bids people abandon their substance, what else would the Lord be doing than exhorting to give and not to give the same things, to feed and not to feed, to take in and to shut out, to share and not to share? which were the most irrational of all things.[19]

Riches, then, which benefit also our neighbours, are not to be thrown away. For they are possessions, inasmuch as they are possessed, and goods, inasmuch as they are useful and provided by God for the use of men; and they lie to our hand, and are put under our power, as material and instruments which are for good use to those who know the instrument. If you use it skillfully, it is skillful; if you are deficient in skill, it is affected by your want of skill, being itself destitute of blame. Such an instrument is wealth. Are you able to make a right use of it? It is subservient to righteousness. Does one make a wrong use of it? It is, on the other hand, a minister of wrong. For its nature is to be subservient, not to rule. That then which of itself has neither good nor evil, being blameless, ought not to be blamed; but that which has the power of

[19] *Ibid.*, par. 13.

using it well and ill, by reason of its possessing voluntary choice. And this is the mind and judgment of man, which has freedom in itself and self-determination in the treatment of what is assigned to it. So let no man destroy wealth, rather than the passions of the soul, which are incompatible with the better use of wealth. So that, becoming virtuous and good, he may be able to make a good use of these riches. The renunciation, then, and selling of all possessions, is to be understood as spoken of the passions of the soul.[20]

I would then say this, since some things are within and some without the soul, and if the soul make a good use of them, they also are reputed good, but if a bad, bad;—whether does He who commands us to alienate our possessions repudiate those things, after the removal of which the passions still remain, or those rather, on the removal of which wealth even becomes beneficial? If therefore he who casts away worldly wealth can still be rich in the passions, even though the material (for their gratification) is absent,—for the disposition produces its own effects, and strangles the reason, and presses it down and inflames it with its inbred lusts—it is then of no advantage to him to be poor in purse while he is rich in passions. For it is not what ought to be cast away that he has cast away, but what is indifferent; and he has deprived himself of what is serviceable, but set on fire the innate fuel of evil through want of the external means [of gratification]. We must therefore renounce those possessions that are injurious, not those that are capable of being serviceable, if one knows the right use of them. And what is managed with wisdom, and sobriety, and piety, is profitable; and what is hurtful must be cast away. But things external hurt not. So then the Lord introduces the use of external things, bidding us put away not the means of subsistence, but what uses them badly. And these are the infirmities and passions of the soul.[21]

The presence of wealth in these is deadly to all, the loss of it salutary. Of which, making the soul pure—that is, poor and bare—we must hear the Saviour speaking thus, "Come, follow

20 *Ibid.*, par. 14.
21 *Ibid.*, par. 15.

Me." For to the pure in heart He now becomes the way. But into the impure soul the grace of God finds no entrance. And that (soul) is unclean which is rich in lusts, and is in the throes of many worldly affections. For he who holds possessions, and gold, and silver, and houses, as the gifts of God; and ministers from them to the God who gives them for the salvation of men; and knows that he possesses them more for the sake of the brethren than his own; and is superior to the possession of them, not the slave of the things he possesses; and does not carry them about in his soul, nor bind and circumscribe his life within them, but is ever labouring at some good and divine work, even should he be necessarily some time or other deprived of them, is able with cheerful mind to bear their removal equally with their abundance. This is he who is blessed by the Lord, and called poor in spirit, a meet heir of the kingdom of heaven, not one who could not live rich.[22]

The point of the parable is evident. Let it teach the prosperous that they are not to neglect their own salvation, as if they had been already foredoomed, nor, on the other hand, to cast wealth into the sea, or condemn it as a traitor and an enemy to life, but learn in what way and how to use wealth and obtain life.[23]

Further Readings

Primary Sources

Oulton, J. E. L., and Chadwick, J. E. (eds.). *Alexandrian Christianity.* (*Library of Christian Classics,* Vol. 2.) Philadelphia: Westminster Press, 1954.

Clement. *Christ the Educator.* Trans. by Simon P. Wood. New York: Fathers of the Church, Inc., 1954.

Secondary Sources

Chadwick, Henry. *Early Christian Thought and the Classical Tradition.* New York: Oxford University Press, 1966. (On Justin, Clement, and Origen.)

22 *Ibid.,* par. 16.
23 *Ibid.,* par. 27.

GONZÁLAZ, JUSTO L. *A History of Christian Thought,* Vol. 1. Nashville: Abingdon Press, 1970.

OSBORN, E. F. *The Philosophy of Clement of Alexandria.* Cambridge (England) University Press, 1957.

Chapter 4

ST. AUGUSTINE

One of the major figures in the history of Christianity, and certainly the most influential in Christian theology between Paul and Thomas Aquinas, was St. Augustine (354-430), bishop of the Christian church in Africa. Out of the confused tendencies of Christian thought in his era, he formulated the normative lines of Western Latin Christian doctrine and ethics. All of medieval law, history, psychology, political theory, and social thought stood in debt to Augustine. Thomas Aquinas of the thirteenth century, who came to be the standard theologian of the Roman Catholic church, looked back to Augustine for much of his inspiration and for more liberal quotation than from any other Church Father. The first reformers of the sixteenth century, too, derived from Augustine insights which they felt medieval Catholicism had obscured. And again in the twentieth century, the new creative revival in theology among Protestant and Catholic theologians has turned with enthusiasm back to his writings. As he spoke to the condition of men in the fifth-century breakdown of Roman civilization, his reflections have taken on a fresh cogency to the students of what appears to many to be the breakdown of Western democratic civilization.

His multiple service to the Christian thought of his time was his synthesis of Latin Christian theology and Platonic philosophy, a synthesis more fully fused than what Clement of Alexandria had attempted two centuries before. He also recovered many of the Pauline insights which had been neglected since Paul's time. Augustine had, moreover, a boldly original mind, full of sharp flashes of insight. He pioneered as well as consolidated the lines of orthodoxy. In him the old and the new found creative and fresh expression.

The Prodigal Pilgrimage

Augustine came to his conclusions about what it means to be a Christian only after a protracted and intense personal struggle of mind and heart, recorded in the *Confessions*. This spiritual autobiography traverses the twisting road which led him to his Christian conviction. Its content is refracted by the glass of Christian faith through which in retrospect he views his experience. It is a long and impassioned commentary on the famous prayer with which it starts: "Thou hast made us for Thyself, and our spirits are restless until they rest in Thee."[1] Its course, amid many side excursions, may be described as a series of stages through which Augustine passed in his spiritual pilgrimage, or a series of "crushes" which held him and then disillusioned him, until he found his true and lasting love in the love of God.

Born of a Christian mother and pagan father at Tagaste in Africa, he had the benefit of a brilliant mind and a thoroughgoing education. Headstrong and independent from boyhood, he rejected the religion of his devout mother, which he thought to be impossibly naive and credulous. As a student he excelled in the subjects of debate, rhetoric, and logic. In his late teens, choosing rhetoric as his profession, he went to Carthage to study and teach. In the big city he enjoyed what he calls his "vagrant liberty" in its sophisticated life and shortly took up with a mistress, whom he loved singly, but deferred to marry.

He was first turned toward the true way of life by reading Cicero's *Hortentius*, which awoke in him the passion to seek truth. But to this sharp-minded and dashing young professor it was clear that truth did not lie in the orthodox Christianity of his mother, with its simple literalism and plain piety. Through his twenties, he was persuaded that the faith of the Manicheans offered the convincing solution to his in-

[1] *Confessions*, Bk. I, chap. i.

tellectual problems. The Manichean religion, a popular self-styled version of Christianity, was in truth a form of Persian dualism. It viewed life as a vast battleground between two equally sovereign principles of Light and Darkness, Good and Evil, God and the Devil. In each man there is a good soul and an evil soul. Every man's career is in perpetual pull-and-haul between these two determinants. Augustine was impressed by the Manichean hardheaded critical method in interpreting the Scriptures, or by what would be called in more recent terms a certain "scientific" spirit. Yet some of the doctrines of the Manicheans left him unsatisfied. Their bishop, Faustus, who was alleged to know all the answers, on a visit to Carthage proved charming and amiable enough, but quite confused and ambiguous in his replies to Augustine's searching questions. So, at twenty-nine, disappointed in his first intellectual love, he tried Scepticism as the only possible answer to life's enigmas: the wise man should suspend judgment on all ultimate questions.

But the ultimate questions would not let him go. One of the issues that troubled his thinking concerned the existence of noncorporeal reality. How could intangible things like "God" and "Spirit" exist in any way subject to empirical check? In this period of his life, turning thirty, he was still restless with himself, in his intellectual quest and in his personal living. In part the tension came from a conflict of loyalties between what he owed to his mother on the one hand, with her patient devotion to the Christian faith, and the appeals of his mistress on the other. In larger part, the tension came out of the hunger of a passionate and yet critical-minded intellectual for a spiritual home. In this mood Augustine went to Rome and shortly thereafter to Milan. To all appearances he was a brilliant and self-assured young professor, but inwardly he was sceptical and tormented by conflicts. He began to read with rising enthusiasm in neo-Platonic philosophy. Here at last he found intellectual peace. The neo-Platonic monistic world view convinced him that ultimate reality is noncorporeal and that evil is not a positive "something," as the Manichees taught, but is rather the absence of good, as silence is the absence of sound. Having crossed this intellectual bridge, he was prepared to accept, through neo-Platonism, the truth of Christian theology with its belief in the goodness of one sovereign God, the eternal reality of unseen things, and the essential unity of the self.

Yet, despite his intellectual conversion, Augustine's moral and emotional life remained one of troubled turbulence. If anything his conflict was intensified, since the good that his mind had now accepted he could not command his will to perform. In this despairing state he came under the influence of Ambrose, the famous Christian preacher of Milan. In Ambrose he found an appealing person and a form of Christianity free from a wooden Biblical literalism. In the year 386 a vivid experience of revelation and insight brought through the reading of a passage of Scripture finally tipped the precarious scales of Augustine's moral life, and he found spiritual and intellectual "oneness" in the Christian faith. He gave up his teaching career as well as his liaison with his mistress and retired from the world with a few friends and his rejoicing mother to study and cultivate spiritual disciplines. He returned thence to become an active priest of the church, rose in rapid time to the bishop's chair, and spent the remainder of his life in Africa, as a busy prelate and apologist for the Christian way, of whose truth he was the more deeply convinced because of the length and pain of his own search for it.

His years of maturity were spent in the exacting tasks of church administration. In a time of disintegrating culture, the church everywhere in the empire found itself heir to a wide range of practical problems which civil administration was incapable of performing. Augustine found himself also, as apologist, wrestling with vital theological issues. Various heresies—Donatism, Pelagianism, as well as Manicheism, self-claimed friends of Christianity—were translating the old beliefs into their own new versions in ways which Augustine painstakingly undertook to show undermined the truth of the old. From the other side orthodoxy was under attack from secular critics, who saw Christianity as the main cause of the breakdown of the empire. To these critics Augustine replied with *The City of God,* in which he set himself to justify the ways of God to man in an era of devastation.

In all his writings there is an intense mind at work on the perennial puzzles of life, searching even as he finds and finding as he searches. His rigorous intellectual training in logic and philosophy keeps him always from shoddy thinking. At the same time, there is the strain of the romantic, even the mystic in him, in his surges of feeling and his reaching toward the Ineffable, which evades the hold of logical grasp, to describe and praise the God who had constantly drawn him, throughout his prodigal pilgrimage, back to Himself.

The Drama of Creation, the Fall, and Salvation

In one of his early dialogues, Augustine is addressed by the Spirit of Truth with this question: What do you want to know? Augustine's answer is: the soul and God, nothing else at all. Around these two foci all of his analysis turns. The Being of God, Augustine finds, forever eludes the limits of human language. God moves on the plane of eternity, which is different from the order of time. Yet he is the Ground of all temporal existence, the Source of all created being. In him is the fullness of being and the fullness of moral good. Further, he is active and dynamic, continually creating and sustaining life, ordering the stars in their courses and men in their history. He is omnipotent sovereign, making even the willful rebellion of men, as well as their obedience, praise him and serve his purposes. In describing the Ultimate One, the King of the Universe, Augustine uses sometimes the more abstract and impersonal vocabulary drawn from the Platonists, but more often he employs the vivid and personal language drawn from the Hebraic tradition of the Bible.

God created the world, along with time, as good in its essential nature. Since the created order is in time, it does not even in its highest form shade into the level of being that God enjoys in eternity, but always stands over against God, as created from Creator. Given with creation is a certain scale or ladder of being. (Here Augustine adopts the idea of the "chain of being" which Plato suggests and the neo-Platonist Plotinus elaborates.) At the top of the scale is the level of "soul," the noncorporeal faculty distinctive of men and angels, whose highest reach is Mind, with its gift of memory, foresight, and intellection. Body, whose essential quality is extension in space, is a good but lesser level of creation. Below Body there exists no Devil, or Evil Sovereign, but only the absence of Being or nothingness.

In this harmonious order of things, man has his distinctive place. He is created "half-way between the angels and the beasts," with a mind to comprehend truth and, above all, a will (*voluntas*) to love. It is so designed by the Creator that it must attach itself to some object; it must always be set on something. Moreover, "where your treasure is, there shall your heart be also"; that is, a man is as he loves. He is good as his will is turned to the higher in the order of Being, evil as it is turned toward the lower.

In the original state of creation, represented by the life in the Garden of Eden, man (Adam) freely loved God in perfect and happy obedience. But through his own voluntary decision, he turned his will away from the Creator to the lower level of created things and particularly to himself. He chose to be under his own dominion, the king of his own castle, rather than under the dominion of God. This is the sin of pride and presumption, the "original" or basic sin. It does not stem from hate, or the absence of love, but from a misdirected love. This dark aspect of human life Augustine underscored, so subtly yet pervasively had he found it present in his own experience and in the behavior of men in history. The inhumanities and miseries of life, then, he ascribed to no metaphysical principle of evil, but to Adam's first misdirection of love, resulting in a dislocation and degradation in which human beings since Adam have been deeply involved.

As "fallen" children of Adam we are caught in a desperate situation. Inwardly we are neurotic, swinging between moods of elevation and depression, simply because in putting ourselves or some other aspect of the created order at the center of our existence, we are literally eccentric, off-center, trying to live a lie. In relations with other men we are given to lusts of the flesh and the eye, wanton licentiousness, aggressive ambition, and personal or group imperialisms by which we try to lord it over others. Inevitably conflicts of rival imperialisms take place, which make a hell on earth. To deepen the darkness of the human situation, as Augustine insists in his criticism of the Pelagians, we are powerless to lift ourselves up out of the morass. We are free to slide down further on the scale, but not to move up. Any self-help program of salvation is doomed from the start, because in trying to turn ourselves away from ego-centricity we are trying to be the lifter and the to-be-lifted, a spiritual as much as a physical impossibility. We lack the leverage point outside ourselves from which alone we can be redeemed.

Salvation is possible only through the grace of God as it comes into history in Jesus Christ and his church. The redemption of man takes place simply when his off-centered existence is abandoned and his will is converted back to God, who is the true Center. The restoring grace of God must be free and unmerited, granted by God to some, denied to others, in ways beyond man's understanding. To have grace contingent on man's own decision for God would cut in on the sovereignty of the Creator. Where the quivering needle of the compass of a man's will is turned again to God, it is the magnetic attraction of the Divine Pole which is really doing the turning. Man comes again to love God as His love pulls him toward Himself.

The redeemed state for man is the recovery of order, the ideal harmony recaptured out of the disharmony of disobedience. Never can this salvation be fully achieved in this temporal life. It is a promise more than a full actuality, a direction more than an arrival. It is no less real for being unfulfilled, however. The redeemed man is freed from the freedom only to sin and now has the freedom not to sin, and he is set on the right road. But there always remains in this life the possibility of bad choices, of detours into bogs, and the nagging discouragements and frustrations that hamper finite existence. The final achievement of salvation, a full recovery of perfect harmony, must therefore await the next life, an eternal bliss to which the saved Christian looks forward in hope. It is that mode of existence where he will be free only to love God and to join with the angels in singing praises to God, the goal of all his conscious and unconscious striving.

This theory of the nature of the God-man relationship Augustine applies socially as well as individually. In *The City of God* he develops the thesis that a society, as well as a person, can best be interpreted by ascertaining its common love, or, to use modern terms, its integrating principle. In the history of the world, Augustine believes, there are two essential communities running parallel in time. One is the *civitas Dei,* that community of men who are bound together by a common love of God. This community he traces from Adam through Christ to its closest approximation in his own time, the Christian church. He is well aware that in the actual church there are others than pure lovers of God. The institutional church cannot be equated by any means with the perfect society. But its motivating spirit qualifies it to stand as the divine community in history. The opposite society is the *civitas terrena,* built upon the love of power, which is the political form of self-love and aggressive pride. This city has been exemplified in the various empires of history, the Roman the latest. Again, the Roman empire cannot be equated with the city of earth as totally bad, since even in its corruption it embodies a relative good, preserving the conditions of civil order and peace in the world against the floods of anarchy and barbarism. Nonetheless, it is a society essentially of the world in its integrating principle. It cannot be the true community to which the Christian gives final allegiance. These two cities will exist down to the end of time. But by the very nature of God's plan the city of earth is even now on the wane—witness the sack of Rome by Alaric—and the city of God will be triumphant in the new order established at the Day of Judgment.

The Christian Life

What constitutes the good life for the Christian? The question of morality centers immediately not upon intellectual perception, nor on outward behavior, but upon the inward will. "For when there is a question as to whether a man is good, one does not ask what he believes, or what he hopes, but what he loves."[2] The single essential to moral goodness is the right direction of the will toward God. The love of God is the ultimate form of Christian decision into which the various contents of specific behavior are to be put, according to the time and circumstances. Augustine went so far as to say, "Love God, and do what you want." This counsel is more exacting than it sounds. If one loved God truly, one would be constrained not to do "any old" thing that whim dictated, but to seek what God willed for the particular new situation.

Such a God-directed love, which Augustine calls *caritas,* is right because it is in keeping with the order of creation. The happiness we seek is a kind of peace, a "coming to rest" in proper place. "The peace of all things is the tranquillity of order."[3] When we love created things, rather than the Creator, our love is disordered, unsatisfying, and insatiable, since it is directed toward relative and contingent reality rather than the Really Real. This sort of love, turned downward away from the Eternal God toward the temporal world, Augustine calls *cupiditas.* Are we, then, to have no love for the created world, the beauty of the turning stars and seasons, our neighbors, and ourselves? Augustine's answer here is important: We are not to love these as final, but to love God as he is evident in these things, or, to put it shortly, to love these "in God" and not in themselves. "If bodies please Thee, praise God on occasion of them, and turn back thy love upon their maker, lest in these things that please thee, thou displease." "So our souls may from their weariness arise toward Thee, leaning on those things which Thou hast

[2] *Enchiridion,* chap. cxvii.
[3] *The City of God,* Bk. XIX, chap. xiii.

created, and passing on to Thyself, who madest them wonderfully."[4]

The love of God also transforms all of the respectable virtues of the civilized man. In Augustine's culture, semi-Christian and semiclassical, the ethical creed of the average pagan citizen was phrased by a fidelity to the four Greek virtues: wisdom, courage, temperance, justice. If a man realized these, said the Greek sages, he would find the highest happiness the world can give. Augustine swings radically away from the Greek tradition in saying, not that these virtues are evil in themselves, but that their worth is determined by the total intention in which they are cultivated. When sought for the sake of self-love, they are self-defeating. They become "splendid vices." When these virtues are transformed by the love of God, turned from their temporal and merely human context in which the Greeks conceived them to an eternal and transcendent object, they become highly worthful. The conversion of the Greek ideals of wisdom, courage, temperance, and justice by the Christian ideal of love typifies sharply a motif that runs through all of Augustine's thought: his belief that the truth of Christianity is not to be laid alongside Greek wisdom, or put on top of it as a superstructure, but is to convert and permeate and redeem it.

The treatise "Of the Morals of the Catholic Church" (pp. 110-18) was written about 388 as one of Augustine's early attacks against the Manicheism from which he had turned. Over against Manichean errors, he sets forth the essentials of the ideal Christian life. At least in the first few pages, he employs the method of rational argument, since he is writing for those who accept reason as their only guide and will take nothing on faith. It is apparent, however, that implicitly he presupposes the Christian-Platonic scale of Being, as an *a priori* assumption of his argument. In the latter part of this treatise Augustine shifts to an open avowal of the authority of Scripture but with no sacrifice of the requirements of logic and rational cogency.

[4] *Confessions,* Bk. IV, chap. xviii; Bk. V, chap. i.

Augustine's ethical theory is set within a world view and a philosophy of history that he spells out in his famous *City of God* (pp. 118-39), which contains his reflections on the tumultuous and despairing times in which he lived. The selections used here are on the themes of the original goodness of creation, the source of evil and the Fall of man (based on Genesis 3), the nature of the two cities, and the Christian's attitude toward this world.

SOURCES

From

St. Augustine: Of the Morals of the Catholic Church[5]

The Chief Good of Man

How, according to reason, ought man to live? We all certainly desire to live happily; and there is no human being but assents to this statement almost before it is made. But the title happy cannot, in my opinion, belong either to him who has not what he loves, whatever it may be, or to him who has what he loves if it is hurtful, or to him who does not love what he has, although it is good in perfection. For one who seeks what he cannot obtain suffers torture, and one who has got what is not desirable is cheated, and one who does not seek for what is worth seeking for is diseased. Now in all these cases the mind cannot but be unhappy, and happiness and unhappiness cannot reside at the same time in one man; so in none of these cases can the man be happy. I find, then, a fourth case, where the happy life exists—when that which is man's chief good is both loved and possessed. For what do we call enjoyment but having at hand the objects of love?

[5] This material is from *The Writings against the Manicheans and against the Donatists* (*A Select Library of the Nicene and Post-Nicene Fathers,* First Series, ed. Philip Schaff, Vol. IV [New York: The Christian Literature Publishing Co., 1886-90]).

And no one can be happy who does not enjoy what is man's chief good, nor is there any one who enjoys this who is not happy. We must then have at hand our chief good, if we think of living happily.

We must now inquire what is man's chief good, which of course cannot be anything inferior to man himself. For whoever follows after what is inferior to himself, becomes himself inferior. But every man is bound to follow what is best. Wherefore man's chief good is not inferior to man. Is it then something similar to man himself? It must be so, if there is nothing above man which he is capable of enjoying. But if we find something which is both superior to man, and can be possessed by the man who loves it, who can doubt that in seeking for happiness man should endeavor to reach that which is more excellent than the being who makes the endeavor. For if happiness consists in the enjoyment of a good than which there is nothing better, which we call the chief good, how can a man be properly called happy who has not yet attained to his chief good? Or how can that be the chief good beyond which something better remains for us to arrive at? Such, then, being the chief good, it must be something which cannot be lost against the will. For no one can feel confident regarding a good which he knows can be taken from him, although he wishes to keep and cherish it. But if a man feels no confidence regarding the good which he enjoys, how can he be happy while in such fear of losing it?[6]

Now if we ask what is the chief good of the body, reason obliges us to admit that it is that by means of which the body comes to be in its best state. But of all the things which invigorate the body, there is nothing better or greater than the soul. The chief good of the body, then, is not bodily pleasure, not absence of pain, not strength, not beauty, not swiftness, or whatever else is usually reckoned among the goods of the body, but simply the soul. For all the things mentioned the soul supplies to the body by its presence, and, what is above them all, life. Hence I conclude that the soul is not the chief good of man, whether we give the name of man to soul and

[6] "Of the Morals of the Catholic Church," chap. iii.

body together, or to the soul alone. For as, according to reason, the chief good of the body is that which is better than the body, and from which the body receives vigor and life, so whether the soul itself is man, or soul and body both, we must discover whether there is anything which goes before the soul itself, in following which the soul comes to the perfection of good of which it is capable in its own kind. If such a thing can be found, all uncertainty must be at an end, and we must pronounce this to be really and truly the chief good of man.[7]

No one will question that virtue gives perfection to the soul. But it is a very proper subject of inquiry whether this virtue can exist by itself or only in the soul. Here again arises a profound discussion, needing lengthy treatment; but perhaps my summary will serve the purpose. In either case, whether virtue can exist by itself without the soul, or can exist only in the soul, undoubtedly in the pursuit of virtue the soul follows after something, and this must be either the soul itself, or virtue, or something else. But if the soul follows after itself in the pursuit of virtue, it follows after a foolish thing; for before obtaining virtue it is foolish. Now the height of a follower's desire is to reach that which he follows after. So the soul must either not wish to reach what it follows after, which is utterly absurd and unreasonable, or, in following after itself while foolish, it reaches the folly which it flees from. But if it follows after virtue in the desire to reach it, how can it follow what does not exist? or how can it desire to reach what it already possesses? Either, therefore, virtue exists beyond the soul, or if we are not allowed to give the name of virtue except to the habit and disposition of the wise soul, which can exist only in the soul, we must allow that the soul follows after something else in order that virtue may be produced in itself; for neither by following after nothing, nor by following after folly, can the soul, according to my reasoning, attain to wisdom.

This something else then, by following after which the soul becomes possessed of virtue and wisdom, is either a wise man or God. But we have said already that it must be something

[7] *Ibid.*, chap. v.

that we cannot lose against our will. No one can think it necessary to ask whether a wise man, supposing we are content to follow after him, can be taken from us in spite of our unwillingness or our persistence. God then remains, in following after whom we live well, and in reaching whom we live both well and happily. If any deny God's existence, why should I consider the method of dealing with them, when it is doubtful whether they ought to be dealt with at all? At any rate, it would require a different starting-point, a different plan, a different investigation from what we are now engaged in. I am now addressing those who do not deny the existence of God, and who, moreover, allow that human affairs are not disregarded by Him. For there is no one, I suppose, who makes any profession of religion but will hold that divine Providence cares at least for our souls.[8]

The Love of God

Let us see how the Lord Himself in the gospel has taught us to live; how, too, Paul the apostle—for the Manichaeans dare not reject these Scriptures. Let us hear, O Christ, what chief end Thou dost prescribe to us; and that is evidently the chief end after which we are told to strive with supreme affection. "Thou shalt love," He says, "the Lord thy God." Tell me also, I pray Thee, what must be the measure of love; for I fear lest the desire enkindled in my heart should either exceed or come short in fervor. "With all thy heart," He says. Nor is that enough. "With all thy soul." Nor is it enough yet. "With all thy mind." What do you wish more? I might, perhaps, wish more if I could see the possibility of more. What does Paul say on this? "We know," he says, "that all things issue in good to them that love God." Let him, too, say what is the measure of love. "Who then," he says, "shall separate us from the love of Christ? Shall tribulation, or distress, or persecution, or famine, or nakedness, or peril, or the sword?" We have heard, then, what and how much we must love; this we must strive after, and to this we must refer all our plans. The

[8] *Ibid.*, chap. vi.

perfection of all our good things and our perfect good is God. We must neither come short of this nor go beyond it: the one is dangerous, the other impossible.[9]

Following after God is the desire of happiness; to reach God is happiness itself. We follow after God by loving Him; we reach Him, not by becoming entirely what He is, but in nearness to Him, and in wonderful and immaterial contact with Him, and in being inwardly illuminated and occupied by His truth and holiness. He is light itself; we get enlightenment from Him. The greatest commandment, therefore, which leads to happy life, and the first, is this: "Thou shalt love the Lord thy God with all thy heart, and soul, and mind." For to those who love the Lord all things issue in good. If, then, to those who love God all things issue in good, and if, as no one doubts, the chief or perfect good is not only to be loved, but to be loved so that nothing shall be loved better, as is expressed in the words, "With all thy soul, with all thy heart, and with all thy mind," who, I ask, will not at once conclude, when these things are all settled and most surely believed, that our chief good which we must hasten to arrive at in preference to all other things is nothing else than God? And then, if nothing can separate us from His love, must not this be surer as well as better than any other good?[10]

The farther the mind departs from God, not in space, but in affection and lust after things below Him, the more it is filled with folly and wretchedness. So by love it returns to God—a love which places it not along with God, but under Him. And the more ardor and eagerness there is in this, the happier and more elevated will the mind be, and with God as sole governor it will be in perfect liberty. Hence it must know that it is a creature. It must believe what is the truth—that its Creator remains ever possessed of the inviolable and immutable nature of truth and wisdom, and must confess, even in view of the errors from which it desires deliverance, that it is liable to folly and falsehood. But then again, it must take care that it be not separated by the love of the other

[9] *Ibid.*, chap. viii.
[10] *Ibid.*, chap. xi.

creature, that is, of this visible world, from the love of God Himself, which sanctifies it in order to lasting happiness. No other creature, then—for we are ourselves a creature—separates us from the love of God which is in Christ Jesus our Lord.[11]

The Conversion of the Greek Virtues

As to virtue leading us to a happy life, I hold virtue to be nothing else than perfect love of God. For the fourfold division of virtue I regard as taken from four forms of love. For these four virtues (would that all felt their influence in their minds as they have their names in their mouths!), I should have no hesitation in defining them: that temperance is love giving itself entirely to that which is loved; fortitude is love readily bearing all things for the sake of the loved object; justice is love serving only the loved object, and therefore ruling rightly; prudence is love distinguishing with sagacity between what hinders it and what helps it. The object of this love is not anything, but only God, the chief good, the highest wisdom, the perfect harmony. So we may express the definition thus: that temperance is love keeping itself entire and incorrupt for God; fortitude is love bearing everything readily for the sake of God; justice is love serving God only, and therefore ruling well all else, as subject to man; prudence is love making a right distinction between what helps it towards God and what might hinder it.[12]

First, then, let us consider temperance, which promises us a kind of integrity and incorruption in the love by which we are united to God. The office of temperance is in restraining and quieting the passions which make us pant for those things which turn us away from the laws of God and from the enjoyment of His goodness, that is, in a word, from the happy life. For there is the abode of truth; and in enjoying its contemplation, and in cleaving closely to it, we are assuredly

[11] *Ibid.*, chap. xii.
[12] *Ibid.*, chap. xv.

happy; but departing from this, men become entangled in great errors and sorrows.

The whole duty of temperance, then, is to put off the old man, and to be renewed in God—that is, to scorn all bodily delights and the popular applause, and to turn the whole love to things divine and unseen.[13]

The man, then, who is temperate in such mortal and transient things has his rule of life confirmed by both Testaments, that he should love none of these things, nor think them desirable for their own sakes, but should use them as far as is required for the purposes and duties of life, with the moderation of an employer instead of the ardor of a lover.[14]

On fortitude we must be brief. The love, then, of which we speak, which ought with all sanctity to burn in desire for God, is called temperance, in not seeking for earthly things, and fortitude, in bearing the loss of them. But among all things which are possessed in this life, the body is, by God's most righteous laws, for the sin of old, man's heaviest bond, which is well known as a fact, but most incomprehensible in its mystery. For the soul loves it from the force of habit, not knowing that by using it well and wisely its resurrection and reformation will, by the divine help and decree, be without any trouble made subject to its authority. But when the soul turns to God wholly in this love, it knows these things, and so will not only disregard death, but will even desire it.

Then there is the great struggle with pain. But there is nothing, though of iron hardness, which the fire of love cannot subdue. And when the mind is carried up to God in this love, it will soar above all torture free and glorious, with wings beauteous and unhurt, on which chaste love rises to the embrace of God. Otherwise God must allow the lovers of gold, the lovers of praise, the lovers of women, to have more fortitude than the lovers of Himself, though love in those cases is rather to be called passion or lust. And yet even here we may see with what force the mind presses on with unflagging energy, in spite of all alarms, towards what it

[13] *Ibid.*, chap. xix.
[14] *Ibid.*, chap. xxi.

loves; and we learn that we should bear all things rather than forsake God, since those men bear so much in order to forsake Him.[15] [There follows a summary treatment of justice and prudence as converted by the love of God.]

Love of Self and Neighbor

To proceed to what remains. It may be thought that there is nothing here about man himself, the lover. But to think this, shows a want of clear perception. For it is impossible for one who loves God not to love himself. For he alone has a proper love for himself who aims diligently at the attainment of the chief and true good; and if this is nothing else but God, as has been shown, what is to prevent one who loves God from loving himself? And then, among men should there be no bond of mutual love? Yea, verily; so that we can think of no surer step towards the love of God than the love of man to man.

Let the Lord then supply us with the other precept in answer to the question about the precepts of life; for He was not satisfied with one as knowing that God is one thing and man another, and that the difference is nothing less than that between the Creator and the thing created in the likeness of its Creator. He says then that the second precept is, "Thou shalt love they neighbor as thyself." Now you love yourself suitably when you love God better than yourself. What, then, you aim at in yourself you must aim at in your neighbor, namely, that he may love God with a perfect affection. For you do not love him as yourself, unless you try to draw him to that good which you are yourself pursuing. For this is the one good which has room for all to pursue it along with thee. From this precept proceed the duties of human society, in which it is hard to keep from error. But the first thing to aim at is, that we should be benevolent, that is, that we cherish no malice and no evil design against another. For man is the nearest neighbor of man.

15 *Ibid.*, chap. xxii.

But as a man may sin against another in two ways, either by injuring him or by not helping him when it is in his power, and as it is for these things which no loving man would do that men are called wicked, all that is required is, I think, proved by these words, "The love of our neighbor worketh no ill." And if we cannot attain to good unless we first desist from working evil, our love of our neighbor is a sort of cradle of our love to God, so that, as it is said, "the love of our neighbor worketh no ill," we may rise from this to these other words, "We know that all things issue in good to them that love God." The main point is this, that no one should think that while he despises his neighbor he will come to happiness and to the God whom he loves.

These things require more than mere good-will, and can be done only by a high degree of thoughtfulness and prudence, which belongs only to those to whom it is given by God, the source of all good.[16]

From

St. Augustine: The City of God[17]

Disorder in the Order of Creation

All natures inasmuch as they are, and have therefore a rank and species of their own, and a kind of internal harmony, are certainly good. And when they are in the places assigned to them by the order of their nature, they preserve such being as they have received. And those things which have not received everlasting being, are altered for better or for worse, so as to suit the wants and motions of those things to which the Creator's law has made them subservient; and thus they tend in the divine providence to that end which is embraced in the general scheme of the government of the universe. So that, though the corruption of transitory and perishable things

[16] *Ibid.*, chap. xxvi.
[17] *The City of God*, trans. Marcus Dods (Edinburgh: T. & T. Clark, 1871).

brings them to utter destruction, it does not prevent their producing that which was designed to be their result. And this being so, God, who supremely is, and who therefore created every being which has not supreme existence (for that which was made of nothing could not be equal to Him, and indeed could not be at all had He not made it), is not to be found fault with on account of the creature's faults, but is to be praised in view of the natures He has made.[18]

Thus the true cause of the blessedness of the good angels is found to be this, that they cleave to Him who supremely is. And if we ask the cause of the misery of the bad, it occurs to us, and not unreasonably, that they are miserable because they have forsaken Him who supremely is, and have turned to themselves who have no such essence. And this vice, what else is it called than pride? For "pride is the beginning of sin." They were unwilling, then, to preserve their strength for God; and as adherence to God was the condition of their enjoying an ampler being, they diminished it by preferring themselves to Him. This was the first defect, and the first impoverishment, and the first flaw of their nature, which was created, not indeed supremely existent, but finding its blessedness in the enjoyment of the Supreme Being; whilst by abandoning Him it should become, not indeed no nature at all, but a nature with a less ample existence, and therefore wretched.

If the further question be asked, What was the efficient cause of their evil will? there is none. For what is it which makes the will bad, when it is the will itself which makes the action bad? And consequently the bad will is the cause of the bad action, but nothing is the efficient cause of the bad will. For if anything is the cause, this thing either has or has not a will. If it has, the will is either good or bad. If good, who is so left to himself as to say that a good will makes a will bad? For in this case a good will would be the cause of sin; a most absurd supposition. On the other hand, if this hypothetical thing has a bad will, I wish to know what

[18] *Ibid.*, Bk. XII, chap. v.

made it so; and that we may not go on for ever, I ask at once, what made the *first* evil will bad? For that is not the first which was itself corrupted by an evil will, but that is the first which was made evil by no other will. For if it were preceded by that which made it evil, that will was first which made the other evil. But if it is replied, "Nothing made it evil; it always was evil," I ask if it has been existing in some nature. For if not, then it did not exist at all; and if it did exist in some nature, then it vitiated and corrupted it, and injured it, and consequently deprived it of good. And therefore the evil will could not exist in an evil nature, but in a nature at once good and mutable, which this vice could injure. For if it did no injury, it was no vice; and consequently the will in which it was, could not be called evil. But if it did injury, it did it by taking away or diminishing good. And therefore there could not be from eternity, as was suggested, an evil will in that thing in which there had been previously a natural good, which the evil will was able to diminish by corrupting it. If, then, it was not from eternity, who, I ask, made it? The only thing that can be suggested in reply is, that something which itself had no will, made the will evil. I ask, then, whether this thing was superior, inferior, or equal to it? If superior, then it is better. How, then, has it no will, and not rather a good will? The same reasoning applies if it was equal; for so long as two things have equally a good will, the one cannot produce in the other an evil will. Then remains the supposition that that which corrupted the will of the angelic nature which first sinned, was itself an inferior thing without a will. But that thing, be it of the lowest and most earthly kind, is certainly itself good, since it is a nature and being, with a form and rank of its own in its own kind and order. How, then, can a good thing be the efficient cause of an evil will? How, I say, can good be the cause of evil? For when the will abandons what is above itself, and turns to what is lower, it becomes evil—not because that is evil to which it turns, but because the turning itself is wicked. Therefore it is not an inferior thing which has made the will evil, but it is itself which has become so by wickedly and inordinately desiring an inferior thing. For if two men, alike in physical and moral constitution, see the same corporal beauty, and one of them is excited by the sight to desire an illicit enjoyment, while the other stedfastly maintains a modest restraint of his will, what do we suppose brings it about, that there is an evil will in the one and not in the other? What produces it in the man in whom it exists? Not the bodily beauty, for that was presented equally to the gaze of both, and yet did not produce in both an evil will. Did the flesh of the one cause the desire as he looked? But why did not the flesh of the other? Or was it the disposition? But why not the disposition of both? For we are supposing that both were of a like temperament of body and soul. Must we, then, say that the one was tempted by a secret suggestion of the evil spirit? As if it was not by his own will that he consented to this suggestion and to any inducement whatever! This consent, then, this evil will which he presented to the evil suasive influence—what was the cause of it, we ask? For, not to delay on such a difficulty as this, if both are tempted equally, and one yields and consents to the temptation, while the other remains unmoved by it, what other account can we give of the matter than this, that the one is willing, the other unwilling, to fall away from chastity? And what causes this but their own wills, in cases at least such as we are supposing, where the temperament is identical?[19]

This I do know, that the nature of God can never, nowhere, nowise be defective, and that natures made of nothing can. These latter, however, the more being they have, and the more good they do (for then they do something positive), the more they have efficient causes; but in so far as they are defective in being, and consequently do evil (for then what is their work but vanity?), they have deficient causes. And I know likewise, that the will could not become evil, were it unwilling to become so; and therefore its failings are justly punished, being not necessary, but voluntary. For its defections are not to evil things, but are themselves evil; that is to say, are not towards things that are naturally and in them-

19 *Ibid.*, Bk. XII, chap. vi.

selves evil, but the defection of the will is evil, because it is contrary to the order of nature, and an abandonment of that which has supreme being for that which has less. For avarice is not a fault inherent in gold, but in the man who inordinately loves gold, to the detriment of justice, which ought to be held in incomparably higher regard than gold. Neither is luxury the fault of lovely and charming objects, but of the heart that inordinately loves sensual pleasures, to the neglect of temperance, which attaches us to objects more lovely in their spirituality, and more delectable by their incorruptibility. Nor yet is boasting the fault of human praise, but of the soul that is inordinately fond of the applause of men, and that makes light of the voice of conscience. Pride, too, is not the fault of him who delegates power, nor of power itself, but of the soul that is inordinately enamoured of its own power, and despises the more just dominion of a higher authority. Consequently he who inordinately loves the good which any nature possesses, even though he obtain it, himself becomes evil in the good, and wretched because deprived of a greater good.[20]

The Nature of Sin

But the character of the human will is of moment; because, if it is wrong, these motions of the soul will be wrong, but if it is right, they will be not merely blameless, but even praiseworthy. For the will is in them all; yea, none of them is anything else than will. For what are desire and joy but a volition of consent to the things we wish? And what are fear and sadness but a volition of aversion from the things which we do not wish? But when consent takes the form of seeking to possess the things we wish, this is called desire; and when consent takes the form of enjoying the things we wish, this is called joy. In like manner, when we turn with aversion from that which we do not wish to happen, this volition is termed fear; and when we turn away from that which has happened against our will, this act of will is called

[20] *Ibid.*, Bk. XII, chap. viii.

sorrow. And generally in respect of all that we seek or shun, as a man's will is attracted or repelled, so it is changed and turned into these different affections. Wherefore the man who lives according to God, and not according to man, ought to be a lover of good, and therefore a hater of evil. And since no one is evil by nature, but whoever is evil is evil by vice, he who lives according to God ought to cherish towards evil men a perfect hatred, so that he shall neither hate the man because of his vice, nor love the vice because of the man, but hate the vice and love the man. For the vice being cursed, all that ought to be loved, and nothing that ought to be hated, will remain.[21]

But because God foresaw all things, and was therefore not ignorant that man also would fall, we ought to consider this holy city in connection with what God foresaw and ordained, and not according to our own ideas, which do not embrace God's ordination. For man, by his sin, could not disturb the divine counsel, nor compel God to change what He had decreed; for God's foreknowledge had anticipated both—that is to say, both how evil the man whom He had created good should become, and what good He Himself should even thus derive from him. For though God is said to change His determinations (so that in a tropical sense the Holy Scripture says even that God repented), this is said with reference to man's expectation, or the order of natural causes, and not with reference to that which the Almighty had foreknown that He would do. Accordingly God, as it is written, made man upright, and consequently with a good will. For if he had not had a good will, he could not have been upright. The good will, then, is the work of God; for God created him with it. But the first evil will, which preceded all man's evil acts, was rather a kind of falling away from the work of God to its own works than any positive work. And therefore the acts resulting were evil, not having God, but the will itself for their end; so that the will or the man himself, so far as his will is bad, was as it were the evil tree bringing forth evil fruit. Moreover, the bad will, though it be not

21 *Ibid.*, Bk. XIV, chap. vi.

in harmony with, but opposed to nature, inasmuch as it is a vice or blemish, yet it is true of it as of all vice, that it cannot exist except in a nature, and only in a nature created out of nothing, and not in that which the Creator has begotten of Himself, as He begot the Word, by whom all things were made. For though God formed man of the dust of the earth, yet the earth itself, and every earthly material, is absolutely created out of nothing; and man's soul, too, God created out of nothing, and joined to the body, when He made a man. But evils are so thoroughly overcome by good, that though they are permitted to exist, for the sake of demonstrating how the most righteous foresight of God can make a good use even of them, yet good can exist without evil, as in the true and supreme God Himself, and as in every invisible and visible celestial creature that exists above this murky atmosphere; but evil cannot exist without good, because the natures in which evil exists, in so far as they are natures, are good. And evil is removed, not by removing any nature, or part of a nature, which had been introduced by the evil, but by healing and correcting that which had been vitiated and depraved. The will, therefore, is then truly free, when it is not the slave of vices and sins. Such was it given us by God; and this being lost by its own fault, can only be restored by Him who was able at first to give it.[22]

Our first parents fell into open disobedience because already they were secretly corrupted; for the evil act had never been done had not an evil will preceded it. And what is the origin of our evil will but pride? For "pride is the beginning of sin." And what is pride but the craving for undue exaltation? And this is undue exaltation, when the soul abandons Him to whom it ought to cleave as its end, and becomes a kind of end to itself. This happens when it becomes its own satisfaction. And it does so when it falls away from that unchangeable good which ought to satisfy it more than itself. This falling away is spontaneous; for if the will had remained stedfast in the love of that higher and changeless good by which it was illumined to intelligence and kindled into love,

[22] *Ibid.*, Bk. XIV, chap. xi.

it would not have turned away to find satisfaction in itself, and so become frigid and benighted; the woman would not have believed the serpent spoke the truth, nor would the man have preferred the request of his wife to the command of God, nor have supposed that it was a venial transgression to cleave to the partner of his life even in a partnership of sin. The wicked deed, then—that is to say, the transgression of eating the forbidden fruit—was committed by persons who were already wicked. That "evil fruit" could be brought forth only by "a corrupt tree." But that the tree was evil was not the result of nature; for certainly it could become so only by the vice of the will, and vice is contrary to nature. Now, nature could not have been depraved by vice had it not been made out of nothing. Consequently, that it is a nature, this is because it is made by God; but that it falls away from Him, this is because it is made out of nothing. But man did not so fall away as to become absolutely nothing; but being turned towards himself, his being became more contracted than it was when he clave to Him who supremely is. Accordingly, to exist in himself, that is, to be his own satisfaction after abandoning God, is not quite to become a nonentity, but to approximate to that. And therefore the holy Scriptures designate the proud by another name, "self-pleasers." For it is good to have the heart lifted up, yet not to one's self, for this is proud, but to the Lord, for this is obedient, and can be the act only of the humble. There is, therefore, something in humility which, strangely enough, exalts the heart, and something in pride which debases it. This seems, indeed, to be contradictory, that loftiness should debase and lowliness exalt. But pious humility enables us to submit to what is above us; and nothing is more exalted above us than God; and therefore humility, by making us subject to God, exalts us. But pride, being a defect of nature, by the very act of refusing subjection and revolting from Him who is supreme, falls to a low condition; and then comes to pass what is written: "Thou castedst them down when they lifted up themselves." For he does not say, "when they had been lifted up," as if first they were exalted, and then afterwards cast down;

but "when they lifted up themselves" even then they were cast down—that is to say, the very lifting up was already a fall. And therefore it is that humility is specially recommended to the city of God as it sojourns in this world, and is specially exhibited in the city of God, and the person of Christ its King; while the contrary vice of pride, according to the testimony of the sacred writings, specially rules his adversary the devil. And certainly this is the great difference which distinguishes the two cities of which we speak, the one being the society of the godly men, the other of the ungodly, each associated with the angels that adhere to their party, and the one guided and fashioned by love of self, the other by love of God.[23]

The Two Cities

Accordingly, two cities have been formed by two loves: the earthly by the love of self, even to the contempt of God; the heavenly by the love of God, even to contempt of self. The former, in a word, glories in itself, the latter in the Lord. For the one seeks glory from men; but the greatest glory of the other is God, the witness of conscience. The one lifts up its head in its own glory; the other says to its God, "Thou art my glory, and the lifter up of mine head." In the one, the princes and the nations it subdues are ruled by the love of ruling; in the other, the princes and the subjects serve one another in love, the latter obeying, while the former take thought for all. The one delights in its own strength, represented in the persons of its rulers; the other says to its God, "I will love Thee, O Lord, my strength." And therefore the wise men of the one city, living according to man, have sought for profit to their own bodies or souls, or both, and those who have known God "glorified Him not as God, neither were thankful, but became vain in their imaginations, and their foolish heart was darkened; professing themselves to be wise"—that is, glorying in their own wisdom, and being possessed by pride—"they became fools, and changed the

[23] *Ibid.*, Bk. XIV, chap. xiii.

glory of the incorruptible God into an image made like to corruptible man, and to birds, and four-footed beasts, and creeping things." For they were either leaders or followers of the people in adoring images, "and worshipped and served the creature more than the Creator, who is blessed for ever." But in the other city there is no human wisdom, but only godliness, which offers due worship to the true God, and looks for its reward in the society of the saints, of holy angels as well as holy men, "that God may be all in all."[24]

We have already stated in the preceding books that God, desiring not only that the human race might be able by their similarity of nature to associate with one another, but also that they might be bound together in harmony and peace by the ties of relationship, was pleased to derive all men from one individual, and created man with such a nature that the members of the race should not have died, had not the two first (of whom the one was created out of nothing, and the other out of him) merited this by their disobedience; for by them so great a sin was committed, that by it the human nature was altered for the worse, and was transmitted also to their posterity, liable to sin and subject to death. And the kingdom of death so reigned over men, that the deserved penalty of sin would have hurled all headlong even into the second death, of which there is no end, had not the undeserved grace of God saved some therefrom. And thus it has come to pass, that though there are very many and great nations all over the earth, whose rites and customs, speech, arms, and dress, are distinguished by marked differences, yet there are no more than two kinds of human society, which we may justly call two cities, according to the language of our Scriptures. The one consists of those who wish to live after the flesh, the other of those who wish to live after the spirit; and when they severally achieve what they wish, they live in peace, each after their kind.[25]

First, we must see what it is to live after the flesh, and what to live after the spirit. For any one who either does not

24 *Ibid.*, Bk. XIV, chap. xxvii.
25 *Ibid.*, Bk. XIV, chap. i.

recollect, or does not sufficiently weigh, the language of sacred Scripture, may, on first hearing what we have said, suppose that the Epicurean philosophers live after the flesh, because they place man's highest good in bodily pleasure; and that those others do so who have been of opinion that in some form or other bodily good is man's supreme good; and that the mass of men do so who, without dogmatizing or philosophizing on the subject, are so prone to lust that they cannot delight in any pleasure save such as they receive from bodily sensations: and he may suppose that the Stoics, who place the supreme good of men in the soul, live after the spirit; for what is man's soul, if not spirit? But in the sense of the divine Scripture both are proved to live after the flesh.

Since, then, Scripture uses the word flesh in many ways, which there is not time to collect and investigate, if we are to ascertain what it is to live after the flesh (which is certainly evil, though the nature of flesh is not itself evil), we must carefully examine that passage of the epistle which the Apostle Paul wrote to the Galatians, in which he says, "Now the works of the flesh are manifest, which are these: adultery, fornication, uncleanness, lasciviousness, idolatry, witchcraft, hatred, variance, emulations, wrath, strife, seditions, heresies, envyings, murders, drunkenness, revellings, and such like: of the which I tell you before, as I have also told you in time past, that they which do such things shall not inherit the kingdom of God." This whole passage of the apostolic epistle being considered, so far as it bears on the matter in hand, will be sufficient to answer the question, what it is to live after the flesh. For among the works of the flesh which he said were manifest, and which he cited for condemnation, we find not only those which concern the pleasure of the flesh, as fornications, uncleanness, lasciviousness, drunkenness, revellings, but also those which, though they be remote from fleshly pleasure, reveal the vices of the soul. For who does not see that idolatries, witchcrafts, hatreds, variance, emulations, wrath, strife, heresies, envyings, are vices rather of the soul than of the flesh? For it is quite possible for a man to abstain from fleshly pleasures for the sake of idolatry or some heretical error; and yet, even when he does so, he is proved by this apostolic authority to be living after the flesh; and in abstaining from fleshly pleasure, he is proved to be practising damnable works of the flesh. Who that has enmity has it not in his soul? or who would say to his enemy, or to the man he thinks his enemy, You have a bad flesh towards me, and not rather, You have a bad spirit towards me? In fine, if any one heard of what I may call "carnalities," he would not fail to attribute them to the carnal part of man; so no one doubts that "animosities" belong to the soul of man. Why then does the doctor of the Gentiles in faith and verity call all these and similar things works of the flesh, unless because, by that mode of speech whereby the part is used for the whole, he means us to understand by the word flesh the man himself?[26]

When, therefore, man lives according to man, not according to God, he is like the devil. Because not even an angel might live according to an angel, but only according to God, if he was to abide in the truth, and speak God's truth and not his own lie. And of man, too, the same apostle says in another place, "If the truth of God hath more abounded through my lie";—"my lie," he said, and "God's truth." When, then, a man lives according to the truth, he lives not according to himself, but according to God; for He was God who said, "I am the truth." When, therefore, man lives according to himself—that is, according to man, not according to God—assuredly he lives according to a lie; not that man himself is a lie, for God is his author and creator, who is certainly not the author and creator of a lie, but because man was made upright, that he might not live according to himself, but according to Him that made him—in other words, that he might do His will and not his own; and not to live as he was made to live, that is a lie. For he certainly desires to be blessed even by not living so that he may be blessed. And what is a lie if this desire be not? Wherefore it is not without meaning said that all sin is a lie. For no sin is committed save by that desire or will by which we desire that it be well with us, and shrink from it being ill with us. That, therefore, is a lie which

[26] *Ibid.*, Bk. XIV, chap. ii.

we do in order that it may be well with us, but which makes us more miserable than we were. And why is this, but because the source of man's happiness lies only in God, whom he abandons when he sins, and not in himself, by living according to whom he sins?

In enunciating this proposition of ours, then, that because some live according to the flesh and others according to the spirit there have arisen two diverse and conflicting cities, we might equally well have said, "because some live according to man, others according to God."[27]

The Harmony of God's Order

Whoever gives even moderate attention to human affairs and to our common nature, will recognise that if there is no man who does not wish to be joyful, neither is there any one who does not wish to have peace. For even they who make war desire nothing but victory—desire, that is to say, to attain to peace with glory. For what else is victory than the conquest of those who resist us? and when this is done there is peace. It is therefore with the desire for peace that wars are waged, even by those who take pleasure in exercising their warlike nature in command and battle. And hence it is obvious that peace is the end sought for by war. For every man seeks peace by waging war, but no man seeks war by making peace. For even they who intentionally interrupt the peace in which they are living have no hatred of peace, but only wish it changed into a peace that suits them better. They do not, therefore, wish to have no peace, but only one more to their mind. And in the case of sedition, when men have separated themselves from the community, they yet do not effect what they wish, unless they maintain some kind of peace with their fellow-conspirators. And therefore even robbers take care to maintain peace with their comrades, that they may with greater effect and greater safety invade the peace of other men. And if an individual happen to be of such unrivalled strength, and to be so jealous of partnership, that he

[27] *Ibid.*, Bk. XIV, chap. iv.

trusts himself with no comrades, but makes his own plots, and commits depredations and murders on his own account, yet he maintains some shadow of peace with such persons as he is unable to kill, and from whom he wishes to conceal his deeds. In his own home, too, he makes it his aim to be at peace with his wife and children, and any other members of his household; for unquestionably their prompt obedience to his every look is a source of pleasure to him. And if this be not rendered, he is angry, he chides and punishes; and even by this storm he secures the calm peace of his own home, as occasion demands. For he sees that peace cannot be maintained unless all the members of the same domestic circle be subject to one head, such as he himself is in his own house. And therefore if a city or nation offered to submit itself to him, to serve him in the same style as he had made his household serve him, he would no longer lurk in a brigand's hiding-places, but lift his head in open day as a king, though the same covetousness and wickedness should remain in him. And thus all men desire to have peace with their own circle whom they wish to govern as suits themselves. For even those whom they make war against they wish to make their own, and impose on them the laws of their own peace.

For the most savage animals encompass their own species with a ring of protecting peace. They cohabit, beget, produce, suckle, and bring up their young, though very many of them are not gregarious, but solitary—not like sheep, deer, pigeons, starlings, bees, but such as lions, foxes, eagles, bats. For what tigress does not gently purr over her cubs, and lay aside her ferocity to fondle them? What kite, solitary as he is when circling over his prey, does not seek a mate, build a nest, hatch the eggs, bring up the young birds, and maintain with the mother of his family as peaceful a domestic alliance as he can? How much more powerfully do the laws of man's nature move him to hold fellowship and maintain peace with all men so far as in him lies, since even wicked men wage war to maintain the peace of their own circle, and wish that, if possible, all men belonged to them, that all men and things might serve but one head, and might, either through love or fear, yield themselves to peace with him! It is thus that pride in its perversity apes God. It abhors equality with other men under Him; but, instead of His rule, it seeks to impose a rule of its own upon its equals. It abhors, that is to say, the just peace of God, and loves its own unjust peace; but it cannot help loving peace of one kind or other. For there is no vice so clean contrary to nature that it obliterates even the faintest traces of nature.

He, then, who prefers what is right to what is wrong, and what is well-ordered to what is perverted, sees that the peace of unjust men is not worthy to be called peace in comparison with the peace of the just. And yet even what is perverted must of necessity be in harmony with, and in dependence on, and in some part of the order of things, for otherwise it would have no existence at all.[28]

The peace of the body then consists in the duly proportioned arrangement of its parts. The peace of the irrational soul is the harmonious repose of the appetites, and that of the rational soul the harmony of knowledge and action. The peace of body and soul is the well-ordered and harmonious life and health of the living creature. Peace between man and God is the well-ordered obedience of faith to eternal law. Peace between man and man is well-ordered concord. Domestic peace is the well-ordered concord between those of the family who rule and those who obey. Civil peace is a similar concord among the citizens. The peace of the celestial city is the perfectly ordered and harmonious enjoyment of God, and of one another in God. The peace of all things is the tranquillity of order. Order is the distribution which allots things equal and unequal, each to its own place. And hence, though the miserable, in so far as they are such, do certainly not enjoy peace, but are severed from that tranquillity of order in which there is no disturbance, nevertheless, inasmuch as they are deservedly and justly miserable, they are by their very misery connected with order. They are not, indeed, conjoined with the blessed, but they are disjoined from them by the law of order. And though they are

[28] *Ibid.*, Bk. XIX, chap. xii.

disquieted, their circumstances are notwithstanding adjusted to them, and consequently they have some tranquillity of order, and therefore some peace. But they are wretched because, although not wholly miserable, they are not in that place where any mixture of misery is impossible. They would, however, be more wretched if they had not that peace which arises from being in harmony with the natural order of things. When they suffer, their peace is in so far disturbed; but their peace continues in so far as they do not suffer, and in so far as their nature continues to exist. As, then, there may be life without pain, while there cannot be pain without some kind of life, so there may be peace without war, but there cannot be war without some kind of peace, because war supposes the existence of some natures to wage it, and these natures cannot exist without peace of one kind or other.

And therefore there is a nature in which evil does not or even cannot exist; but there cannot be a nature in which there is no good. Hence not even the nature of the devil himself is evil, in so far as it is nature, but it was made evil by being perverted. Thus he did not abide in the truth, but could not escape the judgment of the Truth; he did not abide in the tranquillity of order, but did not therefore escape the power of the Ordainer. The good imparted by God to his nature did not screen him from the justice of God by which order was preserved in his punishment; neither did God punish the good which He had created, but the evil which the devil had committed. God did not take back all He had imparted to his nature, but something He took and something He left, that there might remain enough to be sensible of the loss of what was taken. And this very sensibility to pain is evidence of the good which has been taken away and the good which has been left. For, were nothing good left, there could be no pain on account of the good which had been lost. For he who sins is still worse if he rejoices in his loss of righteousness. But he who is in pain, if he derives no benefit from it, mourns at least the loss of health. And as righteousness and health are both good things, and as the loss of any good thing is a matter of grief, not of joy—if, at least, there is no compensation, as spiritual righteousness may compensate for the loss of bodily health—certainly it is more suitable for a wicked man to grieve in punishment than to rejoice in his fault. As, then, the joy of a sinner who has abandoned what is good is evidence of a bad will, so his grief for the good he has lost when he is punished is evidence of a good nature. For he who laments the peace his nature has lost is stirred to do so by some relics of peace which make his nature friendly to itself. And it is very just that in the final punishment the wicked and godless should in anguish bewail the loss of the natural advantages they enjoyed, and should perceive that they were most justly taken from them by that God whose benign liberality they had despised. God, then, the most wise Creator and most just Ordainer of all natures, who placed the human race upon earth as its greatest ornament, imparted to men some good things adapted to this life, to wit, temporal peace, such as we can enjoy in this life from health and safety and human fellowship, and all things needful for the preservation and recovery of this peace, such as the objects which are accommodated to our outward senses, light, night, the air, and waters suitable for us, and everything the body requires to sustain, shelter, heal, or beautify it: and all under this most equitable condition, that every man who made a good use of these advantages suited to the peace of his mortal condition, should receive ampler and better blessings, namely, the peace of immortality, accompanied by glory and honour in an endless life made fit for the enjoyment of God and of one another in God; but that he who used the present blessings badly should both lose them and should not receive the others.[29]

The whole use, then, of things temporal has a reference to this result of earthly peace in the earthly community, while in the city of God it is connected with eternal peace. And therefore, if we were irrational animals, we should desire nothing beyond the proper arrangement of the parts of the body and the satisfaction of the appetites—nothing, therefore, but bodily comfort and abundance of pleasures, that the

[29] *Ibid.*, Bk. XIX, chap. xiii.

peace of the body might contribute to the peace of the soul. For if bodily peace be awanting, a bar is put to the peace even of the irrational soul, since it cannot obtain the gratification of its appetites. And these two together help out the mutual peace of soul and body, the peace of harmonious life and health. For as animals, by shunning pain, show that they love bodily peace, and, by pursuing pleasure to gratify their appetites, show that they love peace of soul, so their shrinking from death is a sufficient indication of their intense love of that peace which binds soul and body in close alliance. But, as man has a rational soul, he subordinates all this which he has in common with the beasts to the peace of his rational soul, that his intellect may have free play and may regulate his actions, and that he may thus enjoy the well-ordered harmony of knowledge and action which constitutes, as we have said, the peace of the rational soul. And for this purpose he must desire to be neither molested by pain, nor disturbed by desire, nor extinguished by death, that he may arrive at some useful knowledge by which he may regulate his life and manners. But, owing to the liability of the human mind to fall into mistakes, this very pursuit of knowledge may be a snare to him unless he has a divine Master, whom he may obey without misgiving, and who may at the same time give him such help as to preserve his own freedom. And because, so long as he is in this mortal body, he is a stranger to God, he walks by faith, not by sight; and he therefore refers all peace, bodily or spiritual or both, to that peace which mortal man has with the immortal God, so that he exhibits the well-ordered obedience of faith to eternal law. But as this divine Master inculcates two precepts—the love of God and the love of our neighbour—and as in these precepts a man finds three things he has to love—God, himself, and his neighbour—and that he who loves God loves himself thereby, it follows that he must endeavour to get his neighbour to love God, since he is ordered to love his neighbour as himself. He ought to make this endeavour in behalf of his wife, his children, his household, all within his reach, even as he would wish his neighbour to do the same for him if he needed it; and consequently he will be at peace, or in well-ordered concord, with all men, as far as in him lies. And this is the order of this concord, that a man, in the first place, injure no one, and, in the second, do good to every one he can reach. Primarily, therefore, his own household are his care, for the law of nature and of society gives him readier access to them and greater opportunity of serving them. And hence the apostle says, "Now, if any provide not for his own, and specially for those of his own house, he hath denied the faith, and is worse than an infidel." This is the origin of domestic peace, or the well-ordered concord of those in the family who rule and those who obey. For they who care for the rest rule—the husband the wife, the parents the children, the masters the servants; and they who are cared for obey—the women their husbands, the children their parents, the servants their masters. But in the family of the just man who lives by faith and is as yet a pilgrim journeying on to the celestial city, even those who rule serve those whom they seem to command; for they rule not from a love of power, but from a sense of the duty they owe to others—not because they are proud of authority, but because they love mercy.[30]

The Earthly Sojourn of the Citizen of Heaven

But the families which do not live by faith seek their peace in the earthly advantages of this life; while the families which live by faith look for those eternal blessings which are promised, and use as pilgrims such advantages of time and of earth as do not fascinate and divert them from God, but rather aid them to endure with greater ease, and to keep down the number of those burdens of the corruptible body which weigh upon the soul. Thus the things necessary for this mortal life are used by both kinds of men and families alike, but each has its own peculiar and widely different aim in using them. The earthly city, which does not live by faith, seeks an earthly peace, and the end it proposes, in the well-ordered concord of civic obedience and rule, is the combina-

[30] *Ibid.*, Bk. XIX, chap. xiv.

tion of men's wills to attain the things which are helpful to this life. The heavenly city, or rather the part of it which sojourns on earth and lives by faith, makes use of this peace only because it must, until this mortal condition which necessitates it shall pass away. Consequently, so long as it lives like a captive and a stranger in the earthly city, though it has already received the promise of redemption, and the gift of the Spirit as the earnest of it, it makes no scruple to obey the laws of the earthly city, whereby the things necessary for the maintenance of this mortal life are administered; and thus, as this life is common to both cities, so there is a harmony between them in regard to what belongs to it. This heavenly city, then, while it sojourns on earth, calls citizens out of all nations, and gathers together a society of pilgrims of all languages, not scrupling about diversities in the manners, laws, and institutions whereby earthly peace is secured and maintained, but recognizing that, however various these are, they all tend to one and the same end of earthly peace. It therefore is so far from rescinding and abolishing these diversities, that it even preserves and adapts them, so long only as no hindrance to the worship of the one supreme and true God is thus introduced. Even the heavenly city, therefore, while in its state of pilgrimage, avails itself of the peace of earth, and, so far as it can without injuring faith and godliness, desires and maintains a common agreement among men regarding the acquisition of the necessaries of life, and makes this earthly peace bear upon the peace of heaven; for this alone can be truly called and esteemed the peace of the reasonable creatures, consisting as it does in the perfectly ordered and harmonious enjoyment of God and of one another in God. When we shall have reached that peace, this mortal life shall give place to one that is eternal, and our body shall be no more this animal body which by its corruption weighs down the soul, but a spiritual body feeling no want, and in all its members subjected to the will. In its pilgrim state the heavenly city possesses this peace by faith; and by this faith it lives righteously when it refers to the attainment of that peace every good action towards God and man; for the life of the city is a social life.[31]

But the peace which is peculiar to ourselves we enjoy now with God by faith, and shall hereafter enjoy eternally with Him by sight. But the peace which we enjoy in this life, whether common to all or peculiar to ourselves, is rather the solace of our misery than the positive enjoyment of felicity. Our very righteousness, too, though true in so far as it has respect to the true good, is yet in this life of such a kind that it consists rather in the remission of sins than in the perfecting of virtues. Witness the prayer of the whole city of God in its pilgrim state, for it cries to God by the mouth of all its members, "Forgive us our trespasses as we forgive those who trespass against us." And this prayer is efficacious not for those whose faith is "without works and dead," but for those whose faith "worketh by love." For as reason, though subjected to God, is yet "pressed down by the corruptible body," so long as it is in this mortal condition, it has not perfect authority over vice, and therefore this prayer is needed by the righteous. For though it exercises authority, the vices do not submit without a struggle. For however well one maintains the conflict, and however thoroughly he has subdued these enemies, there steals in some evil thing, which, if it do not find ready expression in act, slips out by the lips, or insinuates itself into the thought; and therefore his peace is not full so long as he is at war with his vices. For it is a doubtful conflict he wages with those that resist, and his victory over those that are defeated is not secure, but full of anxiety and effort. Amidst these temptations, therefore, of all which it has been summarily said in the divine oracles, "Is not human life upon earth a temptation?" who but a proud man can presume that he so lives that he has no need to say to God, "Forgive us our trespasses?" And such a man is not great, but swollen and puffed up with vanity, and is justly resisted by Him who abundantly gives grace to the humble. Whence it is said, "God resisteth the proud, but giveth grace to the humble." In this, then, consists the righteousness of a man, that he submit himself to God, his body to his soul, and his vices, even when they

31 *Ibid.*, Bk. XIX, chap. xvii.

rebel, to his reason, which either defeats or at least resists them; and also that he beg from God grace to do his duty, and the pardon of his sins, and that he render to God thanks for all the blessings he receives. But, in that final peace to which all our righteousness has reference, and for the sake of which it is maintained, as our nature shall enjoy a sound immortality and incorruption, and shall have no more vices, and as we shall experience no resistance either from ourselves or from others, it will not be necessary that reason should rule vices which no longer exist, but God shall rule the man, and the soul shall rule the body, with a sweetness and facility suitable to the felicity of a life which is done with bondage. And this condition shall there be eternal, and we shall be assured of its eternity; and thus the peace of this blessedness and the blessedness of this peace shall be the supreme good.[32]

Further Readings

Primary Sources

The main writings of St. Augustine are to be found in many editions and translations. The most commonly available are the following:

Fathers of the Church Series, New York: The Fathers of the Church, Inc., 1947– . Various volumes.

Library of Christian Classics, Philadelphia: Westminster Press. Vols. 6 (1958), 7 (1955), 8 (1955).

Basic Writings of St. Augustine. 2 vols. Edited by Whitney V. Oates. New York: Random House, 1948.

Selected Writings of St. Augustine. Edited by Roger Hazelton. New York: Meridian Books, World, 1962.

The Confessions and *The City of God* are available separately in many editions.

Secondary Sources

D'Arcy, M. C. (ed.). *St. Augustine.* New York: Meridian Books, 1957.

Brown, Peter. *Augustine of Hippo: a biography.* Berkeley: University of California Press, 1967.

Gilson, Etienne. *The Christian Philosophy of St. Augustine.* New York: Random House, 1960.

Mourant, John A. *Introduction to the Philosophy of St. Augustine.* University Park: Pennsylvania State University Press, 1964.

TeSelle, Eugene. *Augustine, the Theologian.* New York: Herder and Herder, 1970.

[32] *Ibid.,* Bk. XIX, chap. xxvii.

Chapter 5

ETHICS OF MONASTICISM

When, in 1944, the Italian abbey of Monte Cassino was bombed into rubble, the attention of the world was turned back fourteen hundred years. Journalists pointed out that since A.D. 529 in the seclusion of this abbey a mode of life had been lived by successive generations of Benedictine monks so utterly different in its premises from that of the efficient airmen sent to destroy the ancient walls that it seemed impossible that bombers and bombed could belong to the same civilization. Yet Monte Cassino was the shrine and symbol of the ethical ideal of monasticism, which from the time of Augustine until the Reformation was regarded almost universally as *the* Christian way of life, and for many Christians today it remains so.

Though the monastic movement did not become powerful until the fourth century, it had begun its development long before. After the age of apocalyptic expectation and persecution had passed, the Christian church had settled down into a relatively assured status as the official religion of the empire. It had, in a sense, gained the world but at the price of its own soul. Or so it appeared to a few men who saw in the worldly accommodations and laxities of the church an utter betrayal of the commands of its founder. The church had become so secularized that the behavior of Christians seemed hardly distinguishable from that of nonbelievers. The moral ambiguity involved in being both a citizen of the corrupt empire, the city of earth, and being a "citizen of heaven" became for them intolerable. Under the compulsion of the commands of Christ, of the Greek ideal of the contemplative life, so strong in later Hellenistic culture, and of the natural human inclination to escape from a snarled and compromised situation, many devout laymen, particularly in the East, fled "the world" to recapture the lost vision of God in the solitary and stark isolation of the deserts of Egypt. As with the American Thoreau, who fifteen hundred years later took to the woods "to front only the essential facts of life," these first hermit monks believed that the essential facts of life, God and the soul, could not be found in a crowded culture.

In the remotest mountain lairs and caves the first Christian monks took up their austere abodes, subjecting themselves to ascetic bodily torture, dressing themselves only in the coarsest garments, and eating next to nothing in order to "die to the world" and devote their days to prayer and contemplation. Eastern monasticism was for the most part individualistic and ascetic. But the movement in its Western development did not long remain an individualistic, Robinson Crusoe affair. Practical as well as spiritual requirements soon brought monks together to organize their renunciation of the world into a corporate search under social discipline. The communal (or coenobitic) form of the monastic ideal became the normal form in the West by the time of the fourth century. Cassian, Pachomius, and others experimented with various "rules" for the government of monastic orders. St. Augustine added his blessing to the development, commending it as the highest Christian life. But by the sixth century the various monastic communities which had spread from Italy into Gaul and the North were in sorry decay. Laxity and anarchy were prevalent. This situation was remedied for a time by Benedict of Nursia (480-543), who drew up in his *Rule* the principles which became standard for the monastic orders of subsequent centuries. Benedict's *Rule* was marked particularly by the Latin genius for order and stability, by moderation in discipline in the interests of functional simplicity of life rather than harsh bodily self-denial, and by a flexibility that made the *Rule* adaptable to a wide range of changing circumstances.

The subsequent history of the monastic ideal continued, however, to be one of periodic corruption and reform. This was the cycle: laxity and worldliness brought on by a wave of popular success, then a movement back to the original rigor of the *Rule* at the inspiration of some devoted and saintly monk, then another era of decline. There were minor and major variations of this cycle. The most significant reforms took place (1) in the late tenth century (the Cluniac) when Hildebrand attempted not only to purify monastic life but also to apply its rules to the regular clergy of the church, (2) in the twelfth century (the Cistercian), and (3) in the thirteenth century, when the Dominican and Franciscan reforms swept over Europe. The Franciscan order gave a sharp new turn to the monastic scheme. Francis of Assisi stressed in radical form the ethical ideals of Benedict and even more what he believed to be the message of the Gospels, especially the requirement of absolute poverty. He sent the monk out from the seclusion of the monastery into the world as preacher and missionary. This new monk became a wandering friar, who went about preaching to the common folk the love of the created world, the joys of absolute poverty, and the peaceable humility and devotion of Christ. Even in the lifetime of St. Francis, however, his movement encountered the usual stubborn problems on the matter of property ownership. A fatal schism between rigorists and moderates took place, the latter securing the church's blessing; the old accommodation to "the world and the flesh" that Francis had set his heart on rooting out again followed.

The Monastic Discipline

The *summum bonum* of the monk was spiritual perfection in the contemplation and love of God, to be achieved by the renunciation of the world and the uncompromising imitation of Christ. The distinguishing feature of monasticism lay not so much in that it held this ideal as in its understanding of the way such a goal must be approached. The monk found his clue in such Gospel words as "You lack one thing; go, sell what you have, and give to the poor, and you will have treasure in heaven; and come, follow me."[1] "Disciple" and "discipline" are words of the same root. To follow Christ one must take the narrow way, the way of suffering, self-denial, and chastisement. "A man cannot serve two masters." The world and Christ were irreconcilable sovereigns. To attempt to live in the world with Christian allegiance was impossible. Only the pure in heart could see God; such purity required a cleansing of the self, inward and outward, of all that the world held dear; a cleansing not once, but perpetually, in a lifetime discipline that schooled the soul to habitual renunciation so that it might become rich in things eternal. Three specific disciplines formed the way: poverty, chastity, and obedience.

Poverty was a mark of the monk's renunciation of the world's standard of value. A man's life, in the eyes of God, could not consist in the abundance of things he possessed. Indeed, a man would always be possessed by his possessions, small or great, unless he cut out at the root his inward desire to gain security by ownership. Even a modicum of wealth was a great temptation to selfishness. "If a man calleth aught his own, he maketh himself a stranger to God," wrote Basil, one of the monastic fathers. Private ownership of anything was rigidly prohibited in all the monastic rules. Whatever little property was necessary—shelter, a change of garment, simple fare, a bed, tools to work with, a few books—was corporately owned by the monastery, and administered by the abbot. The collective ownership of property, when coupled with the program of hard manual labor on the soil and in the circumstances of the feudal economic order, proved in time a serious strain on the ideal. Work produced wealth; integrity inspired trust. The monasteries became places of affluence, even of luxury. It was against this corruption that St. Francis, "married to Lady Poverty," directed his attack. Poverty must be complete, he said. If the inward possessive will were absolutely denied, then corporate as well as individual ownership would be automatically abolished.

[1] Mark 10:21.

As the monk's poverty—at least in theory—marked his renunciation of the world, his chastity marked his renunciation of the flesh. The most persistent demand of the flesh, the more compelling the more denied, was that of sex. Some monastic writers looked on the sex drive with horror as demonic and at best "God's one mistake in creation." Others granted sex to be necessary for the continuation of the race, upon which even personnel for the monastery must depend. Yet, as Jerome bluntly put it: "Marriage populates the earth, virginity populates heaven." The perfect way of life, the pursuit of the vision of God, must be untrammeled by the distractions of family life, the yammering of children, as well as by sexual self-indulgence. Sex seemed one of the commonest wiles of the devil whereby a man was led to exploit others for his own self-interest. The vow to celibacy, then, was a vow to deny self-assertion as well as the evil flesh.

The lifelong repression of the sex impulse was no easy task. Some of the measures practiced by the Eastern hermit-monks were strenuous to the extreme: standing up to sleep, for instance, to avoid the thoughts that might surge in on one in a horizontal position. In Benedict's *Rule*, however, a healthier mode of sublimation was maintained: manual labor. Celibacy was so axiomatic for Benedict that it is not even mentioned in the *Rule*. Yet it is apparent that one of the reasons, albeit a minor one, for his incorporation of six hours of manual labor into the monk's daily regimen was to enable him to sustain celibacy with greater health of mind. It should be added that the dignifying of manual labor in the Benedictine pattern had other purposes: the practical necessity of providing food and clothing for a sizeable community "so that there may be no need for the monks to go beyond the gates." The spiritual weal one might acquire from the soil and the craftsman's bench was great. Indolence, mental sloth, and parasitic ease were supplanted by diligence, alertness, and the sense of humble contribution to the common good. Labor was, truly, a form of prayer.

Obedience was the third of the great disciplines. In holy obedience to one's superior the monk renounced his self-will.

No doubt there was practical sagacity in Benedict's requirement of absolute obedience to the abbot. Only so could a cohesive and well-ordered community of men live in close proximity. But the spiritual intention of the vow to obey was more important. It was the road to humility. Monasticism here put into local and specific form a theme of orthodox Hebrew-Christian thought, that pride, "the lifting up of the head," is the root of sin and reverent humility the root of good. "It is a great matter to live in obedience," said Thomas à Kempis, one of the famous apologists of monasticism, "to be under a superior and not at one's own disposing. It is much safer to obey than to govern."

Implicit in this pattern of the good life was the principle of gradation as applied to moral discipline. For each monk the achievement of moral perfection was set forth as a scale or ladder on which he might mount from lower to higher. It was assumed that a man cannot change from evil to good overnight; morality is not a matter of sudden conversion whereby in a twinkling the lost are saved. To learn to imitate Christ required slow and painstaking effort with many setbacks. At best one might hope to achieve only the middle rungs of the ladder. It is important to note that a corollary of the principle of gradation was a stress on human initiative. Moral perfection was a matter of achievement, the perfected doing of spiritual works, more than a matter of the unmerited grace of God. It was this emphasis, among others, which so disquieted the monk Martin Luther and which he came to repudiate as false in his framing of the principles of the Protestant Reformation.

The Monk's Relation to the World

One baffling problem always faced the theorist of the monastic ideal: What should be the relation of the monastic way to the way of the world? How should the monk think of those outside the cloister walls? If he felt that his mode of life was the truly Christian way, would he not be concerned that all men should come under its sway, that the world be "Christianized" or "monasticized"? The monk had to reckon with a tendency common to human nature to universalize one's conception of the right. At certain periods in monastic history, such as the Cluniac, there was strong impetus to extend the monastic life from a minority to a majority rule. Yet by its very nature, the extension of the ideal proved to lead more easily to its corruption. Great numbers could be brought in only by a relaxation of strict discipline or by substituting quantitative standards of worth for qualitative. At the more creative and pure periods of its course, the monastic ideal was held up frankly as a way for the minority, and a small one at that. Monasticism saw itself as a separate and higher vocation, to which only a few were called in the diversity of God's planned economy. It is from diversity, not uniformity of function, it said, that the whole of society prospers. Some men are called to be carpenters, artists, or teachers, but others cannot nor should not perform these roles. Some are called to be parents that society may continue, but not all need be. So the monk, too, had his vocation of seeking moral perfection, while those in the world sought lesser things. Yet the monk was dependent on the world. Celibacy could only be pursued by the children of noncelibates. And the full practice of poverty was dependent in part on the charity of those who had enough of this world's goods to spare.

This relationship did not seem to the monk or to the world to be parasitic. In his way, the monk was performing a service to the world which he could not perform were he to live by the world's ethic. St. Francis put this in pointed words: "God hath called us into this holy religion for the salvation of the world, and has made this compact between the world and us, that we should give it good example and that it should provide for our necessities."[2]

The monastery was as much the servant of the market place as its beneficiary. It gave witness to the authenticity and beauty of the absolute ethic of the Gospel, holding "the candle of the Lord," which shed light for those in a culture

[2] *The Little Flowers of St. Francis of Assisi,* trans. Dom Roger Hudleston (London: Burns Oates, 1953), p. 131.

that lived by the relativities and imperfections of a darker way. No doubt many a monk cultivated the garden of his own soul and was content to let the outside world go to the devil. But the high-minded and authentic monk of the West was not insensitive to the need of the world he had left behind. In his worship at the altar, in his prayers of intercession, in his preservation and cultivation of Latin culture and art, in his charity and hospitality to the world's hungry and disinherited, but above all in his cultivation of purity of life, he looked not only up to heaven but down in love upon the world he had renounced.

The Problem of the Monastic Way

It is almost impossible to make any fair estimate of the monastic version of Christianity from the standpoint of modern Western democratic life. At almost every point the preconceptions of current culture are poles apart from those of the Middle Ages. Those Protestants who think of religion as hearty neighborliness or as the social extension of the ideals of Jesus for the greater happiness of mankind, find monasticism mystical, escapist, otherworldly, socially irresponsible. To those moderns who stress action, busyness, "doing something about it," the preference of the monk for contemplation over action seems empty and idle. To capitalists who regard aggressive and self-seeking individualism as virtuous, the monk's self-denial appears abject and spineless. To socialists, who believe with monks in common ownership, monasticism is outrageously otherworldly. To democrats the monastic cultivation of a spiritual aristocracy living on a higher plane than the common man is blatantly false. To those who think of education as preparation for life, the medieval and monastic concept of education as preparation for death seems morbid.

It is important, however, for the contemporary student to try to escape from his own provincialism in time and attempt to judge the monastic ideal in terms of its own premises. Viewed thus, the common strictures against monasticism may take on less cogency. Was it a "retreat from reality"? Not by the monk's standard of what was most real in the universe. His was a retreat, he felt, from a false to a true world, from things transient and temporal to things abiding and eternal, from a frustrating life of distraction and striving after wind, to the true life of serenity and peace which the "world" could neither give nor take away.

Monastic concentration on God and the soul fostered, more than in any other era of Christian history, profound explorations of the inner life of man, for it provided the soil in which best could flower the great classics of the devotional life. Part of its genius lay in its firm hold on a permanent truth of Christian ethics: The crucial point at which morality begins and ends is the heart of man. Reconstruction of life is from within. Moreover, the place to begin in the moral life is not with the "other," the neighbor, but with the self. Self-conquest is always the first ethical task. So the monastic community was first of all a community of self-discipline, rather than of the discipline of the world. At the risk of some spiritual isolationism, the monk escaped that sin of spiritual imperialism which a Christian community practices when it preaches to secular society a way of life it does not itself follow.

Withal—and judging it again on its own premises—one must recognize the serious shortcomings of monastic ethics as it was usually practiced. The very height of its aim accounted in part for the sullied corruptions into which it perennially fell. Heroic in ideal, it was in practice a spotted reality. First, there was a certain stubbornness in the human stuff it tried to overcome which always blocked the realization of the perfect ethic, a stuff which the monk failed to understand as God-given for right use, not denial. The world and the flesh in one form might be left behind in the market place only to slip in the back door of the monastery in another disguise. This problem we have already noted in regard to the issue of property. The matter of sex illustrates the point even more sharply. In keeping the vow of absolute chastity the monk contended against the demands of a natural order which would out, despite himself. St. Jerome found that the "dancing girls of Rome," whom he could banish from the conscious thoughts of his days, reappeared to haunt his nightly dreams. The difficult dilemma of being at once a human being and a monk is illustrated by the tale of a celibate monk who went so far in his vow as to refuse to look at a woman. Inadvertently he happened to meet a group of nuns on a road and turned his face away as he passed them. At which one of the nuns said to him, "If you were a true monk, you would not know whether we were women or not."[3]

A second shortcoming of the monastic ideal as generally practiced lay in a certain idolatry which substituted the way to the vision of God for God himself. The "end" of living, as we have noted, was the love and contemplation of God. But the monk could never rest easy with the anarchy to which Augustine's dictum, "Love God and do what you want," might lend itself when interpreted by amateurs and beginners. The way to love God truly was in poverty, chastity, and obedience, and the host of regulations which furthered these commands. The monastery was to be a lifelong "school of the Lord's service," where strict discipline and exactly prescribed "steps" might lead to the "commencement" of spiritual perfection. But in the curriculum of salvation the monk could easily become more concerned with his relation to the discipline than to the end for which the discipline was set, or, to speak by analogy, more concerned about getting grades than wisdom. Standing somewhere on the middle rungs of the ladder to heaven, it was too easy for him to lose sight of the heavenly vision in measuring the progress of his own ascent. He was encouraged to try to outdo his fellow monks in humility; hence he might look down on those whom he had surpassed. Thus the deadly sin of pride, in the guise of its opposite, forever shadowed the monk as he struggled to achieve humility, a shadow inevitable in an ethics that conceives blessedness as something to be achieved by the self-conscious self. So also, the self-denying charity of the monk to his in-

[3] H. B. Workman, *The Evolution of the Monastic Ideal* (London: C. H. Kelly, 1913), p. 105.

digent neighbor became, in much practice, a work of perfection, a sort of merit badge, so that the very self he struggled to deny remained at the center of his focus. In the great saints of monasticism, Bernard, Francis, Dominic, and many little saints as well, there was a quality of unself-conscious spontaneity and simplicity derived more from their sense of grace than from the ethics of works. They were not bothered by this dilemma. But many an average monk found that not only the flesh and the world, but also his own self-will—these three devils he struggled most to exorcise—remained with him forever because of the very way of life he was set to follow.

Of the many rich sources from which one might draw illustrations of the spirit of monastic ethics, the *Rule of St. Benedict,* from the early sixth century, and the *Little Flowers of St. Francis,* from the fourteenth, are both the most honored and the most typical. Benedict's *Rule* (pp. 151-62), compiled by him out of a long experience in monastic organization at Monte Cassino, deals in careful detail with the mode of life in the community: the tasks and qualification of every officer from abbot to cook, the manner of worship, dormitory regulations, the rules for dress, eating, and sleeping, the modes of punishment for offenses, and so on. Although the whole is obviously intended not as a treatise on ethics, Benedict makes quite clear what the spirit as well as the letter of the monk's law should be, a spirit which the selected chapters below make evident.

The Little Flowers of St. Francis (pp. 162-74) belongs to a type of literature common to the medieval period when legend and fancy were intermingled with history and fact. St. Francis, who was not a man of letters, left no systematic treatise on theology and ethics—only the few terse sentences of his original Rule, random sayings, and the famous *Canticle* and other poems of praise to God. But around his memory and that of his devoted followers grew up stories and recollections, in time collected and preserved in the *Flowers,* which convey authentically as well as lovingly the spirit of the Franciscan reform. One of the most venerated of the original "poor friars" was Friar Giles, whose sayings in the

Flowers phrase in concise aphorisms the ideals not only of Francis but of monastic ethics in general.

SOURCES

From
THE RULE OF ST. BENEDICT[4]

Hearken continually within thine heart, O son, giving attentive ear to the precepts of thy master. Understand with willing mind and effectually fulfil thy holy father's admonition; that thou mayest return, by the labour of obedience, to Him from Whom, by the idleness of disobedience, thou hadst withdrawn. To this end I now address a word of exhortation to thee, whosoever thou art, who, renouncing thine own will and taking up the bright and all-conquering weapons of obedience, dost enter upon the service of thy true king, Christ the Lord.

Let our loins be girt with faith and the observance of good works, and let us, gospel-led, pursue His paths, that we may be worthy to see Him Who has called us unto His own kingdom.

But if our wish be to have a dwelling-place in His kingdom, let us remember it can by no means be attained unless one run thither by good deeds. For, with the prophet, let us ask the Lord, saying to Him: "Lord, who will dwell in Thy tabernacle, and who will rest in Thy holy mount?" After putting this question, brethren, let us listen to our Lord showing us in answer the way by saying: "He who lives blamelessly and does justice; he who speaks truth from his heart; he who has kept his tongue from guile; he who has done his neighbour no evil and has accepted no slander against his neigh-

[4] *The Rule of St. Benedict*, trans. by W. K. Lowther Clarke, (London: Society for the Promotion of Christian Knowledge, 1931). Copyright 1931 by Society for the Promotion of Christian Knowledge. Reprinted by permission.

bour": he who has brought to naught the malignant slanderer the devil, rejecting from his heart's thoughts him and his efforts to persuade him; and who has taken hold of his suggestions or ever they be come to maturity and has dashed them against the Rock which is Christ. Those who fear the Lord are not puffed up by their own good observance of rule, but reckoning that the good that is in them could not be wrought by themselves but by God, magnify the Lord working in them.

And if we wish to escape the pains of hell and attain to eternal life we must hasten to do such things only as may profit us for eternity, now, while there is time for this and we are in this body and there is time to fulfil all these precepts by means of this light.

We have therefore to establish a school of the Lord's service, in the institution of which we hope we are going to establish nothing harsh, nothing burdensome. But if, prompted by the desire to attain to equity, anything be set forth somewhat strictly for the correction of vice or the preservation of charity, do not therefore in fear and terror flee back from the way of salvation of which the beginning cannot but be a narrow entrance. For it is by progressing in the life of conversion and faith that, with heart enlarged and in ineffable sweetness of love, one runs in the way of God's commandments, so that never deserting His discipleship but persevering until death in His doctrine within the monastery, we may partake by patience in the suffering of Christ and become worthy inheritors of His kingdom. Amen.[5]

The Abbot

Let the abbot be always careful of his own teaching of the obedience of his disciples, of both which matters examination will be made at the dreadful judgment of God; and let the abbot know that to the fault of the shepherd is accounted whatever the father of the family shall have found amiss in the sheep. Only so shall he be free of blame in proportion as

[5] *Ibid.*, Prologue.

the perfect diligence of a shepherd has been applied to the restless and disobedient flock and every careful attention has been manifested towards whatever was corrupt about them.

Therefore when anyone receives the title of abbot he ought to preside over his disciples with twofold manner of teaching: that is, to show forth all that is good and holy by deeds even more than by words, so as by his words to set the commandment of the Lord before the more intelligent disciples: but to those hard of heart and to those of less capacity to show forth the divine precept by his deeds. And all things that he has taught the disciples are contrary to the divine precepts, let his own deeds indicate are things not to be done; lest preaching to others himself be found reprobate.

Let him show no favouritism in the monastery. Let not one be loved more than another, unless it be one whom he has found to excel in good deeds and obedience. Let not one of gentle birth be placed higher than one who was recently a serf, unless there be some other and reasonable cause. For whether bondmen or freemen we are all one in Christ and under the one Lord bear equal rank of subjection, for there is no acceptation of persons with God. In His sight we are differentiated one from the other in respect to this only, namely, if we be found humble and to excel others in good deeds.[6]

What Are the Instruments of Good Work?

In the first place, to love the Lord God with the whole heart, the whole soul and the whole strength. Then one's neighbour as if oneself. Then, not to kill. Not to commit adultery. Not to steal. Not to covet. Not to utter false witness. To honour all men. To do as one would be done by. To deny oneself that one may follow Christ. To chastise the body. Not to embrace delights. To love fasting. To relieve the poor. To clothe the naked. To visit the sick. To bury the dead. To help in tribulation. To console the sorrowing. To become a stranger to worldly deeds. To prefer nothing to the love of Christ.

[6] *Ibid.*, chap. ii.

Not to carry anger into effect. Not to prolong the duration of one's wrath. Not to retain guile in one's heart. Not to make a false peace. Not to abandon charity. Not to swear, lest perchance one forswear. To utter only truth from heart and mouth. Not to return evil for evil. Not to do injury, but to suffer it patiently. To love enemies. Not to curse in return those who curse one, but rather to bless them. To bear persecution for righteousness. Not to be proud. Not to be given to much wine. Not to be gluttonous. Not given to much sleep. Not to be sluggish. Not to be given to gambling. Not to be a detractor. To put one's hope in God.

When one sees any good in oneself to attribute it to God, not to self. But to recognize that evil always comes from self and to refer it to self. To have wholesome fear of the day of judgment. With fear to shrink from hell. To long for eternal life with all spiritual desire. To have the expectation of death daily before one's eyes. Hour by hour to keep guard over one's every act. To know for certain that God sees one everywhere. Forthwith to dash down upon the Rock, even Christ, any evil thoughts approaching the heart: and to lay them open before one's superior. To keep one's mouth from evil or depraved speech. Not to love to speak much. Not to speak useless or mirth-provoking words. Not to love much or excessive laughter. To listen with goodwill to holy reading. To be frequently occupied in prayer. With tears and groaning daily to confess in prayer to God one's past sins and concerning those same sins to amend for the future. Not to fulfil the desires of the flesh: to hate one's own will. To yield obedience in all things to the abbot's precepts, even if he himself act contrary to their spirit, the which be far from him. Not to wish to be called holy before one is, but to be so first, whereby one would be so called the more truly. By deeds daily to fulfil the precepts of God. To love chastity. Not to hate anyone. Not to harbour jealousy. Not to love contention. To avoid elation. To venerate seniors. To love juniors. In the love of Christ to pray for one's enemies. In case of discord with anyone to make peace before the setting of the sun. And never to despair of the mercy of God.

And the cloister of the monastery and stability in the community are the workshop wherein we may diligently effect all these works.[7]

Concerning Obedience

The first degree of humility is obedience without delay. This is becoming to those who value nothing as more dear to them than Christ, on account of the holy servitude they have professed, whether through fear of hell or on account of the glory of life eternal. As soon as any order has been given by a superior, as being the same as if the order were divinely given, they can brook no delay in carrying it out.

But this same obedience will only then be acceptable to God and pleasing to man when that which is ordered be carried out neither with trepidation nor tardily and lukewarmly, nor yet with murmuring and the back answer of one unwilling; for obedience yielded to superiors is an offering laid before God. And with goodwill should disciples yield it because it is the cheerful giver God loves. For if it is with ill-will the disciple obeys, if even he murmur in his heart and not only by actual word of mouth, though he fulfil the command, yet will he not now be accepted as obedient by God, who regardeth the heart of the murmurer.[8]

Concerning Humility

Brethren, the sacred Scriptures cry out to us and say: "Every one who exalts himself will be humbled, and every one who humbles himself will be exalted."

If we wish to attain the highest point of humility and if we wish quickly to reach that heavenly exaltation which is attained through humility in this present life, we must by what we do to attain it set up that ladder which appeared in Jacob's dream and by which angels were shown to be both descend-

[7] *Ibid.*, chap. iv.
[8] *Ibid.*, chap. v.

ing and ascending; for without doubt we are not to understand that descending and ascending but as descending by exaltation and ascending by humility.

For that ladder set up is our life in this world which, when the heart has been humbled by the Lord, is set up to heaven. And we say that the sides of this ladder are our body and soul, into which sides God-given vocation has inserted sundry rungs of humility and discipline by which we may ascend.

The first step, then, of humility is if one set the fear of God always before his eyes and altogether avoid forgetfulness; and be always mindful of everything that God has ordered and always ponder over life eternal, which is prepared for those that fear God; and how hell will consume, for their sins, such as despise God; and if he keep himself at all times from sins and faults, alike of thought, or the tongue, of the eye, of the hand, of the foot, or of self-will; and moreover hasten to cut away the desires of the flesh.

The second step in humility is, if anyone, loving not his own self-will, delight not to fulfil his natural desires, but in his deeds reproduce that word of the Lord Who says: "I did not come to do My will, but His Who sent Me."

The third step in humility is that one for love of God subject himself in all obedience to his superior, imitating the Lord, of Whom the Apostle says: "Made obedient even unto death."

The fourth step in humility is if in that same obedience, though things hard and contrary and even injuries, no matter of what kind, have been inflicted, he keep patience with a quiet conscience and enduring grows not weary nor gives in.

The fifth step in humility is if one shall have confessed to his abbot, by humble admission, any evil thoughts that come to the heart, or evil deeds done by him in secret.

The sixth step in humility is if a monk be content with the meanest and worst of everything and with respect to everything enjoined him adjudge himself a profitless workman and unworthy.

The seventh step in humility is if he not only with his mouth denounce himself as inferior to all and more worthless, but also believe it in his inner consciousness, humbling himself.

The eighth step in humility is if a monk do nothing but what the common rule of the monastery and the example of his seniors suggest.

The ninth step in humility is if a monk restrain his tongue from speaking so as to keep silence and not speak till questioned.

The tenth step in humility is if he be not easily and quickly moved to laughter, because it is written: "The fool lifts up his voice in laughter."

The eleventh step in humility is if when a monk speaks he speak few and reasonable words, calmly and without laughter, humbly and with gravity.

The twelfth step in humility is if a monk not only be humble in heart, but also always in his very body evince humility to those who see him, that is, that in the Work of God, in the oratory, in the monastery, in the garden, on the road, in the field or elsewhere, sitting, walking, or standing, his head be always bent, his eyes cast down, accounting himself at all times as one convicted of his sins.

When then the monk shall have ascended all these steps in humility, he will presently arrive at that love of God which, being perfect, puts fear right outside; and by means of which all that formerly he could not observe but with much fearfulness he will begin to keep without any difficulty, as it were by habit become second nature, no longer through fear of hell, but for love of Christ and a certain good habit and delight in virtue, the which the Lord will deign to manifest by the Holy Spirit to His labourer now cleansed from vices and sins.[9]

Whether Monks Ought to Have Anything of Their Own

Very specially is this vice of private ownership to be cut off from the monastery by the roots; and let not anyone presume to give or accept anything without the abbot's orders, nor to have anything as his own, not anything whatsoever,

[9] *Ibid.*, chap. vii.

neither books, nor writing-tablet, no pen; no, nothing at all, since indeed it is not allowed them to keep either body or will in their own power, but to look to receive everything necessary from their monastic father; and let not any be allowed to have what the abbot has not either given or permitted. And let all things be common to all.[10]

Concerning the Daily Manual Work

Idleness is inimical to the soul; and therefore the brethren ought to be occupied, at fixed seasons, with manual work and again at fixed seasons with spiritual reading: and so we think the hours for each should be arranged on this plan; that is to say that from Easter to the first of October they go out in the morning from Prime and work at whatever has to be done until nearly the fourth hour: And from the fourth hour have time for reading until about the sixth hour. And when they rise from table after the sixth hour let them rest upon their beds in complete silence; or if by chance anyone should wish to read, let him so read as that he may not disturb anyone else. Let None be said in good time, about the middle of the eighth hour, and then again let them work at whatever has to be done, until Vespers. And let them not be distressed if poverty or the needs of the place should require that they busy themselves about gathering the crops with their own hands; for then are they truly monks, when they live by the work of their own hands, as did our fathers and the apostles. Let everything be done in moderation however on account of the faint-hearted.[11] [Benedict then sets a similar routine for the rest of the year.]

Concerning Craftsmen in the Monastery

Let artificers, if there are any in the monastery, with all humility work at their arts, if the abbot shall have given per-

[10] *Ibid.*, chap. xxxiii.
[11] *Ibid.*, chap. xlviii.

mission. But if any one of their number is puffed up by reason of his knowledge of his art, in that he seems to confer some favour upon the monastery, let such an one as this be removed from exercising that art and not engage in it anew unless by chance the abbot again order him to do so when he has become humble. And if any of the artificers' work is to be sold, let those who are to effect the transaction see to it that they presume not to bring about any fraudulent act. And let not the evil of avarice creep in in the matter of the prices charged for the goods; but let them always be sold somewhat more cheaply than they can be sold by others who are seculars, that in all things God may be glorified.[12]

Concerning the Discipline of Those To Be Received as Brethren

In the case of anyone newly come to essay conversion of life, let not an easy entrance be accorded him. If anyone who comes shall have persevered in knocking for admission and after four or five days shall have been found patiently to bear all the injuries inflicted upon him and the difficulty of gaining entrance and shall be found to persist with his petition, let the entrance be granted him and let him be in the guests' house for a few days. After that, let him be in the novices' cell where he may meditate and eat and sleep.

Let there be set before him all the hard and the rough things through which lies the way to God; and if he shall have given promise of stability and perseverance let this rule be read right through to him after the lapse of two months and let this be said to him: "Behold the law under which thou dost wish to serve as a faithful soldier; if thou art able to keep it, enter; but if thou art not able, depart free." If thus far he shall have stood firm, then let him be conducted to the aforenamed novices' cell and be again tested in all patience; and after the lapse of six months let the rule be re-read to him that he may know upon what he is entering: and if thus far

12 *Ibid.*, chap. lvii.

he stand firm, after four months let this same rule again be reread to him: and if, having deliberated of the matter with himself he shall have promised that he will keep it all and observe everything ordered him, then let him be received into the community, knowing himself to be now established by the law of the rule so that it is not lawful for him from that day onwards to go forth from the monastery, nor to shake free his neck from beneath the yoke of the rule which it was permitted him after such prolonged deliberation either to refuse or to accept.

Let him then who is to be received, in the oratory, in the presence of all the brethren, make promise of stability, of conversion of life and of obedience, in the presence of God and of His saints, that if he should ever act otherwise he may know he will be condemned by Him Whom he mocks.

If he has any property, let him either assign it beforehand to the poor, or else by formal donation confer it upon the monastery, reserving nothing at all for himself, as becomes one who must know that thenceforth he will hold no power even over himself. Forthwith, therefore, in the oratory, let him also be stripped of the garments, his own property, with which he is clad and be clothed with such as are the property of the monastery: and let those garments of which he was stripped be put away to be kept in the wardrobe, that if at any time, by suasion of the devil, he should consent to go forth from the monastery, which God forbid, he may then be cast forth unfrocked.[13]

Concerning the Porter of the Monastery

Let there be stationed at the monastery gate a wise and elderly monk who knows how to receive an answer and to give one and whose ripeness of years does not suffer him to wander about. This porter ought to have his cell close to the gate so that those who come may always find someone there from whom they can get an answer; and as soon as anyone

[13] *Ibid.*, chap. lviii.

shall have knocked, or any beggar have called out, let him answer "Thanks be to God" or bid him Godspeed; and with the gentleness of the God-fearing and with fervent charity let him make speed to answer. And let the porter, if he need help, receive it from a junior brother: yet the monastery ought to be so organized, if it can possibly be done, that all necessaries, that is, water, a mill-house, a garden and various crafts may be forthcoming within the monastery, so that there may be no necessity for the monks to go beyond the gates, because that is by no means expedient for their souls. And this rule we will to be somewhat often read in community, lest any of the brethren should hold himself excused on the plea of ignorance.[14]

Concerning the Good Zeal Which Monks Ought to Have

Just as there is an evil zeal of bitterness which separates from God and leads to hell, so there is a good zeal which separates from vices and leads to God and to life eternal. By most fervent love therefore let monks exercise this zeal, that is, let them see to it that in honour they prefer one another. Let them most patiently tolerate their infirmities whether physical or of character; let them compete in yielding obedience; let none follow what he judges convenient to himself, but rather what he judges convenient to another; in chaste love let them exercise fraternal charity; let them fear God; let them love their abbot with sincere and humble affection; on no account let them exalt anything above Christ; and may He bring us all alike to eternal life.[15]

Not Every Observance of Righteousness Is Laid Down in This Rule

Now we have written out this rule in order that by observing it in our monasteries we may show ourselves to have,

14 *Ibid.*, chap. lxvi.
15 *Ibid.*, chap. lxxii.

to some degree, integrity of life, or the beginning at least of conversion. For the rest, for those who hasten to the perfection of conversion, there are the teachings of the holy fathers, the observing of which brings a man to the height of perfection: and indeed what page or what text of the divine authority of the Old and the New Testament is not an unerring rule of human life? Or what book of the holy catholic fathers does not re-echo this, that by a straight course we may come to our Creator? Moreover also the conferences of the fathers and their institutes and their lives and also the rule of our holy father Basil, what else are they but store houses of the virtues of good-living and obedient monks? But to us, indolent, ill-living and negligent, belong shame and confusion. Whosoever therefore thou art who dost hasten to the heavenly country, fully carry out, Christ helping thee, this most elementary rule that we have written out; and then at last thou shalt come, God protecting thee, to the loftier heights of doctrine and of virtue.[16]

From

THE LITTLE FLOWERS OF ST. FRANCIS[17]

Of Vices and Virtues

The grace of God and the virtues which flow therefrom are a way and a ladder that leadeth to heaven; but vices and sins are a ladder and a way that leadeth to the depths of hell. Vices and sins are a venomous and a mortal poison, but virtues and good works are a salutary medicine. One grace leadeth on to another; and one vice leadeth on to another. Grace asketh not to be praised, and vice cannot endure to be

[16] *Ibid.*, chap. lxxiii.

[17] All subsequent material in this chapter is taken from *The Little Flowers of St. Francis of Assisi*, trans. Dom Roger Hudleston (London: Burns Oates, 1953). Copyright 1953 by Burns Oates. Reprinted by permission.

despised. The mind reposeth tranquilly in humility, of whom patience is daughter.

Holy purity of heart seeth God, and true devotion enjoyeth him.

If thou lovest, thou shalt be loved.

If thou servest, thou shalt be served.

If thou fearest, thou shalt be feared.

If thou doest good to others, fitting it is that others should do good unto thee.

But blessed is he who truly loves, and desireth not to be loved again.

Blessed is he who serves, and desireth not to be served.

Blessed is he who fears, and desireth not to be feared.

Blessed is he who doeth good to others, and desireth not that others should do good to him.

But because these things are most sublime and high perfection, therefore they that are foolish cannot understand them nor attain thereto.

Three things there are that are very sublime and very profitable, which he who has once acquired shall never fall.

The first is, that thou bear willingly and gladly, for the love of Jesus Christ, every affliction that shall befall thee.

The second is, that thou humble thyself daily in every thing thou doest, and in every thing thou seest.

The third is, that thou love faithfully with all thy heart that invisible and supreme Good which thou canst not behold with thy bodily eyes.

Those things which are most despised and decried by worldly men are most truly pleasing and acceptable to God and to his saints; and those things which are most loved and esteemed, and are most pleasing in the eyes of worldly men, are most despised, contemned, and hated by God and his saints.

This foul disorder proceedeth from human ignorance and malice; for wretched man loveth most those things which he ought to hate, and hateth those which he ought to love.[18]

[18] *Ibid.*, chap. i.

Of Holy Humility

No man can attain to any knowledge or understanding of God but by the virtue of holy humility; for the direct way to ascend is first to descend. All the perils and grievous falls which have happened in this world have arisen from nothing else but the uplifting of the head—that is, of the mind—by pride. This is proved by the fall of the devil, who was driven out of heaven; and by that of Adam, our first parent, who was banished from paradise by the uplifting of his head—that is, by disobedience. We see it also in the example of the Pharisee, of whom Christ speaketh in the Gospel, and in many others also.

And so also the contrary truth—namely, that all the great blessings which have ever been bestowed upon the world have proceeded from abasement of the head, that is, from the humiliation of the mind—is proved by example of the blessed and most humble Virgin Mary, the publican, the good thief on the cross and many others in Holy Scripture. And, therefore, good it were if we could find some great and heavy weight, which, being tied round our neck, would draw us down to the earth, and force us to humble ourselves.

A friar once said to Brother Giles: "Father, tell me, how can we avoid this pride?" To whom Brother Giles made this reply: "Rest assured, my brother, that thou canst never hope to be free from pride until thou hast first placed thy mouth where thou dost set thy feet; but if thou wilt well consider the gifts of God, thou wilt clearly see that thou hast reason to bow down thy head. And again, if thou wilt meditate on thy defects and thy manifold offences against God, in all this thou wilt find reasons for humbling thyself. But woe to those who desire to be honoured in their unworthiness! He hath one degree of humility, who knoweth himself to be opposed to his own true good. He hath a second, who restoreth the goods of another to their proper owner, and doth not appropriate them to himself. For every virtue and every good thing which a man findeth in himself, instead of appropriating it to himself, he is bound to refer to God, from whom all graces and all good things do proceed. But every sinful passion of the soul, and every vice which a man findeth within himself, he should attribute to himself, considering that they all proceed from himself and his own malice, and from no other source.

"Blessed is the man who knows and accounts himself to be vile in the eyes of God, and also in the sight of men.

"Blessed is he who judges himself always and condemns himself, and none but himself; for he shall not be condemned in that last and terrible eternal judgment.

"Blessed is he who shall submit himself wholly to the yoke of obedience and the judgment of others, as the holy Apostles before and after they received the Holy Spirit."

Brother Giles said also: "Let him who would acquire and possess perfect peace and quiet of mind account every man his superior, and hold himself the inferior and subject to all.

"Blessed is the man who, in his works and in his words, desires neither to be seen nor known for anything else but for that wherewith God hath adorned him.

"Blessed is the man who knows how to keep and hide within his heart divine revelations and consolations; for there is nothing so secret but God can reveal it when it pleaseth him. If the most holy and perfect man in the world were to esteem and account himself to be the vilest and most miserable sinner in the world, this would be true humility.

"Holy humility loves not to talk, nor the holy fear of God to use many words."

Brother Giles said again: "It seems to me that holy humility is like the thunderbolt; for, even as the thunderbolt striketh a terrible blow, crushing, breaking, and burning that whereon it lights, yet can we never find the thunderbolt itself, so does humility strike and disperse, burn up and consume every evil and vice and sin, and yet itself can nowhere be seen.

"He who possesses humility, by that humility finds grace with God, and perfect peace with his neighbour."[19]

[19] *Ibid.*, chap. iii.

Of the Holy Fear of God

He who fears not, shows that he has nothing to lose. The holy fear of God orders, governs, and rules the soul, and prepares it to receive his grace.

If a man possesses any grace or any divine virtue, it is holy fear which preserves it to him.

And he who has not yet acquired grace or virtue, acquires it by holy fear.

The holy fear of God is a channel of divine grace, inasmuch as it quickly leads the soul wherein it dwells to the attainment of holiness and all divine graces. No creature that ever fell into sin would have so fallen had it possessed the holy fear of God. But this holy gift of fear is given only to the perfect, because the more perfect any man is, the more timorous and humble he is.

Blessed is the man who looks upon this world as a prison-house, and bears in mind continually how grievously he has offended his Lord.

Greatly ought a man to fear pride, lest it should give him a sudden thrust, and cause him to fall from the state of grace in which he is; for no man is ever secure from falling, so beset are we by foes; and these foes are the flatteries of this wretched world and of our own flesh, which, together with the devil, is the unrelenting enemy of our soul.

A man has greater reason to fear being deluded and overcome by his own malice than by any other enemy.

It is impossible for a man to attain to any divine grace or virtue, or to persevere therein, without holy fear.

He who has not the fear of God within him is in great danger of eternal perdition.

The fear of God makes a man to obey humbly, and to bow his head beneath the yoke of obedience: and the more a man fears God, the more frequently he adores him.

The gift of prayer is no small gift, to whomsoever it is given.

The virtuous actions of men, how great soever they may seem to us, are not to be reckoned or rewarded after our judgment, but according to the judgment and good pleasure of God; for God looketh not to the number of the works, but to the measure of humility and love. Our surest way, therefore, is always to love and to keep ourselves in humility; and never to trust in ourselves that we do any good, but always to distrust the thoughts which spring up in our own mind under the appearance of good.[20]

Of Holy Patience

He who with steadfast humility and patience endureth tribulations for the fervent love of God, shall soon attain to great graces and virtues; he shall be lord of this world, and shall have an earnest of that glorious world which is to come.

Everything which a man doeth, be it good or evil, he doeth it unto himself. Therefore, be not thou offended with him who injures thee, but rather, in humble patience, sorrow only for his sin, having compassion on him, and praying fervently for him to God. For, in so far as a man is strong to suffer and endure injuries and tribulations patiently for the love of God, so great, and no greater, is he before God; and the weaker a man is to endure sufferings and adversities for the love of God, the less is he in the sight of God.

If any man praise thee, speaking well of thee, render thou that praise unto God alone; and if any man reproach thee, speaking evil of thee, do thou help him by speaking of thyself still worse.

If thou wouldst maintain thine own cause, strive to make it appear evil, and maintain that of thy companion good, ever accusing thyself and sincerely excusing thy neighbour. When anyone strives and contends with thee, if thou wouldst conquer, lose thy case, and losing it thou shalt conquer, for if thou wilt go to law to obtain the victory, when thou believest thou hast obtained it, thou shalt find thyself shamefully defeated. Wherefore, my brother, believe me assuredly that the certain way to gain is to lose. But if we endure not tribulation

20 *Ibid.*, chap. iv.

well, we shall never attain to consolation eternal. It is a meritorious thing and far more blessed to endure injuries and reproaches patiently, without murmuring, for the love of God, than to feed a hundred poor men, or to keep a perpetual fast. But what profits it a man, or how does it benefit him, to afflict his body with many fasts, vigils, and disciplines, if he cannot endure a little injury from his neighbour? And yet from this might he derive greater reward and higher merit than from all the sufferings he could inflict upon himself of his own will; for to endure reproaches and injuries from our neighbour with humble and uncomplaining patience, will purge away our sins more speedily than they could be by a fountain of many tears.

Blessed is the man who has ever before the eyes of his mind the remembrance of his sins and of the favours of God; for he will endure with patience all tribulations and adversities for which he expects so great consolation. The man who is truly humble looketh for no reward from God, but endeavors only to satisfy him in all things, knowing himself to be his debtor; every good thing which he hath he acknowledges to come from the free bounty of God, while every evil that befalleth him proceedeth from his sins alone.[21]

Of the Contempt of Temporal Things

Many sorrows and troubles shall befall the miserable man who sets his heart and desires upon earthly things, for which he forsakes and loses the things of heaven, and at last those of earth also.

We see daily how men of the world toil and labour hard, placing themselves in many bodily dangers, to acquire its false riches; and then, after they have thus laboured and acquired, in a moment they die, and leave behind them all that they have gathered together in their lifetime. Therefore there is no dependence to be placed on this deceitful world,

[21] *Ibid.*, chap. v.

which deceiveth every man who trusteth in it, for it is a liar. But he who desires to be truly great and rich indeed, let him love and seek the true and eternal riches, which never satiate or weary or grow less.

Let us take example from the beasts and birds, who, when they receive their food are content, and seek only what they need from hour to hour: and so also ought man to be content with what is barely sufficient temperately to supply his needs, asking no more. Brother Giles said that St. Francis loved the ants less than any other animal, because of the great care they take in the summer to gather and lay up a store of grain against the winter; but that he said that he loved the birds far better, because they gathered nothing one day for another.

But the ant giveth us an example that we should not remain idle in the summer-time of this present life, lest we be found empty and without fruit in the winter of the last and final judgment.[22]

Of Holy Chastity

Our frail and miserable human flesh is like to the swine that loves to wallow in the mire, and find its delight therein. Our flesh is the devil's knight; for it resists and fights against all those things which are pleasing to God and profitable for our salvation. A certain friar said to Brother Giles: "Father, teach me now to preserve myself from sins of the flesh." And Brother Giles answered him: "My brother, he who wishes to move a large stone, or any other great weight, and carry it to any other place, must try to move it rather by ingenuity than by force. And so, if we desire to overcome the vice of impurity and to acquire the virtue of chastity, we must set to work rather by the way of humility and by a good and discreet method of spiritual discipline, than by a rash penance and presumptuous austerity. Every vice troubles and obscures the fair glory of holy chastity; for it is like a

22 *Ibid.*, chap. vii.

bright mirror which is clouded and darkened, not only by contact with impure and defiling things, but even by the mere breath of man. It is impossible for a man to attain to any spiritual grace, so long as he is inclined to carnal concupiscence; and therefore, withersoever thou turn thyself, thou shalt never be able to attain to spiritual grace until thou canst master all the vices of the flesh. Wherefore, fight valiantly against thy frail and sensual flesh, thine own worst enemy, which wages war against thee day and night. And know that he who shall overcome this mortal enemy of ours has most certainly defeated and discomfited all his other enemies, and shall attain to spiritual grace, and every degree of virtue and perfection."

A friar said once to Brother Giles: "Father, thou dost so often commend the virtue of chastity, that I would fain ask of thee what it is?" And Brother Giles answered: "My brother, chastity is, in very truth, the careful and continual custody of our corporal and spiritual senses, in order to preserve them pure and unstained for God alone."[23]

Of Holy Prayer

Prayer is the beginning, the middle and the end of all good; prayer illuminates the soul, and enables it to discern between good and evil. Every sinner ought to pray daily with fervour of heart, that is, he should pray humbly to God to give him a perfect knowledge of his own miseries and sins, and of the benefits which he has received and still receiveth from the good God. But how can that man know God who knoweth not how to pray? And for all those who shall be saved, it is needful above all things that, sooner or later, they be converted to the use of holy prayer.[24]

23 *Ibid.*, chap. viii.
24 *Ibid.*, chap. xi.

Of Holy Spiritual Prudence

If thou wouldst see well, pluck out thine eyes and become blind; if thou wouldst hear well, become deaf; if thou wouldst speak well, become dumb; if thou wouldst walk well, stand still, and travel only with thy mind; if thou wouldst work well, cut off thy hands, and labour with thy heart; if thou wouldst love well, hate thyself; if thou wouldst live well, mortify thyself; if thou wouldst gain much and become rich, lose and become poor; if thou wouldst enjoy thyself and take thine ease, afflict thyself, and continually fear and distrust thyself; if thou wouldst be exalted and had in honour, humble and reproach thyself; if thou wouldst be reverenced, despise thyself, and do reverence to those who despise and reproach thee; if thou wouldst always receive good, continually endure evil; if thou wouldst be blessed, desire that all men should curse thee and speak evil of thee; if thou wouldst enjoy true and eternal repose, labour and afflict thyself, and desire every kind of temporal suffering. Oh, what great wisdom is it to know and do all these things! But, because it is so high and so sublime, it is granted by God to few. But I say, of a truth, that if any man will study these things and carry them into effect, he will have no need to go to Paris or to Bologna to learn any other theology. For, if a man were to live a thousand years, and have no external action to perform, nor any word to speak with his tongue, I say that he would have enough to do within his own heart, in labouring internally at the purifying, governing, and justifying of his heart and of his mind.

A man should not desire either to see, to hear, or to speak any thing but for the profit of his soul. The man who knows not himself is not known. Woe to us, then, when we receive the gifts and graces of the Lord, and know not how to acknowledge them! Woe still greater to those who neither receive nor acknowledge them, nor care to receive or possess them! Man was made to the image of God, and changes as he wills; but the good God changeth never.[25]

Of Knowledge Useful and Useless

The man who would know much, must labour much and humble himself much, abasing himself and bowing his head until his mouth be in the dust; and then will the Lord bestow on him great wisdom and knowledge. The highest wisdom is to do always that which is good; acting virtuously, and guarding carefully against every sin and every occasion of sin, and ever keeping in mind the judgments of God. Brother Giles said once to a man who desired to go to a school to learn secular knowledge: "My brother, wherefore wouldst thou go to this school? I would have thee to learn that the sum of all knowledge is to fear and to love, and these two things are sufficient for thee; for so much knowledge as he can use, and no more, is sufficient for a man. Busy not thyself in learning those things which may be useful to others, but study always and seek to use those which are profitable to thyself. For we often greatly desire knowledge by which we may aid others, and think little of that by which we may profit ourselves; and I say to thee, that the word of God dwelleth not with the speaker, nor with the hearer, but with the faithful doer thereof. Some men who cannot swim cast themselves in the water to save others from drowning, and so all of them are lost together. If thou dost not work out thine own salvation, how shalt thou work out that of thy neighbour? And if thou doest not thine own work well, how shalt thou do the work of another man? for it is not credible that thou shouldst love the soul of another better than thine own.

"The preachers of God's word ought to be standard-bearers, lights and mirrors to the people.

"Blessed is the man who so guideth others in the way of salvation, that he ceaseth not to walk therein himself.

"Blessed is the man who so teacheth others to run therein,

[25] *Ibid.*, chap. xii.

that he ceaseth not to run himself. More blessed is he who so helps others to become rich that he fails not also to enrich himself.

"I believe that a good preacher admonishes and preaches to himself far more than to other men."[26]

Of True Religious Life

A man of the world asked Brother Giles: "Father, what wouldst thou advise me to do—to enter Religion, or to remain and do good works in the world?" To whom Brother Giles thus replied: "My brother, it is certain that if a man knew of a great treasure lying hidden in a common field, he would not ask counsel of any one to ascertain whether or no he should take possession of it and carry it to his own house: how much more ought a man to strive and hasten with all care and diligence to possess himself of that heavenly treasure which is to be found in holy religious orders and spiritual congregations, without stopping to ask counsel of so many!" The secular, on receiving this answer, immediately distributed all that he possessed to the poor; and having thus stripped himself of all things, entered forthwith into Religion.

Brother Giles said also: "I would choose rather to be in the secular state, continually and devoutly desiring to enter into holy Religion, than to be clothed in the religious habit without the exercise of good works, but persevering in sloth and negligence. And therefore ought the Religious ever to strive to live well and virtuously, knowing that he can be saved in no other state but that of his profession."

On another occasion Brother Giles said: "It seems to me that the Order of the Friars Minor was instituted by God for the utility and great edification of the people; but woe to us friars if we be not such men as we ought to be! Certain it is that there can be found in this life no men more blessed than we; for he is holy who followeth the holy, and he is truly good who walketh in the way of the good, and he is

26 *Ibid.*, chap. xiii.

rich who goeth in the path of the rich; and the Order of Friars Minor is that which follows more closely than any other the footsteps and the ways of the Best, the Richest, and the Most Holy who ever has been or ever will be, even our Lord Jesus Christ."[27]

Further Readings

Primary Sources

Athanasius. *The Life of St. Anthony;* John Cassian. *The Conferences and Institutes;* Gregory. *Pastoral Rule.* (These selections are found in A *Select Library of the Nicene and Post-Nicene Fathers of the Christian Church,* Second Series, Vols. 4, 10, 12.) New York: The Christian Literature Publishing Co., 1890–1900.

Library of Christian Classics, Vol. 12, *Western Asceticism,* edited by Owen Chadwick. Philadelphia: Westminster Press, 1958.

Coulton, G. G. (ed.). *Life in the Middle Ages.* Cambridge (England) University Press, 1967. Part IV: Monks, Friars and Nuns.

The Rule of St. Benedict. (*Library of Christian Classics,* Vol. 12).

The Little Flowers of St. Francis; The Mirror of Perfection. (Many editions available.)

Thomas à Kempis. *The Imitation of Christ.* (Many editions available.)

Secondary Sources

Knowles, David. *Christian Monasticism.* New York: McGraw-Hill, 1969.

Liversidge, Douglas. *Saint Francis of Assisi.* New York: F. Watts, 1968.

Peifer, Claude. *Monastic Spirituality.* New York: Sheed and Ward, 1966.

van Zeller, Dom Hubert. *Approach to Monasticism.* New York: Sheed and Ward, 1960.

Workman, H. B. *The Evolution of the Monastic Ideal.* Boston: Beacon Press, 1962.

[27] *Ibid.*, chap. xvi.

Chapter 6

ETHICS OF MYSTICISM

Though it is a recurring phenomenon in religious history, mysticism eludes precise and clear description. It is as much a temper of mind as a body of belief, as much an approach as a conclusion. Since mystics claim that both the final stages on the road to Truth and the Truth itself are ineffable, inexpressible, beyond the capacity of temporal language to formulate, even a definition of mysticism loses what it tries to catch. Nonetheless, there is a remarkable unanimity among mystics, even as they speak out of different centuries and widely separate cultures, as to what constitutes the mystic's discipline and the prize of his striving. What he seeks is the direct apprehension of and communion with the ultimate being, God. The road to this high goal is a *via negativa:* the elimination of all temporal distractions, so that by purified and disciplined concentration on the divine, the inward self is gradually elevated to the beatific vision and united with God. Meister Eckhart's definition of its essence is characteristic: "The foundation of spiritual blessing is this: that the soul look at God without anything between; here it receives its being and life and draws its essence from the core of God, unconscious of the knowing-process, or love or anything else. Then it is quite still in the essence of God . . . knowing nothing but God."[1]

There are other elements in the experience to which its exponents attest: (1) The experience is positive and optimistic in its affirmation that God, the Force at the heart of the universe, is good and that behind its apparent scattered

[1] *Meister Eckhart, A Modern Translation,* trans. by R. B. Blakney (New York: Harper & Bros., 1941), p. 79.

manyness the universe "hangs together," is truly *one*. (2) With St. Paul, the mystic affirms the priority of the spiritual over the material in the order of being: "the things that are seen are temporal; the things that are unseen are eternal." (3) The attachment to the spiritual can only be achieved by detachment from the material world. (4) The direct encounter of the self with God can be in this life only a transient experience at best, never long sustained. The mystic must live in alternation between the pursuit of his vision and the return to the world of finitude. (5) The instrument to be used in cultivating the mystic discipline is not plain sense awareness, or normal reasoning, but an intuitive, supra-sensible capacity which transcends empirically or rationally derived knowledge.

It is not our present purpose to examine the many implications of these common principles for theology and psychology. The important thing to note in passing is that in much of what the mystic asserts there is a reaffirmation, sometimes expressed in oblique and poetic, sometimes in exaggerated form, of the traditional affirmations of the Christian faith. Christian mysticism is to be distinguished from various Eastern types by its fidelity to certain distinctive Christian doctrines, such as the revelation of God in Christ and the authority of Scripture. Thus it never becomes the pursuit of a great Something-or-other, or a pantheistic faith where all is divine. This fact enables Christian mystics to speak meaningfully of their convictions, at least in part, to other Christians who would not call themselves mystics. But in so far as the latter feel a certain subjective assurance of faith and insight, they are enabled to see and acknowledge, even at a distance, the authenticity of what the extreme mystic is saying.

Mysticism and Monasticism

The ethical importance of Catholic mysticism in the West can be best understood by considering its relation to monasticism. Almost without exception the great mystics of the

Middle Ages are themselves monks. This is a fact of paramount importance. The monastic practice seems to be the soil in which best can grow both that rigorous denial of self and that sensitivity to things spiritual which in exalted form characterize the mystic. In spirit the mystical ideal of the good life differs from the monastic ideal in degree rather than in kind. To put it another way, medieval mysticism intensifies and internalizes the monastic principle.

The whole array of external regulations in the monastic rules are intended as means to the end of cultivating self-denial and inner purity, which themselves are but prerequisites for the true love of God. The outward fulfillment of the commands in themselves would be fruitless if not dangerous unless an inward nonpossessive will, a chastity of spirit, and humility of soul were the result. But in practice, human nature being what it is, the emphasis on outward fulfillment again and again takes precedence. Certainly the mystic recognizes the importance of the Rule. All who would seek the true end of man must go to school within its severe confines. But the mystic's witness is a strong reminder that the monastic discipline is only the elemental beginning of the way to the vision of God. To act "as though the cowl made the monk," as Bernard of Clairvaux says, is the very denial of the monastic ideal. The monk's heart can be so set on obeying the commands that he loses sight of the end toward which the commands point. In the final chapter of his *Rule*, Benedict informs his would-be disciples that to live the *Rule* is only the "beginning of conversion." "The loftier heights of doctrine and virtue"[2] still lie ahead. On these "loftier heights" the mystic concentrates his attention. The writings of Bernard and Eckhart and many another mystic thus constitute internal reformations of monasticism, calling the monk lost in external practices back to his original intention, reminding him that the real transaction of his life is between God and his secret soul.

Thus the monastic mystic turns his attention inwards, to the depths of the human self, where he probes into what con-

[2] *The Rule of St. Benedict,* chap. lxxiii.

temporary psychology would call the dynamics of human motivation. The literature of mysticism is replete with descriptions of the mystic's consciousness, the joy in his sense of God's presence, "the dark night of the soul" experienced in God's absence, and the steps whereby he may return to the Lord.

It is important to note that these descriptions are almost always cast in moral terms, using the common coin of the language of Christian ethical theory. The speculative mysticism of the East tends to be contemplative and intellectualistic, stressing the levels of mental purification and clarification leading up to where the inward eye of the beholder sees ultimate truth. Western mysticism takes a different turn. While contemplative in spirit, certainly, and much indebted to the insights of such Eastern monks as Dionysius, it focuses its attention on the *will* of man. It thinks of the *summum bonum* as conformity of man's will with God's will. Bernard of Clairvaux, for instance, is voluntaristic in his view of the good life: The way of blessedness is not so much the clear mind's apprehension of truth as it is the devoted heart's absorption in God's holy will.

In particular Bernard points out that humility and love are the ways to communion with God. Humility, the overcoming of self-will, is the necessary inner purification (what other mystics call "purgation") which empties the heart of all temporal desire. This is characteristic of much mysticism, which of all the varieties of Christian ethics stresses detachment as essential. In the treatise *The Steps of Humility* he analyzes with psychological skill the various forms of humility, the false and the true. He finds that true humility, as the sense of one's own unworthiness before God, is the precondition for compassionate charity toward other men since it puts all men on a sympathetic and common level as neighbors in creaturely finitude and sin. The meek alone can be truly merciful.

Bernard's analysis of love in his treatise *On the Love of God* is also highly voluntaristic. Here he takes Augustine's moral opposition between the love of self and the love of

God and works it out into a scheme of four stages. In the fourth and highest stage of love the self is so completely given over to the love of God for God's own sake that its will is now one with God's. Here for Bernard is true ecstasy. Even though he confesses for himself to have glimpsed this stage only distantly, he is confident that it is the highest bliss. It is the "deification" of the soul. This unity of the human and the divine wills does not imply a metaphysical fusion of the mystic with God, a melting of the substance of the self into the substance of God. For Bernard, the self retains its separate identity from God and keeps its proper distance. This is one of the distinctive points in Christian mysticism; in Eastern, non-Christian mysticism complete union without separation of knower and known is sought. Whenever in exaltation the Christian mystic begins to talk of "identification" with God, he encounters the prophetic protest that, whatever may be the possibility of the conformity of human wills with that of God, there always remains an infinite distance between creature and Creator, between the finite and the infinite.

The Mystic's Social Concern

We have defined medieval mysticism as moral in quality by virtue of its voluntaristic emphasis on the humbled and loving will. Its moral spirit is even more readily apparent in its social concern. Quite in contradiction to the popular conception of mysticism, its chief representatives do not think of the good life as an exclusively private transaction between God and the secluded self. The relations of man to men are never neglected, for the love of God entails directly the love of neighbor. It is the claim of mysticism that concern for the well-being of one's fellows is both the prerequisite and the fruit of the mystic exaltation. The preparation for mystical communion, says Bernard, entails "good works . . . peace, gentleness, justice, obedience, cheerfulness."[3] Prayer and contemplation without deeds of mercy on behalf of the

[3] *Sermons on the Song of Songs*, chap. xlvi.

needy friend are "inane idleness." Moreover, the signs by which Bernard is assured that he has been visited by the Divine Being are the ethical changes that have been wrought. "Only by the movement of my heart have I been aware of him. In the flight of vices and the restraint of carnal affections I have perceived the power of his virtue. In the renovation and reformation of my mind and spirit, that is, of my inner man, I have seen the fashion of his beauty."[4] Meister Eckhart likewise affirms that the life of service is the corollary of the mystical possession of God. "As I have often said, if a person were in such a rapturous state as St. Paul once entered, and he knew of a sick man who wanted a cup of soup, it would be far better to withdraw from the rapture for love's sake and serve him who is in need."[5]

This represents a good deal more than merely the protection of mysticism against the pathological by surrounding it with moral safeguards and limits; it is the affirmation of the essentially moral character of the experience itself. It is impossible, of course, to be certain whether this claim of the mystic is justified. Some students of mysticism would question the indigenously moral character of the mystic's experience and feel that the ethical emphases come from some Christian source distinct from the character of the experience.

"What a man takes in contemplation he must pour out in love," says Eckhart. This sentence describes the alternation of the mystic's life, a rhythm of activity between "sacred repose and necessary action," to use Bernard's phrasing. The mystic can never sustain for long the absorption in the ineffable. He is called back to work, to attention to detail, to problems of existence no man can escape. But the two activities, work and worship, are diverse expressions of a single will and a single love. The mystic's action is not plain busyness or frantic "do-gooding." It is action interfused with serenity and inward quietude, spontaneously poured out from the awareness of the divine love which the mystic beholds in his contemplation. It is a matter of no small moment that

4 *Sermons on the Song of Songs,* chap. lxxiv.

5 *Op. cit.,* p. 14.

the renowned mystics of the medieval church were not recluses cultivating solitude and looking upon activity as irksome interruption. While they certainly spent extended hours in prayer and contemplation, as befitted all monks, they also led busy lives in the crush and turmoil of public activities. Bernard, "the uncrowned pope" of the church, was one of the busiest executives of twelfth-century Europe. Eckhart was a preacher much in demand and vicar of a large church province. But in all his outward activity, the inner possession of God in tranquillity and devout humility enabled the mystic to affirm that the time of business was no different in essence from the time of prayer.

Christian Detachment

Meister Eckhart, the Dominican preacher-mystic of Germany, may not have been the most representative of the late medieval mystics, but he was certainly one of the most striking and influential. Living at an era of the church's life when monasticism was at a high tide of its external power and at one of its low ebbs of internal purity, Eckhart uttered a forthright message to his time which was contrary in many ways to the prevailing opinion. His writings and sermons (pp. 193-200) play continual and sometimes extravagant variations on a few simple themes. Of first importance for him is the innate kinship of man's essential nature, the "Divine spark," with the nature of God himself. God comes to perpetual birth in the soul of men—but only as men first empty themselves of all worldly, temporal, sensual love and become poor in spirit, "willing nothing, desiring nothing, knowing nothing." This is what Eckhart means by "disinterest" (not "uninterest") or "detachment" (*Abgescheidenheit*), which he daringly poses as the highest virtue, almost to distort beyond recognition the Christian ethic of love. At times his discussion of "disinterest" has the ring of Stoicism, which extolls apathy as the crowning virtue, a valiant indifference to calamity and fortune. But Eckhart is more Christian than

Stoic: the detachment he requires is only a preliminary way of breaking false attachments that the self may find its true attachment to God. At least this is his claim: In so far as a man rules out of his will the desire for any human thing, so far will God possess his nature, for it is God's nature so to do, "just as when the air is clear and pure the sun must pour into it and may not hold back."

Eckhart was critical of the externalism of the monasticism of his time. Though he revered and followed the sacramental practices and monastic disciplines, he made bold to write and preach that renunciation of the world is first and last an inward affair. If a monk has truly overcome the world in himself, his observance of the vows is a matter of minor importance. In light of such sentiments, it is not surprising that at the close of his career he was accused of heresy. His *Defense* to the papal authorities was a humble and sincere avowal of full orthodoxy. Nevertheless, he was put under the ban of the church, though his death came before the final sentence was passed.

His writings did in fact lead him close to the precipice of heresy. At many points he borders on pantheism, and his apparently casual attitude toward the external practices of monasticism must have appeared dangerous to honest defenders of the Catholic faith as well as to some less honest Franciscans, bitter rivals of any and all Dominicans, who were happy to be agents of his downfall. In intention he can hardly be called a precursor of the Reformation, but it is significant that many of the early reformers, as well as eighteenth- and nineteenth-century Protestant philosophers and theologians, were much impressed by his teaching. Yet the final judgment which must be put upon his work is clear: His whole mission was not to destroy the law of the church, or of monasticism, but to fulfil its inward spirit of purity in the love of God.

Of the many writings of Bernard of Clairvaux (1090-1153) —sermons, treatises, and letters—the two works *On the Steps of Humility* and *On the Love of God* are classic statements of the mystical type of Christian ethical theory. The selections below (pp. 183-93) are taken from the latter. This piece was written apparently in reply to an inquiry from a "cardinal-deacon and chancellor of the church of Rome," asking the meaning of "the love of God." The distinctive views of Meister Eckhart (1260-1328) are represented here (pp. 193-200) by selections from his *About Disinterest* and *Sermons.*

SOURCES

From

Bernard of Clairvaux: On the Love of God[6]

Why God Is to Be Loved

You wish, therefore, to hear from me why and how God should be loved? And I: the reason for loving God is God Himself; the way is to love Him beyond measure. There is a twofold reason, I should say, why God should be loved for His own sake: because nothing can be more justly, nothing more profitably, loved. Indeed, when the question is asked why God should be loved it may have one of two meanings: whether it is God's title to our love or our own advantage in loving Him. To be sure, I would give the same answer to both of these questions: I find no other worthy reason for loving Him except Himself. And first let us examine the question of God's title to our love. A very special title to it is His who gave Himself to us despite the fact that we were so undeserving. For, what better than Himself could even He have given? If, then, in asking the reason why we should love God we seek to know His title to our love, it is chiefly this: "because He hath first loved us." He it is who is clearly deserving of being loved in return, especially if one considers who He is that loved, who they are whom He loved and how

[6] This material is taken from St. Bernard, *On the Love of God,* trans. by T. L. Connally (Techny, Ill.: The Mission Press, 1943). Reprinted by permission of the monastery of Our Lady of Gethsemani, Trappist, Kentucky.

much He loved them. And who is He? Is He not the One to whom every spirit bears witness: "Thou art my God, for Thou hast no need of my goods?" And the true love of this Sovereign One lies in this, that it does not seek its own interests.[7]

Those to whom what I have said is plain will also, I think, plainly see why God should be loved: that is, whence He deserves to be loved. But if unbelievers blind themselves to these truths God is still ready to confound their ingratitude with His numberless benefits conferred for man's advantage and manifest to human sense. Who else, forsooth, supplies food to everyone who eats, light to everyone who sees, breath to everyone who breathes? But it is foolish to strive to enumerate what I have just spoken of as innumerable. It is enough, by way of example, to have mentioned the chief ones —bread, sun, and air. The chief ones, I mean, not because they are superior but because they are more necessary since they pertain to the body. Let man seek his higher goods— dignity, knowledge, and virtue—in that higher part of him which excels self, that is, in the soul. By man's dignity I mean his free will in which it is surely given him not only to excel other creatures but also to rule over all other [visible] living things. By knowledge I mean that by which he recognizes that his dignity is within himself but not from himself. By virtue I mean that by which he ardently seeks Him from whom he has his being and valiantly holds fast to Him when found.[8]

Now let us see with what advantage to ourselves God is to be loved. For not without reward is God loved although He should be loved without thought of the reward. True charity cannot be unprofitable nor is it, however, mercenary; certainly it seeketh not its own. It is a matter of affection, not a contract: it neither gains nor is gained by a compact. It exerts influence freely and makes one free. True love finds satisfaction in itself [i.e., is its own satisfaction]. It has its reward, but it is [the possession of] the object it loves. For

[7] Bernard, *On the Love of God,* chap. i.
[8] *Ibid.,* chap. ii.

whatever you seem to love because of something else, you clearly love that to which the end of love ultimately attains and not that [the means] by which it attains it. Paul does not preach the Gospel in order that he may eat, but he eats in order that he may preach the Gospel: because he loves, not food, but the Gospel. True love asks no reward but deserves one. It is when a man has not yet learned to love that reward is set before him; it is due one who loves; it is awarded to him who perseveres. Finally in appealing [to a man] in matters of a lower order, it is the unwilling that we urge on with promises or rewards, but not the willing. For who is there who thinks that a man should be rewarded in order that he may do what he freely desires? No one, for instance, pays a hungry man to eat, or a thirsty man to drink, or a mother to give milk to the child of her womb. Or who thinks that a man ought to be induced by a price or an entreaty to fence in his own vine, to dig about his own tree, or to erect the structure of his own home? How much less does the soul that loves God seek anything besides God as the reward of her love! If she seeks anything else, it is clearly something else and not God that she loves.

I said above: The cause of loving God is God. I spoke the truth, for He is both the efficient and final Cause. It is He who gives the occasion, it is He who creates the affection, He consummates the desire. It is He who wrought, or rather, was made [i.e., is what He is] in order that He might be loved; He, it is hoped, will be so fruitfully loved as not to be loved in vain. His love makes our love ready and rewards it. He goes before more graciously than any other, He is repaid more justly, He is awaited more sweetly. He "is rich unto all who call upon Him"; still He has nothing better than Himself to give. He gave Himself to merit for us, He retains Himself to be our reward, He offers Himself as the food of saintly souls, He gives Himself as the price of the redemption of those [i.e., of every individual soul] in captivity. You "are good, O Lord, to the soul that seeketh" Thee: what, then, to one who finds? But in this is the wonder that no one can seek Thee save him who first has found Thee. Therefore You wish to be found in order that You may be sought, to be sought in order that you may be found.[9]

The Four Stages of Love

We must now state whence our love has its beginning, since we have already told where it has its consummation. Love is a natural affection, one of four. They are well known: love, fear, joy, and sorrow. It would therefore be just that what is natural should serve its own Author before all others. Hence the first commandment is called the greatest: Thou shalt love the Lord thy God, etc. But since nature is rather weak and feeble, it is impelled at the bidding of necessity to serve itself first. And there is carnal love by which before all other things man loves himself for his own sake, as it is written: "first . . . that which is natural; afterwards that which is spiritual." And it is not imposed by a command but implanted in nature; for who ever hated his own flesh? But truly if this love, as is its wont, begins to be too precipitate or too lavish and is not at all satisfied with the river-bed of necessity, overflowing rather widely, it will be seen to invade the fields of pleasure. At once its overflow is held in check by the commandment that opposes itself to it: "Thou shalt love thy neighbor as thyself." It happens very justly indeed, that the sharer in nature should not be excluded from a part in grace as well, especially in that grace which is inborn in nature itself. If man finds it a burden, I do not say to relieve his brother in matters of necessity but to administer to his pleasures, let him restrain his own unless he wishes to be a transgressor of the law. Let him be as indulgent as he likes to himself, so long as he is mindful to show the same degree of indulgence to his neighbor. The bridle of temperance is put upon you, O man, out of the law of life and of discipline lest you should go after your concupiscences and perish; lest in the good of nature you become a slave to your soul's enemy, that is, to lust. How much more justly and honorably

[9] *Ibid.*, chap. vii.

do you give such things to your fellow-sharer, that is, your neighbor, rather than to your enemy! And if indeed, according to the advice of the wise man, you turn away from your own pleasures, and according to the teaching of the Apostle, content with food and raiment, you find it no burden to withhold your love for a little while from carnal desires which war against the soul; surely, I think, what you take away from your soul's enemy you will find no burden to bestow upon the sharer of your nature. Your love will then be both temperate and just if what is taken from your own pleasures is not denied to your brother's needs. Thus carnal love is made to belong to our neighbor when it is extended to the common good.

Nevertheless, in order that it may be perfect justice to love one's neighbor, it is imperative that it be referred to God as its cause. Otherwise how can he love his neighbor without alloy who does not love him in God? He surely cannot love in God who does not love God. God must be loved first, in order that one's neighbor, too, may be loved in God. God, therefore, who makes all else that is good, makes Himself to be loved. And He does it as follows. He who fashioned nature, it is He who shields it from harm as well. For it was so fashioned that it should have as a necessary Protector, Him whom it had as Maker, in order that what could not have come into being save through Him, should not be able to subsist at all without Him. And lest the creature might not know this about itself and consequently (which God forbid) in its pride arrogate to itself the benefits it had received from its Creator, the same Maker in His high and salutary counsel wills that man should be harassed with troubles; so that when man has failed and God has come to his assistance, while man is being delivered by God, God, as is fitting, may be honored by man. For this is what He says: "call upon Me in the day of trouble: I will deliver thee, and thou shalt glorify Me." Thus it comes to pass in this wise that a man, an animal and carnal by nature, who knew how to love no one except himself may begin even for his own sake, to love God too, because in Him beyond a shadow of a doubt, as he has often learned from experience, he can do all things —those, to be sure, which it is good to be able to do—and without Him he can do nothing.[10]

A man, therefore, loves God but still for a while for his own sake, not for Himself. It is, however, a sort of prudence to know what you are able to do by yourself, what with God's help, and to preserve yourself guiltless for Him who keeps you unharmed. But if tribulation assails you again and again, and on this account there occurs an oft-repeated turning towards God; and as often, there follows deliverance obtained from God, is it not true that even though the breast were of steel or the heart of stone in one so many times rescued, it must of necessity be softened at the grace of the Rescuer so that man might love God not merely for his own sake but for God Himself? From the occasion that arises from frequent needs it is necessary that man should frequently, in repeated intercourse, go to God who in such intercourse is tasted, and it is by tasting that it is proved how sweet is the Lord. Thus it happens that when once His sweetness has been tasted, it draws us to the pure love of God more than our need impels. We now love God, not for our necessity; for we ourselves have tasted and know how sweet is the Lord. And so for one who feels thus, it will not now be hard to fulfil the commandment in regard to loving his neighbor. For he truly loves God and in this way also loves the things which are God's. He loves purely and it is no burden for the pure to be obedient to a command; rather, purifying his heart, as it is written, in the obedience of charity. He loves justly and gladly embraces a just command. This love is deservedly acceptable because it is disinterested. It is pure because it is paid neither by word nor tongue, but by deed and truth. It is just, since it is paid back as it is received. For he who loves thus, to be sure, loves in no other wise than he is loved; seeking, in his turn, not the things that are his own but the things that are Jesus Christ's, just as He sought the things that are ours, or rather ourselves and not His own. It is thus He loves who says: "Give praise to the

10 *Ibid.*, chap. viii.

Lord, for He is good." He who gives praise to the Lord not because He is good to him but because He is good, he truly loves God for God and not for his own sake. This is the third degree of love by which God is now loved for His very self.[11]

Happy is He who has deserved to attain as high as the fourth degree where a man does not love even himself except for the sake of God. When will the mind experience such an affection as this, so that inebriated with divine love, forgetful of self, and become in its own eyes like a vessel that is destroyed, the whole of it may continue on to God and being joined to God, become one spirit with Him? Blessed and holy, I would say, is he to whom it has been given to experience such a thing in this mortal life at rare intervals or even once, and this suddenly and scarcely for the space of a single moment. In a certain manner to lose yourself as though you were not, and to be utterly unconscious of yourself and to be emptied of yourself and, as it were, brought to nothing, this pertains to heavenly intercourse, not to human affection. And if, indeed, anyone among mortals is suddenly from time to time (as has been said) even for the space of a moment admitted to this, straightway the wicked world grows envious, the evil of the day throws everything into confusion, the body of death becomes a burden, the necessity of the flesh causes unrest, the fainting away of corruption offers no support, and what is more vehement than these, fraternal charity [i.e., obligations to one's neighbor] recalls one [from the state of contemplation].

Since, however, Scripture says God "hath made all things for Himself," it will certainly come to pass that the creature will at one time or other conform itself to its Author and be of one mind with Him. We ought therefore be transformed into this same disposition of soul, so that as God has willed that everything should be for Himself, so we, too, may deliberately desire neither ourselves nor any other thing to have been in the past, or to be in the future, unless it be equally for His sake, to wit, for His sole will, not for our own pleasure. Just as a little drop of water mixed with a lot of wine seems

[11] *Ibid.*, chap. ix.

entirely to lose its own identity, while it takes on the taste of wine and its color; just as iron, heated and glowing, looks very much like fire, having divested itself of its original and characteristic appearance; and just as air flooded with the light of the sun is transformed into the same splendor of light so that it appears not so much lighted up as to be light itself; so it will inevitably happen that in saints every human affection will then in some ineffable manner melt away from self and be entirely transfused into the will of God. The substance, indeed, will remain, but in another form, another glory, and another power.[12]

The Disinterested Love of God

I remember well that a while ago I wrote a letter to the holy Carthusian brethren and in it, among other matters, I discussed these very grades of love. That, I say, is true and genuine love and must be admitted as proceeding entirely from "a pure heart, a good conscience, and a faith unfeigned," by which we love the good of our neighbor as well as our own. For he who loves only what is his, or loves it more, stands convicted of loving good unchastely, since he loves for his own and not for His sake. And such a one cannot obey the prophet who says: Give praise to the Lord, for He is good. He gives praise, to be sure, because, perhaps, He is good to him but not because He is good in Himself. There is a man who gives praise to the Lord because He is powerful, and there is a man who gives praise to Him because He is good to him, and, again, there is a man who gives praise to Him because He is simply good. The first is a servant and fears for himself; the second, a hireling, desires things for his own sake; the third, a son, gives honor to the father. And so he who is afraid and he who desires things for his own sake, both act for themselves. Only the love which is found in a son "seeketh not her own." For this reason I think that it was of love that it was said: "The law of the Lord is unspotted, converting souls"; for it is she [love] alone which is strong

12 *Ibid.*, chap. x.

enough to convert a soul from love of self and of the world, and direct it to God. For, neither fear nor love of oneself converts the soul. At times they change an expression of countenance or an external act, but an affection, never. Even a servant, to be sure, sometimes does the work of God, but because he does not do it freely he is known still to remain in his hardness. Even the hireling does the work of God, but because he does not do it without recompense he is convicted of being carried along by his own cupidity. But love converts souls whom she makes free agents.[13]

It is not rightly said that the just have no law, or that the just are without the law, but "the law is not made for the just"; that is, it is not imposed upon them as upon unwilling subjects but it is given them as to willing subjects, with a freedom equal to the sweetness with which it is breathed into them. Hence, also, the Lord says beautifully: "Take up My yoke upon you"; as if He would say: I do not place it upon the unwilling, but you, if you are willing, take it up; otherwise you will find not rest but labor for your souls.

The law of love, therefore, is good and sweet. It is not only lightly and sweetly borne but renders the laws even of servants and hirelings bearable and light. It does not destroy these laws, to be sure, but it brings about their fulfillment in accordance with Our Lord's words when He said: "I am not come to destroy (the law) but to fulfill it." It modifies the one, it puts order into the other, and it lightens both of them. Never will love be without fear, but chaste fear; never will it be without its desire of personal gratification, but kept within bounds. Love, therefore, perfects the law of the servant when it imparts devotion, and that of the hireling when it directs aright his desire of reward. Surely devotion mingled with fear does not annihilate those last but purifies them. Dread of punishment, only, is taken away, without which fear can not exist so long as it is servile; and this fear is pure and filial, enduring forever and ever. For, the text which reads, "perfect love casteth out fear," is to be understood of a dread of punishment which (as we have said) is never

[13] *Ibid.*, chap. xii.

wanting to servile fear. This (we said) making use of that sort of speech in which, often, the cause is put for the effect. As for a desire for personal gratification, it is then kept within bounds by the love which is joined to it, when evil is completely rejected, better things are preferred to the good, nor are good things desired save on account of those which are better. When the complete fulfillment of this will have been attained through God's grace, the body and every good that pertains to the body will be loved only for the sake of the soul; the soul for the sake of God; but God for His own sake.[14]

Nevertheless, because we are carnal and are born of the concupiscence of the flesh, it follows as a necessary consequence that our desire for personal gratification, or our love, should have its source in the flesh. But if it is directed according to the right order of things, advancing by its several degrees under the guidance of grace, it will at last be consummated by the spirit because: "that was not first which is spiritual, but that which is natural; afterwards that which is spiritual." First, therefore, man loves himself for his own sake; for, he is flesh and he can have no taste for anything except in relation to himself. And when he sees that he cannot subsist of himself he begins to seek God through faith as something, as it were, necessary for him, and to love Him. Thus he loves God according to the second degree, but for his own sake, not for Himself. But when, in truth, on account of his own necessity he has begun to worship and come to Him again and again by meditating, by reading, by prayer and by being obedient, little by little God becomes known to him through experience, in a sort of familiarity, and consequently He grows sweet; and thus by tasting how sweet is the Lord he passes to the third degree so that he loves God now, not for his own sake but for Himself. Yes, in this degree he stands still for a very long time. And I know not if the fourth degree is attained in its perfection by any man in this life so that, forsooth, a man loves himself only for the sake of God. If there are any who have experience of this, let them declare it; to me, I confess, it seems impossible. But it

[14] *Ibid.*, chap. xiv.

will be so, beyond a doubt, when the good and faithful servant has been brought into the joy of his Lord and inebriated with the plenty of God's house. For, forgetful of himself in a wonderful way, as it were, and as if entirely freed of self he will continue on, wholly, into God, and thereafter being joined to Him he will be one spirit with Him.[15]

From

MEISTER ECKHART: ABOUT DISINTEREST[16]

I have read much of what has been written, both by heathen philosophers and sages and in the Old and New Testaments. I have sought earnestly and with great diligence that good and high virtue by which man may draw closest to God and through which one may best approximate the idea God had of him before he was created, when there was no separation between man and God; and having delved into all this writing, as far as my intelligence would permit, I find that [high virtue] to be pure disinterest, that is, detachment from creatures. Our Lord said to Martha: "Unum est necessarium," which is to say: to be untroubled and pure, one thing is necessary and that is disinterest.

The teachers praise love, and highly too, as St. Paul did, when he said: "No matter what I do, if I have not love, I am nothing." Nevertheless, I put disinterest higher than love. My first reason is as follows. The best thing about love is that it makes me love God. Now, it is much more advantageous for me to move God toward myself than for me to move toward him, for my blessing in eternity depends on my being identified with God. He is more able to deal with me and join me than I am to join him. Disinterest brings God to me and I can demonstrate it this way: Everything likes its

[15] *Ibid.*, chap. xv.

[16] This and all subsequent selections are from *Meister Eckhart, a Modern Translation*, trans. by R. B. Blakney (New York: Harper & Bros., 1941). Copyright 1941 by Harper & Bros. Reprinted by permission.

own habitat best; God's habitat is purity and unity, which are due to disinterest. Therefore God necessarily gives himself to the disinterested heart.

In the second place, I put disinterest above love because love compels me to suffer for God's sake, whereas disinterest makes me sensitive only to God. This ranks far above suffering for God or in God; for, when he suffers, man pays some attention to the creature from which his suffering comes, but being disinterested, he is quite detached from the creature. I demonstrate that, being disinterested, a man is sensitive only to God, in this way: Experience must always be an experience of something, but disinterest comes so close to zero that nothing but God is rarefied enough to get into it, to enter the disinterested heart. That is why a disinterested person is sensitive to nothing but God. Each person experiences things in his own way and thus every distinguishable thing is seen and understood according to the approach of the beholder and not, as it might be, from its own point of view.

The authorities also praise humility above other virtues, but I put disinterest above humility for the following reasons. There can be humility without disinterest but disinterest cannot be perfect without humility; perfect humility depends on self-denial; disinterest comes so near to zero that nothing may intervene. Thus, there cannot be disinterest without humility and, anyway, two virtues are better than one!

The second reason I put disinterest above humility is that in humility man abases himself before creatures, and in doing so pays some attention to the creatures themselves. Disinterest, however, stays within itself. No transference of attention [such as humility] can ever rank so high that being self-contained will not go higher. Perfectly disinterested, a man has no regard for anything, no inclination to be above this or below that, no desire to be over or under; he remains what he is, neither loving nor hating, and desiring neither likeness to this or unlikeness to that. He desires only to be one and the same; for to want to be this or that is to want something; and the disinterested person wants nothing. Thus everything remains unaffected as far as he is concerned.

You may ask: "What is this disinterest that it is so noble a matter?" Know, then, that a mind unmoved by any contingent affection or sorrow, or honor, or slander, or vice, is really disinterested—like a broad mountain that is not shaken by a gentle wind. Unmovable disinterest brings man into his closest resemblance to God. It gives God his status as God. His purity is derived from it, and then his simplicity and unchangeable character. If man is to be like God, to the extent that any creature may resemble him, the likeness will come through disinterest, and man proceeds from purity to simplicity and from simplicity to unchangeableness, and thus the likeness of God and man comes about. It is an achievement of the grace that allures man away from temporal things and purges him of the transitory. Keep this in mind: to be full of things is to be empty of God, while to be empty of things is to be full of God.

Now I ask what the object of pure disinterest is. I reply that it is neither this nor that. Pure disinterest is empty nothingness, for it is on that high plane on which God gives effect to his will. It is not possible for God to do his will in every heart, for even though he is almighty, he cannot act except where he finds preparations made or he makes them himself. I say "or makes them" on account of St. Paul, for God did not find him ready; he prepared St. Paul by an infusion of grace. Otherwise, I say that God acts where he finds that preparations have been made.

Take an illustration from nature. If I wish to write on a white tablet, then no matter how fine the matter already written on it, it will confuse me and prevent me from writing down [my thoughts]; so that, if I still wish to use the tablet, I must first erase all that is written on it, but it will never serve me as well for writing as when it is clean. Similarly, if God is to write his message about the highest matters on my heart, everything to be referred to as "this or that" must first come out and I must be disinterested. God is free to do his will on his own level when my heart, being disinterested, is bent on neither this nor that.

But no man can be sensitive to divine influence except by conforming to God, and in proportion to his conformity he is sensitive to divine influence. Conformity comes of submission to God. The more subject to creatures a man is, the less he conforms to God, but the pure, disinterested heart, being void of creatures, is constantly worshiping God and conforming to him, and is therefore sensitive to his influence.

Among men, be aloof; do not engage yourself to any idea you get; free yourself from everything chance brings to you, things that accumulate and cumber you; set your mind in virtue to contemplation, in which the God you bear in your heart shall be your steady object, the object from which your attention never wavers; and whatever else your duty may be, whether it be fasting, watching, or praying, dedicate it all to this one end, doing each only as much as is necessary to your single end. Thus you shall come to the goal of perfection.[17]

From

MEISTER ECKHART: THE SERMONS. NO. 3

"I must be about my Father's business!" This text is quite convenient to the discussion in which I shall now engage, dealing with the eternal birth, which occurred at one point of time, and which occurs every day in the innermost recess of the soul—a recess to which there is no avenue of approach. To know this birth at the core of the soul it is necessary above all that one should be about his Father's business.

No one can be sure of the experience of this birth, or even approach it, except by the expenditure of a great deal of energy. It is impossible without a complete withdrawal of the senses from the [world of] things and great force is required to repress all the agents of the soul and cause them to cease functioning. It takes much strength to gather them all in, and without that strength it cannot be done.

You may, however, say: Alas, good man, if, to be prepared for God, one needs a heart freed from ideas and activities

[17] *Ibid.*, pp. 82-91.

which are natural to the agents of the soul, how about those deeds of love which are wholly external, such as teaching and comforting those who are in need? Are these to be denied? Are we to forgo the deeds that occupied the disciples of our Lord so incessantly, the work that occupied St. Paul on behalf of the people, so much that he was like a father to them? Shall we be denied the [divine] goodness because we do virtuous deeds?

Let us see how this question is to be answered. The one [contemplation] is good. The other [deeds of virtue] is necessary. Mary was praised for having chosen the better part but Martha's life was useful, for she waited on Christ and his disciples. St. Thomas [Aquinas] says that the active life is better than the contemplative, for in it one pours out the love he has received in contemplation. Yet it is all one; for what we plant in the soil of contemplation we shall reap in the harvest of action and thus the purpose of contemplation is achieved. There is a transition from one to the other but it is all a single process with one end in view—that God is, after which it returns to what it was before. If I go from one end of this house to the other, it is true, I shall be moving and yet it will be all one motion. In all he does, man has only his one vision of God. One is based on the other and fulfills it. In the unity [one beholds] in contemplation, God foreshadows [the variety of] the harvest of action. In contemplation, you serve only yourself. In good works, you serve many people.

God begets his Son or the Word in the soul and, receiving it, the soul passes it on in many forms, through its agents, now as desire, now in good intentions, now in loving deeds, now in gratitude or whatever concerns it. These are all his and not yours at all. Credit God with all he does and take none for yourself.

Above all, claim nothing for yourself. Relax and let God operate you and do what he will with you. The deed is his; the word is his; this birth is his; and all you are is his, for you have surrendered self to him, with all your soul's agents and their functions and even your personal nature. Then at once, God comes into your being and faculties, for you are like a desert, despoiled of all that was peculiarly your own.

Perhaps, however, you object: "What should one do to be as empty as a desert, as far as self and things go? Should one just wait and do nothing? Or should he sometimes pray, read, or do such virtuous things as listening to a sermon or studying the Bible—of course, not taking these things as if from outside himself, but inwardly, as from God? And if one does not do these things, isn't he missing something?"

This is the answer. External acts of virtue were instituted and ordained so that the outer man might be directed to God and set apart for spiritual life and all good things, and not diverted from them by incompatible pursuits. They were instituted to restrain man from things impertinent to his high calling, so that when God wants to use him, he will be found ready, not needing to be brought back from things coarse and irrelevant. The more pleasure one takes in externalities the harder it is to turn away from them. The stronger the love the greater the pain of parting.

See! Praying, reading, singing, watching, fasting, and doing penance—all these virtuous practices were contrived to catch us and keep us away from strange, ungodly things. Thus, if one feels that the spirit of God is not at work in him, that he has departed inwardly from God, he will all the more feel the need to do virtuous deeds—especially those he finds most pertinent or useful—not for his own personal ends but rather to honor the truth—he will not wish to be drawn or led away by obvious things. Rather, he will want to cleave to God, so that God will find him quickly and not have to look far afield for him when, once more, he wants to act through him.

But when a person has a true spiritual experience, he may boldly drop external disciplines, even those to which he is bound by vows, from which even a bishop may not release him. No man may release another from vows he has made to God—for such vows are contracts between man and God. And also, if a person who has vowed many things such as prayer, fasting, or pilgrimages, should enter an order, he is then free from the vow, for once in the order, his bond is to all virtue and to God himself.

I want to emphasize that. However much a person may have vowed himself to many things, when he enters upon a true spiritual experience he is released from them all. As long as that experience lasts, whether a week, or a month, or a year, none of this time will be lost to the monk or nun, for God, whose prisoners they are, will account for it all. When he returns to his usual nature, however, let him fulfill the vows appropriate to each passing moment as it comes, but let him not think for a moment of making up for the times he seemed to neglect, for God will make up for whatever time he caused you to be idle. Nor should you think it could be made up by any number of creature-deeds, for the least deed of God is more than all human deeds together. This is said for learned and enlightened people who have been illumined by God and the Scriptures.

This is easy to prove, for we must look to the fruits, the inward truth, rather than to outward works. As St. Paul says: "The letter killeth (that is, all formal practices) but the spirit maketh alive (that is, inner experience of the truth)." Realize this clearly, that whatever leads you closest to this inner truth, you are to follow in all you do.[18]

From

Meister Eckhart: The Sermons. No. 4

God lies in wait for us with nothing so much as love. Love is like a fisherman's hook. Without the hook he could never catch a fish, but once the hook is taken the fisherman is sure of the fish. Even though the fish twists hither and yon, still the fisherman is sure of him. And so, too, I speak of love: he who is caught by it is held by the strongest bonds and yet the stress is pleasant. He who takes this sweet burden on him-

[18] *Ibid.*, pp. 109-17.

self gets further, and comes nearer to what he aims at than he would by means of any harsh ordinance ever devised by man. Moreover, he can sweetly bear all that happens to him, all that God inflicts he can take cheerfully. Nothing makes you God's own, or God yours, as much as this sweet bond. When one has found this way, he looks for no other. To hang on this hook is to be so [completely] captured that feet and hands, and mouth and eyes, the heart, and all a man is and has, become God's own.

Therefore there is no better way to overcome the enemy, so that he may never hurt you, than by means of love. Thus it is written: "Love is as strong as death and harder than hell." Death separates the soul from the body but love separates everything from the soul. It cannot endure anything anywhere that is not God or God's. Whatever he does, who is caught in this net, or turned in this direction, love does it, and love alone; and whether the man does it or not, makes no difference.

The most trivial deed or function in such a person is more profitable and fruitful to himself and all men, and pleases God better, than all other human practices put together, which, though done without deadly sin, are characterized by a minimum of love. His rest is more profitable than another's work.

Therefore wait only for this hook and you will be caught up into blessing, and the more you are caught the more you will be set free. That we all may be so caught and set free, may he help us, who is love itself. Amen.[19]

Further Readings

Primary Sources

BERNARD OF CLAIRVAUX. *The Steps of Humility.* Edited by G. B. BURCH. Cambridge: Harvard University Press, 1950.

[19] *Ibid.*, pp. 123-24.

BERNARD OF CLAIRVAUX. *Sermons on the Song of Songs.* London: A. R. Mowbray; New York: Morehouse-Gorham, 1952.

Meister Eckhart, a Modern Translation. Trans. by R. B. BLAKNEY. New York: Harper and Row, 1941.

PETRY, RAY (ed.). *Late Medieval Mysticism* in *Library of Christian Classics.* Vol. 13. Philadelphia: Westminster Press, 1957.

TAULER, JOHN. *Spiritual Conferences.* St. Louis: Herder, 1961.

Theologia Germanica (c. 1350). (Available in several translations.)

Secondary Sources

BUTLER, E. C. *Western Mysticism: the teaching of Augustine, Gregory, and Bernard on Contemplation and the Contemplative Life.* 3d ed. New York: Harper and Row, 1967.

CLARK, JAMES M. *Meister Eckhart, an Introduction to the Study of His Works.* London: Nelson, 1957.

DANIEL-ROPS, HENRY. *Bernard of Clairvaux.* New York: Hawthorn Books, 1964.

GRAEF, HILDA. *The Story of Mysticism.* Garden City, N. Y.: Doubleday, 1965.

HAPPOLD, FREDERICK C. *Mysticism: a Study and an Anthology.* Baltimore, Penguin Books, 1963.

A *Thomas Merton Reader.* Edited by THOMAS P. MCDONNELL. New York: Harcourt Brace Jovanovich, 1962. (A contemporary mystic.)

Chapter 7

THOMAS AQUINAS AND SCHOLASTICISM

The writings of St. Thomas Aquinas (1225-74) stand as the high-water mark of medieval Catholic thought. He was the master spokesman for the Christian faith in that era of European history when Catholic theology and the power of the Roman church reached their peak of influence. This thirteenth-century period has been called that of "the medieval unity of civilization." This generalization hides, no doubt, many considerable disunities and tensions that prevailed in this as in any other age. Yet, if contrasted with the "confusion of tongues" that prevails in twentieth-century culture, the prevailing climate of opinion in Thomas' time was one in which Christian principles as to the nature of God, of man, and of man's destiny were generally acknowledged as the basis of culture. In that day a spokesman for the Christian faith like Thomas was not under the necessity of defending the faith as a minority claim against competing non-Christian views. His task was to draw together in synthesis and to articulate in detail the vast body of accepted Christian wisdom that had developed through the Middle Ages.

The monumental structure that Thomas built, though after his death rather neglected, proved in time so persuasive a summation of Christian thought that the Roman Catholic hierarchy in the nineteenth century came to look on him as the "official" theologian of the church. Modern Catholic investigation, in science as in philosophy, is carried on within the general framework set by Thomas. Indeed, any attempt to comprehend the attitude of Rome on such lively issues as private property, labor unions, communism, and contraception leads one back to the Thomistic first principles. The Anglican tradition in the Church of England has also been much indebted to St. Thomas, perhaps more than to any other philosopher.

The unique achievement of St. Thomas was the synthesis of Aristotelian philosophy and Christian theology. Aristotle's philosophy, rediscovered in its original form just prior to Aquinas' time, was creating considerable furor as a challenge to the Platonic and Augustinian traditions, long dominant in Christian theology. The two most influential monastic orders of the day, rivals on many issues, divided sharply also on their attitude toward Aristotle. The Franciscans viewed with scepticism, if not alarm, the kind of rationalism found in Aristotle. The Dominicans, on the other hand, of whom Thomas was one, received Aristotle with respect, not as an enemy but, if truly interpreted, as an ally of the Christian faith. Thomas set out to show how the Aristotelian method and presuppositions were quite in keeping with orthodoxy. His veneration for Aristotle (whom he calls "the Philosopher") is reflected throughout his pages, both as to method and content. From the Christian tradition, Aquinas drew heavily on the Bible, of course, on the church fathers, particularly Augustine, on the medieval monks and mystics, and on his own Dominican teacher, Albertus Magnus, whose germinal insights and enthusiasm for Aristotle had been passed on to his student. In the drawing together of all these elements, Thomas was much more than a mechanical summarizer. His synthesis was a creative one, marked by his own particular genius for a painstaking investigation of every path and bypath of thought and by a rational and orderly arrangement of ideas into an architectonic whole.

The Thomistic Theology

Thomas' main work, the *Summa Theologica,* is voluminous in spread; even the barest lines of the argument are too complex to be sketched here. Certain salient features of this theology, however, need to be reviewed as a background for the understanding of his ethics.

Using Aristotle's philosophical method—his concept of knowledge, teleology, and causation—Aquinas established, at least to his own satisfaction, absolute proof for the existence of God. Quite apart from "faith," sheer logical rigor would be led by a thoroughgoing analysis of the natural world to posit as the necessary basis of temporal existence a Supreme Being and Supreme Good, the First Cause and Intelligent Controller of the universe, by whose hand it is continually sustained in existence. Further, by analogy from human personality, this God can be described as just, merciful, rational, and purposive, if it is recognized that He is "just" and "merciful" not as is any human being but in a supremely excellent and infinite way. Thus far natural reason leads us in establishing the existence and attributes of God. "Faith" goes further to believe that God is Triune, Father, Son, and Holy Spirit. This is a belief which does not go *against* reason, though it goes *beyond* the power of reason to demonstrate on the basis of logical inference from the natural world.

God brings the world into existence as an ordered structure. There are distinct levels in the scale of creation: (1) angels at the top, who are disembodied rational souls, (2) men, in whom soul is conjoined with body but who are distinguished from the lower levels in having rational souls and wills, capable of self-consciousness and free choice based on intellectual comprehension, (3) animals, whose embodied souls are "sensitive" and animating but not rational, (4) plants, whose souls are capable simply of reproduction and growth, and (5) the crude elements of prime matter, which is completely "soul-less" and unorganized. Thus, the type of soul determines the position of different kinds of beings on this ladder of creation.

In order to understand what he must do as an ethical being, man must first recognize his midway status in this order of creation, between the angel and the animal. Thomas affirms that of the two elements conjoined in man, soul and body, the body is not by nature the bad part of him. As much as soul it is created good. Yet it is of lesser worth and good only as ordered by the spiritual element, the soul, which is created to seek the end of perfection in God, to pass through its temporary bodily housing in such fashion that it can be fit for the bodiless angelic state of perfection that lies beyond this life.

It is God's intention that man should be enabled to reach the end for which he was made: perfect happiness or the vision of God. The Creator therefore endows man with an ample variety of equipment whose proper use can lead to perfection, prepared for in this life, consummated in the next. Self-analysis reveals to a person that on the intellectual level he has the gift of reason, the capacity to judge truth, to piece together information derived from sense experience into a coherent whole and a pattern of ends. Man also finds himself imbued with a general capacity to distinguish right from wrong, or *synteresis*. When this is properly schooled by reason in dealing with particulars it is called conscience, the moral skill in applying universal principles to practical situations.

When a man properly disciplines his drives and impulses ("appetitive faculties") into the patterns of behavior which his reason guides, he acquires good habits, or virtues, which are the very stuff of morality. Virtue is "a settled disposition of doing good." Thus does Aquinas combine the will and the reason in describing the inner sources of ethical action: The will is the propulsive drive which seeks the good, but only truly finds it when that good is presented to it by the reason. Morality is as much a matter of head as of heart. The intellectual virtues of "intuition," "science," and "wisdom," involving skilled perception of first principles, are prerequisite for right-minded moral decision in the practical realm. In man-to-man relationships, the life of a good man will be characterized by the practice of the four classical virtues: temperance, courage (or fortitude), justice, and above all wisdom or prudence, that refined ability to judge correctly what is right to know and do. This much can be developed by natural and reasonable man, quite apart from revelation and faith. In all this Thomas does little more than reproduce Aristotle. God endows man, through Christian revelation and the church with its sacraments, with the added gift of the three theological virtues, faith, hope, and love, which direct man to God Himself, and which therefore crown the four natural virtues. These seven cardinal virtues are the internal habits of the good life.

The Creator provides further guide lines to moral perfection of an external sort: the structure of laws. The context in which man practices his morality is a law-abiding universe under the governance of a sovereign God. There are four kinds of law. (1) Eternal law is the ultimate transcendent "blueprint" of the universe in the mind of God. (2) Natural law is the enactment of the eternal law in the created world and there discernible by the reason of man. Though all the levels of creation, inanimate and animate, are ruled by natural law, men alone are consciously subject to it through the responsible participation of their free wills. (3) Human law, which is statute law, positive law, is enacted by human beings. The point to note here is that while human law is created by man, it is valid only in so far as its principles are grounded in natural law, which is to be discovered in the universe. (4) Divine law is the special revealed law found in the Bible, which in part parallels natural law known by reason and in part goes beyond it.

With the guidance of the God-given internal principles of morality and the external constraints of the structure of laws, one might expect men to run easily down the road to perfection. But ever since Adam's fall, men have failed to realize the perfection they might achieve. Their good natures are corrupted, in part through a blindness of their reason, in part through a stubbornness of their wills. Above all they have lost the supernatural gifts of blessedness. To overcome the shortcoming of natural man in sin, there is need for the further and final assistance from God in his activity of grace, in the sending of Jesus Christ to earth to break the power of evil, and through the establishment of his Church to provide in history a continuing channel wherein the forgiveness and sustenance of God can be mediated through the sacraments. As his hand is seen at work at the level of nature and the level of grace, then, God is ever seeking to draw men upward to himself, to realize their true natures as his own creatures, even in this life bound for citizenship in heaven.

The Role of Reason

There are certain characteristic stresses in this synthesis of Aristotelian and Christian thought which mark the distinctive Thomistic variations on the central theme of the Christian view of the good life. For one thing, as to method, Thomas always works through the apparent conflicts of thought to a "both-and" resolution, rather than leaving issues in "either-or" opposition. Unlike many of the more dialectical thinkers in the Christian tradition, Thomas is convinced that the whole of human experience is not paradoxical, at odds with itself. As product of the divine Mind it is a rational unity, and the persevering reason of man can describe the way the parts fit into the whole. So he reconciles the Aristotelian and the Christian world views. Law and grace, faith and reason, nature and supernature, duty and inclination, self-love and the love of others—these have constituted for many a Christian points of polar opposition between which one lives in tension with no hope of resolution on the hither side of eternity. Not so for Thomas. He works them all together in a neatly ordered scheme of salvation.

A second characteristic of the moral theory of Thomas is the high regard he holds for the natural world and natural man. Even without the supernatural activity of grace, any man, since he is endowed with reason, can know God and his natural law, and can achieve a level of natural goodness, such as the Greeks knew apart from Christ. This is only a partial goodness and a flickering vision of God, to be sure, but no less real for being partial. Here may be noted a point of contrast with Augustine, for whom the natural man unconverted by grace was corrupt and sinful and for whom the natural virtues of the Greeks stood in need of conversion by divine love in order truly to be good. But for Thomas, grace completes nature. It brings to fulfillment what a natural man trying to be good can only part way attain. Thus the theological virtues go on from where the natural virtues leave off, to a higher level of moral accomplishment, leading man from earthly goodness to his heavenly destination.

A third motif of Thomas is the emphasis on rationality in ethics. The reason of man is his most exalted natural part. The exercise of reason in ethical choice is the sign of moral stature. The most essential of all the virtues intellectual and moral is prudence, by which Thomas means not a calculating, self-interested caution, but the quality best described by the modern phrase "good judgment." Thomas shares with Aristotle and with Clement of Alexandria a philosopher's prejudice against the extremes of radical, hasty, unthinking action, when even well-meant ardor gets out of the control of deliberation and common sense. Aristotle's "mean" becomes now a rule of Christian ethics. In nothing too much. Good action is the wise action that strikes a proper median between excess and deficiency or achieves a nice balance among various interests. Even in the practice of Christian love one should be sensible about balancing self-love with the love of others in proper degree, for self-regard of an orderly sort has a proper place in the Christian life.

The constant play of the judicious reason which Thomas extols results inevitably in a distinctive treatment of the original ethics of the Sermon on the Mount. The commands of Christ, stated in their unqualified, stark form ("Love your enemies," "Judge not," "Lay not up for yourselves treasure on earth," etc.) are moderated and qualified by Thomas as he explicates them in terms of the particular circumstances in which they are to be practiced. We are to love our enemies, yes, but only in such and such situations, in such and such a manner, with such and such provisos. And it is prudence that draws the fine distinctions. Some Protestant critics of scholasticism have claimed that any "sensible" qualifications of these Christian commands destroy their heroic integrity. Indeed the very genius of the Christian life, they claim, is its absurdity, its nonconformity to the practical ethics of the world which common-sense reason holds. Thus, it is charged, the Thomistic synthesis is faithful more to the mind of Aristotle than to the mind of Christ.

The Pursuit of Happiness

The section on ethics in the *Summa Theologica*[1] starts with Aristotle's question: What is the "end" of man? Since all human action is end-directed, men find themselves involved in a whole complex of ends or targets. Which of these shall be taken as the inclusive or ultimate end and by which shall the worth of lesser, proximate ends be measured? Thomas agrees with Aristotle that the supreme end sought by rational men is *eudaimonia*, usually translated as "happiness," connoting by that not pleasure but a sense of well-being and well-doing. To push the question further, in what does this happiness consist? Various popular candidates are considered: money, honor, reputation, power. They all fall short, since they depend on circumstances external to man and come at the fickle hand of fortune. At best, these are unsought recognitions of an internal quality of life. Looking inward, then, can it be said that happiness lies in any well-being of the body, in pleasure? Certainly not, since the body is secondary in importance to the soul. The good of the soul? Yes, in a sense. "Happiness itself, being a perfection of the soul, is a good inherent in the soul: but that in which happiness consists, or the object that makes one happy, is something outside the soul."[2] Since we do not find the chief constituent of happiness in anything external to man in the temporal world or in anything within man, either body or soul, we look *above* man, to God. "Hence it is clear that nothing can set the will of man at rest but universal good, which is not found in any-

[1] Thomas' chief ethical writings are Part II of the *Summa Theologica*, Book III of the *Summa Contra Gentiles*, and the treatise *On the Governance of Rulers*.

[2] *Summa Theologica*, II-I, Q. 2, art. vii.

thing created, but in God alone."[3] "The last and perfect happiness of man cannot be otherwise than in the vision of the Divine Essence."[4] This end-of-ends, never perfectly realized in this life, is yet the lode-star of the Christian life on earth.

The passages that follow, taken from the *Summa Theologica,* lead the discussion through the psychological analysis of human behavior, the nature of the will and reason, the consideration of the kinds of virtues, to the treatment of the kinds of law. The full text of the material follows the manner of scholastic debate: each Article proposes a question, assembles possible objections to the thesis, which is then stated, and ends with replies to the objections. The selections here reproduce only the principal thesis of each article.

SOURCES

From

THOMAS AQUINAS: THE SUMMA THEOLOGICA[5]

On the Nature and Kinds of Virtues

Is human virtue a habit?

Virtue denotes some perfection of a power. The perfection of everything is estimated chiefly in regard to its end: now the end of power is action: hence a power is said to be perfect inasmuch as it is determined to its act. Now there are powers which are determined of themselves to their acts, as the active powers of physical nature. But the rational powers, which are proper to man, are not determined to one line of action, but

[3] *Ibid.,* II-I, Q. 2, art. viii.

[4] *Ibid.,* II-I, Q. 3, art. viii.

[5] The selections which follow are taken from Joseph Rickaby, *Aquinas Ethicus,* or *The Moral Teaching of St. Thomas,* a translation of the principal portions of the second part of the *Summa Theologica* (London: Burns Oates, 1896).

are open indeterminately to many, and are determined to acts by habits. And therefore human virtues are habits.[6]

Can the intellect be the subject of virtue?

There are two ways in which a habit is directed to a good act: in one way inasmuch as by such a habit a man acquires a readiness for a good act, as by a habit of grammar a man acquires a readiness in speaking correctly: still grammar does not always make a man speak correctly, for a grammarian may use a barbarism, or make a solecism, and the same is the case with other sciences and arts. In another way a habit not only produces a readiness for well-doing, but also makes one use the readiness duly, as justice not only makes a man prompt of will for just deeds, but also makes him act justly. And because goodness is not predicated of a thing absolutely for what it potentially is, but for what it actually is, therefore it is from habits of this latter sort that a man is said absolutely to do good and to be good—for instance, because he is just and temperate. And because virtue is what makes its possessor good and renders his work good, habits of this sort are called *virtues* absolutely and without qualification, because they render a work actually good, and make their possessor good absolutely. But the former habits are not called *virtues* absolutely and without qualification, because they do not render a work good except in point of a certain readiness, neither do they make their possessor good absolutely; for a man is not called absolutely good from the mere fact of his being a man of science or art; but he is called good only in a restricted sense, for instance, a good grammarian or a good smith; and therefore generally science and art are marked off as distinct from virtue, though they are called virtues sometimes. Therefore the intellect—not only the practical, but even the speculative intellect apart from all reference to the will—may be the subject of a habit that is called a virtue in a restricted sense. Thus the Philosopher [Aristotle] lays down *knowledge, wisdom,* and *understanding,* and also *art,* to be intellectual virtues. But the subject of a habit, called virtue

[6] *Summa Theologica,* II-I, Q. 55, art. i.

absolutely, cannot be aught else than the will, or some power inasmuch as it is moved by the will. The reason for this is, that the will moves to their proper acts all the other powers that are in any way rational. And therefore that a man does well in act comes of his having a good will. Hence the virtue that causes a man to do well in act, and not merely be in preparedness for well-doing, must either be in the will itself, or in some power so far forth as that power is moved by the will.[7]

Are speculative habits of intellect virtues?

A habit is called a virtue in two ways: in one way because it produces a readiness for well-doing; in another way because along with the readiness it produces the use of the same to the actual doing of good. This latter characteristic belongs only to those habits which regard the appetitive faculty: because the appetitive faculty it is that brings about the use of all powers and habits. Since then speculative habits of intellect do not perfect the appetitive faculty, nor regard it at all, but only the intellectual faculty, such habits may indeed be called virtues, inasmuch as they make a readiness to that good work, the consideration of truth, which is the good work of the intellect. They are not however called *virtues* in the second sense of the term, as causing one to put a power or habit to actual good use. For a man is not inclined to use the habit of speculative science by the mere fact of possessing it: he simply has the ability of contemplating the truth in the matters upon which his science turns. But his using the science that he has comes of the motion of his will. And therefore a virtue which perfects the will, as charity or justice, also causes one to make good use of speculative habits.[8]

Are there only three speculative habits of intellect, namely wisdom, science, and intuition?

The virtue of the speculative intellect is that which perfects the said intellect for the consideration of truth, such

[7] *Ibid.*, II-I, Q. 56, art. iii.
[8] *Ibid.*, II-I, Q. 57, art. i.

being the good work proper to it. Now truth offers itself to consideration in two shapes: in the shape of something known of *itself,* and in the shape of something known *through something else.* What is known of itself is a principle perceived by the intellect at a glance; and therefore the habit that perfects the intellect for the consideration of such truth is called *intellect,* or *intuition,* which is a hold upon principles. The truth that is known through something else is not taken in by the intellect at a glance, but is gathered by inquiry of reason, and stands as the termination of a reasoning process. This may be in two ways: either that the goal is final in some particular kind; or that it is final in respect of all human knowledge. About the latter goal *wisdom* is conversant, which considers the highest causes, and hence is apt to judge and ordain on all points, because a perfect and universal judgment cannot be got except by carrying matters back to their first causes. *Science,* on the other hand, perfects the intellect in regard of what is a final goal in this or that kind of knowable things; and therefore there are different sciences, according to the different kinds of things to be known, but only one wisdom.[9]

Is prudence a virtue necessary to man?

Prudence is a virtue especially necessary to human life. For to live well is to work well, or display a good activity. Now for activity to be good, care must be taken not only of what the agent does, but of how he does it: to wit, that he go to work according to a right election, not by the mere impetus of passion. But since election is of means to the end, rightness of election requires two things, a due end and a proper direction of means to that due end. Now to the due end man is properly disposed by the virtue which perfects the appetitive part of the soul, the object whereof is that which is good and that which ranks as an end. But towards the proper direction of means to a due end a man must be positively disposed by a habit of reason: because deliberation and election, which are about means to the end, are acts of reason. And therefore

[9] *Ibid.,* I-II, Q. 57, art. ii.

there must be in the reason some intellectual virtue, whereby the reason may be perfected so as suitably to regard the means to the end; and that virtue is prudence.[10]

Is moral virtue distinct from intellectual?

Reason is the first principle of all human acts: all other principles obey reason, though in different degrees. Some obey reason's every beck without any contradiction, as do the limbs of the body if they are in their normal state. Hence the Philosopher says that "the soul rules the body with a despotic command," as the master rules the slave, who has no right to contradict. Some authorities have laid it down that all the active principles in man stand in this way subordinate to reason. If that were true, it would suffice for well-doing to have the reason perfect. Hence as virtue is a habit whereby we are perfected towards well-doing, it would follow that virtue was in reason alone; and thus there would be no virtue but that which is intellectual. Such was the opinion of Socrates, who said that all virtues were modes of prudence. Hence he laid it down that man, while knowledge was present in him, could not sin, but that whoever sinned, sinned through ignorance. This argumentation, however, goes on a false supposition: for the appetitive part is obedient to reason, not to every beck, but with some contradiction. Hence the Philosopher says that "reason commands appetite with a constitutional command," like to that authority which a parent has over his children, who have in some respects the right of contradiction. Hence Augustine says, "sometimes understanding goes before, and tardy or none the affection that follows after": inasmuch as, owing to passions or habits in the appetitive faculty, the use of reason on some particular point is impeded. And to this extent it is in some sort true what Socrates said, that "in the presence of knowledge sin is not," provided that the knowledge here spoken of be taken to include the use of reason on the particular point that is matter of choice. Thus then for well-doing it is required that not only reason be well disposed by the habit of intellectual virtue, but also that the

[10] *Ibid.*, I-II, Q. 57, art. v.

appetitive power be well disposed by the habit of moral virtue. As then appetite is distinct from reason, so is moral virtue distinct from intellectual. Hence as appetite is a principle of human action by being in a manner partaker of reason, so a moral habit has the character of a human virtue by being conformable to reason.[10a]

Is the division of virtues into moral and intellectual an exhaustive division?

Human virtue is a habit perfecting man unto well-doing. Now the principle of human acts in man is only two fold, namely, intellect or reason, and appetite. Hence every human virtue must be perfective of one or other of these two principles. If it is perfective of the speculative or practical intellect towards a good human act, it will be intellectual virtue: if it is perfective of the appetitive part, it will be moral virtue.

Prudence in its essence is an intellectual virtue: but in its subject-matter it falls in with the moral virtues, being a right method of conduct; and in this respect it is counted among the moral virtues.[11]

Can there be moral virtue without intellectual?

Moral virtue may be without some intellectual virtues, as without wisdom, science, and art, but it cannot be without intuition and prudence. Moral virtue cannot be without prudence, because moral virtue is an elective habit, making a good election. Now to the goodness of an election two things are requisite: first, a due intention of the end—and that is secured by moral virtue, which inclines the appetitive powers to good in accordance with reason, which is the due end; secondly, it is required that the person make a right application of means to the end, and this cannot be except by the aid of reason, rightly counselling, judging, and prescribing: all which offices belong to prudence and the virtues annexed thereto. Hence moral virtue cannot be without prudence, and consequently not without intuition either: for by the aid of

10a *Ibid.*, I-II, Q. 58, art. ii.
11 *Ibid.*, I-II, Q. 58, art. iii.

intuition principles are apprehended, such principles as are naturally knowable, both in speculative and in practical matters. Hence as right reason in matters of speculation, proceeding on principles naturally known, presupposes the intuition of principles, so also does prudence, being right reason applied to conduct, presuppose the same intuition or insight.[12]

Can any moral virtue exist without passion?

If by passions we mean inordinate affections, as Stoics laid down, at that rate it is manifest that perfect virtue is without passions. But if by passions we mean all the movements of the sensitive appetite, at that rate it is plain that moral virtues, which are about passions as about their proper matter, cannot be without passions; because otherwise it would follow that moral virtue made the sensitive appetite altogether idle, its occupation gone. Now it is no point of virtue that the powers subject to reason should cease from their proper acts; but that they should follow out the command of reason in doing their proper acts. Hence as virtue directs the limbs of the body to due external acts, so it directs also the sensitive appetite to its proper movements under regulation. But those moral virtues that are not concerned with passions, but with actions, may be without passions. Such a virtue is justice, whereby the will is applied to the proper act of the will, which is not a passion. Yet on the act of justice there follows joy, at least in the will; and though this joy is not a passion, still if this joy be multiplied by the perfection of justice, there will be an overflow of the same on to the sensitive appetite. And thus by such an overflow, the more perfect justice is, the more is it a cause of passion.[13]

The Chief Virtues

Are there four cardinal virtues?

The formal principle of virtue is rational good; and that may be considered in two ways—in one way as consisting in

[12] *Ibid.*, I-II, Q. 58, art. iv.
[13] *Ibid.*, I-II, Q. 59, art. v.

the mere consideration of reason; and in that way there will be one principal virtue, which is called *prudence:* in another way according as a rational order is established in some matter, and that, either in the matter of actions, and so there is *justice;* or in the matter of passions, and so there must be two virtues. For rational order must be established in the matter of the passions with regard to their repugnance to reason. Now this repugnance may be in two ways: in one way by passion impelling to something contrary to reason; and for that, passion must be *tempered,* or repressed: hence *temperance* takes its name; in another way by passion holding back from that which reason dictates; and for that, man must put his foot down there where reason places him, not to budge from thence: and so *fortitude* gets its name.[14]

Do the four cardinal virtues differ one from another?

The four virtues above-mentioned are differently understood by different authors. Some take them as meaning certain general conditions of the human mind which are found in all virtues.

Others better understand these four virtues as being determined to special matters, each of them to one matter, so that every virtue which produces that goodness which lies in the consideration of reason, is called *prudence;* and every virtue which produces that goodness which consists in what is due and right in action, is called *justice;* and every virtue which restrains and represses the passions, is called *temperance;* and every virtue which produces a firmness of soul against all manner of sufferings, is called *fortitude.* On this arrangement it is manifest that the aforesaid virtues are different habits, distinct according to the diversity of their objects.[15]

Are there any theological virtues?

By virtue man is perfected unto the acts whereby he is set in the way to happiness. Now there is a twofold happiness of

[14] *Ibid.,* I-II, Q. 61, art. ii.
[15] *Ibid.,* I-II, Q. 61, art. iv.

man: one proportionate to human nature, whereunto man can arrive by the principles of his own nature. Another happiness there is exceeding the nature of man, whereunto man can arrive only by a divine virtue involving a certain participation in the Deity, according as it is said that by Christ we are made "partakers of the divine nature." And because this manner of happiness exceeds the capacities of human nature, the natural principles of human action, on which man proceeds to such well-doing as is in proportion with himself, suffice not to direct man unto the aforesaid happiness. Hence there must be superadded to man by the gift of God certain principles, whereby he may be put on the way to supernatural happiness, even as he is directed to his connatural end by natural principles, yet not without the divine aid. Such principles are called *theological virtues:* both because they have God for their object, inasmuch as by them we are directed aright to God; as also because it is only by divine revelation in Holy Scripture that such virtues are taught.[16]

Are theological virtues distinct from virtues intellectual and moral?

Habits are specifically distinct according to the formal difference of their objects. But the object of the theological virtues is God Himself, the last end of all things, as He transcends the knowledge of our reason: whereas the object of the intellectual and moral virtues is something that can be comprehended by human reason. Hence theological virtues are specifically distinct from virtues moral and intellectual.[17]

Are faith, hope, and charity fitly assigned as the theological virtues?

The theological virtues set man in the way of supernatural happiness, as he is directed to his connatural end by a natural inclination. This latter direction is worked out in two ways: first, by way of the reason or intellect, as that power holds in its

[16] *Ibid.*, I-II, Q. 62, art. i.
[17] *Ibid.*, I-II, Q. 62, art. ii.

knowledge the general principles of rational procedure, theoretical and practical, known by the light of nature: secondly, by the rectitude of the will naturally tending to rational good. But both these agencies fall short of the order of supernatural good. Hence for both of them some supernatural addition was necessary to man, to direct him to a supernatural end. On the side of the intellect man receives the addition of certain supernatural principles, which are perceived by divine light; and these are the objects of belief, with which *faith* is conversant. Secondly, there is the will, which is directed to the supernatural end, both by way of an affective movement directed thereto as to a point possible to gain, and this movement belongs to *hope;* and by way of a certain spiritual union, whereby the will is in a manner transformed into that end, which union and transformation is wrought by *charity.*[18]

Are moral virtues in a mean?

The proper function of moral virtue is to perfect the appetitive part of the soul with regard to some determinate matter. Now the measure and rule of the movement of the appetite towards its object is reason. But the goodness of everything that comes under measure and rule consists in its being conformed to its rule. Consequently, evil in these things lies in departure from rule or measure either by excess or defect. And therefore it is clear that the good of moral virtue consists in being up to the level of the measure of reason: which condition of being up to the level, or of conformity to rule, evidently lies in the mean between excess and defect.

The mean and the extremes in actions and passions are determined according to circumstances: and circumstances differ. Hence there is nothing to hinder a virtue exhibiting what is an extreme according to one circumstance, and yet is a mean according to other circumstances by conformity to reason; and such is the case with munificence and magnanimity. For if we consider the absolute quantity of that unto which the munificent and magnanimous man tends, it will be

[18] *Ibid.*, I-II, Q. 62, art. iii.

called an extreme and a maximum: but if this same degree is considered in respect of other circumstances, at that rate it has the character of a mean, because the said virtues tend to this maximum according to the rule of reason, where they ought, and when they ought, and for the motive for which they ought: whereas excess would be to tend to this maximum when one ought not, or where one ought not, or for a motive for which one ought not; and defect would be not to tend to this maximum where one ought and when one ought.[19]

Do the theological virtues observe the golden mean?

There are two measures of a theological virtue: one with regard to the virtue itself, and the other in our regard. The measure and rule of the theological virtue in itself, is God. For our faith is ruled by God's truth, our charity by His goodness, and our hope is measured by the greatness of His omnipotence and loving kindness. But this is a measure exceeding all human ability; and therefore never can man love God so much as He ought to be loved; nor believe or hope in Him as much as is due. Much less can there be excess there; and therefore the goodness of such virtue does not consist in any observance of a golden mean, but the observance is all the better the more it is carried to a height.

The other rule or measure of a theological virtue is in regard of ourselves; because though we cannot go out to God as we ought, still we ought to go out to Him, believing in Him, hoping in Him, and loving Him, according to the measure of our condition. Hence a mean and extremes may be made out in a theological virtue incidentally, in regard of ourselves.[20] [From the discussion of the theological virtues, faith, hope, and charity, the selected passages which follow illustrate the way in which "charity" (*caritas*), the supreme virtue of the Christian life, is incorporated by Thomas in his structure of rational morality.]

[19] *Ibid.*, I-II, Q. 64, art. i.
[20] *Ibid.*, I-II, Q. 64, art. iv.

On Charity

Is charity the most excellent of virtues?

The standard of human acts is twofold, namely, human reason and God; but God is the first standard, by which even human reason is to be regulated. And therefore the theological virtues, which consist in attaining that first standard—seeing that their object is God—are more excellent than the moral or intellectual virtues, which consist in attaining to human reason. Therefore, even among theological virtues themselves, that one must be preferable which attains more to God. Now that which has being of itself, is always greater than that which derives its being through another. Faith then and hope attain to God, inasmuch as the knowledge of truth, or the obtaining of good, comes to us of Him: but charity attains to God Himself, to rest in Him, not that anything may accrue to us of Him. And therefore charity is more excellent than faith or hope, and consequently than all other virtues.[21]

Can there be any true virtue without charity?

Virtue aims at good. Now the chief good is the end in view: for the means to the end are not called good except in order to the end. As the end is twofold, one ultimate and one proximate end, so there is also a twofold good, one ultimate and general good, and another good proximate and particular. The ultimate and principal good of man is the enjoyment of God, according to the text: "It is good for me to adhere to my God"; and to this end man is adapted by charity. The secondary and particular good of man is again twofold. There is one variety of it that is truly good, and capable, so far as it goes, of subordination to the principal good, or last end. The other variety is apparent and not true good—not true, because it leads away from final good.

It is clear then that true virtue, absolutely so called, is that which aims at the principal good of man: as the Philosopher also says that "virtue is a disposition of the perfect to the

[21] *Ibid.*, II-II, Q. 23, art. v.

best." And in that way no true virtue can be without charity. But if we consider virtue in reference to some particular end, we may then allow of something in the absence of charity being called virtue, inasmuch as it aims at some particular good. But if that particular good be not true good, but only apparent, then also the virtue that aims at that good will not be true virtue, but a false appearance of virtue. Thus the prudence of the covetous is not true prudence, which devises various ways and means of making money; and the same of the justice of the covetous, which scorns to touch others' possessions for fear of losing heavily thereby; and the same of the temperance of the covetous, by which they abstain from luxury as being an expensive taste; and the same of the fortitude of the covetous, with which, as Horace says, "they cross the sea, over the rocks and through the fire, to escape poverty." But if the particular good that is sought be true good, as the preservation of the State, or something of that sort, the virtue that seeks it will be true virtue, but imperfect, unless it be referred to the formal and perfect good.

Thus without charity there may be an act good of its kind, yet not perfectly good, because the due reference to the last end is wanting.[22]

Ought a man to love himself in charity?

Charity being a friendship, we may speak of charity in two ways: in one way under the general aspect of friendship; and in this light we must say that friendship properly is not entertained towards one's own self, but something greater than friendship: because friendship imports union, but every being has with itself unity, which goes beyond union with another. Hence as unity is the principle of union, so the love wherewith one loves oneself is the form and root of friendship: for our friendship for others consists in bearing them that regard which we bear ourselves. So there is no science of first principles, but something greater than science, namely, intuition, or insight. In another way we may speak of charity in its proper character and essence, as it is a friendship of man with

[22] *Ibid.*, II-II, Q. 23, art. vii.

God primarily, and secondarily with the creatures that are of God; among which the man himself counts who has the charity. In this way, among other things that he loves in charity as belonging to God, he also loves himself in charity.[23]

Are sinners to be loved in charity?

In sinners two things may be considered, their nature and their fault. In the nature that they have from God they are capable of happiness, on the sharing of which charity is founded; and therefore in their nature they are to be loved in charity. But their fault is contrary to God, and is an obstacle to happiness. Hence for the fault whereby they are opposed to God, all sinners are to be hated, even father and mother and kinsmen, as the text has it. For we ought in sinners to hate their being sinners, and love their being men, capable of happiness; and this is to love them truly in charity for God's sake.[24]

Is the love of enemies a necessary point of charity?

The love of enemies may be looked at in three ways. In one way, as though enemies were to be loved for being enemies: that were a wrongheaded proceeding and repugnant to charity, because it would be loving what was evil in another. In another way the love of enemies may be taken as fastening upon the nature that is in them, but only in the general. Thus understood, the love of enemies is a necessary point of charity, to the effect that a man loving God and his neighbour would not exclude his enemies from the general compass of his love of his neighbour. In a third way love of enemies may be looked at as something that is made a special point of, as though one should be moved with a special affection of love towards an enemy; and this is not a necessary point of charity, absolutely speaking, because neither is it a necessary point of charity to have a particular affection for any and every given individual, seeing that such universal particularisation is impossible. It is, however, a necessary point of charity, so far

23 *Ibid.*, II-II, Q. 25, art. iv.
24 *Ibid.*, II-II, Q. 25, art. vi.

as preparedness of mind goes, that a man should have his mind made up to show love to his enemy even as an individual, should necessity occur. But apart from instant necessity, a man's doing an act of love to his enemy for the sake of God, belongs to the perfection of charity. For the more a man loves God, the more love also he shows for his neighbour, and allows no enmity to stand in his way: just as if one had much love for another, he would love also that man's children for love of him, though they were enemies to himself.

To the objection that charity does not take away nature, and that naturally every being, even an irrational agent, hates its own contrary, it is to be said that enemies are contrary to us inasmuch as they are enemies: hence we ought to hate that point in them: for the fact that they are our enemies ought to displease us. But they are not contrary to us inasmuch as they are men, capable of happiness; and in that respect we are bound to love them.[25]

Is one neighbour to be loved more than another?

There have been two opinions on this point. Some have said that all neighbours are to be loved in charity equally as far as affection goes, but not in exterior effect. They allow gradations of love in the matter of outward acts of kindness, which they say we ought to do rather for those nearest to us than for strangers; but as for inward affection, that they say we ought to bestow equally on all, even on enemies. But this is an irrational thing to say. For the affection of charity, which is an inclination of grace, goes not less according to order than natural appetite, which is an inclination of nature, seeing that both the one and the other inclination proceeds from the divine wisdom. We see in natural things that natural inclination is proportionate to the act or movement which is proper to the nature of each. Therefore also the inclination of grace, which is the affection of charity, must be proportioned to what has to be done externally: so that we should have a more intense affection of charity for those who are the more proper objects of our active beneficence. There-

[25] *Ibid.*, II-II, Q. 25, art. viii.

fore we must say that even in affection we ought to love one of our neighbours more than another. And the reason is, because, seeing that the principle of love is God and the subject loving, there must necessarily be greater affection of love according as there is greater nearness to one or other of these two principles.

To the objection taken from Augustine's words, "All men are to be equally loved: but seeing that you cannot do good to all, their interest is to be especially consulted whose lot is more closely bound up with your own, according as place and time and other circumstances give opportunity," it is to be said that love may be unequal in two ways: in one way in respect of the good that we wish to a friend; and so far as this goes, we should love all men equally in charity: because we are to wish for all generically the same good, namely, eternal happiness. In another way love is said to be greater for the act of love being more intense: at that rate we ought not to love all men equally.

Or to put it otherwise, there are two ways in which love for different persons may be unequal. One way would be by loving some and not loving others. Now in actual beneficence we must observe this inequality, because we cannot do good to all; but as regards good wishes, such inequality should not be. The other way consists in loving some more than others. Augustine then does not intend to exclude this latter inequality, but only the former, as is clear from what he says about doing good.[26]

Is it more meritorious to love an enemy than to love a friend?

The reason for loving our neighbour in charity is God. When then we ask which is better or more meritorious, to love a friend or an enemy, these loves may be compared from two points of view: in one way considering the neighbour who is loved, and in another way considering the reason for loving. In the former way, love borne to a friend ranks above love borne to an enemy: because a friend is at once a better man and more allied to you, and therefore affords more suit-

[26] *Ibid.*, II-II, Q. 26, art. vi.

able matter for love. Hence also the opposite act is worse: for it is worse to hate a friend than an enemy. But in the latter way love borne to an enemy ranks first, for two reasons. First of all, because there may be another reason than God for the loving of a friend; but of the loving of an enemy God alone is the reason. Secondly, because supposing that both the one and the other is loved for God's sake, that love of God is shown to be stronger which extends the affections to more remote objects, to wit, even to the loving of enemies; as the force of a fire is shown to be all the stronger, the more remote the objects to which it extends its heat. But as the same fire acts more strongly on nearer than on more remote objects, so also charity loves more ardently persons closely conjoined than others more remote; and in this respect love borne to friends, taken in itself, is a warmer and better love than love borne to enemies.[27]

On the Laws

Is law a function of reason?

A law is a rule and measure of acts, whereby one is induced to act or is restrained from action. Now the rule and measure of human acts is reason: it being the part of reason to direct to the end, which is the first principle of conduct. Hence a law must be some function of reason.[28]

Is law always directed to the general good?

As reason is the principle of human acts, so in reason itself there is something which acts as a principle or mainspring in regard of all the rest; and upon this something law must mainly and chiefly bear. Now in matters of conduct, which are the domain of practical reason, the prime mainspring is the last end in view; and that is happiness. Hence law must especially regard the order that is to be followed in the attainment of happiness.

27 *Ibid.*, II-II, Q. 27, art. vii.
28 *Ibid.*, I-II, Q. 90, art. i.

Again, seeing that every part is referred to the whole as the imperfect to the perfect, and one man is a part of a perfect community, it needs must be that law peculiarly regards the order that is to be followed in view of the general happiness.

Since the name of *law* denotes something bearing upon the general good; every other precept prescribing a particular work lacks the character of law, except inasmuch as it is referred to the general good of the community.[29]

[In Article IV, the definition of law is given thus: "an ordinance of reason for the general good, emanating from him who has the care of the community, and promulgated."]

Is there any Eternal Law?

A law is nothing else than the dictate of practical reason in the sovereign who governs a perfect community. Now it is manifest, supposing that the world is ruled by Divine Providence, that the whole community of the universe is governed by Divine Reason. And therefore the plan of government of things, as it is in God the Sovereign of the universe, bears the character of a law. And because the Divine Reason conceives nothing according to time, but has an eternal concept, therefore it is that this manner of law must be called eternal.[30]

Is there in us any natural law?

Law being a rule and measure, may be in a thing in two ways: in one way as in one ruling and measuring, in another way as in one that is ruled and measured. Hence, since all things subject to Divine Providence are ruled and measured by the Eternal Law, it is manifest that they all participate to some extent in the Eternal Law, inasmuch by the stamp of that law upon them they have their inclinations to their several acts and ends. But among the rest the rational creature is subject to Divine Providence in a more excellent way, being itself a partaker in Providence, providing for itself and others. Hence there is in it a participation of the Eternal

[29] *Ibid.*, I-II, Q. 90, art. ii.
[30] *Ibid.*, I-II, Q. 91, art. i.

Law, whereby it has a natural inclination to a due act and end: such participation in the Eternal Law in the rational creature is called the natural law. Hence it is clear that the natural law is nothing else than a participation of the Eternal Law in the rational creature.[31]

Whether there is human law?

As we have stated above, a law is a dictate of the practical reason. Now it is to be observed that the same procedure takes place in the practical and in the speculative reason, for each proceeds from principles to conclusions. Accordingly, we conclude that, just as in the speculative reason, from naturally known indemonstrable principles we draw the conclusions of the various sciences, the knowledge of which is not imparted to us by nature, but acquired by the efforts of reason, so too it is that from the precepts of the natural law, as from common and indemonstrable principles, the human reason needs to proceed to the more particular determination of certain matters. These particular determinations, devised by human reason, are called human laws, provided that the other essential conditions of law be observed as was stated above.[32]

Was it necessary that there should be any divine law?

Besides the natural law and human law it was necessary for the guidance of human life to have a divine law. And this for four reasons: First, because it is by law that man is guided to the performance of proper acts in view of his last end. And if indeed man were ordained to an end that did not exceed the measure of the natural faculties of man, there would be no need of man's having any guidance on the part of reason beyond that of the natural law, and human law which is derived from it. But because man is ordained to an end of eternal blessedness, which exceeds the measure of the natural human faculties, therefore it was necessary that, over and above natural law and human law, he should be further

[31] *Ibid.*, I-II, Q. 91, art. ii.
[32] *Ibid.*, I-II, Q. 91, art. iii.

guided to his end by a law given from God. Secondly, because of the uncertainty of human judgment, especially on contingent and particular matters, whence it is that different men come to form different judgments on human acts; whence also different and contrary laws arise. In order then that man might know without a doubt what to do and what to avoid, it was necessary for him to be guided in his acts by a law given from God, which can be relied upon for certain not to err. Thirdly, because man can make a law only upon matters of which he can be a judge. Now the judgment of man cannot pass upon interior acts, which are hidden, but only upon exterior movements which appear: and yet for the perfection of virtue rectitude in both sorts of acts is necessary. And therefore human law could not sufficiently restrain and direct interior acts: but to this end it was necessary for a divine law to supervene. Fourthly, because human law cannot punish or prevent all evil doings; for in the wish to take away all evils many good things would be taken away, and the profit of the public good would be impeded, which is necessary for the preservation of society. In order then that no evil might go unforbidden and unpunished, the supervening of the divine law was necessary, whereby all sins are prohibited.[33]

Is the Eternal Law the Sovereign Plan existing in the mind of God?

As with every artificer there pre-exists the plan of the things that are set up by art, so in every governor there must pre-exist a plan of the order of the things that are to be done by those who are subject to his government. And as the plan of things to be done by art is called a pattern or exemplar, so the plan of him who governs subjects has the character of a law, if the other conditions are observed, which we have said to be essential to a law. Now God by his wisdom is the Creator of all things, and stands to them as the artificer to the products of his art. He is also the governor and controller of all the acts and movements that are found in any

[33] *Ibid.*, I-II, Q. 91, art. iv.

creature. And as the plan of divine wisdom has the character of an exemplar, pattern, or idea, inasmuch as by it all things are created, so the plan of divine wisdom moving all things to their due end has the character of a law. And thus the Eternal Law is nothing else than the plan of divine wisdom, as director of all acts and movements.[34]

Are all things human subject to the Eternal Law?

There are two ways in which a being is subject to the Eternal Law. The one is a participation of it by way of knowledge; the other by way of an interior motive principle; and it is in this second way that irrational creatures are subject to the Eternal Law. But because the rational creature, along with what it has in common with all creatures, has also something proper to itself inasmuch as it is rational, it is therefore subject to the Eternal Law in both ways: because on the one hand it has some notion of the Eternal Law; and on the other hand there is in every rational creature some natural inclination to a line of conduct in harmony with the Eternal Law. But both ways are imperfect and more or less destroyed in the wicked; in whom the natural inclination to virtue is corrupted by vicious habits, and again, the natural knowledge of good in them is darkened by passions and habits of sin. But in the good both ways are found in greater perfection: because in them, over and above the natural knowledge of good, there is superadded the knowledge that comes of faith and wisdom; and over and above the natural inclination to good there is superadded in them the inward motive of grace and virtue. Thus then the good are perfectly subject to the Eternal Law, as ever acting according to it: while the wicked are subject to the Eternal Law but imperfectly as to their actions, seeing that their knowledge of good is imperfect, and imperfect their inclination to it. But what is wanting on the side of action is made up on the side of suffering, in that they suffer what the Eternal Law dictates concerning them to that exact extent to which they fail to do what is in accordance with that Law.[35]

[34] *Ibid.*, I-II, Q. 93, art. i.
[35] *Ibid.*, I-II, Q. 93, art. vi.

Does the natural law contain several precepts or one only?

A certain order is found in the things that fall under human apprehension. What first falls under apprehension is being, the idea of which is included in all things whatsoever any one apprehends. And therefore the first principle requiring no proof is this, that there is no affirming and denying of the same thing at the same time: a principle which is founded on the notion of being and not-being; and upon this principle all the rest are founded. As being is the first thing that falls under apprehension absolutely, so good is the first thing that falls under the apprehension of the practical reason. For every agent acts for an end, which end has a character of goodness. And therefore the first principle of practical reason is one founded on the nature of good, good being that which all things seek after. This then is the first precept of law, that good is to be done and gone after, and evil is to be avoided. All the other precepts of the natural law are founded upon this: so that all those things belong to the precepts of the law of nature as things to be done, or avoided, which practical reason naturally apprehends and recognizes as human goods [or evils]. But because good has the character of an end of action, and evil the contrary character, hence all of those things to which a man has a natural inclination are apprehended by reason as good, and consequently as things to be gone after, and followed out in act; and their contraries are apprehended as evils to be avoided. According then to the order of natural inclinations is the order of the precepts of the law of nature. First of all there is in man an inclination to that natural good which he shares along with all substances, inasmuch as every substance seeks the preservation of its own being, according to its nature. In virtue of this inclination there belongs to the natural law the taking of those means whereby the life of man is preserved, and things contrary thereto are kept off. Secondly, there is in man an inclination to things more specially belonging to him, in virtue of the nature which he shares with other animals. In this respect those things are said to be of the natural law, which nature has taught to all animals, as the intercourse of the sexes, the education of offspring, and the like. In a third way there is in man an inclination to good according to the rational nature which is proper to him; as man has a natural inclination to know the truth about God, and to live in society. In this respect there belong to the natural law such natural inclinations as to avoid ignorance, to shun offending other men, and the like.[36]

Was there any use in laws being enacted by man?

Man has a certain innate aptitude for virtue, but the perfection of virtue must accrue to him by discipline and training: as we see that he is aided by industry in his necessities, notably in food and clothing. Nature has given him the beginnings of the satisfaction of his wants in these respects, in giving him reason and a pair of hands; but not complete satisfaction, as to other animals, to whom she has given in sufficiency clothing and food. For the purposes of this training and discipline it is not easy to find a man who suffices for himself: because the perfection of virtue principally consists in withdrawing man from undue pleasures, to which all men are prone, and especially the young, with whom discipline goes further. And therefore one man must receive from another this training and discipline whereby virtue is arrived at. Now for those young people who are prone to acts of virtue by a good natural disposition, or by custom, or rather by the gift of Heaven, the paternal discipline suffices which is by admonitions. But because of wanton and saucy spirits, prone to vice, who cannot easily be moved by words, it was found necessary to provide means of restraining them from evil by force and fear, that so at least they might desist from evil-doing, allow others to live in quiet, and themselves at length be brought by habituation of this sort to do willingly what formerly they accomplished out of fear, and thus might become virtuous. This discipline, coercive by fear of punishment, is the discipline of the laws.[37]

Is every law framed by man derived from the natural law?

Every law framed by man bears the character of a law exactly to that extent to which it is derived from the law of na-

[36] *Ibid.*, I-II, Q. 94, art. ii.
[37] *Ibid.*, I-II, Q. 95, art. i.

ture. But if on any point it is in conflict with the law of nature, it at once ceases to be a law: it is a mere perversion of law. But there are two modes of derivation from the law of nature. Some enactments are derived by way of conclusion from the common principles of the law of nature; as the prohibition of killing may be derived from the prohibition of doing harm to any man. Other enactments are derived by way of determination of what was in the vague: for instance, the law of nature has it that he who does wrong should be punished; but that he should be punished with this or that punishment, is a determination of the law of nature. Both sort of enactments are found in human law. But the former are not mere legal enactments, but have some force also of natural law. The latter sort have force of human law only.[38]

Is the obligation imposed on man by human law binding in the court of conscience?

Laws enacted by men are either just or unjust. If they are just, they have a binding force in the court of conscience from the Eternal Law, whence they are derived. Laws are said to be just in respect to the end, when they are ordained to the general good; in respect of the author, when the law does not exceed the competence of the legislator; and in respect of the form, when burdens are laid upon subjects in proportionate equality in order to the general good. For as one man is a part of a multitude, all that every man is and has belongs to the multitude, as all that every part is, is of the whole: hence also nature inflicts loss on the part to save the whole. Under this consideration, the laws that impose these burdens according to proportion are just, and binding in the court of conscience, and are legal laws.

Laws are unjust in two ways: in one way by being contrary to human good either in respect of the end, as when one in authority imposes on his subjects burdensome laws, that have no bearing on the general good, but make rather for the gratification of his own cupidity or vainglory: or in respect of the author, as when one makes a law beyond the scope of the

[38] *Ibid.*, I-II, Q. 95, art. ii.

power committed to him; or in respect of the form, as when burdens are laid unevenly on the multitude, though the end of the imposition is the public good. Such proceedings are rather acts of violence than laws: because, as Augustine says: "A law that is not just, goes for no law at all." Hence such laws are not binding in the court of conscience, except perhaps for the avoiding of scandal or turmoil, for which cause a man ought to abate something of his right, according to the text: "If a man will take away thy coat, let go thy cloak also unto him; and whosoever will force thee one mile, go with him other two." In another way laws may be unjust by being in conflict with the good that is of God, like the laws of tyrants inducing to idolatry; or to anything else that is against the divine law; and such laws it is nowise lawful to observe, because, as is said: "We ought to obey God rather than men."[39]

Further Readings

Primary Sources

Basic Writings of Saint Thomas Aquinas. 2 vols. Edited by Anton C. Pegis. New York: Random House, 1945.

Bourke, Vernon J. (ed.). *The Pocket Aquinas.* New York: Washington Square Press, 1960.

Thomas. *On Nature and Grace. Library of Christian Classics.* Philadelphia: Westminster Press, Vol. 11, 1954.

Thomas. *Treatise on the Virtues.* Trans. by John Oesterle. Englewood Cliffs, N. J.: Prentice-Hall, 1966.

Secondary Sources

Copleston, Frederick Charles. *Aquinas.* Baltimore: Penguin Books, 1963.

Farrell, Walter. *A Companion to the Summa.* 4 vols. New York: Sheed and Ward, 1938.

Gilleman, Gerard. *The Primacy of Charity in Moral Theology.* Westminster, Md.: Newman Press, 1961.

Gilson, Etienne. *Moral Values and the Moral Life.* St. Louis: B. Herder, 1931.

———. *The Spirit of Thomism.* New York: Harper and Row, 1966.

Maritain, Jacques. *St. Thomas Aquinas.* London: Sheed and Ward, Inc., 1938.

Pittenger, Norman. *St. Thomas Aquinas.* New York: F. Watts, 1969.

[39] *Ibid.*, I-II, Q. 96, art. iv.

Chapter 8

MARTIN LUTHER

Martin Luther (1483-1546) is the key figure, the dominant leader in that profound movement of life and thought, the Reformation, which marked the end of the medieval and the beginning of the modern period in the history of Christianity. Though conjoined with the Renaissance, the rise of nationalities, the growth of capitalism, and the development of modern science, the Reformation was fundamentally a religious revolution. It resulted in a great popular revival of Christian faith and life, in an unprecedented influence of Biblical history and thought on the Western mind, in the adoption of new ethical ideas and ideals, in the organization of the Protestant churches and in the reconstruction—through the Counter Reformation and the constant rivalry with Protestantism—of the Roman Catholic church. The interrelations between the religious and the cultural, political, and economic movements of the periods are so complex, Luther's personality is so challenging, and his activities were so diversified that no consensus on the significance of his achievements is likely to be reached. But for a large part of the Christian church—far larger than that which calls itself by his name—he is a great prophetic figure and a theological genius from whose vital and penetrating utterances ever new insights are gained. In recent times even Roman Catholic theologians have paid tribute to his religious significance.

Luther's understanding of the Christian gospel and of Christian ethics is not so discontinuous with that of the thirteenth century as is often maintained by ardent disciples and ardent critics; it is particularly misleading to interpret him as standing in complete antithesis to Thomas Aquinas. Church, state, and society on the eve of the Reformation in the sixteenth century presented a radically different picture from the one that had obtained in the thirteenth; and Thomas' influence at the time was not great. Nevertheless Luther's ideas and the Reformation impulse were revolutionary in a large sense, for they sought to base Christian faith and practice directly on Biblical foundations without much concern for the conservation of the tradition and usages developed during fourteen centuries. The gospel—the central message of Scriptures—as Luther had discovered it in the course of desperate personal struggles supplied him with a new beginning and led him to call for a far more radical reform of the church and of Christian life than did his contemporaries. Hence the starting point of the Reformation is to be sought in that encounter with the gospel which marked Luther's personal conversion.

This conversion was in many respects similar to Paul's, for Luther, like the man who had been a zealous Pharisee, made his transition to a life of vital faith not from profligacy and moral carelessness but from intense ethical seriousness and religious devotion. The profound desire for a saintly life had come to appearance in the young Luther when he abandoned his plans for a career in law and, at the age of twenty-one, had entered an Augustinian monastery noted for the severity of its discipline. There he had distinguished himself by his asceticism as well as by his abilities that led to his appointment as a professor of Biblical studies in the university at Wittenberg. The combination of Bible study with intense personal concern for saintliness and salvation had led him into an enduring crisis. The Scriptural demand for holiness of life, for the complete fulfillment of the law to love God with heart, soul, mind and strength and to love the neighbor as one's self was irreducible. No less unavoidable was the Biblical picture of the divine wrath against sin. So the young monk had found himself involved in the dilemma of being required to love a fearsome God and of fulfilling for the sake of his own salvation commandments that could not be met by a self concerned for itself. He had found himself involved in what he later described as the "curving in upon itself" of human self-interestedness, that inversion which makes a man consider his own status and profit in everything that he does, be it in the pursuit of truth, in the practice of charity, in worship, or in the exercise of humility. The self curved in upon itself discovers that instead of loving God it is admiring or grieving over its own measure of love; instead of being concerned for the neighbor it is concerned about its acquisition of the virtue of neighbor-love; instead of being humble it seeks to excel in humility.

In consequence of his rigorous self-examination, but above all as a result of the illumination which came when at last the meaning of the Gospel struck home, Luther, more than any theologian since Paul, came to understand the difference between self-conscious moral aspiration after perfection or happiness and genuine goodness. He noted that there was as great an opposition between the self-centeredness of men who wanted to be saints and "the grace of our Lord Jesus Christ" as there was between the latter and the obvious immorality of passionate lovers of wealth or pleasure. In his later writings he often expressed the idea that there are two kinds of sinners, those who go off the road on the right-hand side and those who stray toward the left. The latter, like the publicans and "sinners" of the Gospels, succumb to their passions; the former, like Pharisees and scribes, fall prey to their egotism. Both fall short of the glory of God, and which sort does the greater harm to their companions is questionable. Where Bernard and Thomas had discerned stages of progress between perfectionist morality and the grace of Christ, Luther, with Paul, Augustine, Calvin and Edwards, saw only antithesis. There is no way, he believes, from self-love, though it be love even of one's best self, to love of God and neighbor, except through a radical change of direction—a change which may be easier in some respects for the profligate than for the self-righteous sinner.

This radical understanding of the sinfulness of the "just and the unjust," which became a distinctive characteristic of the Christianity of the Reformation, had not, of course, been achieved by Luther so long as he wrestled only with his own inability to fulfill the commandments and achieve perfection. Insight into it came only in the double experience of despair and of faith. When it dawned upon Luther at last that "the grace of our Lord Jesus Christ" was less an example set for him than a deed done to him and for him, that he was loved and accepted by God prior to any achievement and in his perverseness, then all his ideas and values were subjected to a sharp change and transposition. What had been first became last and the last first. One may look for the secret of Luther's conversion, and so of the beginning of the Reformation, in the reversal of his understanding of the human situation before God. In the dialogue of self and God, present in religion, the self had forever been seeking to make itself heard by God, multiplying its prayers, increasing its efforts so to change itself as to invite divine acknowledgment. It had never been silent long enough to listen to what God was saying; when it appeared to be listening it heard only what its stereotyped preconceptions allowed it to hear. When at last God's word and deed broke through this self-concentration, the whole situation between God and man was altered. The word of God and deed of God, focused in Jesus Christ, became the point of departure for a new relationship, a new self-knowledge, and a new response. Now the self recognized itself as both sinful and beloved, able to live before God in repentance and faith, in daily reliance on forgiveness, and in constant gratitude. The dialogue with God continued; outside it there was no possibility of existence, but in the dialogue God's word was always first, man's word or deed only response; and the word of God, harsh as it might sound at times, was always the word of the Saviour.

Luther's conversion, a relatively long drawn out process, led on his part to a manifold and intense activity. He was absorbed for thirty years and more in the tasks connected with the reformation of ecclesiastical abuses, the reorganization of the churches after the reformers had been rejected by the Roman authorities, the elimination of monasteries and the monastic life from reformed Christendom, the translation and explanation of the Bible, the development of popular religious education and of popular church services, the relations of churches and states. His work in these domains has well been called a "reconstruction of morality." During these busy years he wrote, as occasion demanded, essays, sermons, treatises, and pamphlets without any thought of constructing a system of theology such as that of Thomas or of Calvin. The unity of his thought is, however, apparent in these manifold utterances; and the ethical interest is strong in all of them, for he was never a speculative thinker. Among these writings the following are especially important for the understanding of his view of the Christian life: *The Treatise on Good Works, The Treatise on Christian Liberty,* the commentaries on *Romans* and *Galatians,* and *The Large Catechism.* Special applications of his ideas to the field of political and economic ethics were made in such writings as the essays *Secular Authority, To What Extent It Should Be Obeyed; Whether Soldiers, Too, Can Be Saved; Address to the German Nobility; On Usury; Instructions for the Organization of a Community Chest.*

Justification by Faith

The insights and convictions that come to expression in Luther's writings are psychological as well as ethical and theological. On the psychological side two ideas in particular must be mentioned. The first of these is his voluntaristic, activist understanding of human nature. In distinction from the intellectualist view, which regards the human mind as fundamentally theoretical and for which the will translates the prior purposes of the intellect into action, Luther, with the voluntarists in general, notes that "the being and nature of man cannot for an instant be without doing or not-doing something, enduring or running away from something, for life never rests." Man's moral problem, from this point of view, is less that of choosing the right means for the sake of attaining a chosen end than it is that of doing rightly the actions that issue from his nature. For voluntarism action, though always accompanied by understanding, does not begin with reflection. It is an expression of man's inner nature, of the set and disposition of his will. The voluntarist notes that man will eat, and that his moral problem in this realm is that of regulating his eating, not of choosing between fasting and eating, even though fasting seem to his mind a good means toward the attainment of a spiritual goal. So it is with his sexuality, his political existence, and his religion. The moral question is not about the *what* but about the *how* of our activity.

A second psychological insight of Luther's has been highly developed in modern times, though much ethical theory remains oblivious to it. It is the understanding that in all his actions man is subject to an inner bondage, a conflict and a self-contradiction which does not permit him to live at his full capacity. The internal bondage has many aspects. It appears in the sense of guilt, in anxiety, in self-centeredness and blindness to the values of others, in compulsive cravings for pleasure, and in abnormal scrupulosity. The fundamental moral problem of man is therefore the problem of freedom, not as the problem whether there is such a thing as liberty of choice, but as the problem of achieving liberation from these internal fetters so that man can serve his good causes without hindrance.

Closely connected with these psychological convictions are certain theological ideas which run through all of Luther's writings. Important among these is the principle that "good works do not make a good man but a good man produces good works." In common with a central tradition in Christian ethics Luther emphasizes the importance of good motives as compared with the consequences of action. While careful calculation of consequences is necessary in technical action when men deal with things, such calculation is misplaced when it is applied to persons and to personal relationships. There everything depends on the spirit, the source of the action. Luther illustrates the point in his *Treatise on Good Works.*

When a man and a woman love and are pleased with each other, and thoroughly believe in their love, who teaches them how they are to behave, what they are to do, leave undone, say, not say, think? Confidence alone teaches them all this and more. They make no difference in works: they do the great, the long, the much, as gladly as the small, the short, the little, and that too with joyful, peaceful, confident hearts. But where there is doubt search is made for what is best; then a distinction of works is imagined, whereby a man may win favor; and yet he goes about it with a heavy heart and great disrelish; he is, as it were, taken captive, more than half in despair, and often makes a fool of himself.[1]

As the quotation indicates, Luther believed that the fundamental element in man's personal life, that which gives color and direction and meaning to every action, is man's trust or confidence—his real, not his official, religion. To have a god, says Luther, is to trust in something; whatever it is men trust in to give meaning to their lives, that is actually their god. Men are not either religious or irreligious, for none live without believing in something. They are either believers in the one true God or idolaters who trust in themselves, or in wealth, or reason, or civilization, or any one of the many actual and imagined beings to which they turn for a sense of security in their distrust and suspicion of the ultimate power on which they depend for being. When men distrust God and trust in themselves or in an idol, this becomes apparent in all their actions, no matter how much they profess to being religious or how ardently they try to conform to some ideal code of conduct. On the other hand, when the great gift of confidence in God, as Father and Saviour, is given, all their actions reflect this fundamental reorientation of their lives. In their assurance of being valued and sustained by the One who delivers from all evil they are set free from concern about themselves; their energies are released and integrated in the service of their neighbors. This is the theme of the *Treatise On Christian Liberty*.

Faith, the root-virtue whence all actions draw their goodness, is for Luther completely the gift of God. It is not something under man's control so that he can will to trust as perhaps he can will to believe a proposition about God.

[1] Martin Luther, *Works* (Philadelphia: A. J. Holman Company, 1915), I, 191.

Preparations for the reception of the gift are indeed made by man in his moral struggles to achieve worthiness, since without such struggles he would never be brought to realize the vanity of his trust in himself. But even so, the primary preparations here are made by God who speaks to man through conscience and the commandments. The gift of faith in God is directly given through the gospel, as this is received by those who have been prepared for it. Through the proclamation of his deed in sacrificing his son for the salvation of men, God wins men from distrust of him to confidence and reliance, from the fear of his wrath to the expectation of his love. The Christian life consists now in the daily acceptance of this gift and in its expression through works of gratitude and love of neighbor.

It follows from all this that for Luther being a Christian is not primarily a matter of specifically religious actions. Indeed, in specifically religious matters man is to be receptive rather than active, *hearing* the word of God, *accepting* his forgiveness. On its active side this life is one of doing all the ordinary things demanded by the nature of life itself and the laws of society and conscience as well as those of the Scriptures. But the man of faith does all these things with a difference—in freedom from anxiety, without self-seeking, for the sake of the objective good, not for the sake of the agent. Christian vocation for Luther is, therefore, not religious vocation, though some men are required to preach and to organize churches. Any kind of constructive work in the world is a Christian vocation when it is carried on with confidence in God and with the repentance of a sinner in constant reliance on forgiveness. Although there are a few kinds of activities that evidently cannot be done in the right spirit—such as the activities of thieves and harlots on the one hand, or of seekers after saintliness on the other—there are none that carry the guarantee of the right spirit with them. Even the gospel may be preached in distrust of God and in pride. Every Christian in every vocation is involved in the constant problem of living as a sinner and yet by grace. There are even horrible things he may be required to do for the public good, such as going to war or acting as hangman. But if in a sinful world and as a sinful man he acts in faith, he is justified as the seeker after personal virtue cannot be justified. Luther's conception of Christian vocation, especially as developed by Calvin, came to be of paramount significance in the later history of the Protestant countries. The heart of it is the understanding that a "good tree brings forth good fruit" and that the quarrels of men, including moralists, about the relative values of good pears, good cherries, and good persimmons exhibit human pride rather than knowledge of good and evil.

In political ethics, as the following selections from the *Large Catechism* indicate, Luther, never forgetting the greatness of the monastic virtue of obedience and alarmed by the prospects of anarchy in the breaking up of the medieval system, insisted especially on the importance of yielding to authority. He qualified the principle of obedience to human authorities, however, in the same way that Calvin did, and the latter's teachings upon the subject, presented in the next chapter, largely represent a systematization of Luther's unsystematic thought. The qualifying idea for him, as for all Christians, was contained in the statement, "We must obey God rather than men."

SOURCES

From

MARTIN LUTHER: THE LAW, FAITH AND PRAYER[2]

There are three things which a man must know in order to be saved:

First he must know what he is to do and what he is to avoid. Second, when he realizes that he cannot of his own

[2] This and all subsequent materials in this chapter are from *Luther on Christian Education: Luther's Catechetical Writings*, translated by John Nicholas Lenker (Minneapolis, Minn.: The Luther Press, 1907).

power do what is required of him, nor refrain from that which is forbidden, he must know where he should seek and find the power necessary. In the third place, he must know how to seek and find it. The sick man is a case in point. If he would recover he must first know the nature of his illness, and also what he may do and what he may not do. Then he must know where the remedy is to be found which will enable him to do as a healthy man does. Lastly, he must desire, seek, and secure that remedy. By a similar process the commandments teach a man to recognize his malady, so that he realizes and experiences what he can do and what he cannot do, what he can avoid and what he cannot avoid, with the result that he recognizes himself a sinful and wicked man. Then secondly, the Creed offers grace as a remedy and he is enabled to be godly and keep the commandments. It reveals God and his mercy, made available and offered through Christ. Thirdly, the Lord's Prayer teaches him how to desire and seek this grace, and shows how to secure it, by means of regular, humble, and comforting prayer. Thus grace shall be given him and he shall be saved through the fulfilment of the commandments. These three things virtually comprise the entire Scriptures.[3]

From

Martin Luther: The Large Catechism

Exposition of the Ten Commandments

The First Commandment: "You shall have no other gods before me."[4]

The simple meaning of this commandment is, You shall worship me alone as your God. What do these words mean and how are they to be understood? What is it to have a

[3] The introduction is from the Foreword to *The Law, Faith and Prayer,* a brief exposition of the three principal parts of the Catechism.

[4] Exod. 20:3, Deut. 5:7.

god, or what is God? Answer: A god is that to which we look for all good and where we resort for help in every time of need. To have a god is simply to trust and believe in one with our whole heart. The confidence and faith of the heart make both God and an idol. If your faith and confidence are right, then likewise your God is the true God. On the other hand, if your confidence is false, then you have not the true God. For the two, faith and God, have inevitable connection. Now, I say, whatever your heart clings to and confides in, that is really your God. Therefore, the intent of this commandment is to require true faith and trust of the heart with respect to the only true God.

Many a one thinks he has God and entire sufficiency if he has money and riches; in them he trusts and proudly and securely boasts that he cares for no one. He surely has a god, called mammon, on which he fixes his whole heart. This is a universal idol upon earth. He who is in possession of money and riches deems himself secure. He who has nothing doubts and despairs as if he had no knowledge of God. This desire for wealth cleaves to our natures until we are in our graves. In like manner he who boasts great skill, wisdom, power, and influence, and friends and honors, and trusts in them, has also a god, but not the one true God.

You readily recognize the nature of this commandment and the extent of its requirements. It claims man's whole heart and his trust in God alone. One can easily understand that to have God does not mean to lay hands upon him, nor to put him in a purse or lock him in a safe. But we lay hold of him when our hearts embrace him and cleave to him. Now, to cling to him with the heart is simply fully to trust him.

Idolatry does not consist merely in the act of erecting an image and praying to it. It consists chiefly in the state of a heart that is intent on something else and seeks help and consolation from creatures, saints or devils; that neither cares for God nor looks to him for any good, even for help, nor believes that the good it receives comes from God.

There is, moreover, another false divine service, the greatest idolatry we have as yet practiced; it still reigns in the world. It sways the conscience that seeks in its own works help, consolation, and salvation, that presumes to wrest heaven from God, and reckons how many institutions it has established, how often it has fasted, attended mass, etc. Such a conscience relies upon and boasts of these things, as if it would receive nothing from God gratuitously, but has acquired and earned all by works of supererogation; as if God were under obligation to stand at our service, indebted to us, and we were his lords. What is that but making God an idol, yea, a mere dispenser of apples, and esteeming and exalting ourselves as god?

Let each, then, take heed that he regard this commandment as exalted above every other thing, and treat it not as a light matter. Examine your own heart diligently and inquire of it, and you will surely find whether or no it cleaves to God alone. Do you possess a heart that expects from him nothing but good, especially when in need and distress, and that renounces and forsakes all that is not God? Then you have the only true God. On the contrary, does your heart cleave to something from which it expects more good and more aid than it does from God, and does it flee, not to him, but from him? Then you have another god, an idol.

To instruct us that he will not allow his commandment to be cast to the winds, but that he guards it well, God has attached to this commandment, first a terrible threat, and then a beautiful, comforting promise. "For I the Lord thy God am a jealous God, visiting the iniquity of the fathers upon the children to the third and the fourth generation of those who hate me, and showing steadfast love to thousands of those who love me and keep my commandments."[5] Although these words are related to all the commandments yet they are joined to this chief commandment because it is of first importance that a man's head be right. Where the head is right the whole life must be right. Learn also from these words how angry God is with those who trust in aught but Himself, and how good and gracious he is to those who, with their whole hearts, trust and believe in him alone.

[5] Exod. 20:5-6, Deut. 5:9-10.

Learn all this that you may not live in false security and take your chances as do brutish hearts which imagine that it makes no difference how they live. God has witnessed to this by all history, as the Scriptures amply show and as daily experience abundantly teaches. Let every one take heed that this commandment be not regarded as if spoken by man. It means either eternal blessing, happiness, and salvation, or eternal wrath, misery, and woe. The trouble is, the people of this world believe none of these words nor do they esteem them as words of God. For they see that those who trust in God and not in mammon suffer grief and want and are opposed and attacked of Satan. On the other hand, the servants of mammon have power, favor, honor, and every comfort in the eyes of the world. We must therefore lay hold of these words, even in the face of this apparent contradiction, and remember that they neither lie nor deceive, but that their truth must yet be made manifest.

> *The Second Commandment:* "You shall not take the name of the Lord your God in vain; for the Lord will not hold him guiltless that takes his name in vain."[6]

As the first commandment instructed the heart and taught faith, so this commandment leads us into the outer sphere and trains our lips and tongue Godward. If asked, How do you understand the second commandment and what is meant by taking God's name in vain? answer in the briefest way: It is a misuse of God's name if we call upon the Lord God in any way to support falseness or wrong-doing. Therefore, it commands that we are not to mention God's name falsely or so take it upon our lips, when the heart knows or should know the deception. Now, with this knowledge, each one can easily decide for himself when and how God's name is abused, although it is impossible to name all its misuses. In general, a wrong use is seen in the first place in worldly business and in things relating to money, possessions and honor, be it publicly before the courts of justice, at market or else-

[6] Exod. 20:7, Deut. 5:11.

where whenever men swear or make a false oath by an appeal to God's name or their own souls to support their statements. But its greatest abuse is found in spiritual matters when false preachers arise and present untruthful teachings as the Word of God. Notice, all these are expedients to use the name of God as a veneer in order to appear attractive and commendable, whether in ordinary worldly business or in the high and subtle matters of faith and doctrine.

It is a calamity common in all the world that there are few who do not use God's name in falsehood and all kinds of wickedness. So few are they who in their hearts trust in God alone. We all naturally possess this beautiful virtue: He who has committed a wrong would gladly cover up and disguise his disgrace, that it might come to no one's sight or knowledge. All men would rather work their wickedness secretly than let anyone find it out. Then when we are arraigned, God must give his name and make the rascality appear as an act of righteousness and the disgrace as honorable conduct. This is the universal way of the world. It is a great mercy that the earth still bears and nourishes us.

In the words, "You shall not take the name of the Lord your God in vain," God at the same time gives us to understand that we are to take his name in the right sense. It has been revealed and given to us for constant use and profit. Therefore, since it is here forbidden to use this holy name in the service of falsehood and wickedness, it necessarily follows that we are, on the other hand, commanded to use it in the service of truth and everything that is good; as for example, where one swears to the truth wherever needed and demanded. Likewise, when we teach the truth aright; when we invoke it in trouble or use it in praise and thanksgiving for prosperity, etc. Thereby is solved the question that has troubled many teachers, why swearing is forbidden in the Gospel, Matthew 5:33-34, and yet Christ and Paul and other saints often swore, John 14:12; 16:20 and 23; II Corinthians 1:23. The explanation is briefly this: We are not to swear in support of evil, that is to a falsehood, or unnecessarily; but we are to swear in support of the good, and for the welfare of our neighbor. For that is a truly good work by which God is praised and truth and justice established; by which falsehood is refuted, peace restored, obedience enforced and contentions suppressed.

The Third Commandment: "Remember the sabbath day, to keep it holy."[7]

In the Old Testament God set apart the seventh day and appointed it for rest, commanding it to be kept holy above all other days. In point of outward observance the commandment was given only to the Jews. Therefore, this commandment in its literal, rough, meaning is not for us Christians now. It is wholly an external matter, like the other ordinances of the Old Testament which were bound to particular customs, persons, times and places, from which we are now set free through Christ. But to give to the uninformed a Christian interpretation of what God requires of us in this commandment we remind them that we keep holidays not for the sake of intelligent and learned Christians; for they have no need of it. We keep them, first, for the sake of bodily necessity. Nature teaches and demands that the mass of the people—servants and mechanics, who the whole week attend to their work and trades—retire for a day of rest and recreation. And then, especially, we do keep holydays that people may have time and opportunity to worship with the congregation, which otherwise they could not do. Also, that they may assemble in meetings to hear and discuss God's Word and appropriately praise him with song and prayer. But these concerns are not so bound up with a particular time as they were among the Jews, when it had to be precisely this or that day, for one day in itself is no better than another, and worship should, indeed, be observed daily. But since the mass of the people cannot attend to it daily, one day a week at least must be set apart for the purpose. Sunday was appointed for it in olden times, and we should not change the day. The Sabbath should be uniformly observed as to the day and so no disorder be caused by unnecessary innovations.

[7] Exod. 20:8, Deut. 5:12.

The plain meaning of this commandment is that, since man naturally celebrates festival days, the celebrations be so arranged that he learn God's Word. The Word of God is the holy of holies, yea, the only holy thing we Christians know and have. God's Word is the treasure that sanctifies everything. Whatever be the hour when God's Word is taught or preached, when it is heard, read, or called to mind, then the person, day, and work are thereby sanctified; not because of any outward work, but because of the Word which sanctifies us all. Other labor and employment are not properly called holy unless the doer is himself first holy, but here a work must be performed which makes the doer holy; such a thing occurs only through God's Word. Places, times, individuals, and all the appointments of worship have been instituted and ordered that God's Word may exert its power publicly.

> *The Fourth Commandment:* Thus far we have learned the first three commandments which treat of our duty to God. Now the other seven commandments follow, which treat of our duty to our neighbors. Among these the first and greatest is: "Honor your father and your mother."[8]

God has exalted fatherhood and motherhood above all other relations under his scepter. This appears from the fact that he does not command merely to love the parents but to honor them. As to our brothers, sisters, and neighbors, God generally commands nothing higher than that we love them. He thus distinguishes father and mother above all other persons upon earth and places them next to himself. It is a much greater thing to honor than to love. It includes not only love, but also obedience, humility and reverence, as if we were pointed to some sovereignty hidden there. Thus the young must be taught to reverence their parents in God's stead, and to remember that even though they be lowly, poor, frail, and peculiar, they are still father and mother given by God. Their way of living and their failings cannot

[8] Exod. 20:12, Deut 5:16.

rob them of their honor. Therefore we are not to regard the manner of their persons but God's will that appointed and ordained them to be our parents. Before God we are no doubt all equal, but among ourselves there must be such inequality and rightful distinction as is enjoined by God.

First, then, learn what is meant by honor to parents as required by this commandment. It is that they be esteemed and prized above everything else as the most precious treasure we have on earth. Then, that in conversation with them we measure our words, lest our language be discourteous, domineering, quarrelsome, yielding to them in silence, even if they do go too far. And, thirdly, that we honor them by our actions, both in our bearing and the extension of aid, serving, helping, and caring for them when they are old or sick, frail or poor; and that we not only do it cheerfully, but with humility and reverence, as if unto God.

Observe what a great, good, and sacred function is here assigned to children, which, alas, is totally disregarded and cast aside. No one recognizes it as God's command or as a holy, divine Word and precept. For if we had thus honored this commandment it would have been apparent to all that the call is for holy people who live according to these words. It would not have been necessary to institute monastic life or spiritual orders had every child kept this commandment. For what God has commanded must be better and far nobler than all that we can ourselves devise. Since the commands of God embody his highest wisdom, who am I that I should attempt to improve upon his appointments? Since God's Word and will are to be fulfilled nothing is to be more sacredly regarded than the wills and words of our parents, provided that therein we remain obedient to God and break not the preceding commandments.

While speaking on this commandment it is in place to mention the various instances in which obedience is required by those in authority over us, whose duty it is to command and govern. All authority has its root and warrant in parental authority. All who are called masters stand in the place of parents and from them must obtain authority and power to command. In the Bible they are all called fathers, because in their government they perform the functions of a father and should possess a fatherly heart toward their people. [The Romans] called their princes and magistrates *patres patriae,* fathers of the country; and it is a shame that we who wish to be Christians do not so call our rulers, or, at least, treat and honor them as such. Through civil rulers as through our parents, God gives us food, home and land, protection and security. Therefore since they bear this name and title with all honor as their chief glory, it is our duty to honor them and to esteem them as we would the greatest treasure and the most precious jewel on earth. Now he who is obedient, willing and capable, and cheerfully gives honor wherever due, knows that he pleases God, and receives joy and happiness as a reward. If, on the other hand, one will not serve in love but despises and resists authority—or rebels—he should know that he has no favor or blessing. What we in disobedience seek and merit will be paid to and visited upon us. Why, think you, is the world full of unfaithfulness, shame, misery, and murder? Just because everyone strives to be his own lord and free from authority, to care nothing for anyone, and to do what he pleases. God punishes one rogue by means of another; if you deceive and despise your master, another comes and treats you likewise. We, indeed, feel our misfortune and we murmur and complain of unfaithfulness, violence and injustice; but we are unwilling to see that we ourselves are rogues who justly deserve our punishment, and we are not reformed by what we suffer.

In this connection it would not be amiss to advise parents and others filling their office, as to their treatment of those committed to their authority. Although the duty of superiors is not explicitly stated in the Ten Commandments, it is frequently dwelt upon in many other passages of Scripture, and God intends it even to be included in this commandment, where he mentions father and mother. God does not purpose to bestow the parental office and government upon rogues and tyrants; therefore he does not give them that honor, namely the power and authority to govern, merely to receive homage.

Parents should consider that they are under obligation to obey God and that, first of all, they are conscientiously and faithfully to discharge all the duties of their office; not only to feed and provide for the temporal wants of their children, servants, subjects, etc., but especially to train them to the honor and praise of God. Therefore, think not, you parents, that the parental office is a matter of your pleasure and whim, but remember that God has strictly commanded it and entrusted it to you, and that for the discharge of its duties you must give an account.

The Fifth Commandment: "You shall not kill."[9]

We have thus far explained both the spiritual and civil governments, the exercise of divine and parental authority and obedience. In this commandment, however, we go out of our homes, among our neighbors, in order to learn how each one should conduct himself toward his fellow man. Hence in this commandment neither God nor magistrates are mentioned, nor does it take from them the power they have to put to death. For God has delegated to civil magistrates in place of parents the right to punish evil-doers. Therefore, what is forbidden here is forbidden an individual to do to his fellow man and is not forbidden the civil government.

This commandment is simple enough. We hear it explained in the Gospel text of Matthew 5:21. There Christ interprets it in brief to be the prohibition of murder, either by the hand or by word, or by thought of the heart; by sign or gesture, by help or counsel. It forbids anger, except—as said before—to those who act in the place of God—in the capacity of parental or civil authority. Anger and reproof and punishment are the prerogatives of God and his representatives, to be exercised upon those who transgress this and other commandments.

The occasion and need of this commandment is the wickedness of the world and the wretchedness of this life. God, in the knowledge of these, placed the commandments

[9] Exod. 20:13, Deut. 5:17.

as a defense of godly people against the wicked. In the case of this commandment, as in every other, there are various temptations to transgress. We must live among many people of evil intent toward us, giving us reason to be their enemies. In response to their enmity, anger, pain, and revenge arise in our own hearts. Evil speech ensues between us and our enemies, followed by blows resulting in calamity and death. To forestall such an issue, God, as a loving father, by this commandment intervenes and settles the quarrel for the safety of all. Briefly, God's purpose here is to have all persons protected, set free and enabled to live peaceable lives in the presence of the injustice and violence of all men. This commandment is likewise a wall, a fortress of defense, about our neighbor to protect him in his liberty and to guard him from bodily harm and suffering.

Where murder is forbidden, there also is forbidden everything that may lead to murder. Nature implants the spirit of revenge within each of us, and it is a common thing that no one willingly suffers injury from another. God's purpose is to remove this root and fountain of bitterness. God teaches us a calmness of spirit for anger, and a heart of patience and gentleness toward our enemies, who would arouse our wrath.

Not only he who directly does evil breaks this commandment, but also he who unnecessarily omits a service to his neighbor which he might render by anticipating and restraining, and by protecting and rescuing his fellow man from bodily harm and suffering. The chief design of God is that we permit no injury to befall any person, but that we show to everyone all kindness and love. And this kindness is directed especially toward our enemies.

The Sixth Commandment: "You shall not commit adultery."[10]

Explicit injunction is here given against injury [to the neighbor] by the disgrace of his wife. Adultery is particularly mentioned, because among the Jewish people marriage was obligatory. Young people were advised to marry at the

[10] Exod. 20:14, Deut. 5:18.

earliest age possible. Virginity was not particularly commended; harlots and libertines were never tolerated. There was no form of unchastity more common than that of the breaking of the marriage vow. But since there is among us such a shameful and vile mixture of all forms of vice and lewdness, this commandment is directed against every form of unchastity, under any name. Not only the actual deed is forbidden, but also every prompting and incentive to it. Heart, lips, and the whole body must be chaste and give no occasion, no help or suggestion to unchastity. Further, we are to restrain, protect, and rescue where there is need. We are to assist our neighbors to maintain their honor. In brief, the requirement of this commandment is chastity for one's self and the endeavor to secure it for the neighbor.

But since particular attention is here called to the married state, let us carefully note, first, how God especially honors and commends wedded life, since he confirms and protects it with a special command. Hence he requires us to honor, guard, and observe it as a divine and blessed estate. Significantly he established it as the first of all institutions, and with it in view he did not create man and woman alike. God's purpose, as is plain, was not that they should live a life of wickedness, but that they might be true to each other, beget children, and nourish and rear them to his glory. Therefore God blessed this institution above all others and made everything on earth serve and spring from it, so that it might be well and amply provided for. It is not an exceptional estate but the most universal and the noblest, pervading all Christendom, yea, extending through the whole world.

Remember that marriage is not only an honorable but also a necessary estate, earnestly commanded by God, so that in general men and women of all conditions, created for it, should be found in it. Yet there are some exceptions, although few, whom God has especially exempted, either because they are unfit for wedded life or because, by reason of extraordinary gifts, they have become free to live chaste lives unmarried. To unaided human nature, as God created it, chastity apart from matrimony is an impossibility. For flesh and blood remain flesh and blood, and the natural inclination and excitement run their course without let or hindrance, as everyone's observation and experience testify. Therefore that man might more easily keep his evil lust in bounds, God commanded marriage, that each may have his proper portion and be satisfied; although God's grace is still needed for the heart to be pure.

This commandment requires man not only to live chaste in act, word, and thought in his station, and especially in his married life, but also to love and appreciate the consort God has given him. For love and harmony between husband and wife are above all things essential to conjugal chastity. Heart confidence and perfect fidelity must obtain. They are of chief importance, for thereby is created love and the desire for chastity. From such a condition chastity always follows spontaneously, without commandment.

> *The Seventh Commandment:* "You shall not steal."[11]

Next to our own persons and our wedded companions, our temporal treasures are the dearest to us. God designs protection for them also. He has commanded that no one damage or curtail the possessions of his neighbor. "To steal" signifies nothing else than to obtain another's property by unjust means. It briefly embraces every method in all lines of business by which advantage is taken of a neighbor's disadvantage. Stealing is a widespread, universal vice.

It is stealing when a man-servant or a maid-servant is unfaithful in duty and does, or permits, any injury which could easily have been avoided; or when he or she is otherwise indifferent and careless through laziness, negligence, or wickedness—for I do not speak of taking advantage unintentionally or through oversight. I may say the same of mechanics, workmen, and day-laborers, all of whom act wantonly, knowing not how to cheat their employers enough. In like manner dishonesty is rampant and in full force at the market and in

[11] Exod. 20:15, Deut. 5:19.

every-day business. In barter the one deceives the other with inferior goods, false measures, unjust weights, counterfeit money, dexterous tricks, clever financiering, and plausible tales. Who can mention all the species of fraud? In short thievery is a universal art, the largest guild on earth. Viewing the world in all its vocations, it is a universal den of thieves. Therefore there are also men whom you may call gentlemen-robbers, land-grabbers, and road-agents, quite above the safe-robber or pilferer of petty cash. These occupy seats of honor, are styled great lords and honorable, pious citizens, and under the cloak of honesty they rob and steal. Yea, we might well let the lesser individual thieves alone if we could only arrest the great, powerful arch-thieves.

Let everyone know, then, that he is under obligation, at the risk of incurring God's displeasure, not to harm his neighbor nor take advantage of him in any business transaction. But more than that he is faithfully to protect his neighbor's property and further his interests, especially if he takes remuneration for doing so. He who wilfully disregards God's commandment in respect of these things may persist in his course, but he shall not escape God's wrathful punishment. Although he may practice his defiance and arrogance for a long time, eventually he shall be a vagabond and a beggar and suffer all calamity and misfortune. We have daily evidence that nothing stolen or dishonestly acquired contributes to prosperity. But we do not heed the lesson; we go on unconcerned. Then God is compelled to punish us and teach us ethics in a different way. He permits one civil tax after another to be levied upon us, or a troop of soldiers is quartered upon us, who instantly empty our purses and safes. In brief, however much you steal, twice as much will be stolen from you. For since everyone robs and steals from others, God is a master in punishing one thief by means of another.

To you who show your contempt for us, defrauding and robbing, we will submit. We will endure your insolence and forgive, as the Lord's Prayer teaches. We know that the righteous shall not want, and that the greatest injury you do is to yourselves. But beware how you deal with the poor.

When there comes to you one who must live on the pittance of his daily wage, and you inhumanly exact from and turn away from him who should be the object of your pity, he will go away and in his sorrow and misery, because he can cry to none other for help, will cry to heaven. That appeal of distress will be no light matter. It will be with power beyond you and all the world to sustain. It will reach God, who watches over hearts sorrowful and distressed, and he will avenge this their wrong. If you disregard that cry and defy God, consider whose wrath you have provoked. Then if success is yours, before all the world you may pronounce God and me liars.

> *The Eighth Commandment:* "You shall not bear false witness against your neighbor."[12]

God would guard the honor and character of our neighbor as he guards his other possessions. The first and most evident import of the command is with reference to legal injustice—in the instance of a poor and innocent one being wronged by false evidence for the purpose of punishment in person, possession, or good name. The first requirement of this commandment, then, is that each shall assist his neighbor in maintaining his rights. He must not permit the violation of those rights; rather must he further their security as God approves, be he judge or witness, let the consequences be as they may. Here is presented the end to which jurists should strive to attain—perfect justice in every case. Right is to be always right, not perverted, concealed, or silenced for the sake of gain, honor, or power. This is one meaning of the commandment and the most evident—one which pertains to a court of justice.

All use of the tongue to the injury or offense of our neighbor is forbidden. For false witness is clearly a sin of the tongue. That which is done with the tongue to the injury of our fellow-men, God therefore forbids. It may be accomplished by the erroneous doctrines and blasphemies of false teaching; by the injustice of corrupt judges and wit-

[12] Exod. 20:16, Deut. 5:20.

nesses; or by falsehood and evil words of others than those in authority. Particularly is included that despicable vice, slanderous gossip, with which Satan corrupts us. It is a common vice of human nature, that one would rather hear evil than good of his neighbor. Evil as we are ourselves, we cannot tolerate that it be spoken of us; we want the universal commendation of the world. Yet we are unwilling that only good should be said of others. Wherefore, to avoid sin of the tongue, we must heed the fact that public judgment and reproof of one's neighbor is forbidden, even when one has seen the sin, unless he has authority to judge and reprove. There is a vast difference between judging sin and having knowledge of it. Knowledge of sin does not entail the right to judge it. Though I hear and see my neighbor's sin, I am not commanded to report it. If I recklessly pass sentence upon him, I commit a greater sin than he. If you dare not prefer charges before the appointed authorities and be responsible, keep silence. Every report, that cannot be legally proven, is false witness. That which is not publicly substantiated, no one shall publish as truth. In brief, that which is secret should be allowed to remain so or be privately reproved.

In short, then, we are not in any wise to speak evil of our neighbor. Exception is made in the case of civil authority, pastors, and parents; the commandment must not be understood as permitting evil to go unreproved. So the fifth commandment forbids us to do bodily injury to any, but excepts the executioner. By virtue of his office, he does naught to his neighbor but bodily harm; yet without sin, because his office is instituted by God, who, in the first commandment, reserves to himself the right of punishment. No one has a right of himself to condemn another; but they who, having authority by virtue of office, fail to fulfill their duty, sin as does he who presumes upon authority. It is necessary that evil be charged, that investigation and testimony be employed. So civil authorities, parents, close relatives and friends are under mutual obligation to reprove sin when it is necessary and productive of good.

> *The Ninth and Tenth Commandments:* "You shall not covet your neighbor's house. You shall not covet your neighbor's wife, nor his man-servant, nor his maid-servant, or his ox, or his ass, or anything that is your neighbor's."[13]

The seventh commandment forbids us to appropriate or withhold the property of another when we have no right to do so. Here we are forbidden to deprive our neighbor of anything of his own even when, in the eyes of the world, we could honorably do it, without accusation or blame for fraudulent dealing.

Such is human nature that no one of us desires the other to possess as much as himself, and each secures as much as he can, without regard to his neighbor's interests. Yet we want to be thought upright. We dress ourselves up to conceal our roguery. We seek and invent ingenious devices and clever frauds, such as are now daily contrived with cunning skill, under the guise of justice. We even boast of our roguery with arrogance and want it called shrewdness and foresight instead of roguery. This last commandment, then, is not addressed to those whom even the world recognizes as knaves, but to those most righteous, to such as wish to be commended as honest and upright. Who is ingenious enough to imagine all the various methods by which advantage may be taken under the appearance of fair dealing?

Let us understand the commandment to be particularly directed against envy and wretched avarice, God's purpose being to remove the cause and source of our injuries to our neighbor. In plain words, therefore, he expresses it: "You shall not covet," etc. For, above all, he would have our hearts pure, although so long as we live upon earth we shall not fully succeed in this.

Conclusion to the Ten Commandments. Thus we have in the Ten Commandments a summary of divine teaching. They tell us what we are to do to make our lives pleasing to God. They show us the true fountain from which, and the

[13] Exod. 20:17, Deut. 5:21.

true channel in which, all good works must flow. No deed, no conduct can be good and pleasing to God, however worthy or precious it be in the eyes of the world, unless it accord with the Ten Commandments. Now let us see what our noted saints find to boast in their holy orders and the great and difficult tasks they have invented for themselves, at the same time neglecting the commandments as if they were too trivial or had long ago been fulfilled. My opinion is that we shall have our hands full in keeping these commandments—in practicing gentleness, patience, love towards our enemies, chastity, kindness and whatever other virtues they may include. Is it not detestable presumption in those desperate saints to try to find a higher and better life or estate than the commandments teach? They pretend—as has been said—that the life taught in the commandments is a simple life, for common men, but that theirs is for saints and perfect men! Poor, blind people! they do not see that no one can perfectly observe even so much as one of the Ten Commandments; but the Creed and the Lord's Prayer must help us. Through them we must seek and beseech the grace of obedience, and receive it continually. The boastings of these saints, then, is much the same as if I were to boast: I have not a dime with which to pay, but I venture to make myself responsible for the payment of ten dollars without fail.

On the Creed

The Creed teaches a very different lesson from the Ten Commandments. The latter teach us what we must do, but the Creed teaches us what God does for us and what he gives us. The Ten Commandments are written in the hearts of all men, but no mere human wisdom can comprehend the Creed. It must be taught by the Holy Spirit alone. The law of the commandments does not make us Christians, for God's wrath and displeasure abides upon us because we cannot fulfill his demands. But the Creed brings us full mercy, sanctifies us and makes us acceptable to God.

Through this knowledge we learn to love all God's commandments, for we see that he freely bestows himself upon us, with all that he has, to help us and guide us in keeping the Ten Commandments. The Father gives us all created things; Christ all his works; and the Holy Spirit, all his gifts.

On the Lord's Prayer

Since no human being can keep the Ten Commandments perfectly, though he have made a beginning in believing, and since we must fight against the devil and all his powers, the world and our own flesh, nothing is so necessary as that we should constantly seek the ear of God, invoking him and praying him to give us faith and obedience to the Ten Commandments, to sustain and increase our faith and remove all that opposes and hinders us in this way. That we may know what and how to pray, our Lord Jesus Christ has himself taught us, giving us the very form and words.

Now we will discuss the Lord's Prayer. Here, in seven articles or petitions, are comprehended in connected order all the needs that continually beset us, each of which is so pressing as to become a life-long object of prayer.

Hallowed be thy name. In this petition we pray for just that which God required in the second commandment. Note the great need of such a prayer. Since we see that the world is filled with sects and false teachers, and they all use the holy name as a cover and pretense for their devilish doctrines, we ought constantly to cry unto God against all who preach and believe falsely. Likewise, we need to pray for ourselves, who while we have God's Word, are ungrateful for it and do not live according to it as we should.

Thy Kingdom come. What is the kingdom of God? Simply what we learned in the Creed—that God sent his Son, Jesus Christ our Lord, into the world to redeem and deliver us from the devil's power and to bring us to himself and reign over us a king of righteousness, of life and salvation, defending us from sin, death, and an evil conscience. And further that God gave us his Holy Spirit to teach us through his holy Word, and by his power to enlighten and strengthen us in faith. We pray here then that all this may be realized by us. The kingdom of God comes to us in two different ways: first, in time through the Word and faith; secondly, it shall be revealed in eternity. We pray that it may come to those who are not yet therein, and also that in us who have received the same it may daily increase and remain ours in the life eternal.

Thy will be done, as in heaven, so on earth. We who would be Christians must not fail to calculate upon having the devil with all his angels, as well as the world for our enemies, who will prepare all kinds of sorrow and misfortune for us. For wherever God's Word is preached, is accepted or believed, and bears fruit, there the dear holy cross of persecuting will not be wanting. Let no one think that he will live in peace; rather that he must risk all he has upon earth—possessions, honor, home and estate, wife and child, body and life. Now this causes sorrow to our flesh and the old Adam; for it means that we must continue steadfast and suffer with patience whatever may befall us, and that we must surrender what is taken from us. Hence it is necessary in this as in every other case that we pray without ceasing: Thy will be done, dear Father, and not the will of the devil or of our enemies, nor of those who would persecute and destroy thy Word, or prevent thy kingdom from coming; and grant that all we have to suffer because of it may be borne with patience and be overcome, thus saving our poor flesh from yielding or falling through weakness or indolence.

Give us this day our daily bread. This petition includes all that belongs to our temporal life, since only for its sake we need daily bread. Now, our life requires not only food, clothing and other necessities, but also concord and peace in our daily business—in short a sound regulation of all domestic and civil or political affairs. For where these two relations are not maintained under the right conditions life itself cannot be supported. And it is indeed most necessary to pray for our civil authorities and government, for chiefly through them God provides for our daily bread and every comfort of life. Although we receive from God all good things in abundance, yet we are unable to retain any of them or enjoy them in safety and happiness unless he gives us a stable and peaceful government.

And forgive us our debts as we also have forgiven our debtors. This petition refers to the poverty and wretchedness of our lives. Although we have God's Word and believe and do God's will and submit to it, and though we are nourished by God's gifts and blessings, our lives are not free from sin. We daily stumble and transgress, because we live in a world of people who sorely vex us and give occasion for impatience, anger, revenge and the like. Besides, the devil is after us; he attacks on all sides and so it is not possible always to stand firm in such a constant conflict. Hence there is a great need to pray and cry: Dear Father, forgive us our debts. Not that he does not forgive sins without our prayers and before we pray, for he gave us the Gospel in which there is nothing but forgiveness, before we prayed for it or ever thought of it. But the point here is for us to recognize and accept this forgiveness. For the flesh in which we daily live is so constituted that it neither trusts nor believes in God, and is ever stirred by evil lusts and wicked desires, causing us to sin daily in word and deed by omission and commission. Thus our consciences become restless, fear God's wrath and displeasure, and lose the comfort and confidence the Gospel inspires; therefore it is necessary for us to reassure our consciences by constantly turning to this petition for comfort. God has promised us assurance of complete forgiveness and remission of sins; yet only so far as we forgive our neighbor. If you do not forgive, think not that God will forgive you, but if you forgive, you have in that forgiveness the comfort and assurance that you are pardoned in heaven. Not because you forgave others; for God forgives freely and gratuitously; but that you may be strengthened and assured by such earnest of forgiveness.

And lead us not into temptation. Although we have obtained forgiveness and a good conscience and are wholly absolved, yet such is life that one stands today and falls to-morrow. We dwell in the flesh and the old Adam is always astir in us. Then comes the world to offend and drive us to anger and impatience. In addition to these comes the devil, who especially occupies himself with things pertaining to the conscience and spiritual matters. Being, throughout this troublous life, harassed, hounded, and driven from all sides, we are constrained every hour to plead and to cry that God may not permit us to become indolent and weary, and to relapse into sin, disgrace and unbelief.

But deliver us from evil. In the Greek text this petition reads, Deliver or preserve us from the evil one, or the malicious one. Apparently it refers to the devil as the sum of all evil. Therefore, we sum it all up and say: Dear Father, help us that we may be free from all this misery. The short petition includes all the evil we experience in the devil's kingdom—poverty, shame, death; in short, all wretched misery and heartache, of which there is an infinite amount on earth. The devil, because he is not only a liar but a murderer unceasingly seeks to take our lives and wreaks his anger on us. If God did not support us we would not be secure before him one hour. This petition God has placed last; because if we are to be guarded and freed from all evil, his name must first be hallowed in us, his kingdom be in us and his will be done by us. Then he will finally preserve us from sin and shame and from everything else that harms or injures.

FURTHER READINGS

Primary Sources

ANDERSON, CHARLES S. (ed.). *Readings in Luther for Laymen.* Minneapolis: Augsburg Publishing House, 1967.

LUTHER, MARTIN. *Selected Writings.* 4 vols. Edited by THEODORE TOPPART. Philadelphia: Fortress Press, 1967.

———. *Selections From His Writings.* Edited by JOHN DILLENBERGER. Chicago: Quadrangle Books, 1961.

———. *Three Treatises.* Philadelphia: Muhlenberg Press, 1947.

KERR, H. T. *A Compend of Luther's Theology.* Philadelphia: Westminster Press, 1943.

Secondary Sources

BAINTON, ROLAND. *Here I Stand: A Life of Martin Luther.* Nashville: Abingdon Press, 1950.

FORELL, GEORGE W. *Faith Active in Love.* New York: American Press, 1954.

WATSON, PHILIP S. *Let God Be God! An Interpretation of the Theology of Martin Luther.* Philadelphia: Muhlenberg Press, 1949.

WINGREN, GUSTAV. *Luther on Vocation.* Philadelphia: Muhlenberg Press, 1957.

Chapter 9

JOHN CALVIN

As Luther was the prophetic genius of the Reformation so John Calvin (1509-64) was its greatest organizer. He systematized and related to concrete action the ideas that Luther had propounded and at the same time so intensified some of them that the churches which followed his leadership developed a character distinctively different from the Lutheran churches, though the close kinship of the two wings of the Reformation remains evident.

The son of an influential lawyer and man of affairs in Picardy, Calvin studied at the universities of Paris, Orleans, and Bourges. Abandoning his first intention to prepare for a career in the church, he turned to the study of civil law which he pursued so eagerly and effectively that his legal training left a decided impress on all his later work. A second important factor in his education was the influence of various French humanists and the classical studies to which they directed him. As a humanist he published his first book, a commentary on Seneca's *De Clementia*, and to these studies he was indebted for the development of a remarkable literary style and for a deep appreciation of classical philosophy, science, and art. The humanist interest manifest in his writings is often overlooked by those who approach them with preconceived notions about the exclusiveness of his Biblicism. To be sure, both legal training and classical studies were ultimately overshadowed by the influence on his mind of that inquiry into the Scriptures to which he was directed by teachers and friends who were participating in the new religious movement, the Reformation. Under these influences and in consequence of a profound intellectual and emotional conversion he allied himself with the reform party.

Fleeing persecution in France, Calvin joined the native and emigré Protestants who were making the cities of Switzerland centers of the new movement. At Basel, in 1536, he wrote and published the first version of his highly influential *Institutes of the Christian Religion.* Revised many times and translated into many languages, it became for a large part of Western Christendom the standard statement of Christian faith and practice, next to the Scriptures. In the same year Calvin joined the fiery Farel at Geneva as one of the ministers in a city which had combined political with religious reform. Having achieved independence from its feudal lord, a prince-bishop, it had established self-rule through its city council and undertaken to reform and reorganize its churches. Calvin's insistence on the right of the church to govern its own affairs, in a free city-state no less than in a kingdom, led to conflicts and to his banishment in 1538. Three years later, however, the council begged him to return; reluctantly he abandoned his scholarly and pastoral pursuits to assume the direction of the church in Geneva.

During the ensuing twenty-three years he gave to the city a powerful and dynamic leadership, so that it became the spiritual capital of a large part of Protestant Europe. His opponents often regarded him as ruthless; his allies found him impregnable. His influence on political as well as religious affairs was so great that he has often been called a dictator, while Geneva has been styled a "theocracy," in the wholly un-Calvinist and un-Protestant sense of that word as meaning rule by self-constituted representatives of God. Moreover, the rigorous supervision of morals that prevailed in Geneva and the severity with which heresy as well as crime was punished have been laid at Calvin's door. These judgments are all subject to debate. Rigorousness and severity were part of the temper of the time and not peculiarly characteristic of Geneva. The constant conflicts in which Calvin was involved with other authorities in the city indicate that he was far from being a dictator. As for "theocracy" —Geneva, like other Calvinistically organized communities, was a society which, recognizing the sovereignty of God alone, had a dual organization in church and state. These were independent of each other in theory and largely in practice, but each recognized its responsibility, in its own sphere and for the welfare of all the people, to the one Lord. Tensions are the inevitable accompaniments of such separation and cooperation of church and state in one community. In dealing with them Calvin was undoubtedly more interested in maintaining the independence of the church from the state than vice versa, and in proclaiming the truth of revelation than in upholding the supremacy of natural or common law in politics; but there is little indication that in theory or in practice he sought control of the state by the church. To be sure, their understanding of Christian duty led him and his followers to take a very active interest in civic affairs, the enforcement of prevailing moral standards, the suppression of heresy, the establishment of schools, public health measures, and the promotion of economic welfare. But the Genevan ideal was government by God, not by church or clergy or even Bible.

The Encounter of God and Man

Calvin's strongly ethical theology centers in the principle of "justification by faith" or in the conviction that the God who in holiness and righteousness demands man's complete obedience yet is wholly benevolent toward his elect in their sinfulness, forgiving them their transgressions, healing their deep, spiritual disease, and giving them the great gift of eternal life. A modern philosopher has said that religion "runs through three stages, if it evolves to its final satisfaction. It is transition from God the void to God the enemy, and from God the enemy to God the companion."[1] For Calvin as for Luther the second of these transitions was the

[1] A. N. Whitehead, *Religion in the Making* (New York: The Macmillan Co., 1926), p. 16 f.

focal point. What Jesus Christ has done in history and what he accomplishes in each individual believer when the latter is religiously and morally, intellectually and emotionally, started on a new course is to change man's relation to God. "The principal hinge on which faith turns is this," wrote Calvin, "that we must not suppose that any promises of mercy which the Lord offers are only true out of us, and not at all in us: We should rather make them ours by inwardly embracing them. He only is a true believer who, firmly persuaded that God is reconciled, and is a kind Father to him, hopes everything from his kindness."[2] What distinguishes Calvin's treatment of this common theme of the Reformation is the way in which he sets it in the context of the themes of human depravity, divine sovereignty, and the activity of the redeemed, or, to use Whitehead's formula, between the themes of divine-human animosity and divine-human companionship.

When man regards himself in the light of Scriptures, or when in inner companionship with Christ he remembers what he was without Christ, he notes two things—that God was against him and that he was against God. God was against him as the power which he could not resist, calling him into being and destining him to die; giving him a definite constitution; placing him in a world with a given, unavoidable structure and into a history not subject to man's control; limiting his liberty at every point. God was against him as the righteousness which, through the nature of things, the conscience and the declaration of the moral law, required absolute obedience. On the other hand, man was against God; for though by nature he was a dependent being, he willed to be independent; though by nature he could not live except by loving God above all, he willed to prefer himself to God; though he lived in the kingdom of God, he willed to set up an independent and seceding state. Hence arose the inner contradiction in the human situation. Not only is there animosity between God and man, but man is

[2] John Calvin, *Institutes of the Christian Religion,* trans. Henry Beveridge (2 vols.; London: James Clarke & Co., 1949), Bk. III, ch. 2, sec. 16.

divided against himself. He profoundly distrusts his Maker and Sovereign and at the same time lives in constant fear of God's wrath. His ethics is at the same time an ethics of self-love and of fear. It may be the pleasure-seeking ethics of those who know their time is short and must "gather roses while they may," or it may be virtue-seeking on the part of those who want to save themselves and appease the divine wrath. In any case it is the ethics of despair as well as of self-love. Further consequences of egoism and fear are the evident forms of vice, transgressions of social laws, warfare, and every kind of human inhumanity to man; for the revolt against the kingdom of God involves man in virtual anarchy. Calvin does not believe or say that man in this depravity can do nothing worthwhile. Total depravity does not mean that God has left no goodness to man, but that the total man —in reason, will, religion, politics, etc.—is infected with the corruption. Despite the depravity many excellent gifts are left to man so that he is enabled to regulate the community life, to pursue arts and sciences, to direct thought into logical channels, to develop medicine and law. But so long as man knows the Sovereign power over life and death as the enemy, he carries on all these activities in the context of fear, self-love, and despair.

Calvin's sense of divine sovereignty is almost unmatched in Christian literature outside the pages of Scriptures. By and large, Calvin employs, as does the Bible, political and social images and concepts in presenting this conviction about the absoluteness of God: The world is his kingdom; it is subject in all its activities to his laws; everything that happens in it is known to him and subject to his overruling action; his wisdom and power enable him to use even the actions of his enemies for the sake of achieving his good ends. Occasionally Calvin employs the more modern but less appropriate ideas and symbols of machine and designer in setting forth his sense of the absoluteness of God. In so far as he does so he opens the way to a fatalistic interpretation of the situation. But his fundamental conception of God's absoluteness is of a personal and social character, though the personal nature of God is never allowed to imply limitation of power or presence, and the social nature of the kingdom is never permitted to imply that all the self-wills of the creatures cooperate according to a preordained harmony. The sovereignty of God is being exercised in a world in which there is rebellion, but in which those who are reconciled to him become free citizens, happily consenting to the laws and cooperating to increase the glory of the kingdom.

Calvin understands very clearly what is obscured in some Christian thinkers: that the reconciliation of man to God through the work of Jesus Christ does not result in an automatic, effortless change of man's whole moral and spiritual nature. It is rather the beginning of a new and intense activity. The Christian life, as Calvin sees it, is a continuous and hard struggle to realize in every sphere of existence the consequences of the new beginning. But, since this life is based on the knowledge of the benevolence of the absolutely powerful God and on the sure hope of eternal joy, it is the moral warfare of men who are certain of victory no matter how difficult and painful the battles that must still be fought. As the life of those who are still in enmity against God must be defeatist, in its attitude toward internal sin, social evil, and death, so the life of those who know the love of the righteous and sovereign God is sustained by a great assurance. This sense of assurance came to be one of the fundamental characteristics of the Calvinist and Puritan movements. It was closely united with intense moral effort. The God whose love assures salvation is the righteous God who demands integrity and holiness; forgiveness is the beginning of the reconstruction of life; deliverance from evil is deliverance from hopelessness in the presence of evil and liberation to arduous warfare against it, within the soul and in the world.

Calvin's theology and ethics have deeply influenced the social ideas and institutions of Europe and America, though the extent and nature of that influence remain the subject of much study and debate. In economics his development of the Protestant idea of vocation and his so-called "intra-worldly asceticism" have been regarded as historically very important. With Luther, but in a more militant spirit, he taught every believer to regard his particular work in the world, however humble or exalted in popular regard, however poorly or richly rewarded, as a "station" or a post to which God had assigned him in the warfare against sin and death. Put in other terms, it was a training school of the spirit and a trusteeship for which account would need to be given at the last day. This led, on the one hand, to a sense of the equality and dignity of all work and, on the other, to the release of energies which had been held in check by the sense of inferiority that the monastic doctrine of the more perfect religious life had fostered among those in "secular" walks. With this doctrine of vocation Calvin combined that austere demand for accepting hardship, for restraining the love of ease and luxury, for living laboriously, which later writers have dubbed "intra-worldly asceticism" in distinction from the asceticism of the monastery.

In the political realm Calvin took account, as Luther had done, of the necessity of government because men were wicked and needed restraint. But he also noted that government was a necessity for social, free, and rational men who could not live together without leadership and explicit agreements, "its use among men being not less than that of bread and water, light and air, while its dignity is much more excellent." He believed that all civil powers needed to be limited, because human sinfulness and error were thus best checked; that neither the will of a prince nor of the people was entitled to supremacy, since both were subject to God; that the will of God which formed the ultimate constitution of all civil governments was known to men through both conscience and revelation. Hence for all the strong emphasis on the duty of obedience to constituted authorities, Calvin and Calvinism gave powerful impetus to the development of constitutional and parliamentary government. The ideas expressed at the end of the *Institutes*, on the duties of the three estates in dealing with tyrants and on the necessity of obeying God rather than men, were developed by John Knox and by the French Huguenots into powerful arguments for the defense of liberty against tyrants.[3]

SOURCES

From

JOHN CALVIN: INSTITUTES OF THE CHRISTIAN RELIGION[4]

On Man's Nature

We cannot clearly and properly know God unless the knowledge of ourselves be added. This knowledge is twofold—relating, first, to the condition in which we were at first created; and, secondly, to our condition such at it began to be immediately after Adam's fall. Certainly, before we descend to the miserable condition into which man has fallen, it is of importance to consider what he was at first For there is need of caution, lest we attend only to the natural ills of man, and thereby seem to ascribe them to the Author of nature.

First, it is to be observed, that when he was formed out of the dust of the ground a curb was laid on his pride. God not only having deigned to animate a vessel of clay, but to make it the habitation of an immortal spirit, Adam might well glory in the great liberality of his Maker. Moreover, there can be no question that man consists of a body and a soul: meaning by soul, an immortal though created essence, which is his nobler part. It is true indeed, men cleaving too much to the earth are dull of apprehension, nay, being alienated from the Father of Lights, are so immersed in darkness

[3] Cf. John Knox, "Appellation," *Works,* ed. D. Laing, Vol. IV (Edinburgh: 1846-1864); also *Vindiciae Contra Tyrannos* (attributed to Hubert Languet), trans. as *A Defense of Liberty Against Tyrants,* with an Introduction by H. J. Laski (London: G. Bell & Sons, 1924).

[4] All selections in this chapter are from John Calvin's *Institutes of the Christian Religion,* trans. Henry Beveridge (2 vols.; London: James Clarke & Co., 1949).

as to imagine that they will not survive the grave; still the light is not so completely quenched in darkness that all sense of immortality is lost. Conscience, which, distinguishing between good and evil, responds to the judgment of God, is an undoubted sign of an immortal spirit. The body cannot be affected by any fear of spiritual punishment. This is competent only to the soul, which must therefore be endued with essence. Then the mere knowledge of a God sufficiently proves that souls which rise higher than the world must be immortal. In fine, while the many noble faculties with which the human mind is endued proclaim that something divine is engraven on it, they are so many evidences of an immortal essence. The swiftness with which the human mind glances from heaven to earth, scans the secrets of nature, and, after it has embraced all ages, with intellect and memory digests each in its proper order, and reads the future in the past, clearly demonstrates that there lurks in man a something separated from the body. We have intellect by which we are able to conceive of the invisible God and angels—a thing of which body is altogether incapable. We have ideas of rectitude, justice and honesty—ideas which the bodily senses cannot reach. The seat of these ideas must therefore be a spirit. Let us hold, for the purpose of the present work, that the soul consists of two parts, the intellect and the will. God has provided the soul of man with intellect, by which he might discern good from evil, just from unjust, and might know what to follow or to shun, reason going before with her lamp. To this he has conjoined the will, to which choice belongs. Man excelled in these noble endowments in his primitive condition, when reason, intelligence, prudence, and judgment, not only sufficed for the government of his earthly life, but also enabled him to rise up to God and eternal happiness. In this upright state, man possessed freedom of will, by which, if he chose, he was able to attain eternal life.[5]

It is not difficult to infer in what way Adam provoked the wrath of God. Augustine, indeed, is not far from the mark when he says, that pride was the beginning of all evil. A

[5] *Ibid.*, Bk. I, chap. xv, pars. 1, 2, 7, 8.

further definition, however, must be derived from the kind of temptation which Moses describes. When, by the subtlety of the devil, the woman faithlessly abandoned the command of God, her fall obviously had its origin in disobedience. Hence infidelity was at the root of the revolt. From infidelity, again, sprang ambition and pride, together with ingratitude; because Adam, by longing for more than was allotted him, manifested contempt for the great liberality with which God had enriched him. In fine, infidelity opened the door to ambition, and ambition was the parent of rebellion, man casting off the fear of God, and giving free vent to his lust. As Adam's spiritual life would have consisted in remaining united and bound to his Maker, so estrangement from him was the death of his soul. Nor is it strange that he who perverted the whole order of nature in heaven and earth deteriorated his race by his revolt. This is the hereditary corruption to which early Christian writers gave the name of Original Sin. Original sin may be defined as a hereditary corruption and depravity of our nature, extending to all parts of the soul, which first makes us obnoxious to the wrath of God and then produces in us works which in Scriptures are termed works of the flesh.[6]

I feel pleased with the well-known saying that man's natural gifts were corrupted by sin, and his supernatural gifts withdrawn. Man, when he withdrew his allegiance to God, was deprived of the spiritual gifts by which he had been raised to the hope of eternal salvation. Among these are faith, love to God, charity towards our neighbor, the study of righteousness and holiness. Soundness of mind and integrity of heart were, at the same time, withdrawn, and it is this which constitutes the corruption of natural gifts. For although there is still some residue of intelligence and judgment as well as will, we cannot call a mind sound and entire which is both weak and immersed in darkness. To charge the intellect with perpetual blindness, so as to leave it no intelligence of any description whatever, is repugnant not

[6] *Ibid.*, Bk. II, chap. i, pars. 4, 5. 8.

only to the Word of God, but to common experience. We have one kind of intelligence of earthly things and another of heavenly things. To the former belong matters of policy and economy, all mechanical arts and liberal studies. To the latter belong the knowledge of God and of his will, and the means of framing the life in accordance with them. As to the former, the view to be taken is this: Since man is by nature a social animal, he is disposed, from natural instinct, to cherish and preserve society; and accordingly we see that all men have impressions of civil order and honesty. Hence it is that every individual understands how human societies must be regulated by laws, and also is able to comprehend the principles of those laws. Hence the universal agreement in regard to such subjects, both among nations and individuals, the seeds of them being implanted in the breasts of all without a teacher or lawgiver. While men dispute with each other as to particular enactments, their ideas of equity agree in substance. And this is ample proof, that in regard to the constitution of the present life, no man is devoid of the light of reason. Next come manual and liberal arts, in learning which, as all have some degree of aptitude, the full force of human acuteness is displayed. In reading profane authors the admirable light of truth displayed in them should remind us that the human mind, however much fallen and perverted from its original integrity, is still adorned and invested with admirable gifts from its Creator.[7]

We must now explain what the power of human reason is, in regard to the kingdom of God, and spiritual discernment, which consists chiefly of three things—the knowledge of God, the knowledge of his paternal favor towards us, which constitutes our salvation, and the method of regulating our conduct in accordance with the Divine Law. With regard to the former two, but more properly the second, men otherwise the most ingenious are blinder than moles. In the writings of philosophers we meet occasionally with shrewd and apposite remarks on the nature of God.

[7] *Ibid.,* Bk. II, chap. ii, pars. 12, 13, 14.

Still, though seeing, they saw not. Not one of them even made the least approach to that assurance of the divine favor, without which the mind of man must ever remain a mere chaos of confusion. It remains to consider the third branch of the knowledge of spiritual things, viz., the method of properly regulating the conduct. This is correctly termed the knowledge of the works of righteousness, a branch in which the human mind seems to have somewhat more discernment than in the former two. When you hear of an universal judgment in man distinguishing between good and evil, you must not suppose that this judgment is, in every respect, sound and entire. If we would test our reason by the Divine Law, which is a perfect standard of righteousness, we should find how blind it is in many respects. It certainly attains not to the principles in the First Table, such as trust in God, the ascription to him of all praise in virtue and righteousness, the invocation of his name, and the true observance of his day of rest. As to the precepts of the Second Table, there is considerably more knowledge of them, inasmuch as they are more closely connected with the preservation of civil society. Even here, however, there is something defective. The revenge of injuries is not regarded by philosophers as a vice. But the Lord, condemning this too lofty spirit, prescribes to his people that patience which mankind deem infamous. In regard to the general observance of the law, concupiscence altogether escapes our animadversion. For the natural man cannot bear to recognize diseases in his lusts. The light of nature is stifled sooner than take the first step into this profound abyss. We must repudiate the opinion of those who hold that all sins proceed from preconceived depravity and malice. We know too well from experience how often we fall, even when our intention is good. Our reason is exposed to so many forms of delusion, is liable to so many errors, stumbles on so many obstacles, is entangled by so many snares, that it is ever wandering from the right direction.[8]

[8] *Ibid.*, Bk. II, chap. ii, pars. 18, 22, 24, 25.

We must now examine the will, on which the question of freedom principally turns, the power of choice belonging to it rather than the intellect. The power of free will is not to be considered in any of those desires which proceed more from instinct than mental deliberation. If you attend to what this natural desire of good in man is, you will find that it is common to him with the brutes. They too desire what is good; and when any good capable of moving the sense appears, they follow after it. Here, however, man does not, in accordance with the excellence of his immortal nature, rationally choose and studiously pursue, what is truly for his good. He does not admit reason to his counsel, nor exert his intellect; but without reason, without counsel, follows the bent of his nature like the lower animals. The question of freedom, therefore, has nothing to do with the fact of man's being led by natural instinct to desire good. The question is, Does man, after determining by right reason what is good, choose what he thus knows, and pursue what he thus chooses? The natural desire of happiness in man no more proves the freedom of the will, than the tendency in metals and stones to attain the perfection of their nature. When the will is enchained as the slave of sin, it cannot make a movement towards goodness, far less steadily pursue it. Nevertheless there remains a will which both inclines and hastens on with the strongest affection towards sin; man, when placed under this bondage, being deprived not of will, but of soundness of will. If the free will of God in doing good is not impeded, because he necessarily must do good; if the devil, who can do nothing but evil, nevertheless sins voluntarily; can it be said that man sins less voluntarily because he is under the necessity of sinning? Man, since he was corrupted by the fall, sins not forced or unwilling, but voluntarily, by a most forward bias of the mind; not by violent compulsion, or external force; but by the movement of his own passion; and yet such is the depravity of his nature, that he cannot move and act except in the direction of evil.[9]

[9] *Ibid.*, Bk. II, chap. ii, par. 26; Bk. II, chap. iii, par. 5.

The Functions of the Moral Law

Let us take a succinct view of the office and use of the Moral Law. Now, this office and use seems to me to consist of three parts. First, by exhibiting the righteousness of God,—in other words, the righteousness which alone is acceptable to God,—it admonishes every one of his own unrighteousness, certiorates, convicts, and finally condemns him. This is necessary, in order that man who is blind and intoxicated with self-love, may be brought at once to know and to confess his weakness and impurity. He who is schooled by the law, lays aside the arrogance which formerly blinded him. In like manner he must be cured of pride, the other disease under which we have said that he labors. So long as he is permitted to appeal to his own judgment, he substitutes a hypocritical for a real righteousness. But after he is forced to weigh his conduct in the balance of the Law, renouncing all dependence on this fancied righteousness, he sees that he is at an infinite distance from holiness, and, on the other hand, that he teems with innumerable vices of which he formerly seemed free. As in a mirror we discover any stains upon our face, so in the Law we behold, first, our impotence; then, in consequence of it, our iniquity; and, finally, the curse, as the consequence of both. But while the unrighteousness and condemnation of all are attested by the law it does not follow (if we make the proper use of it) that we are immediately to give up all hope and rush headlong on despair. The Apostle testifies that the law pronounces its sentence of condemnation in order "that every mouth may be stopped, and all the world become guilty before God."[10] In another place, however, the same Apostle declares that "God hath concluded them all in unbelief"; not that he might destroy all, or allow all to perish, but that "he might have mercy upon all":[11] in other words, that divesting themselves of an absurd opinion of their own virtue they may perceive how they are wholly dependent on the hand of God; that feeling how naked and destitute they

[10] Rom. 3:19.
[11] Rom. 11:32.

are, they may take refuge in his mercy, rely upon it, and cover themselves up entirely with it; renouncing all righteousness and merit, and clinging to mercy alone, as offered in Christ, to all who long and look for it in true faith.

The second office of the Law is, by means of its fearful denunciations and the consequent dread of punishment, to curb those who, unless forced, have no regard for rectitude and justice. Such persons are curbed, not because their mind is inwardly moved or affected, but because, as if a bridle were laid upon them, they refrain their hands from external acts, and internally check the depravity which would otherwise petulantly burst forth. It is true, they are not on this account either better or more righteous in the sight of God. Nevertheless, this forced and extorted righteousness is necessary for the good of society, its peace being secured by a provision but for which all things would be thrown into tumult and confusion. Nay, this tuition is not without its use, even to the children of God, who, previous to their effectual calling, being destitute of the Spirit of holiness, freely indulge the lusts of the flesh. For where the Spirit of God rules not, the lusts sometimes so burst forth, as to threaten to drown the soul subjected to them in forgetfulness and contempt of God; and so they would, did not God interpose with this remedy. All who have remained for some time in ignorance of God will confess, as a result of their own experience, that the law had the effect of keeping them in some degree in the fear and reverence of God, till, being regenerated by his Spirit, they began to love him from the heart.

The third use of the Law (being also the principal use and more closely connected with its proper end) has respect to believers in whose hearts the Spirit of God already flourishes and reigns. For although the Law is written and engraven on their hearts by the finger of God, that is, although they are so influenced and actuated by the Spirit that they desire to obey God, there are two ways in which they still profit in the Law. For it is the best instrument for enabling them daily to learn with greater truth and certainty what that will of the Lord is which they aspire to follow, and to confirm them in this knowledge. Then, because we need not doctrine merely, but exhortation also, the servant of God will derive this further advantage from the Law: by frequently meditating upon it, he will be excited to obedience, and confirmed in it, and so drawn away from the slippery paths of sin.[12]

The Life of a Christian Man

My intention in the plan of life, which I now propose to give, is not to extend it so far as to treat of each virtue specially, and expatiate in exhortation. It will be sufficient to point out the method by which a pious man may be taught how to frame his life aright, and briefly lay down some universal rule by which he may not improperly regulate his conduct. As philosophers have certain definitions of rectitude and honesty, from which they derive particular duties and the whole train of virtues; so in this respect Scripture is not without order, but presents a most beautiful arrangement, one too which is in every way much more certain than that of philosophers. The Scripture system of which we speak aims chiefly at two objects. The former is, that the love of righteousness to which we are by no means naturally inclined, may be instilled and implanted into our minds. The latter is, to prescribe a rule which will prevent us while in the pursuit of righteousness from going astray.

With what better foundation can it begin than by reminding us that we must be holy, because "God is holy"?[13] When mention is made of our union with God, let us remember that holiness must be the bond; not that by the merit of holiness we come into communion with him (we ought rather first to cleave to him, in order that, pervaded with his holiness, we may follow whither he calls), but because it greatly concerns his glory not to have any fellowship with wickedness and impurity. If the Lord adopts us for his sons on the condition that our life be a representation of Christ, the bond of our adoption,—then, unless we dedicate and devote ourselves to

[12] *Op. cit.*, Bk. II, chap. vii, pars. 6-12.
[13] Lev. 19:1; I Pet. 1:16.

righteousness, we not only, with the utmost perfidy, revolt from our Creator, but also abjure the Savior himself. Ever since God exhibited himself to us as a Father, we must be convicted of extreme ingratitude if we do not in turn exhibit ourselves as his sons. Ever since Christ purified us by the laver of his blood, and communicated this purification by baptism, it would ill become us to be defiled with new pollution. Ever since he ingrafted us into his body, we, who are his members, should anxiously beware of contracting any stain or taint. Ever since he who is our head ascended to heaven, it is befitting in us to withdraw our affections from the earth, and with our whole soul aspire to heaven. Ever since the Holy Spirit dedicated us as temples to the Lord we should make it our endeavor to show forth the glory of God, and guard against being profaned by the defilement of sin. Ever since our soul and body were destined to heavenly incorruptibility and an unfading crown, we should earnestly strive to keep them pure against the day of the Lord. These, I say, are the surest foundations of a well-regulated life. Doctrine is not an affair of the tongue, but of the life; is not apprehended by the intellect and memory merely, like other branches of learning; but is received only when it possesses the whole soul, and finds its seat and habitation in the inmost recesses of the heart. To doctrine in which our religion is contained we have given the first place, since by it our salvation commences; but it must be transfused into the breast, and pass into the conduct, and so transform us into itself, as not to prove itself unfruitful.[14]

Of Self-denial. Although the Law of God contains a perfect rule of conduct admirably arranged, it has seemed proper to our divine Master to train his people by a more accurate method, to the rule which is enjoined in the Law; and the leading principle in the method is, that it is the duty of believers to present their "bodies a living sacrifice, holy and acceptable unto God, which is their reasonable service."[15] The great point is, that we are consecrated and dedicated to

14 *Op. cit.*, Bk. III, chap. vi, pars. 1-4.
15 Rom. 12:1.

God, and, therefore, should not henceforth think, speak, design, or act, without a view to his glory. If we are not our own, but the Lord's, it is plain both what error is to be shunned, and to what end the actions of our lives ought to be directed. We are not our own; therefore, neither is our own reason or will to rule our acts and counsels. We are not our own; therefore, let us not make it our end to seek what may be agreeable to our carnal nature. We are not our own; therefore, as far as possible, let us forget ourselves and the things that are ours. On the other hand, we are God's; let us therefore, live and die to him. We are God's; therefore, let his wisdom and will preside over all our actions. We are God's; to him, then, as the only legitimate end, let every part of our life be directed. Let this, then, be the first step, to abandon ourselves, and devote the whole energy of our minds to the service of God.

When the Scripture enjoins us to lay aside private regard to ourselves, it not only divests our minds of an excessive longing for wealth, or power, or human favor, but eradicates all ambition and thirst for worldly glory, and other more secret pests. He who has learned to look to God in everything he does, is at the same time diverted from all vain thoughts. This is that self-denial which Christ so strongly enforces on his disciples from the very outset. Self-denial has respect partly to men and partly (more especially) to God. For when Scripture enjoins us, in regard to our fellow men, to prefer them in honor to ourselves, and sincerely labor to promote their advantage he gives us commands which our mind is utterly incapable of obeying until its natural feelings are suppressed. For so blindly do we all rush in the direction of self-love, that every one thinks he has a good reason for exalting himself and despising all others in comparison. If God has bestowed on us something not to be repented of, trusting to it, we immediately become elated, and not only swell, but almost burst with pride. The vices with which we abound we both carefully conceal from others, and flatteringly represent to ourselves as minute and trivial, nay, sometimes hug them as virtues. When the same qualities which we admire in ourselves are seen in others, even though they should be superior, we, in order that we may not be forced to yield to them, maliciously lower and carp at them; in like manner, in the case of vices, not contented with severe and keen animadversion, we studiously exaggerate them. Hence the insolence with which each, as if exempted from the common lot, seeks to exalt himself above his neighbor, confidently and proudly despising others, or at least looking down upon them as his inferiors. For this there is no other remedy than to pluck up by the roots those most noxious pests, self-love and love of victory. This the doctrine of Scripture does. For it teaches us to remember, that the endowments which God has bestowed upon us are not our own, but his free gifts, and that those who plume themselves upon them betray their ingratitude. Then by a diligent examination of our faults let us keep ourselves humble. Thus while nothing will remain to swell our pride, there will be much to subdue it. Again, we are enjoined, whenever we behold the gifts of God in others, so to reverence and respect the gifts, as also to honor those in whom they reside. God having been pleased to bestow honor upon them, it would ill become us to deprive them of it.

How difficult it is to perform the duty of seeking the good of our neighbor! Unless you leave off all thought of yourself, and in a manner cease to be yourself, you will never accomplish it. How can you exhibit those works of charity which Paul describes unless you renounce yourself, and become wholly devoted to others? Scripture, to conduct us to this, reminds us that whatever we obtain from the Lord is granted on the condition of our employing it for the common good of the Church, and that, therefore, the legitimate use of all our gifts is a kind and liberal communication of them with others. Whatever the pious man can do, he is bound to do for his brethren, not consulting his own interest in any other way than by striving earnestly for the common edification of the Church. Let this, then, be our method of showing good will and kindness, considering that, in regard to everything that God has bestowed upon us, and by which we can aid our neighbor, we are his stewards, and are bound to give an account of our stewardship; moreover, that the only right mode of administration is that which is regulated by love. In this way, we shall not only unite the study of our neighbor's advantage with a regard to our own, but make the latter subordinate to the former.

The Lord enjoins us to do good to all without exception, though the greater part, if estimated by their own merit, are most unworthy of it. But Scripture subjoins a most excellent reason, when it tells us that we are not to look to what men in themselves deserve, but to attend to the image of God, which exists in all, and to which we owe all honor and love. Whoever be the man that is presented to you as needing your assistance, you have no ground for declining to give it to him. Say he is a stranger. The Lord has given him a mark which ought to be familiar to you. Say he is mean and of no consideration. The Lord points him out as one whom he has distinguished by the lustre of his own image. If he not only merits no good, but has provoked you by ignorance and mischief, still this is no good reason why you should not embrace him in love, and visit him with offices of love. He has deserved very differently from me, you will say. But what has the Lord deserved? In this way only we attain to what is not to say difficult, but altogether against nature, to love those that hate us, render good for evil, and blessing for cursing, remembering that we are not to reflect on the wickedness of men, but look to the image of God in them.[16]

Of Bearing the Cross: One Branch of Self-denial. The pious mind must ascend still higher, namely whither Christ calls his disciples, when he says, that every one of them must "take up his cross." Those whom the Lord has chosen and honored with his intercourse must prepare for a hard, laborious, troubled life, a life full of many and various kinds of evils; it being the will of our heavenly Father to exercise his people in this way while putting them to the proof. Having begun this course with Christ the first-born, he continues it towards all his children. For though that Son was dear to him above all others,

[16] *Op. cit.*, Bk. III, chap. vii, pars. 1-2, 4-6.

yet we see that far from being treated gently or indulgently, we may say, that not only was he subjected to a perpetual cross while he dwelt on earth, but his whole life was nothing else than a kind of perpetual cross. Hence it affords us great consolation in hard and difficult circumstances, which men deem evil and adverse, to think that we are holding fellowship with the sufferings of Christ; that as he passed to celestial glory through a labyrinth of many woes, so we too are conducted thither through various tribulations.

We may add, that the only thing which made it necessary for our Lord to undertake to bear the cross, was to testify and prove his obedience to the Father; whereas there are many reasons which make it necessary for us to live constantly under the cross. Feeble as we are by nature, and prone to ascribe all perfection to our flesh, unless we receive as it were ocular demonstration of our weakness, we readily estimate our virtue above its proper worth, and doubt not that whatever happens, it will stand unimpaired and invincible against all difficulties. Hence we indulge in stupid and empty confidence in the flesh, and then trusting to it wax proud against the Lord himself; as if our own faculties were sufficient without his grace. Therefore he visits us with disgrace, or poverty, or bereavement, or disease, or other afflictions. Feeling altogether unable to support them, we forthwith, in so far as regards ourselves, give way, and thus humbled learn to invoke his strength, which alone can enable us to bear up under a weight of afflictions. Another end which the Lord has in afflicting his people is to try their patience, and train them in obedience.

There is singular consolation when we are persecuted for righteousness' sake. For our thought should then be, How high the honor which God bestows upon us in distinguishing us by the special badge of his soldiers. By suffering persecution for righteousness' sake, I mean not only striving for the defence of the Gospel, but for the defence of righteousness in any way. Whether, therefore, in maintaining the truth of God against the lies of Satan, or defending the good and innocent against the injuries of the bad, we are obliged to incur the of fence and hatred of the world, so as to endanger life, fortune, or honor, let us not grieve or decline so far to spend ourselves for God; let us not think ourselves wretched in those things in which he with his own lips has pronounced us blessed.[17]

Of Meditating on the Future Life. Whatever be the kind of tribulation with which we are afflicted, we should always consider the end of it to be, that we may be trained to despise the present, and thereby stimulated to aspire to the future life. We duly profit by the discipline of the cross, when we learn that this life, estimated in itself, is restless, troubled, in numberless ways wretched, and plainly in no respect happy; that what are estimated its blessings are uncertain, fleeting, vain, and vitiated by a great admixture of evil. From this we conclude, that all that we have to seek or hope for here is contest; that when we think of the crown we must raise our eyes to heaven. For we must hold, that our mind never rises seriously to desire and aspire after the future, until it has learned to despise the present life. Still the contempt which believers should train themselves to feel for the present life, must not be of a kind to beget hatred of it or ingratitude to God. This life, though abounding in all kinds of wretchedness, is justly classed among divine blessings which are not to be despised. Before openly exhibiting the inheritance of eternal glory, God is pleased to manifest himself to us as a Father by minor proofs, viz., the blessings which he daily bestows upon us. Therefore, while this life serves to acquaint us with the goodness of God, shall we disdain it as if it did not contain one particle of good? And there is a much higher reason when we reflect that here we are in a manner prepared for the glory of the heavenly kingdom. For the Lord hath ordained, that those who are ultimately to be crowned in heaven must maintain a previous warfare on the earth, that they may not triumph before they have overcome the difficulties of war, and obtained the victory. Another reason is that we here begin to experience in various ways a foretaste of the divine benignity, in order that our hope and desire may be whetted for its full manifestation.

17 *Ibid.*, Bk. III, chap. viii, pars. 1, 2, 4, 7.

When the earthly is compared with the heavenly life, it may undoubtedly be despised and trampled under foot. We ought never, indeed, to regard it with hatred, except in so far as it keeps us subject to sin; and even this hatred ought not to be directed against life itself. At all events, we must stand so affected toward it in weariness or hatred as, while longing for its termination, to be ready at the Lord's will to continue in it, keeping far from everything like murmuring or impatience. For it is as if the Lord had assigned us a post, which we must maintain till he recalls us.[18]

How to Use the Present Life. If we are to live, we must use the necessary supports of life; nor can we even shun those things which seem more subservient to delight than to necessity. We must therefore observe a mean, that we may use them with a pure conscience, whether for necessity or for pleasure. Let this be our principle, that we err not in the use of the gifts of Providence when we refer them to the end for which their author made and destined them, since he created them for our good and not for our destruction. Now then, if we consider for what end he created food, we shall find that he consulted not only for our necessity, but also for our enjoyment and delight. The natural qualities of things themselves demonstrate to what end, how far, they may be lawfully enjoyed. Has the Lord adorned flowers with all the beauty which spontaneously presents itself to the eye, and the sweet odor which delights the sense of smell, and shall it be unlawful for us to enjoy that beauty and this odor? Has he not given many things a value without having any necessary use? Have done, then, with that inhuman philosophy which, in allowing no use of the creatures but for necessity, not only maliciously deprives us of the lawful fruit of the divine beneficence, but cannot be realised without depriving man of all his senses, and reducing him to a block. But, on the other hand, let us with no less care guard against the lusts of the flesh, which, if not kept in order, break through all bounds. There is no surer or quicker way of accomplishing this than by despising the present life and aspiring to celestial immortality. He

18 *Ibid.*, Bk. III, chap. ix, pars. 1, 3, 4.

who makes it his rule to use this world as if he used it not, not only cuts off all gluttony in regard to meat and drink, and all effeminacy, ambition, pride and excessive show, and austerity, in regard to his table, his house, and his clothes, but removes every care and affection which might withdraw or hinder him from aspiring to the heavenly life, and cultivating the interest of his soul. Therefore, while the liberty of the Christian in external matters is not to be tied down to a strict rule, it is, however, subject to this law—he must indulge as little as possible; on the other hand, it must be his constant aim not only to curb luxury, but to cut off all show of superfluous abundance, and carefully beware of converting a help into a hindrance.

The last thing to be observed is, that the Lord enjoins every one of us, in all the actions of life, to have respect to our own calling. He knows the boiling restlessness of the human mind, the fickleness with which it is borne hither and thither, its eagerness to hold opposites at one in its grasp, its ambition. Therefore, lest all things should be thrown into confusion by our folly and rashness, he has assigned distinct duties to each in the different modes of life. And that no one may presume to overstep his proper limits, he has distinguished the different modes of life by the name of callings. Every man's mode of life, therefore, is a kind of station assigned him by the Lord, that he may not be always driven about at random. He only who directs his life to this end will have it properly framed; because free from the impulse of rashness, he will not attempt more than his calling justifies, knowing that it is unlawful to overleap the prescribed bounds. He who is obscure will not decline to cultivate a private life, that he may not desert the post at which God has placed him. The magistrate will more willingly perform his office, and the father of a family confine himself to his proper sphere. Every one in his particular mode of life will, without repining, suffer its inconveniences, cares, uneasiness, and anxiety; persuaded that God has laid on the burden. This, too, will afford admirable consolation, that in following your proper calling, no work will be so mean and sordid as not to have a splendor and value in the eye of God.[19]

Of Civil Government

Let us observe that in man government is two-fold: the one spiritual, by which the conscience is trained to piety and divine worship; the other civil, by which the individual is instructed in those duties which, as men and citizens, we are bound to perform. The former has its seat within the soul; the latter only regulates the external conduct. By attending to this distinction, we will not erroneously transfer the doctrine of the gospel concerning spiritual liberty to civil order, as if in regard to external government Christians were less subject to human laws, because their consciences are unbound before God, as if they were exempted from all carnal service, because in regard to the spirit they are free.[20]

He who knows to distinguish between the body and the soul, between the present fleeting life and that which is future and eternal, will have no difficulty in understanding that the spiritual kingdom of Christ and civil government are things very widely separated. The former, in some measure, begins the heavenly kingdom in us, even now upon earth, and in this mortal and evanescent life commences immortal and incorruptible blessedness, while to the latter it is assigned, so long as we live among men, to foster and maintain the external worship of God, to defend sound doctrine and the condition of the Church, to adapt our conduct to human society, to form our manners to civil justice, to conciliate us to each other, to cherish common peace and tranquillity. All these I confess to be superfluous, if the kingdom of God, as it now exists within us, extinguishes the present life. But if it is the will of God that while we aspire to true piety we are pilgrims upon the earth, and if such pilgrimage stands in need of such aids, those who take them away from man rob him of his humanity.

19 *Ibid.*, Bk. III, chap. x, pars. 1-4, 6.
20 *Ibid.*, Bk. III, chap. xix, par. 15.

The reader, by the help of a perspicuous arrangement, will better understand what view is to be taken of the whole order of civil government, if we treat of each of its parts separately. Now these are three: The Magistrate, who is president and guardian of the laws; the Laws, according to which he governs; and the People, who are governed by the laws and obey the magistrate.[21]

With regard to the function of magistrates the Lord has not only declared that he is approved and is pleased with it, but, moreover, has strongly recommended it to us by the very honorable titles which he has conferred upon it. When those who bear the office of magistrates are called gods, let no one suppose that there is little weight in that appellation. It is thereby intimated that they have a commission from God, that they are invested with divine authority, and, in fact, represent the person of God, as whose substitutes they in a manner act. Wherefore no man can doubt that civil authority is, in the sight of God, not only sacred and lawful, but the most sacred, and by far the most honorable, of all stations in mortal life. This consideration ought to be constantly present to the minds of magistrates, since it is fitted to furnish a strong stimulus to the discharge of duty, and also afford singular consolation, smoothing the difficulties of their office, which are certainly numerous and weighty. What zeal for integrity, prudence, meekness, continence, and innocence, ought to sway those who know that they have been appointed ministers of the divine justice! If they remember that they are the vicegerents of God, it behooves them to watch with all care, diligence and industry, that they may in themselves exhibit a kind of image of the Divine Providence, guardianship, goodness, benevolence, and justice. And let them constantly keep the additional thought in view, that if a curse is pronounced on him that "doeth the work of the Lord deceitfully," a much heavier curse must lie on him who deals deceitfully in a righteous calling.

Though among magisterial offices themselves there are different forms, there is no difference in this respect, that all

[21] *Ibid.*, Bk. IV, chap. xx, pars. 1-3.

are to be received by us as ordinances of God. When [the] three forms of government, of which philosophers treat, are considered in themselves, I, for my part, am far from denying that the form which greatly surpasses the others is aristocracy, either pure or modified by popular government, not indeed in itself, but because it very rarely happens that kings so rule themselves as never to dissent from what is just and right, or are possessed of so much acuteness and prudence as always to see correctly. Owing, therefore, to the vices or defects of men, it is safer and more tolerable when several bear rule, that they may thus mutually assist, instruct and admonish each other, and should any one be disposed to go too far, the others are censors and masters to curb his excess. And as I willingly admit that there is no kind of government happier than where liberty is framed with becoming moderation, and duly constituted so as to be durable, so I deem those very happy who are permitted to enjoy that form, and I admit that they do nothing at variance with their duty when they strenuously and constantly labor to preserve and maintain it. But should those to whom the Lord has assigned one form of government, take it upon them anxiously to long for a change, the wish would not only be foolish and superfluous, but very pernicious. For if it has pleased him to appoint kings over kingdoms, and senates or burgomasters over free states, whatever be the form which he has appointed in the places in which we live, our duty is to obey and submit.[22]

In states, the thing next in importance to the magistrates is the laws, the strongest sinews of government. There are some who deny that any commonwealth is rightly framed which neglects the law of Moses and is ruled by the common law of nations. How perilous and seditious these views are, let others see; for me it is enough to demonstrate that they are stupid and false. We must attend to the well-known division which distributes the whole law of God, as promulgated by Moses, into the moral, the ceremonial and the judicial law. The moral law, being contained under two heads, the one of

[22] *Ibid.*, Bk. IV, chap. xx, pars. 4-8.

which simply enjoins us to worship God with true faith and piety, the other to embrace men with sincere affection, is the true and eternal rule of righteousness prescribed to the men of all nations, who would frame their lives agreeably to the will of God. As ceremonies might be abrogated without at all interfering with piety, so also when these judicial arrangements are removed, the duties and precepts of charity can still remain perpetual. But if it is true that each nation has been left at liberty to enact the laws which it judges to be beneficial, still these are always to be tested by the rule of charity, so that while they vary in form, they must proceed on the same principle. Equity, as it is natural, cannot but be the same in all, and therefore ought to be proposed by all laws. Now as it is evident that the law of God which we call moral, is nothing else than the testimony of natural law, and of that conscience which God has engraven on the minds of men, the whole of this equity is prescribed in it. Hence it alone ought to be the aim, the rule and the end of all laws.[23]

The first duty of subjects towards their rulers, is to entertain the most honorable views of their office, recognising it as a delegated jurisdiction from God, and on that account receiving and reverencing them as ministers and ambassadors of God. I speak not of the men, as if the mask of dignity could cloak folly, or cowardice, or cruelty, or wicked and flagitious manners; but I say that the station itself is deserving of honor and reverence, and that those who rule should, in respect of their office, be held by us in esteem and veneration. From this, a second consequence is, that we must with ready minds prove our obedience to them, whether in complying with edicts, or in paying tribute, or in undertaking public offices and burdens which relate to the common defence, or in executing any other orders. Under this obedience, I comprehend the restraint which private men ought to impose on themselves in public, not interfering with public business, or rashly encroaching on the province of the magistrate, or attempting any thing at all of a public nature. If it is proper that any thing in a public ordinance be corrected, let them

[23] *Ibid.*, Bk. IV, chap. xx, pars. 14, 18.

not act tumultuously, or put their hands to a work where they ought to feel that their hands are tied. My meaning is, let them not dare to do it without being ordered. For when the command of the magistrate is given, they too are invested with public authority.

If we have respect to the word of God, it will lead us farther, and make us subject not only to the authority of those princes who honestly and faithfully perform their duty toward us, but all princes, by whatever means they have become so, although there is nothing they less perform than the duty of princes. For although the Lord declares that a ruler to maintain our safety is the highest gift of his beneficence, and prescribes to rulers themselves their proper sphere, he at the same time declares, that of whatever description they may be, they derive their power from none but him. Those, indeed, who rule for the public good, are true examples and specimens of his beneficence, while those who domineer unjustly and tyrannically are raised up by him to punish the people for their iniquity. Still all alike possess that sacred majesty with which he has invested lawful power. Wherefore, if we are cruelly tormented by a savage, if we are rapaciously pillaged by an avaricious or luxurious, if we are neglected by a sluggish, if, in short, we are persecuted for righteousness' sake by an impious and sacrilegious prince, let us first call up the remembrance of our faults, which doubtless the Lord is chastising by such scourges. And let us reflect that it belongs not to us to cure these evils, that all that remains for us is to implore the help of the Lord, in whose hands are the hearts of kings, and inclinations of kingdoms. Before his face shall fall and be crushed all kings and judges of the earth, who have not kissed his anointed, who have enacted unjust laws to oppress the poor in judgment, and do violence to the cause of the humble, to make widows a prey, and plunder the fatherless. At one time he raises up manifest avengers from his own servants, and gives them his command to punish accursed tyranny, and deliver his people from calamity when they are unjustly oppressed; at another time he employs, for this purpose, the fury of men who have other thoughts and other aims. But whatever may be thought of the acts of the men themselves, the Lord by their means equally executed his own work, when he broke the bloody sceptres of insolent kings, and overthrew their intolerable dominations. Let princes hear and be afraid; but let us at the same time guard most carefully against spurning or violating the venerable and majestic authority of rulers. Although the Lord takes vengeance on unbridled domination, let us not therefore suppose that that vengeance is committed to us, to whom no command has been given but to obey and suffer. I speak only of private men. For when popular magistrates have been appointed to curb the tyranny of kings (as the Ephori, who were opposed to kings among the Spartans, or Tribunes of the people to consuls among the Romans, or Demarchs to the senate among the Athenians; and perhaps there is something similar to this in the power exercised in each kingdom by the three orders, when they hold their primary diets); so far am I from forbidding these officially to check the undue license of kings, that if they connive at kings when they tyrannize and insult over the humbler of the people, I affirm that their dissimulation is not free from nefarious perfidy, because they fraudulently betray the liberty of the people, while knowing that, by the ordinance of God, they are its appointed guardians.

But in that obedience which we hold to be due to the commands of rulers, we must always make the exception, nay, must be particularly careful that it is not incompatible with obedience to Him to whose will the wishes of all kings should be subject, to whose majesty their sceptres must bow. We are subject to the men who rule over us, but subject only in the Lord. If they command anything against Him, let us not pay the least regard to it. That our courage may not fail, Paul stimulates us by the additional consideration, that we were redeemed by Christ at the great price which our redemption cost him, in order that we might not yield a slavish obedience to the depraved wishes of men, far less do homage to their impiety.[24]

[24] *Ibid.*, Bk. IV, chap. xx, pars. 22-25, 29-32.

Further Readings

Primary Sources

CALVIN, JOHN. *Institutes of the Christian Religion.* (Vols. 20 and 21 of *Library of Christian Classics,* edited by J. T. MCNEILL.) Philadelphia: Westminster Press, 1960.

———. *On the Christian Faith.* Trans. with introduction by J. T. MCNEILL. New York: Liberal Arts Press, 1957.

———. *Theological Treatises.* (Vol. 22 of *Library of Christian Classics,* edited by J. K. S. REID.) Philadelphia: Westminster Press, 1954.

Secondary Sources

MCNEILL, J. T. *The History and Character of Calvinism.* New York: Oxford University Press, 1967.

SCHMIDT, A. M. *John Calvin and the Calvinistic Tradition.* New York: Harper and Row, 1960.

WALLACE, R. S. *Calvin's Doctrine of the Christian Life.* Edinburgh: Oliver and Boyd, 1959.

WEBER, MAX. *The Protestant Ethic and the Spirit of Capitalism.* New York: Scribner's, 1950.

WENDEL, FRANCOIS. *Calvin: the Origins and Development of His Religious Thought.* New York: Harper and Row, 1963.

Chapter 10

ETHICS OF PURITANISM AND QUAKERISM

The impulse of the Reformation, as it moved into England in the late sixteenth and early seventeenth centuries, produced there as profound a moral revolution as on the Continent. The term "Puritan" can be take in its narrower sense to refer to those of a particular ecclesiastical party, the Presbyterians, who attempted to reform, on Biblical and Calvinistic lines, the organization of church life in England and the relationship of church and state, an attempt in which they were for the most part opposed by the Anglicans. "Puritan" can also be taken in its broader sense to refer to a whole reformation of life and manners which permeated English culture and cut across all party lines, ecclesiastical and political. In this larger sense, Puritanism as an ethic is characteristic of many influential figures such as Oliver Cromwell, John Milton, Jeremy Taylor, the Anglican divine, and John Bunyan, a Baptist tinker, whose *Pilgrim's Progress* is one of the classics of Puritan literature. There were, to be sure, various ethical shadings within Puritanism and distinctive teachings which mark off some sectarian groups such as the Quakers from the others. But in seventeenth-century England there is a prevailing unanimity of belief about the meaning of the Christian life that is far more marked than the internal differences.

As with so many eras of moral revolution in Christian history, Puritanism's ethical seriousness can best be understood in terms of its renewed theological conviction. Its theory of the Christian life derives its peculiar power from the intensity of its faith about the nature of God and his relation to man. By and large, its doctrinal starting point is that of Calvin: the complete and absolute sovereignty of God over all of life. God is conceived not merely as an abstract Principle (or "notionally" as the Puritan put it), such as Aristotelian-Thomistic thought might arrive at as the conclusion of a sequence of logic. For the Puritan, God is a living, active, dynamic Will, "High and Holy and Lifted up," whose omnipotent purpose is ever discernible in nature and the affairs of men. Nothing happens but by his decree. The whole scheme of creation is infused with his power. He foreknows and foreordains all things, even to a man's final destination.

"By the decree of God, for the manifestation of his glory, some men and angels are predestinated unto everlasting life, and others foreordained to everlasting death."[1] Out of the state of sin into which Adam had dragged all men in the Fall, men are powerless to lift themselves. Only by a Divine act of grace, given on the basis of no merit of man's works, are some to be elected to the state of grace in this life and of glory in the next. To one whose logic is based on the assumption that reward should be merited only by effort and work, this doctrine of election would seem to undercut all moral vitality, since one's ultimate fate, so completely foreordained, would remain unaffected by whatever moral excellence one achieved in this world. Yet the psychology of human motivation in Calvinism runs counter to this logic. The Puritan's moral response to this theological doctrine is just the opposite from a fatalistic folding of the hands. The doctrine of election heightens rather than weakens the sense of moral responsibility. Good works are not the strategies for entrance to heaven; they are the fruit, the result of God's prior, unmerited grace, and a possible "sign" of election. Moreover, since no one knows who is elected and who is damned, no one can count himself assuredly saved. It behooves him then to pass his precarious days in this world neither in complacency nor despair, but with earnestness of moral resolve.

[1] *The Westminster Confession*, III.

A Godly, Righteous, and Sober Life

In the Westminster Catechism, memorized and repeated by generations of Puritan children, the essence of Puritan ethics is stated thus:

> Question 1: What is the chief end of man?
> Answer: Man's chief end is to glorify God, and enjoy Him forever.
>
> . . .
>
> Question 39: What is the duty which God requires of man?
> Answer: The duty which God requires of man is obedience to His revealed will.

To glorify God and to obey his revealed will, these traditional Christian imperatives are construed by the Puritan to mean certain specific qualities of dealing with one's self and one's neighbor, qualities perhaps best summarized in the phrase from the Book of Common Prayer: "a godly, righteous, and sober life."

The hero of the Puritan age is the "godly" man, as in the twentieth century of science and technology the hero is the efficient man or the scientist. To be godly means to be "God-ruled" in all the minutiae of daily living. The godly man lives under the eye of the ever-present Lord of Life, unto whom, he believes, all hearts are open and all desires known. The godly man takes as the standard of his life the absolute perfection of God. In the making of his daily decisions, the Puritan does not use the criteria of what will "work," or what the public will approve, or what will give him or others pleasure, or what will suit his own inclinations for comfort and convenience. Such criteria as these are like as not the subtle wiles of the devil. Rather, the yardstick of the godly man's decision is simply what God would have him do.

God commands absolute righteousness. A godly life means a righteous life, since the God of the Bible is not served by the beauties of outward ritual, by the penances of Romanism, or by the commonplaces of church-going. His sovereignty demands a straight moral rectitude which battles every moment against the subtle champions of the devil, the fair vanities of the world, and the pleasant demands of the flesh. In defining righteousness, the Puritan adds nothing new to Christian moral theory. For him it means the old ideas of even-handed justice and open-handed honor; a conformity of outer with inner self, of deed with word, of means with ends —the rendering of what is due by the law of love to all of one's neighbors. The perfection of righteousness is the perfection of a tender and scrupulous conscience. This is the root of the Puritan's reputation, accorded him by all historians, even those unfavorable to him on other counts—a reputation for honor and integrity.

How may one acquire a scrupulous conscience? Chiefly by the discipline of constant self-examination. In the Puritan's schedule, time is always set aside for meditation and prayer, the reading of the Bible, the study of printed sermons and "guides to godliness," the best-sellers of the period. The diaries and journals commonly kept by Puritans contain few references to the external happenings of the day; they record chiefly and at length the struggles of the Puritan with himself and with his God. Curiously, this is rarely of the quality of morbid introspection. It is rather the careful measurement of the soul, in its successes and failures, by the objective standard of God's law as revealed in the Bible, the requirements of the catechism, and the sermons of the pastor. By the strict keeping of the moral ledgers of his career, the Puritan prepares against the Great Day when he will appear before the throne of God to render an account of his stewardship of his days in the world.

Such a stress on strict righteousness may easily lead to the moral pride of the self-righteous and a self-conscious preening in virtue. This is the popular stereotype of the Puritan's manner, but for the most part it is a caricature. In his Calvinistic doctrine heavy emphasis on sin keeps godliness from becoming "God-almightiness" and righteousness from self-righteousness. The Bible informs him unequivocally that *all* men, even those saved by grace, sin and fall short of the glory of God. In this life no man can be perfect, nor finally triumphant over the lusts of the flesh and the lures of the world. To be sure, the Puritan desires to be of the spiritual aristocracy, but his glance of moral comparison is not downward to those whom he surpasses in godliness but upward to the One whose good far transcends his own.

The third characteristic of Puritan life is its sobriety. It is this feature by which it is often remembered in subsequent history and most often misrepresented. Many modern estimates misconstrue the sobriety of Puritanism to be gloominess or dourness. But by a "sober" life the Puritan does not mean a life devoid of laughter and delight. "Felicity" is a word common in Puritan writing, and it is of the chief end of man, according to the catechism, to *enjoy* God forever. When the Puritan calls on men to be sober, he is simply reminding them that this life is a swift and solemn trust, an arena of crucial decision wherein the high values of the religious life are in competition with the cheap and easy values of the world's pleasures. Anyone who fritters away his days in frivolous pastimes not only misses the height of life's meaning but commits a grievous sin against his own nature and God's will. Life should not be wasted by treating its superficial enjoyments as its core.

The Puritan feels the solemn import of every moment because he firmly believes in the reality of Heaven and Hell. These for him are God's ultimate sanctions for his moral law. The fear of Hell and the hope of Heaven are not, it should be noted, the ultimate motivations of his moral action. The true Calvinist serves God for God's own glory, even if he himself should be damned. Yet the presence of these sanctions confirms his knowledge that God intends his moral law to be taken seriously. If God be finally sovereign, if moral choice be a really serious affair, there must be an ultimate reckoning. This reckoning the Puritans spell out in detailed pictures of the "saints' everlasting rest" contrasted with the sizzling tortures of Hell. One misses the point of Puritan thought, however, if one concentrates attention on the vivid pictures of Heaven and Hell as empirical places of space and time.

Through these fancies, as intense as they are naive, the Puritan expresses the insight of historic Christian thought, namely, that the final measurement of a man's life can be fairly made not by the world but by a God transcendent of the world, who never judges by appearances. The world's assignments of rewards and punishments are too fickle and too unjust to be accepted as the last word of God. Only beyond this world can God's judgment be finally vindicated.

This is not to say, of course, that God does not in part punish and reward *during* earthly life. The Puritan does not reserve Heaven and Hell completely for the after-life. There is a quality of heavenly blessedness that is known by the saints and an agony of remorse known by sinners, even here and now. A man's conscience is a kind of "private judgement day before the publicke day of Judgement." An approving conscience is a foretaste of Heaven. An accusing conscience is a "hell-worm," which "shooteth like a stitch in a man's side."

To lead a sober life, one must turn away from the pursuits of the world's enjoyments. Worldliness is the chief enemy of godliness in Puritan morality. Its attitude toward the world appears at first sight to be strangely inconsistent. On the one hand, Puritan preachers never tire of reminding their listeners that this world is "vile," a vale of tears, to which the Christian must die if he be loyal to his other-worldly citizenship. On the other hand, the Puritan attacks the monastic principle of the renunciation of the world. The Christian is to live not in the monastery but in the market place, receiving gratefully the goods of God's creation as they come to him both through nature and through the social structures of family, business, and government. Through all these may come the occasions for righteousness.

In the main, the apparent contradiction here is reconciled, as with Calvin, in the theory of stewardship: the responsible and restrained use of the world's things for the glory of God and the good of the neighbor. It is quite in accord with Puritan thought to seek, in moderation, the necessities of food and shelter, to labor honestly for an income, to raise a family, to participate in scientific, political, and economic enterprises, and indeed to take part with relish in all proper recreations. But all these pursuits are to be held under the stern rule of simplicity and restraint and as subservient to God's service. It is not the world that is evil in itself, but worldliness, that is, attachment to the world's values as of final worth. The senses are not evil; what is abhorrent is sensualism, the worship of the delights of the senses as though they were the source and sustenance of life's meaning. Increase Mather writes in a typically Puritan vein: "Drink is in itself a good creature of God, and to be received with thankfulness, but the abuse of drink is from Satan; the wine is from God, but the drunkard is from the Devil."[2] The balanced and sensitive moderation in the Puritan's attitude toward the world creates a tension in decision not known by the monk who renounces the world for God or by the worldling who renounces God for temporal delights. But the Puritan feels that to live in this tension is God's commission for those of his children who would make godliness the aim of their lives.

Vocation and Economic Ethics

One especial feature of Puritan ethics is its concentration on the doctrine of *vocation.* It takes Luther's twin doctrines of "the priesthood of all believers" and *Beruf* (calling), and works them into the fabric of the common life of the day's work. Each man has a role to fulfill in God's planned economy. Be he artisan, farmer, tradesman, or teacher, the requirements of the religious life are equally imperative. Every "honest calling is a schoole of Christianity." From men in whatever walk of life, the great taskmaster requires integrity of conscience, strict honesty of dealing, unflagging diligence, and the avoidance of all extravagance and idleness. Every moment of time as lived under the shadow of eternity becomes "high" time, crucial time to be up doing the duties

[2] Quoted by Perry Miller and T. H. Johnson (eds.), *The Puritans* (New York: Harper & Row, 1963), p. 2.

of one's job. "Be busy; the soul is at stake, so loiter not," writes Jeremy Taylor. One Puritan preacher forcefully phrases the matter: "They that will not sweat on earth will sweat in hell."

This Puritan treatment of the doctrine of vocation has direct consequences in economic theory and practice. The seventeenth century sees a shift from the feudal-agricultural economy, prevailing through the time of Luther, to a clearly capitalistic economy, with its vast expansion of trade, investment income, and mercantilism. In this context, the Puritans, members chiefly of the rising middle-class, become devoted to a particular combination of virtues. Honesty, thrift, industry, and diligence, the outward signs of the inward sense of vocation, are combined with simplicity and frugality of living, which are the virtues of the sober man living the "ascetic" ideal in the world. This combination tends to foster economic success, whether desired or not. It is almost inevitable, therefore, that the Puritan should find himself faced with an intense problem of conscience: How proper is wealth in the life of a Christian? The answers given are somewhat uncertain and more and more qualified as one moves into the latter Puritan era. But the guiding rule is evident enough. The Puritan whose earthly fortunes flourish knows that he holds his earthly possessions in trust from God, in stewardship for the good of his neighbor. From the one whom God has more blessed with material favor, the more is required in philanthropy to the needy. Economic duties take priority over economic rights. Nowhere in seventeenth-century Puritan writing is Christian sanction given to unlimited gain or *laissez faire;* for the laws of self-denial, scrupulous honesty, and charity must govern the relations of getting and spending. Jeremy Taylor finds covetousness the enemy of mercy, "for when God hath satisfied those needs which He made, that is, all that is natural,—whatsoever is beyond it is thirst and disease; and unless it be sent back again in charity or religion, can serve no end but vice or vanity."[3]

[3] *Holy Living,* chap. iv, sect. 8.

Yet at the same time it is clear that on this issue Puritanism stands far from St. Francis and many Christians of similar conviction, who view poverty as a prerequisite to holiness. The Puritan no longer esteems poverty a Christian virtue. If anything, it is a vice. Chances are that the poor man is poor because of his indolence and irresponsibility to his vocation. God frowns on extreme wealth. But a substantial income may well be considered a sign of heavenly favor. Competition in production, income from interest, dividends from investment, without dishonesty or extortion, are practices quite in accord with Christian ethics. Did not Jesus himself illustrate the good life with the parable of the talents? So long as the economic life is kept under the rule and requirements of religion, and so long as the Puritan preserves an unclouded sense of the transiency of all earthly goods and the priority of eternal concerns over the temporal, he feels in all conscience that his economic ethic represents no compromise with the world.[4]

Richard Baxter (1615-91) typifies the Puritan mind as well as any writer of his age. His life spanned the turbulent events of the seventeenth century in which he labored and wrote incessantly for the cause of the moral revolution of England and for the healing of the dissension of the churches. Though a Presbyterian Puritan and a Nonconformist—he served at one time as chaplain in Cromwell's army—the matters of church government he regarded as secondary to matters of morality. Thus he stood for a broad church policy and might have approved an Anglican as much as a Presbyterian pattern of English church life if either had been comprehensive and morally regenerate. After the Restoration, which brought persecution to all Nonconformists, Baxter was forced to undergo severe deprivations and recurrent imprisonments, during which many of his influential works

[4] Two very important studies of Puritan ethics in relation to economic life are Max Weber's *The Protestant Ethic and the Spirit of Capitalism,* (1904), which construes Calvinism as providing the essential and unqualified morale for capitalism, and R. H. Tawney's *Religion and the Rise of Capitalism,* (1926), which is more cautious in its estimate of the relation.

were written. Fortunately, he lived to see enacted the Edict of Toleration of 1689, an Act which represented not a little the fruit of his own lifetime of effort for the peace of England.

The selections from Baxter given in this chapter (pp. 309-19) are taken from his *Christian Directory*, which is perhaps his most extensive though not his most famous work. A detailed moral guidebook for every conceivable crossroad of conscience, it ranks with Jeremy Taylor's *Ductor Dubitandum* as a major work of Protestant casuistry. Baxter opens his treatise with certain "Grand Directions," the explications of which constitute a kind of profile of the Puritan character.

The Quakers

The Puritan spirit finds one of its most distinctive expressions in the life of the "Society of Friends," called Quakers, who were a small sect, generally despised by the larger church groups, and viciously persecuted as religious anarchists. Though distinctive in some of their ways, the Friends shared many of the Calvinistic premises of the time, and the writings of their leaders, such as George Fox, Isaac Penington, and Robert Barclay, sound thoroughly Puritan in theological and moral teaching. Yet their practices were in some ways an extension of, if not a departure from, the Puritanism of a Richard Baxter. For one thing, they maintained the basis of religion as a mysticism, exalting the Inner Light, "the light that lighteth every man that cometh into the world," as the supreme religious and moral authority, superior to every external authority of book or church. Second, and as an extension of Puritanism, they were guided by a sectarian spirit, which believed that most of the structures of the "world" were inherently evil and inimical to the spirit of Christianity. The true believer, therefore, must withdraw from the world's ways, while yet living in the world, at those points where the world's practices run counter to gospel commands. This has been called the strategy of "selective withdrawal." The Friends followed the Puritan ethic, for instance, of participation in the world of business and trade, but refused to take part in the civil government's practice of waging war. Third, as a corollary of this sectarianism, the Friends were perfectionists in demanding an uncompromising fulfillment of the ethical precepts of Christ. Being a Christian, they said, has nothing to do with formal church practices or with doctrinal exactitude. Being a Christian is simply a matter of the living allegiance of every man to the Divine Light within. As William Penn put it, "That which the people called Quakers lay down as a main fundamental in religion is this, that God, through Christ, hath placed a principle in every man to inform him of his duty, and to enable him to do it; and that those who live up to this principle are the people of God, and those who live in disobedience to it are not God's people, whatever name they may bear, or profession they may make of religion. This is their ancient, first, and standing testimony."[5]

In keeping with these convictions, the Quakers were led to set forth certain "testimonies" against the world. They took pains, after the manner of the age, to justify those testimonies with Biblical support. But the sources of these testimonies were as much the distinctive combination of mystical and democratic themes at the heart of their religion. One important testimony was against the state's compulsion in matters of worship. The conscience of man, they said, is inviolable to trespass by the agencies of government. The Quakers were thus among the earliest advocates of religious liberty, a position in the seventeenth century generally viewed with horror. Further testimonies against "flattering titles" and "kneeling, bowing, and uncovering the head" spring from an equalitarian spirit suspicious of all the polite idolatries whereby men pay deference to each other instead of to God. There are other testimonies against taking oaths, against superfluity of apparel, against "gaming, sporting, and vain recreations." But the most famous witness of the Quaker is against war. The Quaker would not bear arms in any cause, since the waging of war is so clearly contrary to the commands of the Inner Light. The original Quaker pacifism,

[5] William Penn, *Primitive Christianity Revived,* I, i.

it should be noted, held that only the few "pure" Christians could follow the way of nonviolence. It was not an ethic that the world could adopt. Nor did the Quaker expect that his pacifism could be "successful." The way of the Cross was the way of suffering and rejection.

Robert Barclay (1648-90), a man of aristocratic breeding, extensive education, and brilliant intellect, was converted to the Quaker faith at the age of eighteen. His *Apology for the True Christian Divinity* (pp. 319-26), written when he was twenty-eight, has taken its place as the normative statement of Quaker belief. Barclay shared in most of the Calvinistic and Puritan theological premises of his day: the sovereignty of God, the high authority of the Bible, the sinfulness of natural man unenlightened by grace. But the Quaker doctrine of the Seed of Christ in every man, countering the pull of sin, gave him a view of human nature rather more favorable than that of his fellow Puritans.

SOURCES

From

Richard Baxter: The Christian Directory[6]

The Nature of Godliness

Know that true godliness is the best life upon earth, and the only way to perfect happiness. Still apprehend it therefore, and use it as the best; and with great diligence resist those temptations which would make it seem to you a confounding, grievous, or unpleasant thing.

There are all things concurrent in a holy life, to make it the most delectable life on earth, to a rational, purified mind, that is not captivated to the flesh, and liveth not on air or dung. The object of it is the eternal God himself, the

[6] This material is taken from *The Practical Works of Richard Baxter*, (4 vols., London: Arthur Hall & Co., 1847), Vol. I: *A Christian Directory*.

infallible truth, the only satisfactory good; and all these condescending and appearing to us, in the mysterious, but suitable glass of a Mediator; redeeming, reconciling, teaching, governing, sanctifying, justifying, and glorifying all that are his own. The end of it is the pleasing and glorifying of our Maker, Redeemer, and Sanctifier; and the everlasting happiness of ourselves and others. The rule of it is the infallible revelation of God, delivered to the church by his prophets, and his Son, and his apostles, and comprised in the Holy Scriptures, and sealed by the miracles and operations of the Holy Ghost that did indite them. The work of godliness is a living unto God, and preparing for everlasting life, by foreseeing, foretasting, seeking, and rejoicing in that endless happiness which we shall have with God; and by walking after the Spirit, and avoiding the filthiness, delusions, and vexations of the world and the flesh. The nature of man is not capable of a more noble, profitable, and delectable life, than this which God hath called us to by his Son. And if we did but rightly know it, we should follow it with continual alacrity and delight. Be sure, therefore, to conceive of godliness as it is, and not as it is misrepresented by the devil and the ungodly.

As long as a man conceiveth of religion as it is, even the most sweet and delectable life, so long he will follow it willingly and with his heart, and despise the temptations and avocations of fleshly gain and pleasure. He will be sincere, as not being only drawn by other men, or outward advantages, nor frightened into it by a passion or fearfulness, but loving religion for itself, and for its excellent ends: and then he will be cheerful in all the duties, and under all the sufferings and difficulties of it; and he will be most likely to persevere unto the end.[7]

Grand Direction X. Your lives must be laid out in doing God service, and doing all the good you can, in works of piety, justice, and charity, with prudence, fidelity, industry, zeal, and delight; remembering that you are engaged to God, as servants to their lord and master; and are intrusted

[7] *A Christian Directory*, Part I, chap. ii.

with his talents, of the improvement whereof you must give account.

Content not yourselves to do some good extraordinarily on the by, or when you are urged to it; but study to do good, and make it the trade or business of your lives.—Having so many obligations, and so great encouragements, do what you do with all your might. If you would know whether you are servants to Christ, or to the flesh, the question must be, which of these have the main care and diligence of our lives; for as every carnal act will not prove you servants to the flesh, so every good action will not prove you the servants of Christ.

Before you do any work, consider whether you can truly say, it is a service of God, and will be accepted by him. See therefore that it be done, 1. To his glory, or to please him. 2. And in obedience to his command.—Mere natural actions, that have no moral good or evil in them, and so belong not to morality, these belong not to our present subject; as being not the matter of rational (or at least of obediential) choice. Such as the winking of the eye, the setting of this foot forward first, the taking of this or that meat, or drink, or instrument, or company, or action, when they are equal, and it is no matter of rational (or obediential) choice, etc. But every act that is to be done deliberately and rationally, as matter of choice, must be moralized, or made good, by doing it, 1. To a right end; and, 2. According to the rule. All the comforts of food, or rest, or recreation, or pleasure which we take, should be intended to fit us for our Master's work, or strengthen, cheer, and help us in it. Do nothing, deliberately, that belongs to the government of reason, but God's service in the world; which you can say, he set you on.

Set not duties of piety, justice, or charity against each other, as if they had an enmity to each other; but take them as inseparable, as God hath made them.—Think not to offer God a sacrifice of injury, bribery, fraud, oppression, or any uncharitable work. And pretend not the benefit of men, or the safety of societies or kingdoms, for impiety against the Lord.

Acquaint yourselves with all the talents which you receive from God, and what is the use to which they should be improved.—Keep thus a just account of your receivings, and what goods of your Master's is put into your hands. And make it a principal part of your study, to know what every thing in your hand is good for to your Master's use; and how it is that he would have you use it.

Keep an account of your expenses; at least, of all your most considerable talents; and bring yourselves daily or frequently to a reckoning, what good you have done, or endeavoured to do. Every day is given you for some good work. Keep therefore accounts of every day (I mean, in your conscience, not in papers). Every mercy must be used to some good: call yourselves therefore to account for every mercy, what you have done with it for your Master's use. And think not hours and minutes, and little mercies, may be past without coming into the account. The servant that thinks he may do what he list with shillings and pence, and that he is only to lay out greater sums for his master's use, and lesser for his own, will prove unfaithful, and come short in his accounts. Less sums than pounds must be in our reckonings.

Prudence is exceeding necessary in doing good, that you may discern good from evil, discerning the season, and measure, and manner, and among divers duties, which must be preferred.—Therefore labour much for wisdom, and if you want it yourself, be sure to make use of theirs that have it, and ask their counsel in every great and difficult case. Zeal without judgment hath not only entangled souls in many heinous sins, but hath ruined churches and kingdoms, and under pretence of exceeding others in doing good, it makes men the greatest instruments of evil. There is scarce a sin so great and odious, but ignorant zeal will make men do it as a good work.

Prefer a durable good that will extend to posterity, before a short and transitory good.—As to build an alms-house is a greater work than to give an alms, and to erect a school than to teach a scholar; so to promote the settlement of the gospel and a faithful ministry is the greatest of all, as tending to the good of many, even to their everlasting good. This is the pre-eminence of good books before a transient speech, that they may be a more durable help and benefit. Look before you with a judicious foresight; and as you must not do that present good to a particular person, which bringeth greater hurt to many; so you must not do that present good to one or many, which is like to produce a greater and more lasting hurt. Such blind reformers have used the church, as ignorant physicians use their patients, who give them a little present ease, and cast them into a greater misery, and seem to cure them with a dose of opium or the Jesuit's powder, when they are bringing them into a worse disease than that which they pretend to cure.

Keep in the way of your place and calling, and take not other men's works upon you without a call, under any pretence of doing good.—Magistrates must do good in the place and work of magistrates; and ministers in the place and work of ministers; and private men in their private place and work; and not one man step into another's place, and take his work out of his hand, and say, I can do it better: for if you should do it better, the disorder will do more harm than you did good by bettering his work. One judge must not step into another's court and seat, and say, I will pass more righteous judgment. You must not go into another man's school, and say, I can teach your scholars better; nor into another's charge or pulpit, and say, I can preach better. The servant may not rule the master, because he can do it best; no more than you may take another man's wife, or house, or lands, or goods, because you can use them better than he. Do the good that you are called to.

Watchfully and resolutely avoid the entanglements and diverting occasions by which the tempter will be still endeavouring to waste your time and hinder you from your work.—Know what is the principal service that you are called to, and avoid avocations: especially magistrates and ministers, and those that have great and public work, must here take heed. For if you be not very wise and watchful, the tempter will draw you, before you are aware, into such a multitude of diverting care or business, that shall seem to be your duties, as shall make you almost unprofitable in the world: you shall have this or that friend that must be visited or spoken to, and this or that civility that must be performed: so that trifles shall detain you from all considerable works. I confess friends must not be neglected, nor civilities be denied; but our greatest duties having the greatest necessity, all things must give place to them in their proper season. And therefore, that you may avoid the offence of friends, avoid the place or occasions of such impediments; and where that cannot be done, whatever they judge of you, neglect not your most necessary work; else it will be at the will of men and Satan, whether you shall be serviceable to God or not.

Ask yourselves seriously, how you would wish at death and judgment that you had used all your wits, and time, and wealth; and resolve accordingly to use them now.—This is an excellent direction and motive to you for doing good, and preventing the condemnation which will pass upon unprofitable servants. Ask yourselves, Will it comfort me more at death or judgment, to think, or hear, that I spent this hour in plays or idleness, or in doing good to myself or others? How shall I wish then I had laid out my estate, and every part of it? Reason itself condemneth him that will not now choose the course which then he shall wish that he had chosen, when we foresee the consequence of that day.

Expect your reward from God alone, and look for unthankfulness and abuse from men, or wonder not if it befall you. —If you are not the servants of men, but of God, expect your recompence from him you serve. You serve not God indeed, if his reward alone will not content you, unless you have also man's reward. "Verily you have your reward," if, with the hypocrite, you work for man's approbation. Expect, especially if you are ministers or others that labour directly for the good of souls, that many prove your enemies for your telling them the truth; and that if you were as good as Paul, and as unwearied in seeking men's salvation, yet the more you love, the less you will (by many) be loved.

Make not your own judgments or consciences your law, or the maker of your duty; which is but the discerner of the law of God, and of the duty which he maketh you, and of your own obedience or disobedience to him.—There is a dangerous error grown too common in the world, that a man is bound to do every thing which his conscience telleth him is the will of God; and that every man must obey his conscience, as if it were the lawgiver of the world; whereas, indeed, it is not ourselves, but God, that is our lawgiver. And conscience is not appointed or authorized to make us any duty, which God hath not made us; but only to discern the law of God, and call upon us to observe it: and an erring conscience is not to be obeyed, but to be better informed, and brought to a righter performance of its office.[8]

Man's Chief End: To Glorify God

Grand Direction XV. Let thy very heart be set to glorify God, thy Creator, Redeemer, and Sanctifier; both with the estimation of thy mind, the praises of thy mouth, and the holiness of thy life.

The glorifying of God, being the end of man and the whole creation, must be the highest duty of our lives; and therefore deserveth our distinct consideration.

Our lives then glorify God, when they are such as his excellencies most appear in: and that is, when they are most divine or holy; when they are so managed, that the world may see, that it is God that we have chiefly respect unto, and that HOLINESS TO THE LORD is written upon all our faculties and affairs.—So much of GOD as appeareth in our lives, so much they are truly venerable, and advanced above the rank of fleshly, worldly lives. God only is the real glory of every person, and every thing, and every word or action of our lives. And the natural conscience of the world, which, in

[8] *Ibid.*, Part I, chap. iii.

despite of their atheism, is forced to confess and reverence a Deity, will be forced (even when they are hated and persecuted) to reverence the appearance of God in his holy ones.

The more of heaven appeareth in your lives, the more your lives do glorify God.—Worldly and carnal men are conscious, that their glory is a vanishing glory, and their pleasure but a transitory dream, and that all their honour and wealth will shortly leave them in the dust; and therefore, they are forced, in despite of their sensuality, to bear some reverence to the life to come. And though they have not hearts themselves to deny the pleasures and profits of the world, and to spend their days in preparing for eternity, and in laying up a treasure in heaven; yet they are convinced, that those that do so, are the best and wisest men; and they could wish that they might die the death of the righteous, and that their last end might be like his. As heaven exceedeth earth, even in the reverent acknowledgment of the world, though not in their practical esteem and choice; so heavenly christians have a reverent acknowledgment from them, (when malice doth not hide their heavenliness by slanders,) though they will not be such themselves. Let it appear in your lives, that really you seek a higher happiness than this world affordeth, and that you verily look to live with Christ; and that as honour, and wealth, and pleasure command the lives of the ungodly, so the hope of heaven commandeth yours. Let it appear that this is your design and business in the world, and that your hearts and conversations are above, and that whatever you do or suffer, is for this, and not for any lower end; and this is a life that God is glorified by.

It glorifieth God, by showing the excellency of faith, when we contemn the riches and honour of the world, and live above the worldling's life; accounting that a despicable thing, which he accounts his happiness, and loseth his soul for.—As men despise the toys of children, so a believer must take the transitory vanities of this world, for matters so inconsiderable, as not to be worthy his regard, save only as they are the matter of his duty to God, or as they relate to him, or the life to come. The world is under a believer's feet, while his eye is fixed on the celestial world. He travelleth through it to his home, and he will be thankful if his way be fair, and if he have his daily bread: but it is not his home, nor doth he make any great matter, whether his usage in it be kind or unkind, or whether his inn be well adorned or not. He is almost indifferent whether, for so short a time, he be rich or poor, in a high or in a low condition, further than as it tendeth to his Master's service. Let men see that you have a higher birth than they, and higher hopes, and higher hearts, by setting light by that, which their hearts are set upon as their felicity. When seeming christians are as worldly and ambitious as others, and make as great a matter of their gain, and wealth, and honour, it showeth that they do but cover the base and sordid spirit of worldlings, with the visor of the christian name, to deceive themselves, and bring the faith of christians into scorn, and dishonour the holy name which they usurp.

It much honoureth God, when the hopes of everlasting joys do cause believers to live much more joyfully than the most prosperous worldlings.—Not with their kind of doting mirth, in vain sports and pleasures, and foolish talking, and uncomely jests; but in that constant cheerfulness and gladness, which beseemeth the heirs of glory. Let it appear to the world, that indeed you hope to live with Christ, and to be equal with the angels. Do a dejected countenance, and a mournful, troubled, and complaining life, express such hopes? or rather tell men that your hopes are small, and that God is a hard master, and his service grievous? Do not thus dishonour him by your inordinate dejectedness; do not affright and discourage sinners from the pleasant service of the Lord.

When christians live in a readiness to die, and can rejoice in the approach of death, and love and long for the day of judgment, when Christ shall justify them from the slanders of the world, and shall judge them to eternal joys: this is to the glory of God and our profession.—When death, which is the king of fears to others, appeareth as disarmed and conquered to believers; when judgment, which is the terror of others, is their desire; this showeth a triumphant faith, and that godliness is not in vain.

It honoureth God and our profession, when you abound in love and good works; loving the godly with a special love, but all men with so much love, as makes you earnestly desirous of their welfare, and to love your enemies, and put up wrongs, and to study to do good to all, and hurt to none.

The unity, concord, and peace of christians, do glorify God and their profession; when their divisions, contentions, and malicious persecutions of one another, do heinously dishonour him.—Men reverence that faith and practice which they see us unanimously accord in. And the same men will despise both it and us, when they see us together by the ears about it, and hear us in a Babel of confusion, one saying, This is the way, and another, That is it; one saying, Lo here is the true church and worship, and another saying, Lo it is there. Not that one man or a few must make a shoe meet for his own foot, and then say, All that will not dishonour God by discord, must wear this shoe: think as I think, and say as I say, or else you are schismatics. But we must all agree in believing and obeying God.

Justice commutative and distributive, private and public, in bargainings, and in government, and judgment, doth honour God and our profession in the eyes of all: when we do no wrong, but do to all men as we would they should do to us. That a man's word be his master, and that we lie not one to another, nor equivocate or deal subtilly and deceitfully, but in plainness and singleness of heart, and in simplicity and godly sincerity, have our conversation in the world. Perjured persons and covenant-breakers, that dissolve the bonds of human society, and take the name of God in vain, shall find by his vengeance that he holdeth them not guiltless.

If you will glorify God in your lives, you must be chiefly intent upon the public good, and the spreading of the gospel through the world.—A selfish, private, narrow soul brings little honour to the cause of God: it is always taken up about itself, or imprisoned in a corner, in the dark, to the interest of some sect or party, and seeth not how things go in the world: its desires, and prayers, and endeavours go no further than they can see or travel. But a larger soul beholdeth all the earth, and is desirous to know how it goeth with the cause and servants of the Lord, and how the gospel gets ground upon the unbelieving nations; and such are affected with the state of the church a thousand miles off, almost as if it were at hand, as being members of the whole body of Christ, and not only of a sect. They pray for the "hallowing of God's name," and the "coming of his kingdom," and the "doing of his will throughout the earth, as it is in heaven," before they come to their own necessities, at least in order of esteem and desire.

Grand Direction XVI. Let your life on earth be a conversation in heaven, by the constant work of faith and love; even such a faith as maketh things future as now present, and the unseen world as if it were continually open to your sight; and such a love as makes you long to see the glorious face of God, and the glory of your dear Redeemer, and to be taken up with blessed spirits in his perfect, endless love and praise.[9]

From

Robert Barclay: An Apology for the True Christian Divinity[10]

Seeing the chief end of all religion is to redeem men from the spirit and vain conversation of this world, and to lead into inward communion with God, before whom if we fear always we are accounted happy; therefore all the vain customs and habits thereof, both in word and deed, are to be rejected and forsaken by those who come to this fear; such as taking off the hat to a man, the bowings and cringings of the body, and superstitious formalities attending them; all which man hath invented in his degenerate state, to feed his pride in the vain

[9] *Ibid.*, Part I, chap. iii.

[10] All subsequent material in this chapter is taken from Robert Barclay, *An Apology for the True Christian Divinity,* Philadelphia: Friends Book Store, 1908.

pomp and glory of this world: as also the unprofitable plays, frivolous recreations, sportings, and gamings, which are invented to pass away the precious time, and divert the mind from the witness of God in the heart, and from the living sense of his fear, and from that evangelical spirit wherewith Christians ought to be leavened, and which leads into sobriety, gravity, and godly fear; in which as we abide, the blessing of the Lord is felt to attend us in those actions in which we are necessarily engaged, in order to the taking care for the sustenance of the outward man.[11]

There are some singular things, which most of all our adversaries plead for the lawfulness of, and allow themselves in, as no ways inconsistent with the Christian religion, which we have found to be no ways lawful unto us, and have been commanded of the Lord to lay them aside; though the doing thereof hath occasioned no small sufferings and buffetings, and hath procured us much hatred and malice from the world. And because the nature of these things is such, that they do upon the very sight distinguish us, and make us known, so that we cannot hide ourselves from any, without proving unfaithful to our testimony; our trials and exercises have here-through proved the more numerous and difficult, as will after appear. These may more largely be exhibited in these six following propositions:

That it is not lawful to give to men such flattering titles, as Your Holiness, Your Majesty, Your Eminency, Your Excellency, Your Grace, Your Lordship, Your Honour, Etc., nor use those flattering words, commonly called COMPLIMENTS.

That it is not lawful for Christians to kneel, or prostrate themselves to any man, or to bow the body, or to uncover the head to them.

That it is not lawful for a Christian to use superfluities in apparel, as are of no use, save for ornament and vanity.

That it is not lawful to use games, sports, plays, nor among other things comedies among Christians, under the notion of recreations, which do not agree with Christian silence, gravity, and sobriety; for laughing, sporting, gaming, mock-

[11] *Apology for the True Christian Divinity,* Prop. XV.

ing, jesting, vain talking, Etc., is not Christian liberty, nor harmless mirth.

That it is not lawful for Christians to swear at all under the gospel, not only not vainly, and in their common discourse, which was also forbidden under the Mosaical law, but even not in judgment before the magistrate.

That it is not lawful for Christians to resist evil, or to war or fight in any case.

Before I enter upon a particular disquisition of these things, I shall first premise some general considerations, to prevent all mistakes; and next add some general considerations, which equally respect all of them. I would not have any judge, that hereby we intend to destroy the mutual relation that either is betwixt prince and people, master and servants, parents and children; nay, not at all: we shall evidence, that our principle in these things hath no such tendency, and that these natural relations are rather better established, than any ways hurt by it. Next, Let not any judge, that from our opinion in these things, any necessity of levelling will follow, or that all men must have things in common. Our principle leaves every man to enjoy that peaceably, which either his own industry, or his parents, have purchased to him; only he is thereby instructed to use it aright, both for his own good, and that of his brethren: and all to the glory of God.

I would seriously propose unto all such, as choose to be Christians indeed, and that in nature, and not in name only, whether it were not desirable, and would not greatly contribute to the commendation of Christianity, and to the increase of the life and virtue of Christ, if all superfluous titles of honour, profuseness and prodigality in meat and apparel, gaming, sporting and playing, were laid aside and forborne? And whether such as lay them aside, in so doing, walk not more like the disciples of Christ and his apostles, and are therein nearer their example, than such as use them? Whether the laying them aside would hinder any from being good Christians? Or if Christians might not be better without them, than with them? Certainly the sober and serious among all sorts will say, Yea. Then surely such as lay them aside, as reckoning them unsuitable for Christians, are not to be blamed, but rather commended for so doing: because that in principle and practice they effectually advance that, which others acknowledge were desirable, but can never make effectual, so long as they allow the use of them as lawful. And God hath made it manifest in this age, that by discovering the evil of such things, and leading his witnesses out of them, and to testify against them, he hath produced effectually in many that mortification and abstraction from the love and cares of this world, who daily are conversing in the world, but inwardly redeemed out of it, both in wedlock, and in their lawful employments, which was judged could only be obtained by such as were shut up in cloisters and monasteries.[12]

Quaker Pacifism

The last thing to be considered, is revenge and war, an evil as opposite and contrary to the Spirit and doctrine of Christ as light to darkness. For, as is manifest by what is said, through contempt of Christ's law the whole world is filled with various oaths, cursings, blasphemous profanations, and horrid perjuries; so likewise, through contempt of the same law, the world is filled with violence, oppression, murders, ravishing of women and virgins, spoilings, depredations, burnings, devastations, and all manner of lasciviousness and cruelty: so that it is strange that men, made after the image of God, should have so much degenerated, that they rather bear the image and nature of roaring lions, tearing tigers, devouring wolves, and raging boars, than of rational creatures endued with reason. And is it not yet much more admirable, that this horrid monster should find place, and be fomented, among those men that profess themselves disciples of our peaceable Lord and master Jesus Christ, who by excellency is called the Prince of Peace, and hath expressly prohibited his children all violence; and on the contrary, commanded

[12] *Ibid.*, Defense of Proposition XV.

them, that, according to his example, they should follow patience, charity, forbearance, and other virtues worthy of a Christian?

It is as easy to reconcile the greatest contradictions, as these laws of our Lord Jesus Christ with the wicked practices of wars: for they are plainly inconsistent. Whoever can reconcile this, "Resist not evil," with, Resist violence by force: again, "Give also thy other cheek," with, Strike again; also "Love thine enemies," with, Spoil them, make a prey of them, pursue them with fire and sword; or, "Pray for those that persecute you, and those that calumniate you," with, Persecute them by fines, imprisonments, and death itself; and not only such as do not persecute you, but who heartily seek and desire your eternal and temporal welfare: whoever, I say, can find a means to reconcile these things, may be supposed also to have found a way to reconcile God with the devil, Christ with Anti-christ, light with darkness, and good with evil.

And although this thing be so much known, yet it is as well known that almost all the modern sects live in the neglect and contempt of this law of Christ, and likewise oppress others, who in this agree not with them for conscience' sake towards God: even as we have suffered much in our country, because we neither could ourselves bear arms, nor send others in our place, nor give our money for the buying of drums, standards, and other military attire. And lastly, because we could not hold our doors, windows, and shops close, for conscience' sake, upon such days as fasts and prayers were appointed, to desire a blessing upon, and success for, the arms of the kingdom or commonwealth under which we live; neither give thanks for the victories acquired by the effusion of much blood. By which forcing of the conscience, they would have constrained our brethren, living in divers kingdoms at war together, to have implored our God for contrary and contradictory things, and consequently impossible: for it is impossible that two parties fighting together, should both obtain the victory. And because we cannot concur with them in this confusion, therefore we are subject to persecution. Yea, and others, who with us do witness that the use of arms is unlawful to Christians, do look asquint upon us; but which of us two do most faithfully observe this testimony against arms? Either they, who at certain times, at the magistrate's order, do close up their shops and houses, and meet in their assembly, praying for the prosperity of their arms, or giving thanks for some victory or other, whereby they make themselves like to those that approve wars and fighting; or we, who cannot do these things for the same cause of conscience, lest we should destroy, by our works, what we establish in words, we shall leave to the judgment of all prudent men.

Since nothing seems more contrary to man's nature, and seeing of all things the defence of one's self seems most tolerable, as it is most hard to men so it is the most perfect part of the Christian religion, as that wherein the denial of self and entire confidence in God doth most appear; and therefore Christ and his apostles left us hereof a most perfect example. As to what relates to the present magistrates of the Christian world, albeit we deny them not altogether the name of Christians, because of the public profession they make of Christ's name, yet we may boldly affirm, that they are far from the perfection of the Christian religion; because in the state in which they are, they have not come to the pure dispensation of the gospel. And therefore, while they are in that condition, we shall not say, that war, undertaken upon a just occasion, is altogether unlawful to them. For even as circumcision and the other ceremonies were for a season permitted to the Jews, not because they were either necessary of themselves, or lawful at that time, after the resurrection of Christ, but because that Spirit was not yet raised up in them, whereby they could be delivered from such rudiments; so the present confessors of the Christian name, who are yet in the mixture, and not in the patient suffering spirit, are not yet fitted for this form of Christianity, and therefore cannot be undefending themselves until they attain that perfection. But for such whom Christ has brought hither, it is not lawful to defend themselves by arms, but they ought over all to trust to the Lord.

If to revenge ourselves, or to render injury, evil for evil, wound for wound, to take eye for eye, tooth for tooth; if to fight for outward and perishing things, to go a warring one against another, whom we never saw, with whom we never had any contest, nor any thing to do; being moreover altogether ignorant of the cause of the war, but only that the magistrates of the nations foment quarrels one against another, the causes whereof are for the most part unknown to the soldiers that fight, as well as upon whose side the right or wrong is; and yet to be so furious, and rage one against another, to destroy and spoil all, that this or the other worship may be received or abolished; if to do this, and much more of this kind, be to fulfil the law of Christ, then are our adversaries indeed true Christians, and we miserable heretics, that suffer ourselves to be spoiled, taken, imprisoned, banished, beaten, and evilly entreated, without any resistance, placing our trust only in GOD, that he may defend us, and lead us by the way of the cross unto his kingdom. But if it be otherways, we shall certainly receive the reward which the Lord hath promised to those that cleave to him, and, in denying themselves, confide in him.

And to sum up all, if to use all these things, and many more that might be instanced, be to walk in the strait way that leads to life, be to take up the cross of Christ, be to die with him to the lusts and perishing vanities of this world, and to arise with him in newness of life, and sit down with him in the heavenly places, then our adversaries may be accounted such, and they need not fear they are in the broad way that leads to destruction, and we are greatly mistaken, that have laid aside all these things for Christ's sake, to the crucifying of our own lusts, and to the procuring to ourselves shame, reproach, hatred, and ill-will from the men of this world: not as if by so doing we judged to merit heaven, but as knowing they are contrary to the will of Him who redeems his children from the love of this world, and its lusts, and leads then in the ways of truth and holiness, in which they take delight to walk.[13]

Further Readings

Primary Sources

Barclay, Robert. *Barclay's Apology in Modern English.* Edited by Dean Freiday. Alburtis, Pa.: Hemlock Press, 1967.

Baxter, Richard. *The Saints' Everlasting Rest.* Introduction by John Wilkinson. London: Epworth Press, 1962.

Bunyan, John. *The Pilgrim's Progress.* (Many editions available.) See also *God's Knotty Log: Selected Writings.* Edited by Henri Talon. Cleveland: World, 1961.

Donne, John. *The Showing Forth of Christ: Sermons.* Selected with an Introduction by Edmund Fuller. New York: Harper and Row, 1964.

Miller, Perry, and Johnson, Thomas (eds.). *The Puritans.* 2 vols. New York: Harper and Row, 1963.

Penn, William. *The Witness of William Penn.* Edited with introduction by Frederick B. Tolles and Gordon Alderfer. New York: Macmillan, 1957.

Taylor, Jeremy. *Holy Living and Holy Dying.* London: Longmans, Green, 1938.

West, Jessamyn (ed.). *The Quaker Reader.* New York: Viking Press, 1962.

Secondary Sources

Barbour, Hugh. *The Quakers in Puritan England.* New Haven: Yale University Press, 1964.

Dickens, Arthur G. *The English Reformation.* New York: Schocken Books, 1964.

George, Charles H., and George, Katherine. *The Protestant Mind of the English Reformation, 1570–1640.* Princeton: Princeton University Press, 1961.

Haller, William. *The Rise of Puritanism.* New York: Harper and Row, 1957.

———. *Liberty and Reformation in the Puritan Revolution.* New York: Columbia University Press, 1955.

Nuttall, Geoffrey. *The Holy Spirit in Puritan Faith and Experience.* Oxford: Blackwell, 1946.

13 *Ibid.*, Defense of Prop. XV.

Chapter 11

JOSEPH BUTLER AND ANGLICAN RATIONALISM

It would be difficult to find a more extreme contrast within Christian ethical theory than that between the spirit of Puritanism and the thinking of Joseph Butler (1692-1752), bishop of the Church of England. In part the difference is due to the contrasting tempers of the seventeenth and the eighteenth centuries. As preacher and scholar, Butler addressed himself to an England in which the Puritan fires of moral zeal and reform had died down, and the religious life of England had considerably settled into a state of placid respectability. Puritanism itself, in this era, had hardened into a kind of Biblical scholasticism, which, as is so often true in the second generation of religious reforms, lost the dynamic of the Puritan revolution in the careful keeping of the rules.

The "Age of Reason" has been the term given to Butler's century, a term not entirely apt, since there was a strong emotionalism in the evangelical revivals of the time. But in a general way, the reaction against "enthusiasm" (especially of the sectarians), the stress on sobriety and calm, and in particular the attempt to validate the claims of Christianity by the standards of natural reason are all characteristic of the period. In theology, the prevailing wind of doctrine was Deism, the view which, briefly put, maintained that the existence of God and the truths of Christianity are to be established on the grounds of natural reason, rather than on the ground of revelation and miracle. Bishop Butler himself was not a Deist. His *Analogy of Religion* is an effort to confute the Deistic treatment of Christianity and to vindicate the claims of the orthodox faith for supernatural revelation. Yet even in this anti-Deistic debate, Butler is thoroughly the rationalist, in showing how "revealed" Christianity is in keeping with natural religion and how even its supernaturalism is perfectly reasonable. With his Deistic opponents, he subscribes to the tenet of his age: the authority of reason.

The contrast between Puritanism and Butler is to be accounted for also by the Anglican theological tradition in which Butler stands. In the previous chapter mention was made of Puritanism as a term referring both to a moral spirit generally characteristic of the seventeenth century and more narrowly to a specific reform movement arising first within the Church of England, then developing into an ecclesiastical and political party, supporting a Presbyterian mode of church government and the cause of Parliament against the Crown. In this, the Puritans (in the specific sense of the word) were countered by the Anglicans, by far the majority element, who stood politically for the Crown and for episcopacy in church government. The most influential and able spokesman for the Anglican position, Richard Hooker (1554?-1600) had formulated at the end of the sixteenth century the main lines of Anglican thought in his *Laws of Ecclesiastical Polity*. Dealing especially with the problem of religious authority, this treatise of Hooker displays the characteristic Anglican *via media* (the phrase is John Donne's), a middle way between Calvinism and Roman Catholicism. Hooker fully appreciates Calvin's stature and accepts the authority of the Bible in matters pertaining to salvation. He is Protestant, too, in standing against the authority of Rome. Yet at the same time he is opposed to such a hard and fanatic Puritanism on the rise within England as would make the Bible the complete and sole authority for all the minutiae of life. This bibliolatry he challenges in the name of natural reason and the very nature of law. He bespeaks the authority of reason as the ground on which all Englishmen of good will, Anglican and Puritan, might come together. His treatment of the kinds of law (Book I of *Ecclesiastical Polity*) is a precise rephrasing of Thomas' philosophy of the laws in the *Summa,* with a certain pragmatic flexibility which makes it suitable to the English situation. Man has recourse, under God's providence, Hooker claims, to other kinds of law than the divine law of Scripture. Nature's law, the law of reason, provides guidance for novel needs where the application of the Bible as law book would be inappropriate. The long historic tradition of the church may also contain wisdom for present perplexities.

Hooker puts his discussion of law to main use on matters of church polity and church-state relations, rather than in broad problems of ethics. But his influence upon the ethical writing of Anglicans after him is very evident. Throughout the seventeenth century and into the eighteenth, where it is apparent in Butler, the ultimate reasonableness of Christian morality is a note repeated frequently. The Christian life is one of ordered harmony, wherein the master principle of cool reason fits the various demands of the self into a well-regulated whole, where the realms of nature and supernature, body and spirit, are regarded as supplementary, not opposed, and where self-love and benevolence both find their due place in Christian living. Thus the perennial Aristotelian and Thomistic ideal of the good life finds its renewed expression in Anglicanism.

Human Nature the Basis of Morality

Butler's ethical theory is set forth in his *Fifteen Sermons Preached at the Rolls Chapel* and in a brief essay, *On the Nature of Virtue,* appended to his *Analogy of Religion.* His method of analysis of the moral life is especially significant, for he belongs with all those moral theorists who look first at something primal and self-evident in human nature upon which the "oughts" of good action, they claim, must be built. Unlike those Christian thinkers who begin by affirming a truth about God's nature, or the incarnation, or the revealed will of God in church or Bible, or who begin with the Pauline situation of man at war with himself, Butler wants to make a new start on the problem of what it means to be a Christian.

Just as Descartes commences afresh in a theory of knowledge with his *cogito, ergo sum,* so Butler takes as his point of departure the most plain, indubitable fact about human nature in action which universally makes him a moral agent. As with Aristotle's beginning point, that man is rational, or that of the Utilitarians, that man seeks pleasure and avoids pain, it is a matter for discussion whether Butler's starting point is indeed a fact or a posited faith, every much as dogmatic as the bottom faith that another might hold in the incarnation, or the moral law, or the ultimacy of the state. In any case, Butler's ethics is autonomous, not theonomous, in its foundation.

What man should do, according to Butler, is to live according to his true nature. This by no means allows, any more than for the Greeks, the casual yielding to any whim or animal impulse that seems "natural." For precisely what is natural to man are certain moral qualities with which he is created by God. To be sure, he shares with the animals basic propulsions and appetites. But he also has a conscious impulse of "self-love," the elemental sense of responsibility of each self for its own needs and happiness. Moreover, he has a natural benevolence, a concern for the well-being of those in society entrusted to his care. Supremely, and in distinction from the animal, man has a conscience, a rational principle of reflection which passes judgment on his own actions and those of others, which controls the basic propulsions and appetites, and balances self-love with benevolence in an ordered, sensible whole. This principle of conscience is the superior element in the constitution of human nature. To be good is to live by its governance. "The very constitution of our nature requires, that we bring our whole conduct before this superior faculty; wait its determination; enforce upon ourselves its authority, and make it the business of our lives, as it is absolutely the whole business of a moral agent, to conform ourselves to it. This is the true meaning of that ancient precept, *Reverence thyself.*"[1]

Thus far Butler traverses the lines of classical Greek moral

[1] Joseph Butler, *Sermons* (New York: Robert Carter & Bros., 1858), p. xii.

theory. The distinctively Christian element follows in his attempt to show that the moral theory of the gospels is the fullest and most convincing expression of this natural morality that one could find. The ethical teachings of Jesus Christ are normative for Christians, not because they go counter to human nature but because obedience to them fulfills our true natures and brings the happiness all men seek. "To love thy neighbor as thyself" is the great moral commandment precisely in that it harmonizes private and public interest, self-love and benevolence. Even the radical and strenuous requirement of love to our enemies, Butler takes pains to show, is "in truth the law of our nature" as we are benevolent creatures: revenge and retaliation compound rather than cancel the injury to social happiness: forgiveness brings self-realization and public concord.

Finally, Butler links this description of the moral life to religion by pointing out that the love of God is rightly the other part of the great commandment since the final fulfillment of man's moral and affectional nature can be in nothing less than the sum and perfection of all goodness, which is God himself. The vision of God, the last and surpassing end of man, awaits the next life, however, since the limited and partial nature of this life renders impossible the face-to-face encounter of the creature with his Creator.

The Reasonableness of Christian Ethics

The manifold significance of Butler's interpretation of Christian morality lies in part in the historical context in which he undertakes to justify the Christian faith. As the sources below indicate, much of his thought turns around the problem of self-love and benevolence, a perennial problem for moral deliberation, but one debated with especial urgency in his day. On the one hand, the blunt scepticism of Thomas Hobbes had challenged traditional piety and morality with the claim that man is after all an egoist, and his pretensions to kindness and virtue are mere costumes for self-interest. Hobbes thoroughly shocked the defenders of tradition and touched off a long chain-sequence of complex debate about the place of egoism in morality, in which Butler's thought is one chapter and in which he takes the side against Hobbes. On the other hand, the kind of fanatic sectarian Christianity which makes a fetish of self-denial ("one-half of religion" according to the Calvinists) Butler finds equally untenable. He urges Christian morality as the true guide of life, since it so sanely balances proper self-love with benevolence. A sheer unqualified egoism is inadequate as the basis for a moral theory, since it overlooks undeniable empirical facts: that men do act out of concern for others and that they naturally commend such benevolence in their neighbors as they deplore its absence. Nor is the Christian life a matter of miserable, unrequited cross-bearing. The pursuit of happiness and self-satisfaction for the self parallels benevolence, according to the constitution of human nature. Thus Butler would solve the problem of self-realization in ethics not so much by way of saying that spiritual satisfaction is the unconscious and unsought byproduct of selfless devotion ("He that loses his life shall find it."), as by way of deliberately making both self-satisfaction and benevolence, private and public benefit, the twin goals of Christian behavior.

It is apparent from what has been said that Butler belongs to that tradition within Christian history, classically represented by St. Thomas, which represents the whole of reality as a good and rational harmony. There is no sharp division in Butler between the realms of the natural and supernatural, between the demands of Christ and the demands of human nature and of a decent culture, between sinful life and redeemed life. Man's nature he takes to be essentially good, and his conscience, his inward monitor of reflection, he does not find to be twisted or perverted by sin as have darker theologians in Christian thought. The dictates of the natural conscience are inherently right and good. Man "hath the rule of right within; what is wanting is only that he honestly attend to it."[2]

[2] *Ibid.*, p. 48.

Butler's favorable estimate of human nature is illustrated by his treatment of sin. Though some of the sermons give sign of Butler's canny insight into human self-deceit and self-righteousness, for the larger part he describes human sin in essentially Greek terms: as disproportion and lack of harmonious order in living, or as the failure of the principle of conscience to maintain the passions in their rightful place, and "in having an unreasonable and too great regard for ourselves, in comparison of others."[3] Salvation, then, if the term can be properly used, consists in taking greater thought, and in paying closer heed to the dictates of conscience.

We have noted earlier the autonomous starting point of Butler's moral reconstruction, his commencement with natural man. In what sense now may his ethical theory be called Christian, if the theological element be an ingredient necessary for Christian ethics? Butler's own theological position is somewhat uncertain. In one sense, it is plain that he assumes a supernatural Creator of all the parts of man's being and the source and sanction of his conscience. It is also evident that he expects a "final distribution of things," a Judgment of God, when all virtue will be rewarded and the moral books balanced out of the imbalances of finite life. He speaks at length of the life of virtue as "obedience to the will of God." Yet withal, the theological element in Butler's thinking is rather more a supplement to his moral theory than a foundation. In contrast to Luther, for whom God judges and condemns natural morality, or to a Puritan for whom the moral life is sustained and renewed by God's present active grace, for Butler religion completes morality rather than judges and sustains it. Butler's God is less the living wilful sovereign of the Puritan and more the abstract Principle of Perfect Goodness, who sees to the final coincidence of virtue and happiness, who presides over human operations, but remotely, and who, it may not be too much to say, himself partakes of the character of the kind and calm reasonableness of the English gentleman. It becomes interesting to compare

[3] *Ibid.*, p. 117.

this faith of Butler's, as an answer to the Deism of the day, with that of the evangelical revivals of Wesley and Edwards in the same century.

SOURCES

From

JOSEPH BUTLER: FIFTEEN SERMONS PREACHED AT THE ROLLS CHAPEL[4]

Upon Human Nature

> For as we have many members in one body, and all members have not the same office: so we being many are one body in Christ, and every one members one of another.—Rom. 12:4, 5.

The relation which the several parts or members of the natural body have to each other and to the whole body, is here compared to the relation which each particular person in society has to other particular persons and to the whole society; and the latter is intended to be illustrated by the former. And if there be a likeness between these two relations, the consequence is obvious: that the latter shows us we were intended to do good to others, as the former shows us that the several members of the natural body were intended to be instruments of good to each other and to the whole body. But as there is scarce any ground for a comparison between society and the mere material body, this without the mind being a dead unactive thing; much less can the comparison be carried to any length. And since the apostle speaks of the several members as having distinct offices, which implies the mind; it cannot be thought an unallowable liberty, instead of the body and its members, to substitute the whole nature of man, and all the variety of

[4] The material following is taken from Joseph Butler: *Sermons* (New York: Robert Carter & Bros., 1858).

internal principles which belong to it. And then the comparison will be between the nature of man as respecting self, and tending to private good, his own preservation and happiness; and the nature of man as having respect to society, and tending to promote public good, the happiness of that society. These ends do indeed perfectly coincide; and to aim at public and private good are so far from being inconsistent, that they mutually promote each other: yet in the following discourse they must be considered as entirely distinct; otherwise the nature of man as tending to one, or as tending to the other, cannot be compared. There can no comparison be made, without considering the things compared as distinct and different.

From this review and comparison of the nature of man as respecting self, and as respecting society, it will plainly appear, that there are as real and the same kind of indications in human nature, that we were made for society and to do good to our fellow creatures; as that we were intended to take care of our own life and health and private good: and that the same objections lie against one of these assertions, as against the other. For,

First, There is a natural principle of benevolence in man; which is in some degree to society, what self-love is to the individual. And if there be in mankind any disposition to friendship; if there be any such thing as compassion, for compassion is momentary love; if there be any such thing as the paternal or filial affections; if there be any affection in human nature, the object and end of which is the good of another; this is itself benevolence, or the love of another. Be it ever so short, be it in ever so low a degree, or ever so unhappily confined; it proves the assertion, and points out what we were designed for, as really as though it were in a higher degree and more extensive. I must however remind you that though benevolence and self-love are different; though the former tends most directly to public good, and the latter to private: yet they are so perfectly coincident, that the greatest satisfactions to ourselves depend upon our having benevolence in a due degree; and that self-love is one chief security of our right behaviour towards society. It may be added, that their mutual coinciding, so that we can scarce promote one without the other, is equally a proof that we were made for both.

Secondly, This will further appear, from observing that the several passions and affections, which are distinct both from benevolence and self-love, do in general contribute and lead us to public good as really as to private. It might be thought too minute and particular, and would carry us too great a length, to distinguish between and compare together the several passions or appetites distinct from benevolence, whose primary use and intention is the security and good of society; and the passions distinct from self-love, whose primary intention and design is the security and good of the individual. It is enough to the present argument, that desire of esteem from others, contempt and esteem of them, love of society as distinct from affection to the good of it, indignation against successful vice, that these are public affections or passions; have an immediate respect to others, naturally lead us to regulate our behaviour in such a manner as will be of service to our fellow creatures. If any or all of these may be considered likewise as private affections, as tending to private good; this does not hinder them from being public affections too, or destroy the good influence of them upon society, and their tendency to public good. It may be added, that as persons without any conviction from reason of the desirableness of life, would yet of course preserve it merely from the appetite of hunger; so by acting merely from regard (suppose) to reputation, without any consideration of the good of others, men often contribute to public good. In both these instances they are plainly instruments in the hands of another, in the hands of Providence, to carry on ends, the preservation of the individual and good of society, which they themselves have not in their view or intention. The sum is, men have various appetites, passions, and particular affections, quite distinct both from self-love and from benevolence: all of these have a tendency to promote both public and private good, and may be considered as respecting others and ourselves equally and in common: but some of them seem most immediately to respect others, or tend to public good; others of them most immediately to respect self, or tend to private good: as the former are not benevolence, so the latter are not self-love: neither sort are instances of our love either to ourselves or others; but only instances of our Maker's care and love both of the individual and the species, and proofs that he intended we should be instruments of good to each other, as well as that we should be so to ourselves.

Thirdly, There is a principle of reflection in men, by which they distinguish between, approve and disapprove their own actions. We are plainly constituted such sort of creatures as to reflect upon our own nature. The mind can take a view of what passes within itself, its propensions, aversions, passions, affections, as respecting such objects, and in such degrees; and of the several actions consequent thereupon. In this survey it approves of one, disapproves of another, and towards a third is affected in neither of these ways, but is quite indifferent. This principle in man, by which he approves or disapproves his heart, temper, and actions, is conscience; for this is the strict sense of the word, though sometimes it is used so as to take in more. And that this faculty tends to restrain men from doing mischief to each other, and leads them to do good, is too manifest to need being insisted upon. Thus a parent has the affection of love to his children: this leads him to take care of, to educate, to make due provision for them; the natural affection leads to this: but the reflection that it is his proper business, what belongs to him, that it is right and commendable so to do; this added to the affection becomes a much more settled principle, and carries him on through more labour and difficulties for the sake of his children, than he would undergo from that affection alone, if he thought it, and the course of action it led to, either indifferent or criminal. This indeed is impossible, to do that which is good and not to approve of it; for which reason they are frequently not considered as distinct, though they really are: for men often approve of the actions of others, which they will not imitate, and likewise do that which they approve not. It cannot possibly be denied, that there is this principle of reflection or conscience in human nature. Suppose a man to relieve an innocent person in great distress; suppose the same man afterwards, in the fury of anger, to do the greatest mischief to a person who had given no just cause of offence; to aggravate the injury, add the circumstances of former friendship, and obligation from the injured person; let the man who is supposed to have done these two different actions, coolly reflect upon them afterwards, without regard to their consequences to himself: to assert that any common man would be affected in the same way towards these different actions, that he would make no distinction between them, but approve or disapprove them equally, is too glaring a falsity to need being confuted. There is therefore this principle of reflection or conscience in mankind. It is needless to compare the respect it has to private good, with the respect it has to public; since it plainly tends as much to the latter as to the former, and is commonly thought to tend chiefly to the latter. This faculty is now mentioned merely as another part in the inward frame of man, pointing out to us in some degree what we are intended for, and as what will naturally and of course have some influence. The particular place assigned to it by nature, what authority it has, and how great influence it ought have, shall be hereafter considered.

From this comparison of benevolence and self-love, of our public and private affections, of the courses of life they lead to, and of the principle of reflection or conscience as respecting each of them, it is as manifest, that we were made for society, and to promote the happiness of it; as that we were intended to take care of our own life, and health, and private good.

I am afraid it would be thought very strange, if to confirm the truth of this account of human nature, and make out the justness of the foregoing comparison, it should be added, that, from what appears, men in fact as much and as often contradict that part of their nature which respects self, and which leads them to their own private good and happiness; as they contradict that part of it which respects society, and tends to public good: that there are as few persons, who attain the greatest satisfaction and enjoyment which they might attain in the present world; as who do the good to others which they might do; nay, that there are as few who can be said really and in earnest to aim at one, as at the other. Take a survey of mankind: the world in general, the good and bad, almost without exception, equally are agreed, that were religion out of the case, the happiness of the present life would consist in a manner wholly in riches, honours, sensual gratifications; insomuch that one scarce hears a reflection made upon prudence, life, conduct, but upon this supposition. Yet on the contrary, that persons in the greatest affluence of fortune are no happier than such as have only a competency; that the cares and disappointments of ambition for the most part far exceed the satisfactions of it; as also the miserable intervals of intemperance and excess, and the many untimely deaths occasioned by a dissolute course of life; these things are all seen, acknowledged, by every one acknowledged; but are thought no objections against, though they expressly contradict, this universal principle, that the happiness of the present life consists in one or other of them. Whence is all this absurdity and contradiction? Is not the middle way obvious? Can any thing be more manifest, than that the happiness of life consists in these possessed and enjoyed only to a certain degree; that to pursue them beyond this degree, is always attended with more inconvenience than advantage to a man's self, and often with extreme misery and unhappiness. Whence then, I say, is all this absurdity and contradiction? Is it really the result of consideration in mankind, how they may become most easy to themselves, most free from care, and enjoy the chief happiness attainable in this world? Or is it not manifestly owing either to this, that they have not cool and reasonable concern enough for themselves to consider wherein their chief happiness in the present life consists; or else, if they do consider it, that they will not act conformably to what is the result of that consideration: i.e. reasonable concern for themselves, or cool self-love is prevailed over by passion and appetite. So that from what appears, there is no ground to assert that those principles in the nature of man, which most directly lead to promote the good of our fellow creatures, are more generally or in a greater degree violated, than those, which most directly lead us to promote our own private good and happiness.

The sum of the whole is plainly this. The nature of man, considered in his single capacity, and with respect only to the present world, is adapted and leads him to attain the greatest happiness he can for himself in the present world. The nature of man, considered in his public or social capacity, leads him to a right behaviour in society to that course of life which we call virtue. Men follow or obey their nature in both these capacities and respects to a certain degree, but not entirely: their actions do not come up to the whole of what their nature leads them to in either of these capacities or respects: and they often violate their nature in both, i.e. as they neglect the duties they owe to their fellow creatures, to which their nature leads them; and are injurious, to which their nature is abhorrent; so there is a manifest negligence in men of their real happiness or interest in the present world, when that interest is inconsistent with a present gratification; for the sake of which they negligently, nay, even knowingly, are the authors and instruments of their own misery and ruin. Thus they are as often unjust to themselves as to others, and for the most part are equally so to both by the same actions.[5]

Upon the Love of our Neighbour

> And if there be any other commandment, it is briefly comprehended in this saying, namely, Thou shalt love thy neighbour as thyself.—Rom. 13:9.

The love of our neighbour is the same with charity, benevolence, or good-will: it is an affection to the good and happi-

[5] *Ibid.*, Sermon I.

ness of our fellow creatures. This implies in it a disposition to produce happiness: and this is the simple notion of goodness, which appears so amiable wherever we meet with it. From hence it is easy to see, that the perfection of goodness consists in love to the whole universe. This is the perfection of Almighty God.

But as man is so much limited in his capacity, as so small a part of the creation comes under his notice and influence, and as we are not used to consider things in so general a way; it is not to be thought of, that the universe should be the object of benevolence to such creatures as we are. Thus in that precept of our Saviour, "Be ye perfect, even as your Father which is in heaven is perfect," the perfection of the divine goodness is proposed to our imitation as it is promiscuous, and extends to the evil as well as the good; not as it is absolutely universal, imitation of it in this respect being plainly beyond us. The object is too vast. For this reason moral writers also have substituted a less general object for our benevolence, mankind. But this likewise is an object too general, and very much out of our view. Therefore persons more practical have, instead of mankind, put our country; and this is what we call a public spirit; which in men of public stations is the character of a patriot. But this is speaking to the upper part of the world. Kingdoms and governments are large; and the sphere of action of far the greatest part of mankind is much narrower than the government they live under: or, however, common men do not consider their actions as affecting the whole community of which they are members. There plainly is wanting a less general and nearer object of benevolence for the bulk of men, than that of their country. Therefore the scripture, not being a book of theory and speculation, but a plain rule of life for mankind, has with the utmost possible propriety put the principle of virtue upon the love of our neighbour; which is that part of the universe, that part of mankind, that part of our country, which comes under our immediate notice, acquaintance, and influence, and with which we have to do.

This is plainly the true account or reason, why our Saviour

places the principle of virtue in the love of our neighbour; and the account itself shows who are comprehended under that relation.

Let us now consider in what sense we are commanded to love our neighbour as ourselves.

This precept, in its first delivery by our Saviour, is thus introduced: "Thou shalt love the Lord thy God with all thine heart, with all thy soul, and with all thy strength; and thy neighbour as thyself." These very different manners of expression do not lead our thoughts to the same measure or degree of love, common to both objects; but to one, peculiar to each. Supposing then, which is to be supposed, a distinct meaning and propriety in the words, *as thyself;* the precept we are considering will admit of any of these senses: that we bear the same kind of affection to our neighbour, as we do to ourselves: or, that the love we bear to our neighbour should have some certain proportion or other to self-love: or, lastly, that it should bear the particular proportion of equality, that it be in the same degree.

First, The precept may be understood as requiring only, that we have the same kind of affection to our fellow creatures, as to ourselves: that, as every man has the principle of self-love, which disposes him to avoid misery, and consult his own happiness; so we should cultivate the affection of good-will to our neighbour, and that it should influence us to have the same kind of regard to him. This at least must be commanded: and this will not only prevent our being injurious to him, but will also put us upon promoting his good. There are blessings in life, which we share in common with others; peace, plenty, freedom, healthful seasons. But real benevolence to our fellow creatures would give us the notion of a common interest in a stricter sense: for in the degree we love another, his interest, his joys and sorrows, are our own. It is from self-love that we form the notion of private good, and consider it as our own: love of our neighbour would teach us thus to appropriate to ourselves his good and welfare, to consider ourselves as having a real share in his happiness. Thus the principle of benevolence would be an advocate within our own breasts, to take care of the interests of our fellow creatures in all the interfering and competitions which cannot but be, from the imperfection of our nature, and the state we are in. It would likewise, in some measure, lessen that interfering; and hinder men from forming so strong a notion of private good, exclusive of the good of others, as we commonly do. Thus, as the private affection makes us in a peculiar manner sensible of humanity, justice or injustice, when exercised towards ourselves; love of our neighbour would give us the same kind of sensibility in his behalf. This would be the greatest security of our uniform obedience to that most equitable rule; "Whatsoever ye would that men should do unto you, do ye even so unto them."

Secondly, The precept before us may be understood to require, that we love our neighbour in some certain proportion or other, according as we love ourselves. And indeed a man's character cannot be determined by the love he bears to his neighbour, considered absolutely: but the proportion which this bears to self-love, whether it be attended to or not, is the chief thing which forms the character, and influences the actions. For, as the form of the body is a composition of various parts; so likewise our inward structure is not simple or uniform, but a composition of various passions, appetites, affections, together with rationality; including in this last both the discernment of what is right, and a disposition to regulate ourselves by it. There is greater variety of parts in what we call a character, than there are features in a face: and the morality of that is no more determined by one part, than the beauty or deformity of this is by one single feature: each is to be judged of by all the parts or features, not taken singly, but together. In the inward frame the various passions, appetites, affections, stand in different respects to each other. The principles in our mind may be contradictory, or checks and allays only, or incentives and assistants to each other. And principles, which in their nature have no kind of contrariety or affinity, may yet accidentally be each other's allays or incentives.

Further, the whole system, as I may speak, of affections

(including rationality), which constitute the heart, as this word is used in Scripture and on moral subjects, are each and all of them stronger in some than in others. Now the proportion which the two general affections, benevolence and self-love, bear to each other, according to this interpretation of the text, denominates men's character as to virtue. Suppose then one man to have the principle of benevolence in an higher degree than another: it will not follow from hence, that his general temper, or character, or actions, will be more benevolent than the other's. For he may have self-love in such a degree as quite to prevail over benevolence; so that it may have no influence at all upon his actions; whereas benevolence in the other person, though in a lower degree, may yet be the strongest principle in his heart; and strong enough to be the guide of his actions, so as to denominate him a good and virtuous man. The case is here as in scales: it is not one weight, considered in itself, which determines whether the scale shall ascend or descend; but this depends upon the proportion which that one weight hath to the other.

Thirdly, if the words, *as thyself,* were to be understood of an equality of affection; it would not be attended with those consequences, which perhaps may be thought to follow from it. Suppose a person to have the same settled regard to others, as to himself; that in every deliberate scheme or pursuit he took their interest into the account in the same degree as his own, so far as an equality of affection would produce this: yet he would in fact, and ought to be, much more taken up and employed about himself, and his own concerns, than about others, and their interests. For, besides the one common affection toward himself and his neighbour, he would have several other particular affections, passions, appetites, which he could not possibly feel in common both for himself and others: now these sensations themselves very much employ us; and have perhaps as great influence as self-love. So far indeed as self-love, and cool reflection upon what is for our interest, would set us on work to gain a supply of our own several wants; so far the love of our neighbour would make us do the same for him: but the degree in which we are put upon seeking and making use of the means of gratification, by the feeling of those affections, appetites, and passions, must necessarily be peculiar to ourselves.

The general temper of mind which the due love of our neighbour would form us to, and the influence it would have upon our behaviour in life, is now to be considered.

The happy influence of this temper extends to every different relation and circumstance in human life. It plainly renders a man better, more to be desired, as to all the respects and relations we can stand in to each other. The benevolent man is disposed to make use of all external advantages in such a manner as shall contribute to the good of others, as well as to his own satisfaction. His own satisfaction consists in this. He will be easy and kind to his dependents, compassionate to the poor and distressed, friendly to all with whom he has to do. This includes the good neighbour, parent, master, magistrate: and such a behaviour would plainly make dependence, inferiority, and even servitude, easy. So that a good or charitable man of superior rank in wisdom, fortune, authority, is a common blessing to the place he lives in: happiness grows under his influence. This good principle in inferiors would discover itself in paying respect, gratitude, obedience, as due. It were therefore, methinks, one just way of trying one's own character, to ask ourselves, am I in reality a better master or servant, a better friend, a better neighbor, than such and such persons; whom, perhaps, I may think not to deserve the character of virtue and religion so much as myself?

I proceed to consider lastly, what is affirmed of the precept now explained, that it comprehends in it all others; i.e. that to love our neighbour as ourselves includes in it all virtues.

First, It is manifest that nothing can be of consequence to mankind or any creature, but happiness. This then is all which any person can, in strictness of speaking, be said to have a right to. We can therefore owe no man any thing, but only to further and promote his happiness, according to our abilities. And therefore a disposition and endeavor to do good to all with whom we have to do, in the degree and manner which the different relations we stand in to them require, is a discharge of all the obligations we are under to them.

As human nature is not one simple uniform thing, but a composition of various parts, body, spirit, appetites, particular passions, and affections; for each of which reasonable self-love would lead men to have due regard, and make suitable provision: so society consists of various parts, to which we stand in different respects and relations; and just benevolence would as surely lead us to have due regard to each of these, and behave as the respective relations require. Reasonable good-will, and right behaviour towards our fellow creatures, are in a manner the same: only that the former expresseth the principle as it is in the mind; the latter, the principle as it were become external, i.e. exerted in actions.

And so far as temperance, sobriety, and moderation in sensual pleasures, and the contrary vices, have any respect to our fellow creatures, any influence upon their quiet, welfare, and happiness; as they always have a real, and often a near influence upon it; so far it is manifest those virtues may be produced by the love of our neighbour, and that the contrary vices would be prevented by it. Indeed if men's regard to themselves will not restrain them from excess; it may be thought little probable, that their love to others will be sufficient: but the reason is, that their love to others is not, any more than their regard to themselves, just, and in its due degree. There are however manifest instances of persons kept sober and temperate from regard to their affairs, and the welfare of those who depend upon them. And it is obvious to every one, that habitual excess, a dissolute course of life, implies a general neglect of the duties we owe towards our friends, our families, and our country.

From hence it is manifest that the common virtues, and the common vices of mankind, may be traced up to benevolence, or the want of it. And this entitles the precept, "Thou shalt love thy neighbour as thyself," to the pre-eminence given to it; and is a justification of the Apostle's assertion, that all other commandments are comprehended in it: whatever cautions and restrictions there are, which might require to be considered, if we were to state particularly and at length, what is virtue and right behaviour in mankind.

Secondly, It might be added, that in a higher and more general way of consideration, leaving out the particular nature of creatures, and the particular circumstances in which they are placed, benevolence seems in the strictest sense to include in it all that is good and worthy; all that is good, which we have any distinct particular notion of. We have no clear conception of any positive moral attribute in the supreme Being, but what may be resolved up into goodness. And, if we consider a reasonable creature or moral agent, without regard to the particular relations and circumstances in which he is placed; we cannot conceive any thing else to come in towards determining whether he is to be ranked in a higher or lower class of virtuous beings, but the higher or lower degree in which that principle, and what is manifestly connected with it, prevail in him.

That which we more strictly call piety, or the love of God, and which is an essential part of a right temper, some may perhaps imagine no way connected with benevolence: yet surely they must be connected, if there be indeed in being an object infinitely good. Human nature is so constituted, that every good affection implies the love of itself; i.e. becomes the object of a new affection in the same person. Thus, to be righteous, implies in it the love of righteousness; to be benevolent, the love of benevolence; to be good, the love of goodness; whether this righteousness, benevolence, or goodness, be viewed as in our own mind, or in another's: and the love of God as a being perfectly good, is the love of perfect goodness contemplated in a being or person. Thus morality and religion, virtue and piety, will at last necessarily coincide, run up into one and the same point, and love will be in all senses the end of the commandment.[6]

[6] *Ibid.*, Sermon XII.

Upon the Love of God

> Thou shalt love the Lord thy God with all thy heart, and with all thy soul, and with all thy mind.—Matt. 22:37.

By the love of God, I would understand all those regards, all those affections of mind which are due immediately to him from such a creature as man, and which rest in him as their end. As this does not include servile fear; so neither will any other regards, how reasonable soever, which respect any thing out of or besides the perfection of divine nature, come into consideration here. But all fear is not excluded, because, his displeasure is itself the natural proper object of fear. Reverence, ambition of his love and approbation, delight in the hope or consciousness of it, come likewise into this definition of the love of God; because he is the natural object of all those affections or movements of mind, as really as he is the object of the affection, which is in the strictest sense called love; and all of them equally rest in him, as their end. And they may all be understood to be implied in these words of our Saviour, without putting any force upon them: for he is speaking of the love of God and our neighbour, as containing the whole of piety and virtue.

It is plain that the nature of man is so constituted, as to feel certain affections upon the sight or contemplation of certain objects. Now the very notion of affection implies resting in its object as an end. And the particular affection to good characters, reverence and moral love of them, is natural to all those who have any degree of real goodness in themselves. This will be illustrated by the description of a perfect character in a creature; and by considering the manner, in which a good man in his presence would be affected towards such a character. He would of course feel the affections of love, reverence, desire of his approbation, delight in the hope or consciousness of it. And surely all this is applicable, and may be brought up to that Being, who is infinitely more than an adequate object of all those affections: whom we are commanded to love with all our heart, with all our soul, and with all our mind. And of these regards towards Almighty God, some are more particularly suitable to and becoming so imperfect a creature as man, in this mortal state we are passing through; and some of them, and perhaps other exercises of the mind, will be the employment and happiness of good men in a state of perfection.

Resignation to the will of God is the whole of piety: it includes in it all that is good, and is a source of the most settled quiet and composure of mind. There is the general principle of submission in our nature. Man is not so constituted as to desire things, and be uneasy in the want of them, in proportion to their known value: many other considerations come in to determine the degrees of desire; particularly whether the advantage we take a view of be within the sphere of our rank. Who ever felt uneasiness, upon observing any of the advantages brute creatures have over us? And yet it is plain they have several. It is the same with respect to advantages belonging to creatures of a superior order. Thus, though we see a thing to be highly valuable, yet that it does not belong to our condition of being, is sufficient to suspend our desires after it, to make us rest satisfied without such advantage. Now there is just the same reason for quiet resignation in the want of every thing equally unattainable, and out of our reach in particular, though others of our species be possessed of it. All this may be applied to the whole of life; to positive inconveniences as well as wants; not indeed to the sensations of pain and sorrow, but to all the uneasinesses of reflection, murmuring, and discontent. Thus is human nature formed to compliance, yielding, submission of temper. We find the principles of it within us; and every one exercises it towards some objects or other; i.e. feels it with regard to some persons, and some circumstances. Now this is an excellent foundation of a reasonable and religious resignation. Nature teaches and inclines us to take up with our lot: the consideration, that the course of things is unalterable, hath a tendency to quiet the mind under it, to beget a submission of temper to it. But when we can add, that this unalterable course is appointed and continued by infinite wisdom and goodness; how absolute should be our submission, how entire our trust and dependence!

Our resignation to the will of God may be said to be perfect, when our will is lost and resolved up into his; when we rest in his will as our end, as being itself most just, and right, and good. And where is the impossibility of such an affection to what is just, and right, and good, such a loyalty of heart to the Governor of the universe, as shall prevail over all sinister indirect desires of our own? Neither is this at bottom any thing more than faith, and honesty, and fairness of mind; in a more enlarged sense indeed, than those words are commonly used. And as in common cases, fear and hope and other passions are raised in us by their respective objects: so this submission of heart and soul and mind, this religious resignation, would be as naturally produced by our having just conceptions of Almighty God, and a real sense of his presence with us. In how low a degree soever this temper usually prevails amongst men, yet it is a temper right in itself: it is what we owe to our Creator: it is particularly suitable to our mortal condition, and what we should endeavour after for our own sakes in our passage through such a world as this; where is nothing upon which we can rest or depend; nothing but what we are liable to be deceived and disappointed in. Thus we might "acquaint ourselves with God, and be at peace." This is piety and religion in the strictest sense, considered as an habit of mind; an habitual sense of God's presence with us; being affected towards him, as present, in the manner his superior nature requires from such a creature as man: this is to walk with God.

Let us then suppose a man entirely disengaged from business and pleasure, sitting down alone and at leisure, to reflect upon himself and his own condition of being. He would immediately feel that he was by no means complete of himself, but totally insufficient for his own happiness. One may venture to affirm, that every man hath felt this, whether he hath again reflected upon it or not. It is feeling this deficiency, that they are unsatisfied with themselves, which makes men look out for assistance from abroad; and which has given rise to various kinds of amusements, altogether needless any otherwise than as they serve to fill up the blank spaces of times, and so hinder their feeling this deficiency, and being uneasy with themselves. Now, if these external things we take up with were really an adequate supply to this deficiency of human nature, if by their means our capacities and desires were all satisfied and filled up; then it might be truly said, that we had found out the proper happiness of man; and so might sit down satisfied, and be at rest in the enjoyment of it. But if it appears, that the amusements, which men usually pass their time in, are so far from coming up to or answering our notions and desires of happiness, or good, that they are really no more than what they are commonly called, somewhat to pass away the time; i.e. somewhat which serves to turn us aside from, and prevent our attending to, this our internal poverty and want; if they serve only, or chiefly, to suspend, instead of satisfying our conceptions and desires of happiness; if the want remains, and we have found out little more than barely the means of making it less sensible; then are we still to seek for somewhat to be an adequate supply to it. It is plain that there is a capacity in the nature of man, which neither riches, nor honours, nor sensual gratifications, nor any thing in this world can perfectly fill up, or satisfy: there is a deeper and more essential want, than any of these things can be the supply of. Yet surely there is a possibility of somewhat, which may fill up all our capacities of happiness; somewhat, in which our souls may find rest; somewhat, which may be to us that satisfactory good we are inquiring after. But it cannot be any thing which is valuable only as it tends to some further end. Those therefore who have got this world so much into their hearts, as not to be able to consider happiness as consisting in any thing but property and possessions, which are only valuable as the means to somewhat else, cannot have the least glimpse of the subject before us; which is the end, not the means; the thing itself, not somewhat in order to it. But if you can lay aside that general, confused, undeterminate notion of happiness, as consisting in such possessions; and fix in your thoughts, that it really can consist in nothing but in a faculty's having its proper object; you will clearly see, that in the coolest way of consideration, without either the heat of fanciful enthusiasm, or the warmth of real devotion, nothing is more certain, than that an infinite Being may himself be, if he pleases, the supply to all the capacities of our nature. All the common enjoyments of life are from the faculties he hath endued us with, and the objects he hath made suitable to them. He may himself be to us infinitely more than all these: he may be to us all that we want. As our understanding can contemplate itself, and our affections be exercised upon themselves by reflection, so may each be employed in the same manner upon any other mind: and since the supreme Mind, the Author and Cause of all things, is the highest possible object to himself, he may be an adequate supply to all the faculties of our souls; a subject to our understanding, and an object to our affections.[7]

Further Readings

Primary Sources

Butler, Joseph. *Butler's Fifteen Sermons and a Dissertation of the Nature of Virtue.* Edited by T. A. Roberts. London: Society for the Promotion of Christian Knowledge, 1970.

———. *Five Sermons, and A Dissertation Upon the Nature of Virtue.* New York: Liberal Arts Press, 1950.

Hooker, Richard. *Of the Laws of Ecclesiastical Polity.* 2 vols. London: J. M. Dent (Everyman's Library), 1954.

Secondary Sources

Duncan-Jones, Austin. *Butler's Moral Philosophy.* Harmondsworth, Eng.: Penguin Books, 1952.

More, P. E., and Cross, F. L. (eds.). *Anglicanism, the Thought and Practise of the Church of England.* Milwaukee: Morehouse Publishing Co., 1935.

Mossner, E. C. *Bishop Butler and the Age of Reason.* New York: Macmillan, 1936.

Norton, William J. *Bishop Butler, Moralist and Divine.* New Brunswick: Rutgers University Press, 1940.

[7] *Ibid.*, Sermons XIII, XIV.

Chapter 12

JOHN WESLEY

Another type of response to the religious needs of eighteenth-century England, very different in spirit from that of Butler, is to be found in what is called the Evangelical Revival, a reformation of faith and morals as significant as Puritanism in the previous century. Although generally associated with the work of John Wesley and his Methodist preachers, he was not the sole leader in the movement; there were others, Spener, Franck, the Moravians on the Continent, and especially George Whitefield in England, who were at work even before Wesley. He stands, therefore, as one among many representing the revival of the faith of the Reformation. The development of the new denomination of Methodism, which Wesley himself resisted, incidentally, is quite secondary to the profound transformation of English life and manners, permeating all churches, the established Church of England as much as any, which was the fruit of this renewal.

The culture into which Wesley came was, by the common testimony of historians, in the throes of an economic transition to urban industrialism accompanied by political corruption and religious decline. The Church of England had lost prestige since the revolution. Its clergy was accused of corruption and ignorance by the Deists, of dead traditionalism by the modernists of the day. Indeed it had probably lost touch with large masses of the people, not only with the strong middle class, which had an affinity with nonconformity, but also with the new industrial workers. Its natural connection seemed to lie with the old landed classes and the rural workers. It represented old England and in outlook and concern was quite inept in meeting the spiritual needs of the new industrialism.

Wesley's life (1703-91) almost spans the century. The son of a high-church Anglican divine, brought up in an atmosphere of devout piety, the young Wesley first gave signs of his later development during his graduate days at Oxford. Along with his brother Charles and a few others who were troubled by the casual manner of religious and moral observances in the university community, John Wesley joined a club whose purpose was the methodical development of religious self-discipline and works of charity. This "Holy Club," as it was sneeringly called by more easy-going fellow students, may have been characterized by some prim self-righteousness, but its members were profoundly serious, self-critical men.

At the age of thirty-two Wesley ventured with his brother on a missionary enterprise to Georgia, under Governor Oglethorpe, to establish churches among the white settlers and to bring Christianity to the Indians. In this task he was almost a complete failure. Neither Indians nor colonists took to the stiff high-church ways of the young missionary. Wesley became increasingly uncertain of his own faith, and this uncertainty was deepened by his shipboard contact with some Moravian missionaries, who lived by a kind of intellectually simple and unself-conscious trust which both troubled and attracted him.

Returning to England in this mood he made further explorations into Moravian piety and the mysticism that lay behind it. Some resolution of his inner turmoil he experienced in 1738 at a mission chapel at Aldersgate, where he found a new emotional assurance of faith which served to undergird, though not displace, his intellectualism and methodical moral self-discipline. Still another conversion, perhaps as significant for the subsequent revival as Aldersgate, took place when, against all his churchly inclinations, he was persuaded by George Whitefield to follow his example in preaching to the people in the streets and fields of western England.

Field preaching was regarded by proper Englishmen of Wesley's day much as modern Protestants would look on tent-meeting revivalism or "store-front" churches. Yet it proved enormously successful. Wesley records crowds of ten and fifteen thousand who came to hear him preach, sometimes at five in the morning before going to work. What these folk heard was solid Christian doctrine and Biblical morality, cast in clear and cogent language. As one reads Wesley's or Whitefield's sermons today, laden as they are with Biblical quotations and unrelieved by dramatic illustration, one wonders what it was about them that constituted such a striking appeal. In part, no doubt, their success was due to the dramatic situation in which they were preached: Wesley standing on a stump or a tombstone in a churchyard, talking to people largely unnoticed by the church, emotionally and intellectually starved. In greater part it was due to the inward appeal of the message which Wesley preached in all seasons: God's saving grace available for all individuals, the lowly and the dispossessed as much as the privileged.

Wesley's unconventional activity, and that of his lay fellow preachers, at the first brought sharp opposition. He was often the target for heckling, rotten fruit, and bricks to the peril of his life. Protest came not only from the rowdy element of the mob, and grog-shop keepers who were losing trade, but also from the dignitaries and officials of the church, who were horrified at the informal, not to say riotous, goings-on and the "enthusiasm" of the revival. Things were not being done in decency and good order when the faith was entrusted to "a ragged legion of preaching barbers, cobblers, tinkers, scavengers, draymen, and chimney-sweepers."

From 1739 when he began his field preaching until his death, Wesley was prodigiously active in travel, preaching, study, and writing. He was a student of contemporary science and philosophy as well as theology. He crisscrossed England many times, traveling some 225,000 miles altogether, in a day when travel was a hardship, at first on horseback (with a loose rein, so that he could study his books as he rode), later by carriage. He had a genius for practical organization. He set up and administered a wide network of "class meetings" or "bands" whose discipline, in financial as much as in moral matters, he controlled with great pastoral skill and a firm hand.

The Theology of the Revival

Wesley nowhere gives a systematic *summa* of Christian theology and ethics. Though he regarded his *Standard Sermons* as normative doctrine for his societies, they are themselves occasional pieces. An over-all analysis of his writings, however, reveals an inner integrity to his thought, with certain distinctive stresses which taken together characterize the evangelical ideal of the Christian life.

In the main, Wesley lays no claim to novel doctrine; he calls his listeners back to the essential principles of Biblical Christianity. The distress of England, he feels, lies not in the inadequacy of its professed standards, but in its moral defection in practice from the principles it acknowledges in theory. As with so many periods of reformation in the history of Christianity, familiar but neglected doctrines are brought to life again for the common people. In his sermons and letters and treatises he treats the traditional tenets of the Christian faith not as intellectual abstractions, to be logically debated and tidily arranged into a philosophy, but as matters of life and death to be experienced in the heart and seriously lived out.

The tradition of Christianity has many facets. Wesley's particular understanding of tradition is something different from that of the scholasticism of the Roman church, or from mysticism, either of the medieval or Quaker sort, which Wesley disclaimed as too quietistic. There is much of the Puritan in Wesley: He said of himself he was "within a hair's breadth of Calvinism." But his stress on human free will, over against the Calvinistic theory of divine decree, and on the possibility of perfection in this life, puts him at considerable remove from the Puritanism of his day and in a somewhat median position between Calvinism and Arminianism, the view which, shortly speaking, lays responsibility for human salvation as much upon man as upon God. Nor does Wesley ever lose the marks of his Anglican training. Thus one can detect many different strands in his thought.

What seems to be the genius of the Methodist revival is a particular combination of (1) Puritanism with (2) the sectarian ideal of a "scriptural holiness" to be lived perfectly in this life, and with (3) the pietism typified by the Moravians, which holds the inward change of heart in conversion, as the simple trust of the believer in Christ, to be the essence of religion.

The sectarian ideal is seen in the fact that the early Methodists feel themselves to be a "new community," "going on to perfection," who had made a radical break with their own past and the ways of the world. They are not more-or-less Christians, treating religion as a healthful hobby or a pleasant cultural adornment. They strive to be "total" Christians, saved by faith in Christ and living now under his tutelage in strict moral group and self discipline. Whereas one type of sectarianism tends toward an actual physical withdrawal from the world into some sort of separate and insulated mode of living, the new community of Methodists lives within English culture, as leaven in the lump, "in the world but not of the world." Wesley made it his goal "to reform the nation, and more especially the Church, and to spread Scriptural Holiness over the land." He countenanced no separation from the Church of England, though the inner sectarian impetus of his revival led after his death to the formation of a new church. The members of his societies were not to forego their citizenship in the economic and political life of England, but to work within it heartily and patriotically. Such an ideal is clearly akin to the Puritanism of Richard Baxter, which goes its way physically amid the world, subscribing to its laws, buying and selling in its markets, yet withal separating itself spiritually from all the world's lusts and prides.

Pietism provides also a strong influence. Wesley's own

contact with the Moravians and his conversion at Aldersgate, a "heart-warming" rather than a head-clearing experience, leads him to stress the inward consecration of the devoted heart over doctrinal exactitude or a moral legalism, important though doctrine and morality are, as the *sine qua non* of true religion. Though the Anglican in him resists the excesses of emotionalism which came with his revival, the ardent hymn-singing and the testimonials of Methodist meetings seem to him valid expressions of new conviction. The fervency of the Methodist's faith is not something opposed to reason: Wesley consistently justifies the Christian way to the eighteenth-century mind as the truly reasonable one. But this inner religion of the heart is something underneath reason which the simple can experience while the experts debate. He decries not the forms of the Anglican worship of his day but its formalism, which substitutes the externals of its worship and the proprieties of polite behavior for authentic religion. "I take religion to be," he once wrote in a letter, "not the bare saying over so many prayers, morning and evening, in public or in private, nor anything superadded now and then to a careless or worldly life; but a constant ruling habit of soul, a renewal of our minds in the image of God, a recovery of the divine likeness, a still-increasing conformity of heart and life to the pattern of our most holy Redeemer."

Christian Perfection

The passage quoted above suggests one of the distinctive elements of Wesley's preaching: the doctrine of Christian perfection. The term itself is a troublesome one, and the long controversy over this doctrine in which Wesley finds himself is due to the misunderstanding of his opponents about what he means and to some confusion of his own about its implications. For the idea of Christian perfection Wesley is indebted to certain New Testament passages, but more especially to three devotional classics, William Law's *Christian Perfection*, Jeremy Taylor's *Holy Living*, and *The Imitation of Christ* by the medieval mystic Thomas à Kempis.

By the term "Christian perfection" Wesley does not mean that natural man is innocent and pure, or that he can make himself perfect through the use of intelligence or a discipline of moral gymnastics. Wesley acknowledges, with the orthodox theology of his day, that "natural" man since Adam is corrupt, a child of self-will and pride. For the strict Calvinist, however, the saving grace brought to sinful man by Jesus Christ is only partially and precariously possessed now by the believer, who needs to await the next life for the "state of glory." Wesley, on the other hand, is prepared to say that if Jesus Christ is to be called the Saviour of men, he really saves them from sin in a way that is certain and that can be enjoyed even within the bounds of finite life. There is, to be sure, an after-life (as there is a "wrath to come"), into which one may go from glory into glory, but perfection need not await that day. To Wesley, the message of the Gospel ("the good news") indubitably assures this as possible in this life for those who are born again.

Perfection for Wesley is a dominantly volitional concept. That is, the truly saved or "justified" man is one whose will is rightly turned toward God, away from self, an orientation which cleanses man from the essential sin and gives his life a primally right direction. It is a perfection of intention, not a state of arrival or completion. He writes: "In one view, it is purity of intention, dedicating all the life to God. It is giving God all our heart; it is one desire and design ruling all our tempers. It is the devoting, not a part, but all, our soul, body, and substance to God. In another view, it is all the mind which was in Christ, enabling us to walk as Christ walked. It is the circumcision of the heart from all filthiness, all inward as well as outward pollution. It is a renewal of the heart in the whole image of God, the full likeness of Him that created it. In yet another, it is the loving God with all our heart, and our neighbor as ourselves."[1]

"Love" is thus the key word in Wesley's understanding of perfection, "the very essence of it," as he affirmed. Christian

[1] John Wesley, *A Plain Account of Christian Perfection*, sec. 27.

love, as a gift from God felt in the heart of the believer, issues in "the love of our neighbor; a calm, generous, disinterested benevolence to every child of man. This earnest, steady good-will to our fellow-creatures never flowed from any fountain but gratitude to our Creator."

Perfection does not mean deliverance from mistaken judgments, from bodily infirmities, "the thousand natural shocks that flesh is heir to," or from temptation. Moreover, there is no guarantee that once gained, it may not be lost. On the moot question whether perfection means an actual incapacity to commit sin, Wesley is somewhat uncertain. At times, in his more extravagant moments, he implies that perfection means a state of assured sinlessness; in more cautious moments, he admits that the saved Christian may morally err. Of one thing he is certain: "There is no perfection . . . which does not admit of a continual increase. So that now how much soever any man has attained, . . . he hath still need to 'grow in grace' and daily to advance in the knowledge and love of God his Saviour." He is equally sure that the "new life" of man in Christ, achieved in the radical about-face of conversion, also entails continual discipline in the moral life. There is no ground to support the claim of a sceptic that Wesley substitutes a "justification by feeling" for the Reformation principle of "justification by faith." For the element of moral discipline is indigenous to the experience of conversion, and Wesley spells out that discipline in specific form. It has been noted that Wesley here conjoins the Protestant emphasis on sudden conversion with the Catholic element of gradual discipline. Perhaps it is more simply explained by saying that he reasserts the Biblical motif that the Kingdom of God is both gift and demand and that grace does not dispense with law. Both the conversion by God's grace and the discipline of scrupulous moral improvement are necessary—the former to save the Christian life from an anxious and calculating spirit of self-salvation by "works"; the latter to save it from a lawlessness which might claim that "to feel saved" is all that is necessary.

Individual and Social Salvation

One of the central and perennial questions of Christian ethics, as well as sociological theory, has to do with the mode of social change. Put oversimply, is society to be reconstructed from within, by the changed individuals within it, or reconstructed from without, by institutional changes which will provide a context favorable to the development of individuals? The Wesleyan revival, and its impact on English and American culture, is important to study in terms of this alternative, "individual" or "social" salvation.

At first glance it appears that Wesley follows the line of traditional Protestantism, over against environmentalism, in choosing the "changed heart" as the all-important thing. "You have nothing to do but to save souls," he told his Methodist preachers. Wesley had no notion of seeking to redeem society through legislation. On the contrary, he would have opposed the whole philosophy of the "welfare state" had it been suggested in his day. Politically he was a conservative Tory, thoroughly loyal to the Crown, in an era when the Georges on the throne were hardly models of Christian perfection. His *Calm Address to our American Colonies* was a highly influential tract popularizing the common arguments against the American Revolution. He counseled his ministers against preaching on politics, except where they might support the king; certainly they were not "to meddle with those given to change." He feared the poor of England as a political bloc as much as he loved them individually. It becomes quite false, then, to claim Wesley as an intentional contributor to the democratic political ferment of that century, at least in so far as democracy is defined in terms of the French Revolution.

On the other hand, there were factors in the evangelical revival which proved in time socially revolutionary. Its spiritual reformation of life worked out from within to effect as its by-product economic amelioration and improved cultural institutions. The evangelical pietism of the Methodists means primarily an inward change of heart. But such change is not a private affair. True faith involves works of charity, just as the love of God, "the one perfect good," involves the love of neighbor. Methodism is as intensely social as it is intensely inward. Salvation does not mean a private preparation for heaven; it means a life of moral purity and social concern.

Wesley was by no means blind to the tragic maladjustments which the Industrial Revolution brought in his lifetime. In traditional Protestant fashion he located the source of this maladjustment not in the machine, nor in industrialism itself, but in "ungodliness" and vice. But his *Journal* records his burning concern with the bleak poverty and the coarse living of the crowds who came to hear him. He himself was unflaggingly busy in all sorts of social salvage and social reform enterprises. He visited English prisons many times, preaching to their inmates and commenting bitterly in his letters on the misery of prison conditions. He set up a simple loan society among his Methodists to help keep his poor followers from the clutches of the pawnbrokers and out of debtors' prisons. He fought hard liquor as much for economic as for moral reasons. He edited a *Christian Library*, fifty volumes of extracts from Christian literature, for popular use. He established a free medical dispensary and wrote a book of simple home remedies for sickness called *Primitive Physic*, which ran to twenty-three editions. He established a home for widows and a school for poor children. He joined with a few valiant Quakers in the unfashionable opposition to slavery. In his last letter, written to William Wilberforce, encouraging him in the battle to abolish slavery in England and even America, he wrote: "A man who has a black skin, being wronged or outraged by a white man, can have no redress; it being a *law* in all our Colonies that the oath of a black against a white goes for nothing. What villainy is this." For Wesley, it would seem clear that "saving souls" involves personal love and social justice.

In the twentieth century, when the Christian conscience

X Bob Hughes would say principally for economic and social reasons (not so much for "moral" reasons) has become sensitive as much to the dangers of uninhibited capitalism as to communism, Wesley's economic ethics, set forth in the sermon *On the Use of Money,* may seem an unwarranted baptism of free enterprise with the holy water of Christianity. At the least it looks like a clear example of the theses of Weber and of Tawney discussed in Chapter 10: that the Protestant spirit gives a moral sanction to capitalistic pursuits. Yet if one examines this economic morality in terms of the historical context in which it was set forth, one may grasp more readily its ameliorative influence. Wesley's message—"gain all you can, save all you can, give all you can"—is addressed not to "capitalists," well-dressed vestrymen in "uptown" churches, but to manual workers and the disinherited, who have a hard time scraping up the one-penny dues used by the Methodist societies for charity work. Wesley preaches to these folk essentially the principle of vocation and Calvinistic stewardship. What one acquires by way of earthly goods is to be acquired diligently and honestly without hurt to another. "Save all you can" does not mean to invest or hoard. It means simplicity of living: to waste nothing, to spend nothing on cheap or degrading pastimes. And "give all you can" means the sacrificial mutual sharing among the poor, not the handouts of the rich from their superfluity. The practice of this ethic gives a religious impetus to Methodists to combat the depressing economic and cultural forces arrayed against them, to become self-respecting and reliable workers, to buy books instead of gin, to rise economically, and to educate their children.

In consequence, even in Wesley's lifetime, Methodism began to take on the "middle-class" features which it has today. Many Methodists became wealthy. This was a result Wesley had not anticipated. Towards the close of his career he became as concerned about the danger of riches as he had been earlier about the misery of poverty. He saw an inverse ratio between material prosperity and religious zeal. His economic ethic may in retrospect seem as quite too simple a solution to a problem which is the perennial bafflement of the conscientious Christian. But if one measures the England before Wesley against the England after Wesley by the yardstick of economic equality, it would be difficult to gainsay the cultural benefits of his teaching.

There is partial truth in the claim often made that Wesley saved England from such a revolution as tore France asunder. Wesley's political conservatism had the effect of quenching any politically revolutionary sparks that might have ignited in his societies. At the same time, his spiritual message had the effect of removing the economic ceiling put upon the poor, thus counteracting the polarization of classes which was in part the source of the revolt of the French proletariat. In this economic sense, and in the spiritual sense that it gave an increased self-respect to those who thought they had no place in society, the effect of Methodism was a democratizing one. There is testimony to this in the horrified statement of the Duchess of Buckingham, who described the doctrines of the Methodist preachers as "most repulsive and tinctured with impertinence and disrespect toward their superiors, in perpetually endeavoring to level all ranks and do away with all distinctions. It is monstrous to be told that you have a heart as sinful as the common wretches that crawl the earth. This is highly offensive and insulting."

The Evangelical Revival is of great importance both in its own right as a resurgence of the serious, self-disciplined Christianity manifested over and over again in history, and also in its ethics as a kind of transitional link between the Puritanism of the seventeenth century and the "social" Christianity of the nineteenth. It retains much of Puritanism: its strict discipline of "innerworldly ascetism," its sharp dualism between the way of the Christian and the way of the world, its individualism, its stress on godliness. But Wesley's ethic, though as much in by-product as in intention, has new social features which go beyond the spirit of John Bunyan, Jeremy Taylor, or Richard Baxter. There is considerably more domestication of the Christian in his culture, less preoccupation with the life beyond. The requirements of Christian perfection and of the moral purifying of life apply now to economic, cultural, and recreational practices, not merely to the self in private. The disciplines of charity, feeding the hungry, welcoming the stranger, clothing the naked, visiting the sick and imprisoned, were given a special urgency as the marks of true conversion. In all these things, the Methodist revival foreshadows—while it remains significantly different from—the Christian Socialist movement in nineteenth-century England and the Social Gospel in America.

SOURCES

From
John Wesley: Christian Perfection[2]

> Not as though I had already attained, either were already perfect.—Phil. 3:12.

There is scarce any expression in holy writ, which has given more offence than this. The word "perfect" is what many cannot bear. The very sound of it is an abomination to them; and whosoever preaches perfection (as the phrase is), that is, asserts that it is attainable in this life, runs great hazard of being accounted by them worse than a heathen man or a publican.

And hence, some have advised, wholly to lay aside the use of those expressions, "because they have given so great offence." But are they not found in the oracles of God? If so, by what authority can any messenger of God lay them aside, even though all men should be offended? We have not so learned Christ; neither may we thus give place to the devil. Whatsoever God hath spoken, that will we speak, whether

[2] This and the following sermon are taken from John Wesley, *Standard Sermons*, ed. E. H. Sugden (2 vols.; London: Epworth Press, 1921).

men will hear, or whether they will forbear; knowing, that then alone can any minister of Christ be "pure from the blood of all men," when he hath "not shunned to declare unto them all the counsel of God."

We may not, therefore, lay these expressions aside, seeing they are the words of God and not of man. But we may and ought to explain the meaning of them; that those who are sincere of heart may not err to the right hand or left, from the mark of the prize of their high calling. And this is the more needful to be done, because, in the verse already repeated, the Apostle speaks of himself as not perfect: "Not," saith he, "as though I were already perfect." And yet immediately after, in the fifteenth verse, he speaks of himself, yea, and many others, as perfect: "Let us," saith he, "as many as be perfect, be thus minded."

In What Sense Christians Are Not Perfect

In the first place, I shall endeavour to show, in what sense Christians are not perfect. And both from experience and Scripture it appears, first, that they are not perfect in knowledge: they are not so perfect in this life as to be free from ignorance. They know, it may be, in common with other men, many things relating to the present world; and they know, with regard to the world to come, the general truths which God hath revealed. They know likewise (what the natural man receiveth not; for these things are spiritually discerned) "what manner of love" it is, wherewith "the Father" hath loved them, "that they should be called the sons of God." They know the mighty working of His Spirit in their hearts; and the wisdom of His providence, directing all their paths, and causing all things to work together for their good. Yea, they know in every circumstance of life what the Lord requireth of them, and how to keep a conscience void of offence both toward God and toward man.

But innumerable are the things which they know not. Touching the Almighty Himself, they cannot search Him out to perfection. Neither is it for them to know the times which He hath in part revealed by His servants and prophets since the world began. Much less do they know when God, having "accomplished the number of His elect, will hasten His kingdom"; when "the heavens shall pass away with a great noise, and the elements shall melt with fervent heat."

They know not the reasons even of many of His present dispensations with the sons of men; but are constrained to rest here: Though "clouds and darkness are round about Him, righteousness and judgment are the habitation of His seat." Yea, often with regard to His dealings with themselves, doth their Lord say unto them, "What I do, thou knowest not now; but thou shalt know hereafter." And how little do they know of what is ever before them, of even the visible works of His hands; how "He spreadeth the north over the empty place, and hangeth the earth upon nothing"; how He unites all the parts of this vast machine by a secret chain, which cannot be broken. So great is the ignorance, so very little the knowledge, of even the best of men!

No one, then, is so perfect in this life, as to be free from ignorance. Nor, secondly, from mistake; which indeed is almost an unavoidable consequence of it; seeing those who "know but in part" are ever liable to err touching the things which they know not. It is true, the children of God do not mistake as to the things essential to salvation: they do not "put darkness for light, or light for darkness"; neither "seek death in the error of their life." For they are "taught of God"; and the way which He teaches them, the way of holiness, is so plain, that "the wayfaring man, though a fool, need not err therein." But in things unessential to salvation they do err, and that frequently. The best and wisest of men are frequently mistaken even with regard to facts; believing those things not to have been which really were, or those to have been done which were not. Or, suppose they are not mistaken as to the fact itself, they may be with regard to its circumstances; believing them, or many of them, to have been quite different from what, in truth, they were. And hence cannot but arise many farther mistakes. Hence they may believe either past or present actions which were or are evil, to be good; and such as were or are good, to be evil.

Nay, with regard to the holy Scriptures themselves, as they are to avoid it, the best of men are liable to mistake, and do mistake day by day; especially with respect to those parts thereof which less immediately relate to practice. Hence, even the children of God are not agreed as to the interpretation of many places in holy writ; nor is their difference of opinion any proof that they are not the children of God, on either side; but it is a proof that we are no more to expect any living man to be infallible, than to be omniscient.

Even Christians, therefore, are not so perfect as to be free either from ignorance or error: we may, thirdly, add, nor from infirmities. Only let us take care to understand this word aright: only let us not give that soft title to known sins, as the manner of some is. So, one man tells us, "Every man has his infirmity, and mine is drunkenness"; another has the infirmity of uncleanness; another, that of taking God's holy name in vain; and yet another has the infirmity of calling his brother, "Thou fool," or returning "railing for railing." It is plain that all you who thus speak, if ye repent not, shall, with your infirmities, go quick into hell! But I mean hereby, not only those which are properly termed bodily infirmities, but all those inward or outward imperfections which are not of a moral nature. Such are the weakness or slowness of understanding, dullness or confusedness of apprehension, incoherency of thought, irregular quickness or heaviness of imagination. Such (to mention no more of this kind) is the want of a ready or retentive memory. Such, in another kind, are those which are commonly, in some measure, consequent upon these; namely, slowness of speech, impropriety of language, ungracefulness of pronunciation; to which one might add a thousand nameless defects, either in conversation or behaviour. These are the infirmities which are found in the best of men, in a larger or smaller proportion. And from these none can hope to be perfectly freed, till the spirit returns to God that gave it.

Nor can we expect, till then, to be wholly free from temptation. Such perfection belongeth not to this life. It is true, there are those who, being given up to work all uncleanness with greediness, scarce perceive the temptations which they resist not; and so seem to be without temptation. There are also many whom the wise enemy of souls seeming to be fast asleep in the dead form of godliness, will not tempt to gross sin, lest they should awake before they drop into everlasting burnings. But this state will not last always; as we may learn from that single consideration, that the Son of God Himself, in the days of His flesh, was tempted even to the end of His life. Therefore, so let his servant expect to be; for "it is enough that he be as his Master."

Christian perfection, therefore, does not imply (as some men seem to have imagined) an exemption either from ignorance, or mistake, or infirmities, or temptations. Indeed, it is only another term for holiness. They are two names for the same thing. Thus, every one that is holy is, in the Scripture sense, perfect. Yet we may, lastly, observe, that neither in this respect is there any absolute perfection on earth. There is no "perfection of degrees," as it is termed; none which does not admit of a continual increase. So that how much soever any man has attained, or in how high a degree soever he is perfect, he hath still need to "grow in grace," and daily to advance in the knowledge and love of God his Saviour.

In What Sense Christians Are Perfect

In what sense, then, are Christians perfect? This is what I shall endeavor, in the second place, to show. But it should be premised, that there are several stages in Christian life, as in natural; some of the children of God being but new-born babes, others having attained to more maturity.

But even babes in Christ are in such a sense perfect, or born of God (an expression taken also in divers senses), as, first, not to commit sin.

Now, the Word of God plainly declares, that even those

who are justified, who are born again in the lowest sense, "do not continue in sin"; that they cannot "live any longer therein"; that they are "planted together in the likeness of the death" of Christ; that their "old man is crucified with Him," the body of sin being destroyed, so that henceforth they do not serve sin; that, being dead with Christ, they are free from sin; that they are "dead unto sin, and alive unto God"; that "sin hath no more dominion over them," who are "not under the law, but under grace"; but that these, "being free from sin are become the servants of righteousness."

The very least which can be implied in these words, is, that the persons spoken of therein, namely, all real Christians, or believers in Christ, are made free from outward sin. For this ceasing from sin, if it be interpreted in the lowest sense, as regarding only the outward behaviour, must denote the ceasing from the outward act, from any outward transgression of the law.

In conformity, therefore, to the whole tenor of the New Testament, we fix this conclusion,—a Christian is so far perfect, as not to commit sin.

This is the glorious privilege of every Christian; yea, though he be but a babe in Christ. But it is only of those who are strong in the Lord, "and have overcome the wicked one," or rather of those who "have known Him that is from the beginning," that it can be affirmed they are in such a sense perfect, as, secondly, to be freed from evil thoughts and evil tempers. First, from evil or sinful thoughts. But here let it be observed, that thoughts concerning evil are not always evil thoughts; that a thought concerning sin, and a sinful thought, are widely different. A man, for instance, may think of a murder which another has committed; and yet this is no evil or sinful thought.

Every one of these can say with St. Paul, "I am crucified with Christ: nevertheless I live; yet not I, but Christ liveth in me,"—words that manifestly describe a deliverance from inward as well as from outward sin.

He, therefore, who liveth in true believers hath "purified

their hearts by faith"; insomuch that every one that hath Christ in him, the hope of glory, "purifieth himself, even as He is pure." He is purified from pride; for Christ was lowly of heart. He is pure from self-will or desire; for Christ desired only to do the will of His Father, and to finish His work. And he is pure from anger, in the common sense of the word; for Christ was meek and gentle, patient and long-suffering. I say, in the common sense of the word; for all anger is not evil.

"God is light, and in Him is no darkness at all. If we walk in the light, . . . we have fellowship one with another, and the blood of Jesus Christ His Son cleanseth us from all sin." And again: "If we confess our sins, He is faithful and just to forgive us our sins, and to cleanse us from all unrighteousness." Now, it is evident, the Apostle here also speaks of a deliverance wrought in this world. For he saith not, The blood of Christ will cleanse at the hour of death, or in the day of judgment; but, it "cleanseth," at the time present, "us," living Christians, "from all sin." And it is equally evident, that if any sin remain, we are not cleansed from all sin; if any unrighteousness remain in the soul, it is not cleansed from all unrighteousness. Neither let any sinner against his own soul say, that this relates to justification only, or the cleansing us from the guilt of sin; first, because this is confounding together what the Apostle clearly distinguishes, who mentions first, to forgive us our sins, and then to cleanse us from all unrighteousness. Secondly, because this is asserting justification by works, in the strongest sense possible; it is making all inward as well as outward holiness necessarily previous to justification. For if the cleansing here spoken of is no other than the cleansing us from the guilt of sin, then we are not cleansed from guilt, that is, are not justified, unless on condition of "walking in the light, as He is in the light." It remains, then, that Christians are saved in this world from all sin, from all unrighteousness; that they are now in such a sense perfect, as not to commit sin, and to be freed from evil thoughts and evil tempers. [3]

[3] *Ibid.*, II, 147-78.

From
JOHN WESLEY: THE USE OF MONEY

> I say unto you, Make to yourselves friends of the mammon of unrighteousness; that, when ye fail, they may receive you into everlasting habitations.—Luke 16:9.

An excellent branch of Christian wisdom is here inculcated by our Lord on all His followers, namely, the right use of money,—a subject largely spoken of, after their manner, by men of the world; but not sufficiently considered by those whom God hath chosen out of the world. These, generally, do not consider, as the importance of the subject requires, the use of this excellent talent. Neither do they understand how to employ it to the greatest advantage; the introduction of which into the world is one admirable instance of the wise and gracious providence of God. It has, indeed, been the manner of poets, orators, and philosophers, in almost all ages and nations, to rail at this, as the grand corrupter of the world, the bane of virtue, the pest of human society.

But is not all this mere empty rant? Is there any solid reason therein? By no means. For, let the world be as corrupt as it will, is gold or silver to blame? "The love of money," we know, "is the root of all evil," but not the thing itself. The fault does not lie in the money, but in them that use it. It may be used ill: and what may not? But it may likewise be used well: it is full as applicable to the best, as to the worst uses. It is of unspeakable service to all civilized nations, in all the common affairs of life: it is a most compendious instrument of transacting all manner of business, and (if we use it according to Christian wisdom) of doing all manner of good. It is true, were man in a state of innocence, or were all men "filled with the Holy Ghost," so that, like the infant church at Jerusalem, "no man counted anything he had his own," but "distribution was made to every one as he had need," the use of it would be superseded; as we cannot conceive there is anything of the kind among the inhabitants of heaven. But, in the present state of mankind, it is an excellent gift of God, answering the noblest ends. In the hands of His children, it is food for the hungry, drink for the thirsty, raiment for the naked: it gives to the traveller and the stranger where to lay his head. By it we may supply the place of an husband to the widow, and of a father to the fatherless. We may be a defence for the oppressed, a means of health to the sick, of ease to them that are in pain; it may be as eyes to the blind, as feet to the lame; yea, a lifter up from the gates of death.

It is, therefore, of the highest concern, that all who fear God know how to employ this valuable talent; that they be instructed how it may answer these glorious ends, and in the highest degree. And, perhaps, all the instructions which are necessary for this may be reduced to three plain rules, by the exact observance whereof we may approve ourselves faithful stewards of "the mammon of unrighteousness."

The first of these is: "Gain all you can." Here we may speak like the children of the world: we meet them on their own ground. And it is our bounden duty to do this: we ought to gain all we can gain, without buying gold too dear, without paying more for it than it is worth. But this it is certain we ought not to do; we ought not to gain money at the expense of life, nor at the expense of our health. Therefore, no gain whatsoever should induce us to enter into, or to continue in, any employ, which is of such a kind, or is attended with so hard or so long labour, as to impair our constitution. Neither should we begin or continue in any business which necessarily deprives us of proper seasons for food and sleep, in such a proportion as our nature requires. Indeed, there is a great difference here. Some employments are absolutely and totally unhealthy; as those which imply the dealing with arsenic, or other equally hurtful minerals, or the breathing an air tainted with streams of melting lead, which must at length destroy the firmest constitution. Others may not be absolutely unhealthy, but only to persons of a weak constitution. Such are those which require many hours to be spent in writing; especially if a person write sitting, and lean upon his stomach, or remain long in an uneasy posture. But whatever it is which reason or experience shows to be destructive of health or strength, that we may not submit to; seeing "the life is more" valuable "than meat, and the body than raiment": and, if we are already engaged in such an employ, we should exchange it, as soon as possible, for some which, if it lessen our gain, will, however, not lessen our health.

We are, secondly, to gain all we can without hurting our mind, any more than our body. For neither may we hurt this: we must preserve, at all events, the spirit of an healthful mind. Therefore, we may not engage or continue in any sinful trade; any that is contrary to the law of God, or of our country. Such are all that necessarily imply our robbing or defrauding the king of his lawful customs. For it is, at least, as sinful to defraud the king of his right, as to rob our fellow subjects: and the king has full as much right to his customs as we have to our houses and apparel. Other businesses there are which, however innocent in themselves, cannot be followed with innocence now; at least not in England, such, for instance, as will not afford a competent maintenance without cheating or lying, or conformity to some custom which is not consistent with a good conscience: these, likewise, are sacredly to be avoided, whatever gain they may be attended with, provided we follow the custom of the trade; for, to gain money, we must not lose our souls.

We are, thirdly, to gain all we can, without hurting our neighbor. But this we may not, cannot do, if we love our neighbor as ourselves. We cannot, if we love every one as ourselves, hurt any one in his substance. We cannot devour the increase of his lands, and perhaps the lands and houses themselves, by gaming, by overgrown bills (whether on account of physic, or law, or anything else), or by requiring or taking such interest as even the laws of our country forbid. Hereby all pawnbroking is excluded: seeing, whatever good we might do thereby, all unprejudiced men see with grief to be abundantly overbalanced by the evil. And if it were otherwise, yet we are not allowed to "do evil that good may come." We cannot, consistent with brotherly lové, sell our goods below the market price; we cannot study to ruin our neighbor's trade, in order to advance our own; much less can we entice away, or receive, any of his servants or workmen whom he has need of. None can gain by swallowing up his neighbor's substance, without gaining the damnation of hell!

Neither may we gain by hurting our neighbor in his body. Therefore we may not sell anything which tends to impair health. Such is, eminently, all that liquid fire, commonly called drams, or spirituous liquors. It is true, these may have a place in medicine; they may be of use in some bodily disorders; although there would rarely be occasion for them, were it not for the unskilfulness of the practitioner. Therefore, such as prepare and sell them for this end may keep their conscience clear. But all who sell them in the common way, to any that will buy, are poisoners general. They murder His Majesty's subjects by wholesale, neither does their eye pity or spare.

So is whatever is procured by hurting our neighbor in his soul; by ministering, suppose, either directly or indirectly, to his unchastity or intemperance; which certainly none can do who has any fear of God, or any real desire of pleasing Him. It nearly concerns all those to consider this, who have anything to do with taverns, victualling-houses, opera-houses, play-houses, or any other places of public, fashionable diversion. If these profit the souls of men, you are clear; your employment is good, and your gain innocent; but if they are either sinful in themselves, or natural inlets to sin of various kinds, then, it is to be feared, you have a sad account to make.

These cautions and restrictions being observed, it is the bounden duty of all who are engaged in worldly business to observe that first and great rule of Christian wisdom, with respect to money, "Gain all you can." Gain all you can by honest industry. Use all possible diligence in your calling. Lose no time. If you understand yourself, and your relation to God and man, you know you have none to spare. If you understand your particular calling, as you ought, you will

X can be misinterpreted: Wesley's focus is economic and social here (Hughes)

have no time that hangs upon your hands. Every business will afford some employment sufficient for every day and every hour. That wherein you are placed, if you follow it in earnest, will leave you no leisure for silly, unprofitable diversions. You have always something better to do, something that will profit you, more or less. And "whatsoever thy hand findeth to do, do it with thy might." Do it as soon as possible: no delay! No putting off from day to day, or from hour to hour! Never leave anything till to-morrow, which you can do to-day. And do it as well as possible. Do not sleep or yawn over it: put your whole strength to the work. Spare no pains. Let nothing be done by halves, or in a slight and careless manner. Let nothing in your business be left undone, if it can be done by labour or patience.

Gain all you can, by common sense, by using in your business all the understanding which God has given you. It is amazing to observe how few do this; how men run on in the same dull track with their forefathers. But whatever they do who know not God, this is no rule for you. It is a shame for a Christian not to improve upon them in whatever he takes in hand. You should be continually learning, from the experience of others, or from your own experience, reading, and reflection, to do everything you have to do better to-day than you did yesterday. And see that you practise whatever you learn, that you may make the best of all that is in your hands.

Having gained all you can, by honest wisdom, and unwearied diligence, the second rule of Christian prudence is "Save all you can." Do not throw the precious talent into the sea: leave that folly to heathen philosophers. Do not throw it away in idle expenses, which is just the same as throwing it into the sea. Expend no part of it merely to gratify the desire of the flesh, the desire of the eye, or the pride of life.

Do not waste any part of so precious a talent, merely in gratifying the desires of the flesh; in procuring the pleasures of sense, of whatever kind; particularly, in enlarging the pleasure of tasting. I do not mean, avoid gluttony and drunkenness only: an honest Heathen would condemn these. But there is a regular, reputable kind of sensuality, an elegant epicurism, which does not immediately disorder the stomach, nor (sensibly at least) impair the understanding; and yet it cannot be maintained without considerable expense. Cut off all this expense! Despise delicacy and variety, and be content with what plain nature requires.

Do not waste any part of so precious a talent, merely in gratifying the desire of the eye, by superfluous or expensive furniture; in costly pictures, painting, gilding, books; in elegant rather than useful gardens.

Lay out nothing to gratify the pride of life, to gain the admiration or praise of men. This motive of expense is frequently interwoven with one or both of the former. Men are expensive in diet, or apparel, or furniture, not barely to please their appetite, or to gratify their eye, or their imagination, but their vanity too. "So long as thou doest well unto thyself, men will speak good of thee." Rather be content with the honour that cometh from God.

But let not any man imagine that he has done anything, barely by going thus far, by "gaining and saving all he can," if he were to stop here. All this is nothing, if a man go not forward, if he does not point all this at a farther end. Nor, indeed, can a man properly be said to save anything, if he only lays it up. You may as well throw your money into the sea, as bury it in the earth. And you may as well bury it in the earth, as in your chest, or in the Bank of England. Not to use, is effectually to throw it away. If, therefore, you would indeed "make yourselves friends of the mammon of unrighteousness," add the third rule to the two preceding. Having, first, gained all you can, and, secondly, saved all you can, then "give all you can."

In order to see the ground and reason of this, consider, when the Possessor of heaven and earth brought you into being, and placed you in this world, He placed you here, not as a proprietor, but a steward: as such He entrusted you, for a season, with goods of various kinds; but the sole property of these still rests in Him, nor can ever be alienated from Him. As you yourself are not your own, but His, such is, likewise, all that you enjoy. Such is your soul and your body, not your own, but God's. And so is your substance in particular. And He has told you, in the most clear and express terms, how you are to employ it for Him, in such a manner, that it may be all an holy sacrifice, acceptable through Christ Jesus. And this light, easy service, He hath promised to reward with an eternal weight of glory.

The directions which God has given us, touching the use of our worldly substance, may be comprised in the following particulars. If you desire to be a faithful and a wise steward, out of that portion of your Lord's goods which He has for the present lodged in your hands, but with the right of resuming whenever it pleases Him, first, provide things needful for yourself; food to eat, raiment to put on, whatever nature moderately requires for preserving the body in health and strength. Secondly, provide these for your wife, your children, your servants, or any others who pertain to your household. If, when this is done, there be an overplus left, then "do good to them that are of the household of faith." If there be an overplus still, "as you have opportunity, do good unto all men." In so doing, you give all you can; nay, in a sound sense, all you have: for all that is laid out in this manner is really given to God. You "render unto God the things that are God's," not only by what you give to the poor, but also by that which you expend in providing things needful for yourself and your household.

If, then, a doubt should at any time arise in your mind concerning what you are going to expend, either on yourself or any part of your family, you have an easy way to remove it. Calmly and seriously inquire, "(1) In expending this, am I acting according to my character? Am I acting herein, not as a proprietor, but as a steward of my Lord's goods? (2) Am I doing this in obedience to His Word? In what scripture does He require me so to do? (3) Can I offer up this action, this expense, as a sacrifice to God through Jesus Christ? (4) Have I reason to believe, that for this very work I shall have a reward at the resurrection of the just?" You will seldom need anything more to remove any doubt which arises on this head; but, by this four-fold consideration, you will receive clear light as to the way wherein you should go.[4]

Further Readings

Primary Sources

A *Compend of Wesley's Theology*. Edited by R. W. Burtner and R. E. Chiles. Nashville: Abingdon Press, 1954.

Watson, Philip (comp.). *The Message of the Wesleys: A Reader of Instruction and Devotion*. Compiled with introduction by Philip S. Watson. New York: Macmillan, 1964.

Secondary Sources

Bready, J. Wesley. *England Before and After Wesley*. New York: Harper and Row, 1938.

Jeffery, Thomas Reid. *John Wesley's Religious Quest*. New York: Vantage Press, 1960.

Lee, Umphrey. *The Lord's Horseman: John Wesley, the Man*. Nashville: Abingdon Press, 1954.

Monk, Robert C. *John Wesley; His Puritan Heritage*. Nashville: Abingdon Press, 1966.

4 *Ibid.*, II, 309-27.

Chapter 13

JONATHAN EDWARDS

Jonathan Edwards, America's greatest theologian, is widely regarded as the most profound and original religious thinker of the eighteenth century. In him are illustrated both the historical variability and the essential constancy of Christian ethical thought. Historically he represents an American, Puritan, eighteenth-century version of Calvinism developed in conflict with the utilitarian "business ethics" of rising "Yankee" secularism, as well as in relation to Newtonian science, Lockean philosophy, and the religious evangelicalism of the Great Awakening. Yet Edwards so states the great themes of Christian faith and life that his writings are intelligible, without a special historical introduction, to a thoughtful reader who comes to them directly from the study of the Scriptures and the Christian classics. The greatness, holiness, and love of God, the misery of man without God, the universality and inescapability of the divine rule, the redemption of man by Jesus Christ from slavery to sonship, the new life of uncoerced love of God and neighbor—these are the themes that he develops. Hence one can understand him on the basis of general Christian experience without reference to the fact that he was born in Connecticut in 1703, died at Princeton in 1758, studied Locke, Newton, and the Cambridge Platonists under his father's guidance, and at Yale was one of the chief leaders of the Great Awakening in America, and the founder of the New England school of theology.

His life contained some dramatic episodes, and he exercised wide influence through his preaching, but it was through his writings that he was most effective and his fame rests on them. Published in Scotland, England, and the

Netherlands as well as in America, they were widely circulated for a century after his death and continue to receive the close attention of students of American philosophy, literature, and social history no less than of theologians. Edwards' works may be divided into three main groups: early notes in which, while student and tutor at Yale, he laid the foundations of his theology and philosophy; descriptions and critiques of religious experience and the sermons written while he participated, as pastor in Northampton, Massachusetts, in the great revival movement of the 1730's and 1740's; and, finally, the remarkable treatises produced during the last seven or eight years of his life in the frontier village of Stockbridge, Massachusetts, where he was missionary to the Indians and pastor of a small group of settlers.

Edwards' intensively reflective and studious nature, further developed by a strict discipline of thought and life, led him to record in boyhood and youth the results of his observations of natural phenomena, his introspective inquiries into the nature of knowledge and of the mind, his reasonings about the structure of being, and his study of the Scriptures and Christian doctrine. His notes on "The Natural History of the Mental World, or of the Internal World" constitute a fascinating chapter in the history of philosophical idealism. An early essay on the habits of flying spiders and the "Notes on Natural Science" manifest an interest like that of Benjamin Franklin and other lay scientists of the eighteenth century; the "Notes on the Scriptures" and the "Miscellanies" (mostly on Christian doctrine) represent the fruits of reflections he carried on throughout his life, in the course of which he developed ideas that were systematically presented in the sermons and treatises. The variety of subjects covered in these series of notes is important, for much of Edwards' greatness as a theologian is due to the fact that he was able to unite in one consistent vision and system of thought convictions gained from studies of the self, of nature, of the Scriptures, and of Christian doctrine.

Even at an early age Edwards came to see the universe as one unified, interdependent system of being in which, as he wrote, "perhaps there is not one leaf of a tree, nor a spire of grass, but what produces effects all over the Universe and will produce them to the end of eternity." Reflections on the nature of knowledge and of being, on the one hand, and the study of Scriptures, on the other, convinced him that this universe is constituted in each moment by the power of God. The fitness and appropriateness of its various parts to each other are grounded in the unity of the divine thought, while the stability of part and whole is the effect of the constantly active divine will. When scientists such as Sir Isaac Newton seek to understand the structure and dynamics of physical events they are literally trying "to think the thoughts of God after him." Men's ability to do this is severely restricted so that, like Plato's cave-dwellers, they mistake shadows for reality; yet, by the same token, the realm of human experience is a realm of "the images and shadows of divine things." Nothing in that experience is merely itself; everything participates in and is symbolic of larger meanings. Revelation has indeed made plain that the universe is created, governed, and sustained by God; yet what Scripture teaches can be seen to be true by a human intelligence that gives proper attention to the nature of things and reflects critically on its own operations. Reason in this sense—empirical, critical, and reflective reason—not only verifies revelation but adds to it a knowledge of the wonderful complexity and excellence of God's work in the creation. It can never take the place of revelation, but, honestly employed, it is not only illuminated by revelation but illuminates it. Some of these ideas, to be sure, are only suggested in the early writings and wait for development in the later treatises. But in Edwards' early as well as late views the universe proceeds from God as light proceeds from the sun and as thought issues from a mind; creation is never an artificial making of things. He contended throughout his life against the Deistic view that thinks of the world as existing independently of the constant activity of the creator and against the kind of humanism which believes that man exists in any moment by his own power, separate from the ground of his being.

The *Personal Narrative* indicates how much religious experience combined in young Edwards with philosophic, scientific, and theological inquiries to produce this apprehension of the universe and God.

> The first instance, that I remember, of that sort of inward sweet delight in God and divine things, that I have lived in much since, was on reading these words, I. Tim. i, 17, *Now unto the King, eternal, immortal, invisible, the only wise God, be honor and glory, forever and ever. Amen.* As I read the words there came into my soul, and was, as it were, diffused through it, a sense of the glory of the Divine Being. . . . I walked abroad alone, in a solitary place in my father's pasture, for contemplation. And as I was walking there, and looking upon the sky and clouds, there came into my mind so sweet a sense of the *glorious majesty* and *grace* of God, as I know not how to express. . . . The appearance of everything was altered; there seemed as it were, a calm, sweet, cast, or appearance of divine glory in almost everything. God's excellency, his wisdom, his purity and love seemed to appear in everything; in the sun, moon, and stars; in the clouds and blue sky; in the grass, flowers, trees; in the water and all nature.[1]

There are intimations in this confession of the romantic spirit that was to flower later in Wordsworth; it also contains echoes of St. Francis, of Augustine, and of the Psalms. Edwards' thought about God and the universe has been described by many adjectives—mystical, idealistic, Neo-Platonic, Newtonian, Calvinistic, pantheistic, and Augustinian. One thing is certain: He knew that God was great and that the strange, wonderful universe was infinitely dependent upon him. What was wrong with believers and unbelievers in general, he thought, was that they had little ideas about a little God.

The Great Awakening

While he was pastor in Northampton (1727-50) Edwards participated very actively in the Great Awakening, the American form of the religious movement which, like Pietism

[1] C. H. Faust and T. H. Johnson (eds.), *Jonathan Edwards, Representative Selections* (New York: American Book Co. 1935), p. 59.

in Germany, Wesleyanism and Evangelicalism in England, and the Catholic revival in France, affected most of Western Christendom profoundly and for centuries. In the Awakening, Christian faith was radically and inwardly appropriated by thousands of previously nominal Christians or nominal unbelievers. Being damned and being saved became for them not the remote possibilities of a distant future but present real experiences of despair and of joyful release from internal conflict and guilt. Instead of regarding God as a being who might or might not be real, they apprehended him as the present, omnificent power on whom the self and all the world immediately depended for existence. His holiness, which tolerated no knavery or venality, open or secret, and his love, which brought the repentant to genuine integrity and to the joy of the forgiven, were no longer ideas but were personally experienced—"tasted" and "felt." This revival, which began in Edwards' Northampton church, soon spread to many towns in New England and New Jersey. Under the leadership of George Whitefield, it developed into a movement that affected almost all the colonies. It had its bright and its dark sides. Constructive for the most part, it led to the reintegration and invigoration of many persons, to the growth of churches, the increase of religious seriousness, the stimulation of humanitarian activities, and the reformation of manners. It also contributed to the rise of the democratic spirit and to the development of an intercolonial culture. But sometimes emotions were whipped up to the point of hysteria, guilt feelings magnified to the point of despondency, frenzy confounded with ecstasy and fanaticism with faith. Moreover the undisciplined enthusiasm of many traveling preachers, on the one side, and conservative reaction against the interruption of ecclesiastical routine, on the other, led to dissension in many churches.

In the ensuing conflict Edwards served at one and the same time as the chief critic and the chief defender of the Awakening. In various accounts of the revival, but chiefly in his *Treatise on the Religious Affections,* he pointed out how much religion was an affair of the "heart," a matter of personal, direct experience of divine reality rather than of merely intellectual assent to propositions about it. It was, when genuine, a loving of God rather than a believing that one ought to love him, active concern for the neighbor rather than acceptance of the statement that love of neighbor is very good.

Edwards developed three points especially in discussing religious affections. First, affections or emotions are the springs of all action. "Take away all love and hatred, all hope and fear, all anger, zeal and affectionate desire, and the world would be, in a great measure, motionless and dead; there would be no such thing as activity amongst mankind, or any earnest pursuit whatsoever." Second, if God is to be known in his objective goodness there must be in man a corresponding subjective principle of evaluation or love. The natural love of men for natural good, such as is present in the love of parents for their children, furnishes no point of contact for religion; there is even less connection here, Edwards might have said, than there is between human ability to take delight in food and the ability to rejoice in the beauty of a great symphony. "Those gracious influences," he wrote, "which the saints are subject of, and the effects of God's spirit which they experience, are entirely above nature, altogether of a different kind from anything that men find in themselves by nature, or only in the exercise of natural principles. . . . The inward principle from whence they [the gracious affections] flow, is something divine, a communication of God, a participation of the divine nature, Christ living in the heart, the Holy Spirit dwelling there, in union with the faculties of the soul." In the third place, Edwards pointed out, it is necessary to test the authenticity of emotions, to distinguish between what is "spiritual" and what is merely imaginary. In much greater detail than Paul, who had dealt with a similar problem in the case of the spiritualists at Corinth, Edwards undertook to "test the spirits," to distinguish between merely subjective experience and genuine affections without rejecting the emotional just because it was emotional and not conceptual in character. His test was funda-

fruits of the Spirit

mentally a moral one. Emotional experience is specious if it does not issue in genuine love of God and neighbor; if it produces these fruits it is not spurious even though it is accompanied by unusual physical manifestations. The test was the same as Paul's: "If any man have not the spirit of Christ he is none of his" and, "Though I speak with the tongues of men and of angels and have not love, I am a noisy gong."

One result of the revival was great concern on the part of many that the church should be made up only of deeply convinced, converted Christians. Edwards himself took this position and so came into conflict with the lay leaders of his Northampton church who thought less rigorous requirements more proper. A harsh debate followed; Edwards was dismissed after twenty-three years of service. Eventually he found a new, apparently very restricted field of labor in the Indian mission at Stockbridge, Massachusetts. There he wrote his major treatises and from thence he was called in 1758 to the presidency of the College of New Jersey, now Princeton University. The latter event had no other consequence than that he became known to history as President Edwards, for he died of smallpox a few weeks after assuming office. But the treatises continued to exercise great influence. In them he summed up the reflections of a lifetime and constructed one of the main systems of divinity of modern times. Their titles indicate the directions of his thought without making wholly evident how unified and consistent it was: *The Freedom of the Will, The Great Christian Doctrine of Original Sin Defended, Concerning the End for which God Created the World,* and *The Nature of True Virtue.*

Christian Morality

Though Edwards was a master metaphysician, his primary interest as it appears in these works was ethical. He presents the system of Christian ethics here in its distinction from and agreement with both the naturalistic and the idealistic movements of thought with which in one form or another, it has debated throughout its history, not least in the eighteenth century. The main points of his analysis may be summarized as follows:

1. The source of human action lies neither in an abstract will nor in an abstract intelligence but primarily in emotions directed toward objective goods: in approving, disapproving, liking, disliking, loving, hating, being pleased and displeased, choosing and refusing.

2. The idea of liberty is applicable to man in the sense that as a moral being he is free from external compulsion, free to do what he pleases. He is not free to choose what he hates or to refuse what he loves. He can move only toward the "apparent good." Human freedom means self-determination rather than liberty of choice between alternatives; "the will is as its strongest motive is."

3. Though man was created with the possibility of loving universal good for its own sake, since the fall he is free only to love himself. Everything else that he loves he loves in the context of self-interest. Men differ in the degree to which their self-interest is enlightened, but no man, except as moved by supernatural grace, is able to get out of the circle of self-interest, that is, of loving whatever he loves for his own sake.

4. Even though it were true, as Edwards does not believe it to be, that conscience or some special moral sense and natural instincts are separable from self-interest and that men motivated by these do not act strictly from self-interest, yet it is clear that actions which have their source in such principles are akin to those which arise out of self-interest. They also are directed toward the good of a *partial* being to the exclusion of other beings. This is evident in parental love and patriotism and even in most interest in justice, which is concern for justice in a limited society, such as the whole of mankind.

5. The ethics of universal good will stands in contrast to man's natural ethics, whether this be founded on self-interest, instinct, conscience, or moral sense. It seeks the good of all beings in their interrelationship; it desires justice in the universal community; it is free from concern for the self. This

is the ethics of the love of God, of delight and joy in him as the source of all existence; it is the ethics of the love of all being as united in God and by him. This ethics of universal benevolence cannot be achieved by moving from the particular to the universal, from the finite to the infinite, but only by the reverse movement. Yet it transforms all particular loves, as when sex love, parental love, and patriotism are transformed by universal loyalty.

6. True virtue—universal good will—which was possible to man before his fall is again made possible and actual in redemption. Morally redemption means the restoration to man of love to God and to all beings in relation to him. Objectively, that is on God's side, it is his disclosure of himself in his great goodness, his being and his value; subjectively, the redemption is the gift to man of the internal principle of desire for and movement toward God without which divine goodness cannot be apprehended.

7. The gift of true virtue—love to God and universal benevolence—makes apparent to man the self-interestedness and partiality of his natural ethics; but where God is recognized and loved in his greatness and holiness, it is also seen that he governs the world through this natural ethics. Self-interest, conscientiousness, moral sense, and so on, keep the world in a kind of disordered order. In them, too, one may see the distorted "shadows of divine things." Yet this relative goodness of natural morality is, from the point of view of true virtue, a more than relative badness. It is the kind of "goodness" which, in Augustine's simile, characterizes a robber band; there must be some loyalty and justice in the band if it is to survive for even a little while so that it can rob.

There is a remarkable kinship, on the whole, between Edwards' understanding of the two moralities and Augustine's theory of the two cities. It is noteworthy also how meaningful this view is in the context of modern controversies about ethics, theoretical and practical. Edwards agrees with Hobbes—and with the analysts of power politics—that man is primarily motivated by self-interest; he agrees with naturalists of every sort that conscience is on the whole a psychological phenomenon, more the voice of society than of God; he agrees also with sociologists and anthropologists in noting the historical and cultural relativity of the content of moral codes. But beyond all this he discerns, under the illumination of revelation, that there is something profoundly contradictory to the human spirit in this relative morality; it is the morality of *fallen* man who feels that he ought not be as he is, that something is required of him which exceeds his present ability, namely, to be just and loyal in a truly universal sense with complete disinterestedness. Hence Edwards' Christian ethics, like that of many another theologian, is both radically realistic in its acceptance of human self-interestedness and moral relativity and also radically idealistic in its insistence on the presence of a requirement and a possibility in life exceeding the possibilities of human achievement.

The paradoxes we seem to encounter here do not represent contradictions except for an atheism that denies the God who is all in all and to whom all things are possible. Man, in the Edwardean view, is a rebel in the universe who sets up his private empires, large and small, never learning that he can make none of them endure in the face of the rule of universal justice. Yet this man is also the subject of the infinite mercy which reconciles the rebel to the universal kingdom, to his enemies, and to himself—mercy which implants in his heart a delight in the glory of God, in the gloriousness of all that is. Those who are so called to universal citizenship become the pioneers of a new humanity. This was history as Edwards saw it, though he mixed with it some gloomy, sinister reflections on eternal punishment that are hard to reconcile with the central vision. Human history was for him fundamentally the story of redemption from self-love to the love of all being, from self-glorification to the glorification of God, from pettiness and smallness of mind in theology and politics to wide vistas of being beyond being, from the provincialism of town, nation, and humanity to citizenship in universal society, from the love of profit to the love of God.

SOURCES

From

Jonathan Edwards: The Nature of True Virtue[2]

Showing Wherein the Essence of True Virtue Consists

Whatever controversies and variety of opinions there are about the nature of virtue, yet all (excepting some sceptics, who deny any real difference between virtue and vice) mean by it something *beautiful,* or rather some kind of *beauty* or excellency. It is not *all* beauty that is called virtue; for instance, not the beauty of a building, of a flower, or of the rainbow; but some beauty belonging to beings that have *perception* and *will.* It is not all beauty of *mankind* that is called virtue; for instance, not the external beauty of the countenance, or shape, gracefulness of motion, or harmony of voice, but it is a beauty that has its original seat in the mind. But yet perhaps not *every* thing that may be called a beauty of mind is properly called virtue. There is a beauty of understanding and speculation. There is something in the ideas and conceptions of great philosophers and statesmen that may be called beautiful which is a different thing from what is most commonly meant by virtue. But virtue is the beauty of those qualities and acts of the mind that are of a *moral* nature, i.e. such as are attended with desert or worthiness of *praise* or *blame.* Things of this sort, it is generally agreed, so far as I know, do not belong merely to speculation, but to the *disposition* and *will,* or (to use a general word I suppose commonly well understood) to the *heart.* Therefore I suppose I shall not depart from the common opinion when I say, that virtue is the beauty of the qualities and exercises of the heart, or those actions which proceed from them. So that when it is inquired, what is the nature of true *virtue?* this is

[2] Excerpts are from Vol. II of *The Works of President Edwards.* Ed. Samuel Austin. (8 vols.; Worcester: Isaiah Thomas, 1808).

the same as to inquire what that is which renders any habit, disposition, or exercise of the heart truly *beautiful?*

I use the phrase *true* virtue, and speak of things *truly* beautiful, because I suppose it will generally be allowed that there is a distinction to be made between some things which are *truly* virtuous and others which only *seem* to be virtuous, through a partial and imperfect view of things. . . . There is a general and particular beauty. By a *particular* beauty I mean that by which a thing appears beautiful when considered only with regard to its connection with, and tendency to some particular things within a limited, and, as it were, a private sphere. And a *general* beauty is that by which a thing appears beautiful when viewed most perfectly, comprehensively and universally, with regard to all its tendencies and its connections with everything it stands related to. The former may be without and against the latter. As, a few notes in a tune, taken only by themselves and in their relation to one another, may be harmonious, which, when considered with respect to all the notes in the tune, or the entire series of sounds they are connected with, may be very discordant, and disagreeable. *That only,* therefore, is what I mean by *true* virtue, which is *that,* belonging to the *heart* of an intelligent Being, that is beautiful by a *general* beauty, or beautiful in a comprehensive view, as it is in itself, and as related to everything that it stands in connection with. And therefore when we are inquiring concerning the nature of true virtue—viz. wherein this true and general beauty of the heart does most essentially consist—this is my answer to the inquiry:—

True Virtue most essentially consists in benevolence to Being in general. Or perhaps, to speak more accurately, it is that consent, propensity and union of heart to Being in general, which is immediately exercised in a general good will.

When I say true virtue consists in love to Being in general, I shall not be likely to be understood, that no one act of the mind or exercise of love is of the nature of true virtue, but what has Being in general, or the great system of universal existence, for its direct and immediate object; so that no exercise of love, or kind affection to any one particular Being, that is but a small part of this whole, has anything of the nature of true virtue. But that the nature of true virtue consists in a disposition to benevolence towards Being in general: though from such a disposition may arise exercises of love to particular beings, as objects are presented and occasions arise. My meaning is, that no affections towards particular persons, or Beings, are of the nature of true virtue, but such as arise from a generally benevolent temper, or from that habit or frame of mind, wherein consists a disposition to love Being in general.

Love is commonly distinguished into love of benevolence, and love of complacence. Love of *benevolence* is that affection or propensity of the heart to any Being, which causes it to incline to its well-being, or disposes it to desire and take pleasure in its happiness. And if I mistake not, it is agreeable to the common opinion, that beauty in the object is not always the ground of this propensity; but that there may be such a thing as benevolence, or a disposition to the welfare of those that are not considered as beautiful, unless mere existence be accounted a beauty. And benevolence or goodness in the divine Being is generally supposed, not only to be prior to the beauty of many of its objects, but to their existence; so as to be the ground both of their existence and their beauty, rather than they the foundation of God's benevolence; as it is supposed that it is God's goodness which moved him to give them Being and beauty. So that if all virtue primarily consists of that affection of heart to being, which is exercised in benevolence, or an inclination to its good, then God's virtue is so extended as to include a propensity not only to Being actually existing, and actually beautiful, but to possible Being, so as to incline him to give Being, beauty and happiness.

What is commonly called love of *complacence* presupposes beauty. For it is no other than delight in beauty; or complacence in the person or Being beloved for his beauty. If virtue be the beauty of an intelligent being, and virtue consists in love, then it is a plain inconsistence, to suppose that virtue primarily consists in any love to its object *for its beauty;* either in a love of complacence, which is delight in a Being for its beauty, or in a love of benevolence, that has the beauty of its object for its foundation. For that would be to suppose, that the beauty of intelligent Beings primarily consists in love to beauty; or, that their virtue first of all consists in their love to virtue. Which is an inconsistence, and going in a circle. If virtue consists primarily in love to virtue, then virtue, the thing loved is the love of virtue: so that virtue must consist in the love of the love of virtue—and so on *in infinitum.* Therefore if the essence of virtue or beauty of mind, lies in love, or a disposition to love, it must primarily consist in something *different* both from complacence, which is a delight in beauty, and also from any benevolence that has the beauty of its object for its foundation. Nor can virtue primarily consist in *gratitude;* or one Being's benevolence to another for his benevolence to him. Because this implies the same inconsistence. For it supposes a benevolence prior to gratitude, that is the cause of gratitude. Therefore there is room left for no other conclusion, than that the primary object of virtuous love is Being, simply considered; or, that true virtue primarily consists, not in love to any particular Beings because of their virtue or beauty, nor in gratitude because they love us, but in a propensity and union of heart to Being simply considered; exciting absolute benevolence (if I may so call it) to Being in general. I say true virtue *primarily* consists in this. For I am far from asserting that there is no true virtue in any other love than this absolute benevolence. But I would express what appears to me to be the truth on this subject, in the following particulars.

The *first* object of a virtuous benevolence is Being, simply considered; and if being, *simply* considered, be its object, then being *in general* is its object; and the thing it has an ultimate propensity to is the *highest good* of Being in general. And it will seek the good of every *individual* being unless it be conceived as not consistent with the highest good of Being in general. In which case the good of a particular Being, or some Beings, may be given up for the sake of the highest good of Being in general. And particularly if there be any Being that is looked upon as statedly and irreclaimably opposite, and an enemy to Being in general, then consent and adherence to Being in general will induce the truly virtuous heart to forsake that Being and to oppose it.

Further, if Being, simply considered, be the first object of a truly virtuous benevolence, then that Being who has the *most* of Being, or has the greatest share of existence, other things being equal, so far as such a being is exhibited to our faculties, or set in our view, will have the *greatest* share of the propensity and benevolent affection of the heart. I say *other things being equal,* especially because there is a *secondary* object of virtuous benevolence, that I shall take notice of presently. Pure benevolence in its first exercise is nothing else but Being's uniting consent, or propensity to Being; appearing true and pure by its extending to Being in general, and inclining to the general highest good, and to each Being, whose welfare is consistent with the highest general good, in proportion to the degree of existence;[3] understood, other things being equal.

The *second* object of a virtuous propensity of heart is *benevolent* Being. A secondary ground of pure benevolence is virtuous benevolence itself in its object. When any one under the influence of general benevolence, sees another Being possessed of the like general benevolence, this attaches his heart to him, and draws forth greater love to him, than merely his having existence; because so far as the Being beloved has love to Being in general, so far his own Being is, as it were, enlarged, extends to, and in some sort comprehends Being in general. Therefore, he that is governed by love to Being in general must of necessity have complacence in him, and the greater degree of benevolence to him, as it

[3] I say, "in proportion to the degree of *existence*" because one Being may have more *existence* than another, as he may be *greater* than another. That which is *great* has more existence, and is further from nothing, than that which is *little.* One Being may have everything positive belonging to it, or everything which goes to its positive existence (in opposition to defect) in a higher degree than another; or a greater capacity and power, greater understanding, every faculty and every positive quality in a higher degree. An *Archangel* must be supposed to have more existence, and to be every way further removed from *nonentity,* than a *worm,* or a *flea.* (Edwards' note.)

were out of gratitude to him for his love to general existence, that his own heart is extended and united to, and so looks on its interest as its own.

It must be noted, that the *degree* of the *amiableness* or *valuableness* of true virtue, primarily consisting in consent and a benevolent propensity of heart to Being in general, in the eyes of one that is influenced by such a spirit, is not in the *simple* proportion of the degree of benevolent affection seen, but in a proportion *compounded* of the greatness of the benevolent Being, or the degree of *Being*, and the degree of benevolence. One that loves Being in general will necessarily value good will to Being in general wherever he sees it. But if he sees the same benevolence in *two* Beings he will value it *more* in two than in one only. Because it is a greater thing, more favorable to Being in general, to have two Beings to favor it than only one of them. For there is more Being that favors Being; both together having more Being than one alone. So if one Being be as great as two, has as much existence as both together, and has the same degree of general benevolence, it is more favorable to Being in general, than if there were general benevolence in a Being that had but half that share of existence. As a large quantity of gold, with the same degree of preciousness, is more valuable than a small quantity of the same metal.[4]

Showing How That Love, Wherein True Virtue Consists, Respects the Divine Being and Created Beings

From what has been said it is evident that true virtue must chiefly consist in love to God; the Being of Beings, infinitely the greatest and best of Beings. This appears whether we consider the primary or secondary ground of virtuous love. It was observed that the *first* objective ground of that love, wherein true virtue consists, is Being, simply considered; and as a necessary consequence of this, that Being who has the most of Being or the greatest share of universal ex-

[4] *Ibid.*, chap. i.

istence, has proportionably the greatest share of virtuous benevolence, so far as such a Being is exhibited to the faculties of our minds, other things being equal. But God has infinitely the greatest share of existence or is infinitely the greatest Being. So that all other Being, even that of all created things, is as nothing in comparison of the divine Being.

And if we consider the *secondary* ground of love, viz. beauty, or moral excellency, the same thing will appear. For as God is infinitely the greatest Being, so he is allowed to be infinitely the most beautiful and excellent. All beauty to be found throughout the whole creation is but the reflection of the diffused beams of that Being who hath an infinite fulness of brightness and glory. God's beauty is infinitely more valuable than that of all other Beings upon both those accounts mentioned, viz. the *degree* of his virtue and the greatness of the Being possessed of this virtue. And God has sufficiently exhibited himself, in his Being, his infinite greatness and excellency, and has given us faculties whereby we are capable of plainly discovering his immense superiority to all other beings in these respects. Therefore, he that has true virtue, consisting in benevolence to *Being* in general and in that complacence in virtue, or moral beauty, and benevolence to *virtuous* being, must necessarily have a supreme love to God, both of benevolence and complacence. And all true virtue must radically and essentially, and as it were summarily, consist in this. Because God is not only infinitely greater and more excellent than all other Being, but he is the head of the universal system of existence; the foundation and fountain of all Being and all Beauty; from whom all is perfectly derived, and on whom all is most absolutely and perfectly dependent; *of whom* and *through whom* and *to whom* is all Being and all perfection; and whose Being and beauty is, as it were, the sum and comprehension of all existence and excellence, much more than the sun is the fountain and summary comprehension of all the light and brightness of the day.

If it should be objected that virtue consists primarily in

benevolence, but that our fellow-creatures, and not God, seem to be the most proper objects of our benevolence; inasmuch as our goodness extendeth not to God, and we cannot be profitable to him:—To this I answer,

1. A benevolent propensity of heart is exercised not only in seeking to promote the happiness of the Being towards whom it is exercised but also in *rejoicing in* his happiness. Even as gratitude for benefits received will not only excite endeavors to requite the kindness we receive, by equally benefiting our benefactor, but also if he be above any need of us, or we have nothing to bestow, and are unable to repay his kindness, it will dispose us to rejoice in his prosperity.

2. Though we are not able to give anything to God, which we have of our own, independently; yet we may be the instruments of promoting his *glory*, in which he takes a true and proper delight. (As was shown at large in the treatise, on God's end in creating the world, Chap. I, sect. 4, whither I must refer the reader for a more full answer to this objection.) Whatever influence such an objection may have on the minds of some, yet is there any that owns the Being of a God, who will deny that any love or benevolent affection is due to God, and proper to be exercised towards him? If no *benevolence* is to be exercised towards God, because we cannot profit him, then for the same reason, neither is *gratitude* to be exercised towards him for his benefits to us, because we cannot requite him. But where is the man who believes a God and a providence, that will say this?

There seems to be an inconsistence in some writers on morality in this respect, that they do not wholly exclude a regard to the Deity out of their schemes of morality, but yet mention it so slightly, that they leave me room and reason to suspect they esteem it a less important and a subordinate part of true morality: and insist on benevolence to the *created system* in such a manner as would naturally lead one to suppose they look upon that as by far the most important and essential thing. But why should this be? If true virtue consists partly in a respect to God, then doubtless it consists chiefly in it. If true morality requires that we should have some regard, some benevolent affection to our Creator, as well as to his creatures, then doubtless it requires the first regard to be paid to him; and that he be every way the supreme object of our benevolence. If his being above our reach, and beyond all capacity of being profited by us, does not hinder but that nevertheless he is the proper object of our love, then it does not hinder that he should be loved according to his dignity, or according to the degree in which he has those things wherein worthiness of regard consists so far as we are capable of it. But this worthiness none will deny consists in these two things, *greatness* and moral *goodness*. And those that own a God, do not deny that he infinitely exceeds all other Beings in these. If the Deity is to be looked upon as within that system of Beings which properly terminates our benevolence, or belonging to that whole, certainly he is to be regarded as the *head* of the system, and the *chief* part of it, if it be proper to call him a *part*, who is infinitely more than all the rest, and in comparison of whom and without whom all the rest are nothing, either as to beauty or existence. And therefore certainly, unless we will be atheists, we must allow that true virtue does primarily and most essentially consist in a supreme love to God, and that where this is wanting there can be no true virtue.

But this being a matter of the highest importance, I shall say something further to make it plain that love to God is most essential to true virtue; and that no benevolence whatsoever to other Beings can be of the nature of true virtue without it.

And therefore, let it be supposed that some Beings, by natural instinct or by some other means, have a determination of mind to union and benevolence to a particular person, or private system,[5] which is but a small part of the

[5] It may be here noted, that when hereafter I use such a phrase as *private system* of Beings, or others similar, I thereby intend any system or society of Beings that contains but a small part of the great system, comprehending the universality of existence. I think *that* may well be called a *private system*, which is but an infinitely small part of this great whole we stand related to. I therefore also call that affection *private affection*, which is limited to so narrow a circle; and that *general* affection or benevolence which has *Being in general* for its object. (Edwards' note.)

universal system of Being, and that this disposition or determination of mind is independent on, or not subordinate to benevolence to *Being in general.* Such a determination, disposition, or affection of mind is not of the nature of true virtue.

This is allowed by all with regard to *self-love,* in which good will is confined to one single person only. And there are the same reasons why any other private affection or good will, though extending to a society of persons, independent of, and unsubordinate to, benevolence to the universality, should not be esteemed truly virtuous. For notwithstanding it extends to a number of persons, which taken together are more than a single person, yet the whole falls infinitely short of the universality of existence; and if put in the scales with it, has no greater proportion to it than a single person.

However it may not be amiss more particularly to consider the reasons why *private affections,* or good will limited to a particular circle of Beings, falling infinitely short of the whole existence, and not dependent upon it, nor subordinate to general benevolence, cannot be of the nature of true virtue.

1. Such a private affection, detached from general benevolence, and independent on it, as the case may be, will be *against* general benevolence, or of a contrary tendency; and will set a person *against* general existence, and make him an enemy to it. As it is with *selfishness,* or when a man is governed by a regard to his own private interest, independent of regard to the public good, such a temper disposes a man to act the part of an enemy to the public. As in every case wherein his private interest seems to clash with the public; or in all those cases wherein such things are presented to his view that suit his personal appetites or private inclinations but are inconsistent with the good of the public. On which account a selfish, contracted, narrow spirit is generally abhorred, and is esteemed base and sordid. But if a man's affection takes in half a dozen more, and his regards extend so far beyond his own single person as to take in his children and family; or if it reaches further still, to a larger circle, but

falls infinitely short of the universal system, and is exclusive of Being in general, his private affection exposes him to the same thing, viz. to pursue the interest of its particular object in *opposition* to general existence; which is certainly contrary to the tendency of true virtue; yea directly contrary to the main and most essential thing in its nature, the thing on account of which chiefly its nature and tendency is good.

2. Private affection, if not subordinate to general affection, is not only liable, as the case *may* be, to issue in enmity to Being in general, but has a *tendency* to it, as the case certainly *is,* and must necessarily be. For he that is influenced by private affection, not subordinate to a regard to Being in general, sets up its particular and limited object above Being in general; and this most naturally tends to enmity against the latter, which is by right the great, supreme, ruling, and absolutely sovereign object of our regard. Even as the setting up another prince as supreme in any kingdom, distinct from the lawful sovereign, naturally tends to enmity against the lawful sovereign. Wherever it is sufficiently published, that the supreme, infinite, and all-comprehending Being requires a supreme regard to himself; and insists upon it, that our respect to him should universally rule in our hearts, and every other affection be subordinate to it, and this under the pain of his displeasure, (as we must suppose it is in the world of intelligent creatures, if God maintains a moral kingdom in the world) then a consciousness of our having chosen and set up another prince to rule over us and subjected our hearts to him, and continuing in such an act, must unavoidably excite enmity, and fix us in a stated opposition to the supreme Being. This demonstrates that affection to a private society or system, independent on general benevolence, cannot be of the nature of true virtue. For this would be absurd, that it has the nature and essence of true virtue, and yet at the same time has a *tendency opposite* to true virtue.

3. Not only would affection to a private system, unsubordinate to a regard to Being in general, have a tendency to opposition to the supreme object of virtuous affection, as its effect and consequence, but would become *itself,* an opposi-

tion to that object. Considered by itself, in its nature, detached from its effects, it is an instance of great opposition to the rightful supreme object of our respect. For it exalts its private object above the other great and infinite object; and sets that up as supreme in opposition to this. It puts down Being in general, which is infinitely superior in itself and infinitely more important, in an inferior place; yea, subjects the supreme general object to this private infinitely inferior object; which is to treat it with great contempt, and truly to act in opposition to it, and to act in opposition to the true order of things, and in opposition to that which is infinitely the supreme interest; making this supreme and infinitely important interest, as far as in us lies, to be subject to, and dependent on an interest infinitely inferior. This is to act against it and to act the part of an enemy to it.

From these things I think it is manifest, that no affection limited to any private system, not dependent on, nor subordinate to Being in general, can be of the nature of true virtue; and this, whatever the private system be, let it be more or less extensive, consisting of a greater or smaller number of individuals, so long as it contains an infinitely little part of universal existence, and so bears no proportion to the great all-comprehending system. And consequently, that no affection whatsoever to any creature, or any system of created Beings, which is not dependent on, nor subordinate to a propensity or union of the heart to God, the supreme and infinite Being, can be of the nature of true virtue.

With respect to the manner in which a virtuous love in *created* beings, *one to another,* is dependent on and is derived from love to *God,* this will appear by a proper consideration of what has been said: that it is sufficient to render love to any created Being virtuous, if it arise from the temper of mind wherein consists a disposition to love God supremely. Because it appears from what has already been observed, all that love to *particular Beings,* which is the fruit of a benevolent propensity of heart to *Being in general,* is virtuous love. But, as has been remarked, a benevolent propensity of heart to Being in general, and a temper or disposition to love God supremely, are in effect the same thing. Therefore, if love to a created being comes from that temper or propensity of the heart, it is virtuous. However, every particular exercise of love to a creature may not *sensibly* arise from any exercise of love to God, or an explicit consideration of any similitude, conformity, union, or relation to God in the creature beloved.

A truly virtuous mind, being as it were under the sovereign dominion of *love to God,* does above all things seek the *glory of God,* and makes *this* his supreme, governing, and ultimate end; consisting in the expression of God's perfections in their proper effects, and in the manifestation of God's glory to created understandings, and the communications of the infinite fulness of God to the creature, in the creature's highest esteem of God, love to God, and joy in God, and in the proper exercises and expressions of these. And so far as a virtuous mind exercises true virtue in benevolence to created beings, it chiefly seeks the good of the creature, consisting in its knowledge or view of God's glory and beauty, its union with God, conformity to him and love to him, and joy in him. And that temper or disposition of heart, that consent, union, or propensity of mind to Being in general, which appears chiefly in such exercises, is virtue, truly so called; or, in other words, true grace and real holiness. And no other disposition or affection but this is of the nature of virtue.

Corollary. Hence it appears that those *schemes* of religion or moral philosophy, which, however well in some respects they may treat of benevolence to *mankind* and other virtues depending on it, yet have not a supreme regard to God, and love to him, laid in the *foundation,* and all other virtues handled in a *connection* with this, and in *subordination* to this, are not true schemes of philosophy, but are fundamentally and essentially defective. It may be asserted in general, that nothing is of the nature of true virtue, in which God is not the *first* and the *last;* or which, with regard to their exercises in general, have not their first foundation and source in apprehensions of God's supreme dignity and glory, and in answerable esteem and love of him, and have not respect to God as the supreme end.[6]

Concerning the Secondary and Inferior Kind of Beauty

Though this which has been spoken of alone is justly esteemed the true beauty of moral agents or spiritual Beings . . . yet there are other qualities, other sensations, propensities and affections of mind and principles of action that often obtain the epithet of *virtuous,* and by many are supposed to have the nature of true virtue, which are entirely of a distinct nature from this, and have nothing of that kind, and therefore are erroneously confounded with real virtue.

That consent, agreement, or union of Being to Being which has been spoken of, viz. the union or propensity of *minds* to mental or spiritual existence, may be called the highest and primary beauty that is to be found among things that exist, being the proper and peculiar beauty of spiritual and moral Beings, which are the highest and first part of the universal system, for whose sake all the rest has existence. Yet there is another, inferior, secondary beauty, which is some image of this, and which is not peculiar to spiritual Beings, but is found even in inanimate things; which consists in a mutual consent and agreement of different things, in form, manner, quantity, and visible end or design; called by the various names of regularity, order, uniformity, symmetry, proportion, harmony, etc. Such is, as it were, the mutual consent of the different parts of the periphery of a circle. Such is the beauty of the figures on a piece of chintz or brocade. Such is the beautiful proportion of the various parts of a human body or countenance. And such is the sweet mutual consent and agreement of the various notes of a melodious tune.

The reason, or at least one reason, why God has made this kind of mutual agreement of things beautiful and grateful to those intelligent Beings that perceive it, probably is that there is in it some image of the true, spiritual, original,

6 *Ibid.,* chap. ii.

beauty which has been spoken of. It pleases God to observe analogy in his works, as is manifest in fact in innumerable instances.

This secondary kind of beauty, consisting in uniformity and proportion, not only takes place in material and external things, but also in things immaterial; and is, in very many things, plain and sensible in the latter as well as the former. There is a beauty of order in society, besides what consists in benevolence or can be referred to it, which is of the secondary kind: As, when the different members of society have all their appointed office, place and station, according to their several capacities and talents, and every one keeps his place, and continues in his proper business. There is the same kind of beauty in immaterial things, in what is called wisdom, consisting in the united tendency of thoughts, ideas and particular volitions to one general purpose, which is a distinct thing from the goodness of that general purpose, as being useful and benevolent.

So there is a beauty in the virtue called *justice*, which consists in the agreement of different things that have relation to one another, in nature, manner and measure, and therefore is the very same sort of beauty with that uniformity and proportion, which is observable in those external and material things that are esteemed beautiful. Things are in natural regularity and mutual agreement, in a literal sense, when he whose heart opposes the general system, should have the hearts of that system, or the heart of the head and ruler of the system against him; and that in consequence, he should receive evil in proportion to the evil tendency of the opposition of his heart. So there is an agreement in nature and measure, when he that loves has the proper returns of love; when he that from his heart promotes the good of another has his good promoted by the other; for there is a kind of justice in a becoming gratitude.

Indeed most of the duties incumbent on us, if well considered, will be found to partake of the nature of justice. There is some natural agreement of one thing to another; some adaptedness of the agent to the object; some answerableness of the act to the occasion; some equality and proportion in things of a similar nature, and of a direct relation one to another. So it is in relative duties: duties of children to parents and of parents to children; duties of husbands and wives; duties of rulers and subjects; duties of friendship and good neighborhood; and all duties that we owe to God, our Creator, preserver and benefactor; and all duties whatsoever, considered as required by God. But there is another and higher beauty in true virtue and in all truly virtuous dispositions and exercises than what consists in any uniformity or similarity of various things, viz. the *union of heart* to *Being in general,* or to God the Being of Beings, which appears in those virtues, and which those virtues, when true, are the various expressions or effects of. It is true that benevolence to Being in general, when a person hath it, will naturally incline him to justice, or proportion in the exercises of it. He that loves Being, simply considered, will naturally, other things being equal, love particular Beings in a proportion compounded of the degree of Being and the degree of virtue, or benevolence to Being, which they have. So that, after benevolence to Being in general exists, the proportion which is observed in objects may be the cause of the proportion of benevolence to those objects; but no proportion is the cause or ground of the existence of such a thing as benevolence to Being.

From all that has been observed concerning this secondary kind of beauty, it appears that that disposition which consists in determination of the mind to approve and be pleased with this beauty, considered simply and by itself, has nothing of the nature of true virtue, and is entirely a different thing from a truly virtuous taste.[7]

Of Self-Love, and Its Various Influence to Cause Love to Others, Or the Contrary

Self-love, as the phrase is used in common speech, most commonly signifies a man's regard to his confined *private*

[7] *Ibid.*, chap. iii.

self, or love to himself with respect to his *private interest.* By *private* interest I mean that which most immediately consists in those pleasures, or pains, that are *personal.* For there is a comfort and a grief that some have in others' pleasures or pains, which are in others originally, but in some measure become theirs by virtue of a benevolent union of heart with others. And there are other pleasures and pains that are originally our own, and not what we have by such a participation with others. Such is the natural disposition in men to be pleased in a perception of their being the objects of the honor and love of others, and displeased with others' hatred and contempt. It is easy to see that a man's love to himself will make him love love to himself, and hate hatred to himself. And as God has constituted our nature, self-love is exercised in no one disposition more than in this.

If we take self-love in this sense, love to some others may truly be the effect of self-love. By order of nature, a man's love to those that love him is no more than a certain expression or effect of self-love. Therefore there is no more true virtue in a man's thus loving his friends merely from self-love, than there is in self-love itself. As men may love persons and things from self-love so may their love to qualities and characters arise from the same source. Is it a strange thing that men should from self-love like a temper of character, which in its nature and tendency falls in with the nature and tendency of self-love and which we know by experience and self-evidence, without metaphysical refining, in the general tends to men's pleasure and benefit? And, on the contrary, should dislike what they see tends to men's pain and misery? If a man from self-love disapproves the vices of malice, envy and others of that sort, which naturally tend to the hurt of mankind, why may he not from the same principle approve the contrary virtues of meekness, peaceableness, benevolence, charity, generosity, justice, and the social virtues in general which he as easily and clearly knows, naturally tend to the good of mankind? It is undoubtedly true that some have a love to these virtues from a higher principle. But yet I think it certainly true, that there is generally in mankind a sort of approbation of them, which arises from self-love.[8]

Of Natural Conscience, and the Moral Sense

There is yet another disposition or principle of great importance, natural to mankind, which, if we consider the consistence and harmony of nature's laws, may also be looked upon as in some sense arising from self-love or self-union. That is a disposition in man to be uneasy in a consciousness of being inconsistent with himself, and as it were, against himself in his own actions. In pure love to others (i.e. love not arising from self-love) there is an union of the heart with others, a kind of enlargement of the mind, whereby it so extends itself as to take others into a man's self. And therefore it implies a disposition to feel, to desire, and to act as though others were one with ourselves, which naturally renders a sensible inconsistence with ourselves and self-opposition in what we ourselves choose and do to be uneasy to the mind.

Thus approving actions, because we therein act as in agreement with ourselves or as one with ourselves, and thus disapproving and being uneasy in the consciousness of disagreeing and being inconsistent with ourselves in what we do, is quite a different thing from approving or disapproving actions because in them we agree and are united with Being in general, which is loving or hating actions from a sense of the primary beauty of true virtue, and odiousness of sin. The former of these principles is private; the latter is public and truly benevolent in the highest sense. The former is a natural principle; but the latter is a divine principle.

In that uneasiness now mentioned consists very much of that inward trouble men have from reflections of conscience. Natural conscience consists in these two things. 1. In that disposition to approve or disapprove the moral treatment which passes between us and others from a determination of the mind to be easy or uneasy in a consciousness of our being

[8] *Ibid.*, chap. iv.

consistent or inconsistent with ourselves. 2. The sense of desert, consisting in a natural agreement, proportion and harmony, between malevolence or injury, and resentment or punishment; or between loving and being loved, between showing kindness and being rewarded, etc. Both these kinds of approving or disapproving concur in the approbation or disapprobation of conscience, the one founded on the other. Thus when a man's conscience disapproves of his treatment of his neighbor, in the first place he is conscious, that if he were in his neighbor's stead, he should resent such treatment, from a sense of justice, or from a sense of uniformity and equality between such treatment and resentment and punishment. And then in the next place, he perceives that therefore he is not consistent with himself, in doing what he himself should resent in that case.

Approbation and disapprobation of conscience, in the sense now explained, will extend to all virtue and vice, to everything whatsoever that is morally good or evil, in a mind which does not confine its view to a private sphere but will take things in general into consideration and is free from speculative error. For as all virtue or moral good may be resolved into love to others, either God or creatures, so men easily see the uniformity and natural agreement there is between loving others and being accepted and favored by others. And all vice, sin, or moral evil, summarily consisting in the want of this love to others, or in the contrary, viz. hatred or malevolence, so men easily see the natural agreement there is between hating and doing ill to others and being hated by them, and suffering ill from them, or from him that acts for all and has the care of the whole system. Thus natural conscience, if the understanding be properly enlightened, and errors and blinding stupifying prejudices are removed, concurs with the law of God, and is of equal extent with it, and joins its voice with it in every article.

And thus in particular we may see in what respect this natural conscience extends to true virtue, consisting of union of heart to Being in general, and supreme love to God. For although it sees not, or rather does not taste its primary and essential beauty, i.e. it tastes no sweetness in benevolence to Being in general, simply considered (for nothing but general benevolence itself can do that), yet this natural conscience, common to mankind, may approve of it from that uniformity, equality and justice which there is in it.

Thus has God established and ordered that this principle of *natural conscience,* which though it implies no such thing as actual benevolence to Being in general, nor any delight in such a principle, simply considered, yet should approve and condemn the same things that are approved and condemned by a spiritual sense or virtuous taste.

The conscience may see the natural agreement between opposing and being opposed, between hating and being hated, without abhorring malevolence from a benevolent temper of mind, or without loving God from a view of the beauty of his holiness. These things have no necessary dependence one on the other.[9]

Of Particular Instincts of Nature, Which in Some Respects Resemble Virtue

There are various dispositions and inclinations natural to man which depend on particular laws of nature, determining their minds to certain affections and actions towards particular objects; which laws seem to be established chiefly for the preservation of mankind . . . and their comfortably subsisting in the world. Which dispositions may be called *instincts.*

If any Being or Beings have by natural instinct, or by any other means, a determination of mind to benevolence, extending only to some particular persons or private system, however large that system may be, or however great a number of individuals it may contain, so long as it contains but an infinitely small part of universal existence, and so bears no proportion to this great and universal system—such limited private benevolence, not arising from, nor being subordinate to benevolence to Being in general cannot have the nature of true virtue.

[9] *Ibid.,* chap. v.

These private affections, if they do not arise from general benevolence, and they are not connected with it in their first existence, have no tendency to produce it. Being not dependent on it, their detached and unsubordinate operation rather tends to and implies opposition to Being in general than general benevolence; as every one sees and owns with respect to self-love. And there are the very same reasons why any other private affection confined to limits infinitely short of universal existence should have that influence, as well as love that is confined to a single person. If persons by any means come to have a benevolent affection limited to a party that is very large or to the country or nation in general, of which they are a part, or the public community they belong to, though it be as large as the Roman empire was of old; yea, if there could be an instinct or a cause determining a person to benevolence towards the whole world of mankind, or even all created sensible natures throughout the universe, exclusive of union of heart to general existence and of love to God, nor derived from that temper of mind which disposes to a supreme regard to him, nor subordinate to such divine love, it cannot be of the nature of true virtue.[10]

The Reasons Why Those Things That Have Been Mentioned, Which Have Not the Essence of Virtue, Have Yet by Many Been Mistaken for True Virtue

The first reason may be this, that although they have not the specific and distinguishing nature and essence of virtue, yet they have something that *belongs to the general nature* of virtue. The general nature of virtue is love. There is something of the general nature of virtue in those natural affections and principles that have been mentioned. In many of these natural affections there is something of the appearance of love to persons. In some of them there appears the tendency and effect of benevolence in part. Pity to others in distress though not properly of the nature of love, yet has

[10] *Ibid.*, chap. vi.

partly the same influence and effect with benevolence. Natural gratitude . . . has the same or like operation and effect with friendship, in part, for a season, and with regard to so much of the welfare of its object as appears a deserved requital of kindness received. So that many times men from natural gratitude do really with a sort of benevolence love those who love them. The natural disposition there is to mutual affection between the sexes often operates by what may properly be called love. There is oftentimes truly a kind both of benevolence and complacence. As there is also between parents and children.

Thus these things have something of the general nature of virtue. What they are essentially defective in is, that they are private in their nature; they do not arise from any temper of benevolence to Being in general, nor have they a tendency to any such effect in their operation. But yet agreeing with virtue in its general nature, they are beautiful within their own private sphere, i.e. they appear beautiful if we confine our views to that private system. The reason why men are so ready to take these private affections for true virtue, is the narrowness of their views; and above all, that they are so ready to leave the divine Being out of their view, and to neglect him in their consideration, or to regard him in their thoughts as though he were not properly belonging to the system of real existence, but as a kind of shadowy, imaginary Being. We are apt, through the narrowness of our views, in judging of the beauty of affections and actions, to limit our consideration to only a small part of the created system. When private affections extend themselves to a considerable number, we are very ready to look upon them as truly virtuous. Thus it is with respect to a man's love to a large party or a man's love to his country. Hence among the Romans love to their country was the highest virtue, though this affection of theirs, so much extolled among them, was employed as it were for the destruction of the rest of mankind.

Another reason why these natural principles and affections are mistaken for true virtue is that in several respects they have the same effect which true virtue tends to; especially in these two ways: 1. The present state of the world is so ordered and constituted by the wisdom and goodness of its supreme ruler, that these natural principles, for the most part, tend to the good of the world of mankind. Herein they agree with the tendency of general benevolence which seeks and tends to the general good. But this is no proof that these natural principles have the nature of true virtue. 2. These principles have a like effect with true virtue in this respect that they tend several ways to restrain vice, and prevent many acts of wickedness. So is this present state of mankind ordered by a merciful God, that men's self-love does in innumerable ways restrain from acts of true wickedness; and not only so but puts men upon seeking true virtue; yet is not itself true virtue, but is the source of all the wickedness that is in the world.

Another reason why these inferior affections, especially some of them, are accounted virtuous, is that there are affections of the same denomination which are truly virtuous. Thus, for instance, there is a truly virtuous pity from general benevolence. It excites compassion in cases that are overlooked by natural instinct. And even in those cases to which instinct extends, it mixes its influence with the natural principle and guides and regulates its operations. So there is a virtuous *gratitude;* or a gratitude that arises not only from self-love, but from a superior principle of disinterested general benevolence. So there is a virtuous love of *justice,* arising from pure benevolence to Being in general . . . and so a virtuous *conscientiousness,* or a sanctified conscience. And as, when *natural affections* have their operations mixed with the influence of virtuous benevolence, and are directed and determined thereby, they may be called virtuous, so there may be a virtuous love of parents to their children, and between other near relatives; a virtuous love of our town, or country, or nation. Yea, and a virtuous love between the sexes, as there may be the influence of virtue mingled with instinct. A principle of general benevolence softens and sweetens the mind, makes it more susceptible of the proper influence and exercise of the gentler natural instincts, and directs every one into its proper channels, and determines the exercise to the proper manner and measure, and guides all to the best purposes.[11]

Further Readings

Primary Sources

Edwards, Jonathan. *Puritan Sage, Collected Writings of Jonathan Edwards.* Edited by Virgilius Ferm. New York: Library Publishers, 1953.

———. *Religious Affections.* Edited by John E. Smith. New Haven: Yale University Press, 1959.

———. *Selected Writings.* Edited with introduction by Harold Simonson. New York: F. Ungar, 1970.

———. *Basic Writings.* Edited by Ola Winslow. New York: New American Library, 1966.

Secondary Sources

Cherry, Conrad. *The Theology of Jonathan Edwards: a Reappraisal.* Garden City, N. Y.: Anchor Books, 1966.

Davidson, Edward H. *Jonathan Edwards.* Boston: Houghton Mifflin, 1966.

Levin, David (comp.). *Jonathan Edwards: a Profile.* New York: Hill and Wang, 1969.

[11] *Ibid.*, chap. viii.

Chapter 14

SØREN KIERKEGAARD

Among the many distinguished nineteenth-century Protestant thinkers there is none who is so singular in intent and accomplishment as Søren A. Kierkegaard. Some thirty-odd published works, a many-volumed journal, and a fistful of slashing polemical pamphlets and articles—these were the work of a lifetime. Though an ardent church-going Lutheran and rather well read in the theology of the day, Kierkegaard's writings were not calculated to the intellectual stride of nineteenth-century life. He wrote from personal concern about his own religious life but with such pathos and enthusiasm on the one hand and with such delicacy and intellectual poise on the other that his writings constitute in a single compass both a devotional literature delineating the ethical content and pragmatic significance of God in Christ and a philosophic literature delineating the nature and province of reflection.

"Better well-hung than ill-wed" is the motto chosen by Kierkegaard for his *Philosophical Fragments*, but it might well have been used for his entire authorship. For he did not choose to write so that he would be supported by "the omnipotence of public opinion." Where almost everyone took for granted the answer, Kierkegaard chose to ask again: What is Christianity? An intellectual and studied detachment kept him "well-hung" within the rationalistic and Hegelian and Lutheran context and permitted him to write in remarkable independence of the modes of the day. But a constant personal concern about his own relation to God provided sufficient motivation for an authorship which was so demanding that it consumed in the writing the author's life.

Kierkegaard's years were very few. He was born in 1813 and died, forty-two years later, in 1855. Born in a home of some intellectual and financial means—the father retired in his early forties to devote the rest of his life to intellectual pursuits—Søren was enabled to live the life of a gentleman man of letters on the patrimony provided. This aristocratic status, however, was itself the occasion for severe scrutiny of his own life. From Søren's twenty-second year and continuing through the next twenty years, we can note him perspicuously threading his way among the difficulties that opulence of talent and fortune provided for him. The possibilities implicit in the abilities which he very early recognized to exist in himself and the freedom which moderate means allowed seemed to Kierkegaard to be an instance, rare to be sure, where a life, his own, might gain its religious significance and justification by a life of authorship. Dare he claim a divine governance for a life of authorship? The question was not easy to answer. Eight years of desultory study at the University of Copenhagen (1830-38) gave him opportunity for the study of literature, philosophy, and theology. A deathbed promise exacted by his father in 1838 brought Søren through two years of disciplined study to a theological degree *cum laude* in 1840. But this latter period was so uninteresting that Søren called it "the great parenthesis." Try as he would, Kierkegaard did not become integrated into what he called "the universal," and neither family, state, nor church could as yet attract him sufficiently to provide a pattern for his life.

The single diversion from theological study during the "parenthesis" was Regina Olsen. "During this time I let her existence twine itself about mine," he said in a later account of his love affair.[1] But in September, 1840, began the overt wooing. During the ensuing year Kierkegaard wrote a massive dissertation for the Master's degree and courted Regina with a briskness that seemed to promise an early marriage. By October, 1841, the engagement was broken and the dis-

1 Walter Lowrie, *A Short Life of Kierkegaard* (Princeton: Princeton University Press, 1944), p. 131.

sertation completed and given honors by the University faculty. With these events came a break in the external fortunes of Kierkegaard's life. He believed himself to be an exception to the rule of marriage and, on the other hand, quite clearly destined for a life of religiously oriented authorship. A trip to Germany lasting several months gave him opportunity to hear Schelling at the University of Berlin and to think about his life in some freedom from youthful conventions. He began to write with a new zeal and enthusiasm. He was launched as an author! And except for a brief period of reconsideration a few years later when his literature reached a turning point, he was quite content to expend all of his talents, time, and money in a vocation that was an exception but nonetheless was conceived as God's will for him.

The Religious Vocation of Authorship

On February 29, 1843, *Either/Or* appeared in Copenhagen. It was a large book, somewhat fantastic in appearance. Purporting to be the accidentally discovered papers of "A," a glowing young intellectual aesthete, and of "B," a decorous and responsible representative of staid community morality, *Either/Or* was something of a sensation. Even though it juxtaposed two qualitatively distinct views of life against one another, the work did not resolve the issue by direct polemic, and many readers were troubled by the lack of conclusive argument and definitive results. Kierkegaard's remarkable literary gifts gave this work and most of the rest an obvious intrinsic merit and perhaps accounted for the immediate popularity of his writings.

In rapid succession, from late 1843 until early 1846, there appeared under various pseudonyms, *Fear and Trembling, Repetition, The Concept of Dread, The Philosophical Fragments, Stages on Life's Way, Prefaces,* and *The Concluding Unscientific Postscript.* This very rich literature explored many issues: the faith of Abraham, the psychological significance of a moral lapse, the meaning of anxiety and dread in relation to the doctrine of original sin, the Incarnation claim of Christianity, the relations between the logic of thought and the attitudes and commitments by which men evaluate—these as well as other topics. This array of subject matter is surprising enough; but this entire literature does something more—it provides varying points of view in the created pseudonymous authors whereby almost every topic is treated from at least two, and sometimes more, vantage points. This proliferation of standpoints and subject matter, and the fact that the author Kierkegaard refused to take responsibility for the views expressed but admitted only to the responsibility of inventing the authors, all of this indicates that the entire literature to the year 1846 had a purpose not evident in any single work.

Readers of Kierkegaard have sometimes disregarded this involved mode of writing and have fallen into the very trap that Kierkegaard said they would. Perhaps it is true that the plot became a little too involved and that the books aroused curiosity instead of inciting the moral and religious spirit of the reader. In any case, Kierkegaard disclosed in several places the plot of the authorship and detailed his intentions as a religious and Christian thinker. He said that there was a point of view on the authorship and that it was "out of the aesthetic, through the ethical and the philosophical, and into the religious." He began with a religious purpose, he said, but a pedagogical wisdom demanded that he begin where the reader was. He therefore wrote the first volume of *Either/Or* in such a way as to depict the categories of life viewed as enjoyment as well as its correlative structure of personality. All of the later pseudonymous works played a corresponding role in the enormous evangelical task of bringing an individual reader first to the consciousness of what he would be if he shared the common-sense commitments of Danish cultured life and subsequently to the consciousness of other significant and alternative commitments including Christianity. Kierkegaard was troubled by the apostasy of his day and, like Schleiermacher, a contemporary German theologian, he chose to address himself to the cultured despisers of Christianity. But his weapons were not the same.

Kierkegaard had to expend his immense creative poetic gifts in a detailed and closely controlled argument with the age. This he conceived to be his religious vocation. And should any one doubt the veracity of the claim to a religious intention—especially while reading about seduction, Mozart's operas, the essay on kissing, and so on—Kierkegaard pointed to the use of pseudonymity and also to the publication of twenty-one religious discourses in seven small volumes, each a companion to one of the pseudonymous works, each bearing his own name and each verifying that he was religious from the beginning.

His authorship was conceived then as a new mode of presenting the Christian faith. It entailed as a matter of fact that Kierkegaard should become sensitive to the value structures in his culture and give them conceptual form. It required further that he come to grips with the most influential philosophy of the day, objective idealism, particularly as it was expressed by Hegel and his followers. These two tasks were done in the pseudonymous literature. Kierkegaard's doctrine of the "stages" is an attempt to state the significant and competing alternative modes of evaluating and living one's life, and this doctrine gives form and structure to his entire literature. But in order to argue that the intelligence can entertain alternative possibilities, including Christianity, without thereby being necessarily committed to any one of them, it became necessary for Kierkegaard to evolve a theory concerning the nature and limits of reflection. In his theories of knowledge and logic he penned what are perhaps the most telling criticisms of idealistic metaphysical logic yet seen. His own theories, even though they are imbedded in his literature and nowhere a topic for extended and separate treatment, are only now being appreciated for their intrinsic intellectual precision and merit.

Kierkegaard actually proposed a new standpoint from which Christianity as well as other views of life could be described and understood. He argued the possibility of a neutral and disinterested standpoint for the intelligence and at the same time the impossibility of neutrality and disinterestedness for the tasks of living. He did not seek to reduce one to the other but only to delineate the provinces respectively of reason and the passions in order that one should violate neither the passions by urging their inferiority in respect to reflection, nor reflection by urging that it was the means of solving the mysteries attendant upon existing and valuing.

But this was only half of Kierkegaard's authorship. After 1846 he began to write another series of works. These were less a part of a plot. They represent instead a filling out of the religious and Christian categories with an almost infinite detail. As rich as other views of life are, a fact to which his writings themselves attest, Kierkegaard was at pains to show that what faith produces need not be "a coarse and common work, only for the more clumsy natures"[2] but could, in virtue of its character, be artistically and dialectically refined. From 1847 through 1851, Kierkegaard wrote *Works of Love, Edifying Discourses in Various Spirits, The Christian Discourses, The Sickness Unto Death, Training in Christianity, Judge for Yourself, For Self-Examination,* and a number of briefer essay-like discourses. Kierkegaard believed these later works to be a part of the larger evangelical task served by the total authorship. He even suggested that his entire literature could be conceived as a long single work of which these later works were but the final chapters.

Becoming a Christian in Christendom

As Kierkegaard's writing went on, new motifs were expressed. Without exaggeration he tells us that he was "strictly brought up in the Christian religion" and that he heard nothing of angels, the child Jesus, and sundry pleasantries of Christianity. Instead he learned about a crucified Saviour and became "old as a child." As he matured, this picture of God began to require more and more of him, and the claim became more inward as years went by. Even

[2] *Fear and Trembling,* trans. by Walter Lowrie (Princeton: University Press, 1945), p. 48.

though he was somewhat critical of what he called this "crazy upbringing," he sought to express this claim by considering how it is that one becomes a Christian. Living in an environment where the church was a national institution and where baptism and observance of certain religious proprieties were taken for granted, Kierkegaard felt the problem to be one of becoming a Christian in Christendom where everyone takes Christianity for granted. Increasingly he called attention to the fact that the categories were no longer clear and that what looked like a "Christianizing" of the culture might also be conceived as a secularizing and attenuating of true Christianity. He found too that many motives, some of them irrelevant, were now present for becoming a Christian, and he deemed it his task to separate these motives and determine their fittingness to a Christian and/or other views of life.

It was within these additional interests that the later religious works were written. Their content provides a severe scrutiny of many of the easy and conventional practices of Christian church life. He agrees that Luther was right in the Reformation period in pushing back "works" in order that the nature of faith be made clear. But he will not agree with what he thinks is in his own day the evasion of the ethics of Jesus for the theology of Paul. He urges therefore that works be brought up again for consideration—at least as the minor premise—in order that all can see that Christianity presupposes an expression of faith in God in the conduct of everyday life. From many different points of view and with all the richness his aesthetic and intellectual capacities permitted, he explored many facets of Christian life and thought, always addressing himself to that cultivated reader who like himself was intent upon becoming a Christian in Christendom.

By 1851, only a few years but many books from *Either/Or*, which started the formal authorship, Kierkegaard's patrimony was spent and his writing had reached a kind of summary point. The enthusiastic readers of his literature he had known had not impressed him with their grasp of his intention. Just as in 1846 he had decried that kind of praise given him in virtue of misunderstanding so now too he sought no followers and refused even to consider that his responsibility was to become a moulder of public opinion. Kierkegaard did not believe that any reformative measures could express the ideality which Christianity, as he understood it, demanded. He refrained, therefore, from all overt measures to instrumentalize his own thought. He never cried out for disestablishment of the national church nor did he look longingly towards reunion with the Roman communion. Those readers who see him as sectarian or as Catholic or as Lutheran do so only by a careful selection of his writings and by studied disregard of the major intention governing the entire productivity. Rightly or wrongly, Kierkegaard saw the issues of the moral and religious life in terms of which kind of inner enthusiasm and passion a man might let rule his life. Every man had to overcome his own world, and all that one man could do for another was not to overcome it for him, but free him by the indirection of compassion, love, mercy, and even thought, to the high honor of facing the choice and working out his own salvation by the help of God.

Amid all of this strenuous reflection and writing, Kierkegaard remained a faithful churchman. He attended services regularly and even preached on occasion. He never courted favor by pretending to be orthodox nor did he seek notoriety by defining himself in opposition. He was quite content to let the church stand as it was—he believed his own personal and religious problems capable of solution without a change in the environment. But with a well-earned leisure on hand he began to reflect upon the relations which he previously had noted between theology and pastor, pastor and layman, church and state, the self-adopted New Testament standard of the Lutheran church and Lutheran practice, and the thought of a deed and the deed itself. In virtue of what he had written and in complete consistency therewith he began to probe more deeply into the relation that obtained between New Testament Christianity and the church in history. Again, and as in his other religious writings, he saw that the deedful expression of Christian faith was the most difficult for the individual believer to attain and the church to advocate. With care and exactness, Kierkegaard examined many facets of religious life. Much of this can be found in the rich journal that was kept from late 1851 through 1855. At the same time he was practicing with complete poise and deep religious joy the presence of God with such intensity as to occasion the view widely current that he had achieved a kind of saintliness. He said during 1854:

> But the thing Christianity teaches is what a man can become in life. Here then there is hope that a tame goose may become a wild goose . . . but for the love of God in heaven, take care of this: so soon as thou dost observe that the tame geese are beginning to acquire power over thee, then off, off and away with the flock! lest it end with thy becoming a tame goose blissfully content with a pitiable condition.[3]

Instead of the church bringing men into the new life in Christ, the godly "wildness," the daring of a life in which one lived as if God, the spirit, existed and all men were to be loved—instead of this, the church seemed to domesticate both the faith and the believers to make of Christianity only the divine justification of those values and commitments which one would have had anyway!

The funeral eulogy of Bishop Mynster, primate of the Danish Lutheran Church, by Hans Martensen, the greatest of Denmark's theologians, seemed to Kierkegaard to epitomize the state of affairs. Martensen's generous description of the Bishop as "irreplaceable," "a genuine witness for the truth," and a link in "the holy chain of witnesses" piqued Kierkegaard, though himself an admirer of Mynster, as quite overdone. After waiting long months for the election and consecration of Martensen as Mynster's successor, Kierkegaard finally made his disapproval public. For nine months thereafter Kierkegaard shocked northern European Christendom by his many satirical pamphlets and articles. He became popular again but, as he noted repeatedly, for wrong reasons. One need neither justify nor defend him at this date, but it is well to remember that he sought no external reforms and proposed no ecclesiastic novelties. He asked only for

[3] Walter Lowrie, *A Short Life of Kierkegaard* (Princeton: Princeton University Press), p. 259.

that which he believed would permit the church to help others into the presence of God. As through his whole life so now too he was unconventional and something of an exception. He denied that he or his thought was a model for anyone else, but he did, nonetheless, move with resoluteness and sure step to the criticism of what he deemed to be the compromises of the church. His onslaught was directed against the state of affairs whereby, in the interest of winning men, the ethical content of the culture is paraded as the ethics of Christianity. Kierkegaard never denied a relation between God and society, but he did deny that the values relevant to either were necessarily homogeneous with one another. He urged therefore a recognition of the heterogeneity of the Christian ethical content. He asked no return to early Christian faith but urged instead that a sensitivity to value structures in his day would be corroborative of the long-standing heterogeneity of Christianity and Christians in history.

In recent years Kierkegaard has been rediscovered. He has been used by many current theologians as the nineteenth-century spokesman of a twentieth-century view. His emphasis upon the qualitative distinctness of Christian morality has given impetus to recent critiques of the socially oriented theologies of Europe and America. But his day is yet to come. The finesse of his thought has engaged relatively few minds, and it may be that his greatest influence will come when theologians find it necessary to reflect upon the elemental problems of the nature of thought and relate these problems to the broader questions which concern the ethical dimension of the Christian religion.

Kierkegaard's significance can be variously assessed. It has been said about him that he was too many-sided to be the founder of a school. And certainly it is difficult ever to imagine that a sect or denomination might be the fruit of his efforts. But it is true that he rethought the philosophical nature of supernaturalism with such acumen that one scholar has claimed that Kierkegaard has repudiated the Protestant scholastic traditions of the seventeenth and eighteenth centuries and reaffirmed a Luther-like philosophical position.[4] He endeavored to describe the nature of Christianity in ethical categories rather than in either the metaphysical-logical categories of idealism or the Biblical and empirical and historical categories of traditional theism. Whether this was a significant endeavor only further reflection of many persons can tell. But whether or not this was an unconventional form of an evangelical ministry, a ministry of writing, seems already to be answered in the affirmative. Whether anyone else would admit the latter or not, Kierkegaard could repeat in the stress of the attack upon the church what he had said before: "I see Christianity from the inside" and "my writings are my own education." If no other person should find significance in Kierkegaard's life and thought, certainly Kierkegaard would not have been disappointed; for his entire life was spent in understanding what it meant to be an individual before God. Before death took him in 1855, his writings were the very means by which he believed himself to have found himself not only in Christendom but becoming a Christian within Christendom. This was enough!

SOURCES

From

THE WRITINGS OF SØREN KIERKEGAARD[5]

Contemporaneity with Christ

If the teacher serves as an occasion by means of which the learner is reminded, he cannot help the learner to recall that he really knows the Truth; for the learner is in a state

[4] Jaroslav Pelikan, *From Luther to Kierkegaard* (St. Louis: Concordia Publishing House, 1950).

[5] The materials below are taken from several of Kierkegaard's books, arranged under appropriate headings by the editor. The location of the sources and the acknowledgment of publishers' permissions are indicated by footnote reference at the close of the first excerpt from each book.

of Error.[6] What the teacher can give him occasion to remember is, that he is in Error. Now if the learner is to acquire the Truth, the Teacher must bring it to him; and not only so, but he must also give him the condition necessary for understanding it. For if the learner were in his own person the condition for understanding the Truth, he need only recall it. The condition for understanding the Truth is like the capacity to inquire for it: the condition contains the conditioned, and the question implies the answer.

But one who gives the learner not only the Truth, but also the condition for understanding it, is more than teacher. All instruction depends upon the presence, in the last analysis, of the requisite condition; if this is lacking, no teacher can do anything. Insofar as the learner exists he is already created, and hence God must have endowed him with the condition for understanding the Truth. For otherwise his earlier existence must have been merely brutish, and the Teacher who gave him the Truth and with it the condition was the original creator of his human nature. But insofar as the moment is to have decisive significance, the learner is destitute of this condition, and must therefore have been deprived of it. This deprivation cannot have been due to an act of God (which would be a contradiction), nor to an accident; . . . it must therefore be due to himself. Error is then not only outside the Truth, but polemic in its attitude toward it; which is expressed by saying that the learner has himself forfeited the condition, and is engaged in forfeiting it.

The Teacher is then God himself, who in acting as an occasion prompts the learner to recall that he is in Error, and that by reason of his own guilt. But this state, the being in Error by reason of one's own guilt, what shall we call it? Let us call it *Sin*.

The Teacher is God, and he gives the learner the requisite condition and the Truth. What shall we call such a Teacher? for we are surely agreed that we have already far transcended the ordinary functions of a Teacher. Insofar as the learner is

[6] The words "teacher," "learner," and "error" refer in the context of the *Philosophical Fragments* to Jesus Christ, the believer, and sin, respectively.

in Error, but in consequence of his own act (and in no other way can he possibly be in this state, as we have shown above), he might seem to be free; for to be what one is by one's own act is freedom. And yet he is in reality unfree and bound and exiled; for to be free from the Truth is to be exiled from the Truth, and to be exiled by one's own self is to be bound. But since he is bound by himself, may not he loose his bonds and set himself free? . . . No. And so it is in very truth; for he forges the chains of his bondage with the strength of his freedom, since he exists in it without compulsion; and thus his bonds grow strong, and all his powers unite to make him the slave of sin. What now shall we call such a Teacher, one who restores the lost condition and gives the learner the Truth? Let us call him *Saviour,* for he saves the learner from his bondage and from himself; let us call him *Redeemer,* for he redeems the learner from the captivity into which he had plunged himself. And when the Teacher gives him the condition and the Truth he constitutes himself an *Atonement,* taking away the wrath impending upon that of which the learner has made himself guilty.

Such a Teacher the learner will never be able to forget. For the moment he forgets him he sinks back again into himself, just as one who while in original possession of the condition forgot that God exists, and thereby sank into bondage.

When the disciple is in a state of Error . . . but is nonetheless a human being, and now receives the condition and the Truth, he does not become a human being for the first time, since he was a man already. But he becomes another man, not in the frivolous sense of becoming another individual of the same quality as before, but in the sense of becoming a man of a different quality, or as we may call him: *a new creature.*

Insofar as he was in Error he was constantly in the act of departing from the Truth. In consequence of receiving the condition in the moment the course of his life has been given an opposite direction, so that he is now turned about. Let us call this change *Conversion.* The sadness in this case, however, is on account of his having so long remained in his former state. Let us call such grief *Repentance;* for what is repentance but a kind of leave-taking . . . ?

Insofar as the learner was in Error, and now receives the Truth and with it the condition for understanding it, a change takes place within him like the change from non-being to being. But this transition from non-being to being is the transition we call birth. Let us call this transition the *new birth,* in consequence of which the disciple enters the world quite as at the first birth . . . ; for while it is indeed possible to be baptized *en masse* it is not possible to be born anew *en masse.*[7]

Now if we assume that it is as we have supposed . . . , that the Teacher himself contributes the condition to the learner, it will follow that the object of faith is not the *teaching* but the *Teacher.*[8]

Let us assume that it is otherwise, that the contemporary generation of disciples had received the condition from God, and that the subsequent generations were to receive it from these contemporaries—what would follow? No, if the contemporary disciple gives the condition to the successor, the latter will come to believe in him. He receives the condition from him, and thus the contemporary becomes the object of faith for the successor; for whoever gives the individual this condition is *eo ipso* the object of faith, and God.[9]

When the believer is the believer and knows God through having received the condition from God himself, every successor must receive the condition from God himself in precisely the same sense, and cannot receive it at second hand; for if he did, this second hand would have to be the hand of God himself, and in that case there is no question of a second hand. But a successor who receives the condition from God

[7] *Philosophical Fragments,* trans. by David F. Swenson (Princeton: Princeton University Press, 1942), pp. 9-14. Copyright 1942 by Princeton University Press. Reprinted by permission of the American-Scandinavian Foundation.

[8] *Ibid.,* p. 50.

[9] *Ibid.,* pp. 84-85.

himself is a contemporary, a real contemporary; a privilege enjoyed only by the believer, but also enjoyed by every believer.[10]

Christianity did not come into the world (as the parsons snivellingly and falsely introduce it) as an admirable example of the gentle art of consolation, but as the *absolute*. It is out of love God wills it so, but also it is *God* who wills it. He will not suffer Himself to be transformed by men and be a nice . . . human God: He will transform men, and that He wills out of love.

For in relation to the absolute there is only one tense: the present. For him who is not contemporary with the absolute —for him it has no existence. And as Christ is the absolute, it is easy to see that with respect to him there is only one situation; that of contemporaneousness. The past is not reality—for me; only the contemporary is reality for me. What then thou dost live contemporaneous with is reality—for thee. And thus every man can be contemporary only with the age in which he lives—and then with one thing more: with Christ's life on earth; for Christ's life on earth, sacred history, stands for itself alone outside of history. His earthly life accompanies the race, and accompanies every generation in particular, as eternal history; His earthly life possesses the eternal contemporaneousness. If thou canst not endure contemporaneousness, . . . if thou art unable to go out in the street and perceive that it is God in this horrible procession, and that this is the case wert thou to fall down and worship Him—then thou art not essentially a Christian.[11]

Truth and Reality

Existence constitutes the highest interest of the existing individual, and his interest in his existence constitutes his

[10] *Ibid.*, p. 56.

[11] *Training in Christianity,* trans. by Walter Lowrie (London: Oxford University Press, 1941; Princeton: Princeton University Press, 1944), pp. 66-69. Copyright 1944 by Princeton University Press. This and all subsequent quotations from this volume are reprinted by permission of Princeton University Press.

reality. What reality is, cannot be expressed in the language of abstraction. The only reality to which an existing individual may have a relation that is more than cognitive, is his own reality, the fact that he exists; this reality constitutes his absolute interest. The ethical demand is that he become infinitely interested in existing.

The only reality that exists for an existing individual is his own ethical reality. To every other reality he stands in a cognitive relation. The real subject is not the cognitive subject . . . ; the real subject is the ethically existing subject. The maximum of attainment in the sphere of the intellectual is to become altogether indifferent to the thinker's reality. A believer is one who is infinitely interested in another reality. This is a decisive criterion for faith, and the interest in question is not just a little curiosity, but an absolute dependence upon faith's object.

The object of faith is the reality of another, and the relationship is one of infinite interest. The object of faith is not a doctrine, for then the relationship would be intellectual. The object of faith is not a teacher with a doctrine. The object of faith is the reality of the teacher, that the teacher really exists. The object of faith is thus God's reality in existence as a particular individual, the fact that God has existed as an individual human being.[12]

Let us now call the untruth of the individual *Sin*.[13] Above all let us not forget that not only theft and murder and drunkenness and the like are sins, but that properly sin is: *in time to lose eternity.* Because man has in him something eternal, therefore he can lose the eternal, but this is not to lose, it is to be lost; if there were nothing eternal in man, he could not be lost.

On the one hand this: only the temporal is lost temporally.

[12] *The Concluding Unscientific Postscript,* trans. by David F. Swenson and Walter Lowrie (Princeton: Princeton University Press, 1941), pp. 279-90. Copyright 1941 by Princeton University Press. This and subsequent quotations from this volume are reprinted by permission of Princeton University Press.

[13] *Ibid.,* p. 186.

On the other hand: *only the eternal can be gained eternally.*[14]

So then: to live on in complete ignorance of oneself, or entirely to misunderstand oneself, or to venture with blind reliance upon one's own powers and such-like . . . that is not to come to oneself, it is to be drunken. But then, to live on, having accurate knowledge of and shrewd calculation upon one's own powers, talents, qualifications, possibilities, and in the same measure familiar with what human and worldly shrewdness teaches the initiated—is that to come to oneself? Yes, according to the opinion of the merely human view. But not according to the Christian opinion; for this is not to come to oneself, it is to come to the probable; on that road one never gets any farther. It is only in the sense of selfishness that it brings him nearer and nearer to himself—this is what the merely human view calls sobriety: Christianity calls it drunkenness. Only by being before God can a man entirely come to himself in the transparency of sobriety.[15]

And so it is in fact, the absolute precisely is the only thing that can make a man entirely sober.[16] Christianity . . . says that just the fact that one's knowing turns against one inwardly, that just this is what makes one sober, that only that man is sober whose understanding, whose knowing, is action, that therefore it is not at all necessary to expend so much effort upon developing one's understanding, if only care be taken to ensure that it gets an inward direction, that it is craftiness to direct all one's attention and concentrate all one's powers upon developing one's understanding, that a man with only a slender understanding, but with this turned inward and so translated into action, is sober, and that a man

[14] *Christian Discourses,* trans. by Walter Lowrie (London: Oxford University Press, 1939), pp. 141-42. Copyright 1939 by Oxford University Press. Reprinted by permission of Oxford University Press.

[15] *For Self-Examination* and *Judge for Yourselves,* trans. by Walter Lowrie (Princeton: Princeton University Press, 1944), pp. 120-22. Copyright 1944 by Princeton University Press. This and subsequent quotations from this volume are reprinted by permission of Princeton University Press.

[16] *Ibid.,* p. 123.

with the greatest understanding, but turned in the opposite direction, is completely drunk.[17]

Is "truth"[18] the sort of thing one might conceivably appropriate without more ado by means of another man? For what is Truth? and in what sense was Christ the truth? Christ's life upon earth, every instant of this life was the truth. Every other man, a thinker, a teacher of science, etc., indeed any other man you please, a serving-man, a letter-carrier—to ask of him what truth is, that makes sense in a way; but to ask it of Christ who stands bodily before one, to ask this of Christ is the most complete confusion possible. No man, with the exception of Christ, is the truth.

Christ is the truth in such a sense that to *be* the truth is the only true explanation of what truth is. Hence one may ask an Apostle, one may ask a Christian, what truth is, and then the Apostle or the Christian will point to Christ and say, "Behold Him, learn of Him, He was the Truth." That is to say, the truth, in the sense in which Christ was the truth, is not a sum of sentences, not a definition of concepts, etc., but a life. Truth in its very being is not the duplication of being in terms of thought, which yields only the thought of being. No, truth in its very being is the reduplication in me, in thee, in him, so that my, that thy, that his life, approximately, in the striving to attain it, expresses the truth, so that my, that thy, that his life, approximately, in the striving to attain it, is the very being of truth, is a *life*, as the truth was in Christ, for He was the Truth.

And hence, Christianly understood, the truth consists not in knowing the truth but in being the truth. That is to say, knowledge has a relation to truth, but with that I am (untruly) outside of myself; within me (that is, when I am truly within myself . . .) truth is, if it is at all, a being, a life. Therefore it is said, "This is life eternal, to know the only true God and Him whom He hath sent," the Truth. That is

[17] *Ibid.*, p. 134.

[18] Kierkegaard distinguishes between propositional truth (empirical or logical) and ethico-religious truth. Here the reference is to the latter.

to say, only then do I truly know the truth when it becomes a life in me. Therefore Christ compares truth with food and appropriation of it with eating. . . .[19]

But the eternal is not a thing which can be had regardless of the way in which it is acquired; no, the eternal is not really a thing, but is the way in which it is acquired. The eternal is acquired in *one* way, and the eternal is different from everything else precisely for the fact that it can be acquired only in one single way; conversely, what can be acquired in only one way is the eternal—it is acquired only in one way, in the difficult way which Christ indicated by the words: "Narrow is the gate and straitened the way, that leadeth unto life, and few are they that find it."[20]

Now it is well enough known that Christ constantly uses the expression "follower"; He never says anything about wanting admirers, admiring worshipers, adherents; and when he uses the expression "disciples," He always so explains it that we can perceive that followers are meant, that they are not adherents of a doctrine but followers of a life.[21]

Christianity proposes to endow the individual with an eternal happiness, a good which is not distributed wholesale, but only to one individual at a time. Though Christianity assumes that there inheres in the subjectivity of the individual, as being the potentiality of the appropriation of this good, the possibility for its acceptance, it does not assume that the subjectivity is immediately ready for such acceptance, or even has, without further ado, a real conception of the significance of such a good. The development or transformation of the individual's subjectivity, its infinite concentration in itself over against the conception of an eternal happiness, that highest good of the infinite—this constitutes the developed potentiality which subjectivity as such presents. In this way Christianity protests every form of ob-

[19] *Training in Christianity*, pp. 198-202.

[20] *The Instant*, No. 2, in *Attack Upon "Christendom,"* trans. by Walter Lowrie (Princeton: Princeton University Press, 1944), p. 100. Copyright 1944 by Princeton University Press. This and subsequent quotations from this volume reprinted by permission of Princeton University Press.

[21] *Training in Christianity*, p. 231.

jectivity; it desires that the subject should be infinitely concerned about himself. It is subjectivity that Christianity is concerned with, and it is only in subjectivity that its truth exists, if it exists at all.

Faith is the highest passion in the sphere of human subjectivity.[22] The ethical is . . . a correlative to individuality, and that to such a degree that each individual apprehends the ethical essentially only in himself, because the ethical is his complicity with God.[23] The thing is that we cannot form any idea of God's exaltation. We always get stuck in our aesthetic accountancy: the marvellous, the great, the far-reaching, etc. Whereas God is so infinitely exalted that the only thing he looks upon is ethics.[24]

That subjectivity, inwardness, is the truth, was my thesis. I have sought to show how the pseudonymous authors in my view move in the direction of this principle, which in its maximum is Christianity.[25] The truth can neither be communicated nor be received except as it were under God's eyes, not without God's help, not without God's being involved as the middle term, He himself being the Truth.[26]

Faith and Works

There is always with us a worldliness which would have the name of being Christian, but would have it at a price as cheap as possible. This worldliness became observant of Luther. It listened, and it took the precaution to listen a second time for fear it might have heard amiss, and thereupon it said, "Capital!" That suits us exactly. Luther says,

22 *Concluding Unscientific Postscript,* pp. 116, 118.

23 *Ibid.,* p. 138.

24 *The Journals,* trans. by Alexander Dru (London: Oxford University Press, 1938), entry no. 997, p. 346. Copyright 1938 by Oxford University Press. This and subsequent quotations from this volume are reprinted by permission of Oxford University Press.

25 *Concluding Unscientific Postscript,* p. 248.

26 "That Individual," *Two Notes Concerning My Work as An Author,* included in *The Point of View,* trans. by Walter Lowrie (London: Oxford University Press, 1939), p. 119. Copyright 1939 by Oxford University Press. Reprinted by permission of Oxford University Press.

"It is faith alone that matters"; the fact that his life expresses works he does not himself say, and now he is dead, so that this is no longer an actuality. Let us take then his word, his doctrine—and we are liberated from all works. Long live Luther! And although all did not take Luther in vain in quite so worldly a way—yet every man has a disposition *either* to want to have merit from works when they are to be done; *or*, when faith and grace are to be stressed, to want to be as far as possible liberated entirely from works. Christianity's requirement is: Thy life shall as strenuously as possible give expression to works—and then one more thing is required: that thou humble thyself and admit, "But none the less I am saved by grace."[27]

So then we "Christians" are living, and are loving our life, just in the ordinary human sense. If then by "grace" God will nevertheless regard us as Christians, one thing at least must be required: that we, being precisely aware of the requirement, have a true conception of how infinitely great is the grace that is showed us. "Grace" cannot possibly stretch so far, one thing it must never be used for, it must never be used to suppress or to diminish the requirement; for in that case "grace" would turn Christianity upside down.[28]

In truth I understand it perfectly: to wish to build one's eternal happiness upon any action whatsoever, to dare to come before God with such things—that is the most horrible sin, for it is to scorn Christ's atonement.

Christ's atonement is everything, unconditionally, to that extent what a man does is all one. But then the infinity of the atonement should neither make a man completely indolent nor stifle the simple and child-like wish to do what one can as well as possible, always, be it noted, with God's permission, never off one's own bat, always gratefully and always treating it as nothing where the infinity of the atonement is concerned.[29]

Which is it? Is God's meaning, in Christianity, simply to

[27] *For Self-Examination*, pp. 41-42.
[28] *The Attack Upon "Christendom,"* p. 38.
[29] *The Journals*, entry no. 935, p. 318.

humble man through the model (that is to say by putting before us the ideal) and to console him with "Grace," but in such a way that through Christianity there is expressed the fact that between God and man there is no relationship, that man must express his thankfulness like a dog to a man, so that the adoration becomes more and more true, and more and more pleasing to God, as it becomes less and less possible for man to imagine that he could be like the model? Is that the meaning of Christianity?

Or is it the very reverse, that God's will is to express that He desires to be in relation with man, and therefore desires the thanks and the adoration which is in spirit and in truth: imitation.

The latter is certainly the meaning of Christianity. But the former is a cunning invention of us men (although it may have its better side) in order to escape from the real relation to God, because in its beginnings it is really suffering.[30]

Imitation must be introduced, to exert pressure in the direction of humility. It is to be done quite simply in this way: everyone must be measured by the Pattern, the ideal. We must get rid of all the bosh about this being said only to the Apostles, and this only to the disciples, and this only to the first Christians, etc. Christ no more desires now than He did then to have admirers (not to say twaddlers), He wants only disciples. The "disciple" is the standard: imitation and Christ as the Pattern must be introduced. It shall not be so that we men are permitted to abrogate the ideal requirement, saying that the thing is not for us, and then to hunt up a certain mediocrity, and then begin there and make that the standard, and then perhaps become distinguished . . . merely because the standard has been altered to suit us.

What is spiritual apathy? It means to have the standard changed by leaving out the ideals, it means to have the standard changed to correspond with what we men who now live in this place actually are.

But when the price of becoming a Christian is so cheap, then comes idleness, and then comes doubt, and then the

[30] *Ibid.*, entry no. 1272, p. 474.

real truth comes to evidence, that one cannot conceive why Christianity need be. And that is perfectly true; for if the requirement is no greater, then a saviour, a redeemer, grace, etc., become fantastic luxuries. What Christianity presupposes, namely, the tortures of a contrite conscience, the need of grace, the deeply felt need, all these frightful inward conflicts and sufferings—what Christianity presupposes in order to introduce and apply grace, salvation, the hope of eternal blessedness—all this is not to be found, or is to be found only in burlesque abridgment—at bottom it is sheer superfluity which at the most one imagines the need of. And so in the end one becomes tired of Christianity; for the pressure of imitation was lacking, the ideal, Christ as Pattern.[31]

The requirement, by humbling a man, should exert a stress which results in exaltation, in rejoicing at "grace," and in boldness through grace. No, in order to worship aright and rightly to have joy in worshipping, a man must so comport himself: he strives with might and main, spares himself neither day nor night, he tries to produce as many as possible of what upright men, humanly speaking, might call "good works." And then when he takes them and, deeply humbled before God, beholds them transformed to wretchedness and vileness, that is to worship God—and that is exaltation.[32]

Imitation and Love

We see therefore why Christ was born and lived in humiliation; no man, absolutely no man contemporary with him lived in such humiliation, there never lived a man so humiliated, and therefore it was absolutely impossible for any man to shirk the claims made upon him with the excuse or evasion that "the Pattern" was in possession of earthly and worldly advantages which he had not. In His actual life there was absolutely nothing to admire in that sense, unless one would admire poverty, wretchedness, the suffering of contempt, etc.

[31] *For Self-Examination* and *Judge for Yourselves!* pp. 207-9.
[32] *Ibid.*, pp. 165-66.

And in the situation of contemporaneousness there was not the least occasion to admire; for Christ had only the same conditions to offer to the man who would join Him, and on those conditions there was never any admirer who would take part. The same conditions: to become just as poor, as despised, as much scorned and mocked, and if possible even a little more.

What, then, is the distinction between "an admirer" and "a follower"? A follower is or strives *to be* what he admires; an admirer holds himself personally aloof, consciously or unconsciously, he does not discern that the object of his admiration makes a claim upon him to be or to strive to be the thing he admires.[33]

So the distinction holds good nevertheless: the admirer is not willing to make any sacrifices, to give up anything worldly, to reconstruct his life, to be what he admires or let his life express it—but in words, verbal expressions, asseverations, he is inexhaustible in affirming how highly he prizes Christianity. The follower, on the other hand, aspires to be what he admires—and so (strange to say!) even though he lives in established Christendom he will encounter the same danger which once was involved in confessing Christ. Only the "followers" are the true Christians.[34]

Seek *first* the kingdom of God. There is no time to gather riches in advance, there is no time to reflect on this question, there is no time to lay up a penny in advance, for the beginning is: to seek first the kingdom of God.

"God's kingdom and His righteousness." Through the latter the former is described. For God's kingdom is "righteousness, peace and joy in the Holy Spirit." Therefore there is here no question of setting forth to discover the kingdom of God, for God's kingdom is righteousness.

Nor does righteousness consist of extraordinary abilities, for it is precisely for those that righteousness will call you to account, if righteousness requires it of you; nor is it earthly obscurity, for no man is so humble that he cannot do wrong;

[33] *Training in Christianity,* p. 234.
[34] *Ibid.,* pp. 245, 247.

and as no coin is so small that it cannot bear the image of the emperor so no man is so humble that he cannot bear God's image. Righteousness consists in seeking the kingdom of God first. If you give every man his due, but forget God: do you practice righteousness? To practice righteousness in this way, is this not as when a thief gives every man his due with the money he has stolen? To forget God, is not this like stealing the whole of your existence?[35]

Luther is right again in this. No one can see faith, it is invisible so that no one can decide whether a man has faith. But faith shall be known by love. Now people have of course tried to make love into something invisible, but against that Luther protests with the Scriptures; for to the Christian love is the works of love. To say that love is a feeling or anything of the kind is really an unchristian conception of love. Christ's love was not an inner feeling, a full heart and what not, it was the work of love which was his life.[36]

To defraud oneself of love is the most terrible deception of all. It is an eternal loss for which there is no compensation either here or in eternity. What is it which connects the temporal and the eternal, what except love, which just for this reason is before everything, and which abides when everything else is past? But precisely because love is the bond of the eternal, and because the temporal existence and eternity are heterogeneous, for that reason love may sometimes seem burdensome to the earthly prudence of the temporal existence, and therefore in this existence it may seem a tremendous relief to the sensual man to cast off this bond of the eternal.

Love's secret life is in the heart, unfathomable, and it also has an unfathomable connection with the whole of existence. As the peaceful lake is grounded deep in the hidden spring

[35] *What We Learn From the Lilies of the Field and the Birds of the Air*, in *The Gospel of Suffering*, trans. by David F. Swenson and Lillian M. Swenson (Minneapolis: Augsburg Publishing House, 1948), pp. 232-34. Copyright 1948 by Augsburg Publishing House. Reprinted by permission of Augsburg Publishing House.

[36] *Journals*, entry no. 932, p. 317.

which no eye can see, so a man's love is grounded even deeper in the love of God. If there were at bottom no well-spring, if God were not love, then there would be no quiet lake or human love. As the quiet lake is grounded darkly in the deep spring, so is human love mysteriously grounded in God's love.[37]

The Christian teaching is to love the neighbor, to love the whole race, all men, even one's enemy, and to make no exception, either of partiality or of dislike.

Who then is one's neighbor? "Neighbor" presses as closely as possible upon the selfishness in life. If there are only two men, the other man is the neighbor; if there are millions, each one of these is the neighbor, who is again closer to one than "the friend" and "the beloved," insofar as those, as being the objects of preferential love, gradually become analogous to the self-love in one. To choose a beloved, to find a friend, those are indeed complicated tasks, but a neighbor is easy to know, easy to find, if we will only—recognize our duty.

To love one's self in the right way and to love one's neighbor are absolutely analogous concepts, are at bottom one and the same. When the "as thyself" of the commandment has taken from you the selfishness which Christianity, sad to say, must presuppose as existing in every human being, then you have rightly learned to love yourself.[38]

Earthly goods are in an external sense *a reality,* therefore one can own them even while being as one who does not own them; but spiritual goods exist only inwardly, exist only in *being possessed,* and therefore one cannot, if one really possesses them, be as one who does not possess them.[39] If, on the contrary, love has undergone the change of eternity by becoming duty, then it does not know the force of habit, then habit can never get power over it. As it is said of eternal life,

[37] *Works of Love,* trans. by David E. Swenson and Lillian M. Swenson (Princeton: Princeton University Press, 1949), pp. 5-6, 8. Copyright 1949 by Princeton University Press. This and subsequent quotations from this volume reprinted by permission of Princeton University Press.

[38] *Ibid.,* pp. 17-19.

[39] *Ibid.,* pp. 22-23.

that there is neither sighing nor weeping, so we might add that there is also no habit. The eternal never becomes old and never becomes habit.

Only when it is a duty to love, only then is love everlastingly free in blessed independence. Such a love stands and falls not by some accidental circumstance of its object, it stands and falls by the law of eternity—but then it never falls; such a love does not depend upon this or that, it depends only on—the one liberating force, consequently it is eternally independent. Love abides, it is independence. The unchangeableness is the true independence.[40]

For consider the most cultured man you know, about whom we all admiringly say, "He is so cultured," and then consider Christianity which says to him, "Thou shalt love thy neighbor!" Moreover, a certain urbanity in all relations, a courtesy toward all men, a friendly condescension toward inferiors, a confident bearing toward the influential, an admirably controlled freedom of spirit: truly that is culture—do you believe that it is also loving your neighbor?[41]

For ultimately love to God is the decisive thing; from it stems love to the neighbor, but paganism never suspected this. They left God out; they made earthly love and friendship into love, and abominated selfishness. But the Christian commandment of love commands men to love God above all else, and next to love the neighbor. In earthly love and friendship partiality is the middle term. In love to the neighbor, God is the middle term; if you love God above all else, then you also love your neighbor and in your neighbor every man. Only by loving God above all else can one love his neighbor in the other man. "Love to the neighbor is therefore the eternal equality in loving," but the eternal equality is the opposite of partiality.[42]

As the joyous message of Christianity is contained in the teaching about mankind's kinship with God, so is its problem man's likeness to God. But God is love, therefore we can re-

[40] *Ibid.*, pp. 31-33.
[41] *Ibid.*, p. 50.
[42] *Ibid.*, p. 48.

semble God only in loving, as we also, according to the Apostle's word, can only be "God's fellow-laborers in—love." When you love your neighbor, then you resemble God.[43]

But Christian love . . . is sheer action, and each of its deeds is sacred, for it is the fulfillment of the law.

Such is ideal Christian love; even if it does not or did not manifest itself in this way in any man (while yet every Christian by continuing in love, strives that his love may become such), yet it still was true in Him who was love, in our Lord Jesus Christ. Therefore the same Apostle [Paul] says about Him, that "Christ was the end of the law." Moreover, He was love, and His love was the fullness of the law. What the law could not bring to pass, any more than it could save a man, that Christ could do.[44]

As the blood pulses in every nerve, so Christianity in the conscience-relation wishes to penetrate everything. The change is not in the external, not in the obvious, and yet the change is infinite. And there within, there far within, where the Christian dwells in the conscience-relation, there is everything changed. There Christianity transforms every relation between men into a conscience-relationship, and thus also into a love-relationship.[45]

Conclusion

Love is from the Christian standpoint commanded; but the commandment of love is the old commandment which is always new.

The matter is simple enough. Christianity has abolished the Jewish like for like: "An eye for an eye, and a tooth for a tooth"; but it has substituted in its place the like for like of eternity. Christianity always directs the attention entirely away from the external, turns it inward, and makes each one of your relationships with other men into a God-relationship: so you will surely in both senses get like for like. From the Christian standpoint a man has ultimately and essentially to

[43] *Ibid.*, p. 52.
[44] *Ibid.*, p. 81.
[45] *Ibid.*, pp. 110-11.

do only with God, although he will still remain in the world and in the earthly relationships as they are allotted to him. But the fact of having to do with God . . . makes at one and the same time for the highest consolation and the greatest exertion, the greatest mildness and the greatest severity. This is man's education; for the true God-relationship is an education, God is the Teacher. But true education must be just as strict as it is mild, and conversely. And when a human teacher has many children to train at the same time, how does he carry this on? To do all this, there is naturally not time for much talking and reproof and verbosity, and if there were time, that education becomes bad as a matter of course where there is too much talk. No, the efficient teacher trains preferably by means of the eyes. He takes the individual child's eyes away from him, that is, he compels the child to look to him for everything. God does just this. He rules the whole world, and He trains these innumerable men by His glance. For what is conscience? In the conscience it is God who looks at a man, so the man must in everything see God. Thus does God educate. But the child who is being educated easily imagines that his relationship to his companions, the tiny world they form, is actuality, whereas the teacher by his glance teaches him that all this is used for the purpose of educating the child.

The older man also thus easily imagines that what he has to do with the world is actuality; but God teaches him to understand that all this is used only for his education. So God is the Teacher; His love combines the greatest mildness with the greatest strictness. So is God's strictness mildness in the lover and the humble, but to the hard of heart his mildness is severity. The fact that God has wished to save the world, this mildness is to the one who will not accept salvation the greatest severity, an even greater severity than if God had never wished it, but wished only to judge the world. Lo, this is the synthesis of the severity and the mildness; the fact that in everything you lay hold on God, the greatest mildness and the greatest severity.[46]

[46] *Ibid.*, pp. 303-04.

Further Readings

Primary Sources

AUDEN, W. H. (ed.). *Living Thoughts of Kierkegaard.* New York: David McKay, 1952.

BRETALL, ROBERT (ed.). *A Kierkegaard Anthology.* Princeton: Princeton University Press, 1947.

KIERKEGAARD, SOREN. *Works of Love.* Trans. by HOWARD and EDNA HONG. New York: Harper and Row, 1962.

Secondary Sources

COLLINS, JAMES. *The Mind of Kierkegaard.* Chicago: Regnery, 1953.

ELLER, VERNARD. *Kierkegaard and Radical Discipleship.* Princeton: Princeton University Press, 1968.

CROXALL, THOMAS HENRY. *Kierkegaard Commentary.* New York: Harper and Row, 1956.

JOHNSON, HOWARD and THULSTRUP, NIELS (eds.). *A Kierkegaard Critique.* New York: Harper and Row, 1962.

SIKES, WALTER. *On Becoming the Truth: An Introduction to the Life and Thought of Soren Kierkegaard.* St. Louis: Bethany Press, 1968.

Chapter 15

WALTER RAUSCHENBUSCH

The thinking of Søren Kierkegaard, as indicated by the preceding chapter, is certainly not characteristic of nineteenth-century moral theory in general. His radical stress on the individual and his interest in the psychology of faith run counter to a strong interest, among Christian thinkers of his age, in the problem of the social order and the Christian responsibility for social reform. The ethics of the Kingdom of God movement (in its American form sometimes called the "Social Gospel" or, rather loosely, "liberalism") was on the rise by the middle of the nineteenth century and reached its peak of influence in the first quarter of the twentieth.

Among the many historic roots of this version of Christian ethical theory, the influence of Immanuel Kant (1724-1804) should be recalled particularly. As a giant figure in eighteenth-century philosophy, casting a long shadow over subsequent Christian and non-Christian thought, Kant combined in his thinking an inheritance of Protestant piety with the rationalism of the Enlightenment. The effect of his work in epistemology was to throw doubt on the possibility of securing knowledge of the realm of ultimate reality. God, freedom, and immortality—which had been the rock-bottom assumptions of all Christian thinking about the world—could now by Kant's principles be treated at best as the "practical" postulates of moral endeavor and decision. They could no longer be taken as the basis of a "scientific" exploration of the universe. Kant urged that men should treat moral laws *as if* they were divine commands, but the validity of moral obligations must finally rest on the floor of human rationality. Christian morality, he felt, stands on reason, not revelation.

Under the influence of Kant's dualism and his rethinking of the relation of morality to theology, many Christian thinkers turned their attention to the human and the moral elements in theology and away from the metaphysical and speculative. The theology of Friedrich Schleiermacher (1768-1834) represents such a trend, and that of Albrecht Ritschl (1822-89) even more. Ritschl was not one to deny, of course, the objective existence of a creating and redeeming God. But he was doubtful about drawing metaphysical conclusions about the nature of God and preferred to speak of the human effects of God's work. "We know the nature of God and Christ only in their worth for us." Value-judgments, not fact-judgments, are the business of religion.

Ritschl was influential also in that he centered his attention on the historic Jesus of Nazareth, rather than on a metaphysical God-man, as the Saviour of man through the moral perfection of his personality. The significance of Christ's work lies both in the reconciliation with God that he provides for the individual believer and also in that he came as the founder of the Kingdom of God on earth. The classic Biblical phrase, the Kingdom of God, had been variously interpreted in Christian history to denote many things: the cosmic and eternal sovereignty of God, the reign of Christ, or eternal blessedness. Ritschl gave a new emphasis to the phrase. He made of it an earthly goal, "the moral unification of the human race, through action prompted by universal love to our neighbor." Among later Ritschlian thinkers the evangelical note of individual forgiveness and salvation in Christ is rather played down, and Ritschl's social ideal of the temporal kingdom of love and righteousness is played up. It captured the imagination of many continental Protestants, such as Adolf von Harnack, whose *What Is Christianity?* was a highly influential restatement of the Ritschlian view. The new trend took hold no less in England and especially in America.

The Kingdom of God movement in America began its definite rise after the Civil War. This era of mechanization and industrialization, with the enormous upswing of urban populations swollen by immigration from abroad, brought problems of social maladjustment and poverty to which the traditional message of Protestant churches seemed remote and inept. Here and there arose prophets such as Washington Gladden, Lyman Abbott, and George Herron, who saw industrial capitalism and the crowded cities of America crushing the spirits of men *en masse*, while the churches were attempting pathetically to "save souls" one by one for a life beyond. These few leaders called the church to turn from its complacency and escapism to the social problems of industrialism, to fight the real powers of darkness, economic corruption in high places and grinding poverty in low. By slow institutional change men could create a democratic order of brotherhood and mutual service, where common labor would recover its dignity and beauty, where the Kingdom of God would be realized on earth as in heaven. The message of the Social Gospel made enough headway against the opposition of a conservative Protestantism to lead its major spokesman, Walter Rauschenbusch, to say in the first decade of the twentieth century, "The Social Gospel has arrived." As matters turned out, this proved an overconfident claim, but certainly the influence of the Kingdom of God ideal was strongly felt among many leaders of the mainline Protestant churches. It inspired, among many things, the formation of the Federal Council of Churches (now the National Council) in 1908. However at variance church leaders found themselves in doctrinal matters, they could make common cause on the ethical convictions of the Social Gospel, and they voiced them in the Social Creed (1912), which for its day represented a radical economic position.

The New and the Old in the Kingdom of God Ideal

The judgment is frequently made that the Social Gospel lacks a theological interest and that it reduces the Christian faith to a program of humanitarian reform. True, the Social Gospel has little interest in certain of the traditional credal doctrines. But it has its own theology. In this as in all types of ethical thinking there are certain theological assumptions, implicit or explicit, faiths about the character of the universe and man, which give to the Kingdom of God ethics its distinctive tone. If indeed it is heavily indebted to certain secular nineteenth-century faiths, on the basis of which it attempts to revise traditional theology, it also, and at a more profound level, is to be credited with recovering certain elements from the historic Christian tradition which had been lost or perverted in the prevailing Christian thought and practice of the day.

Its concept of the nature of God is a mixture of Biblical and, more especially, prophetic motifs with ideas derived from scientific and intellectual currents of nineteenth-century secular thought. In the name of Amos and Isaiah the proponents of the Social Gospel remind men that the Lord of the nations requires public justice and righteousness, not the "burnt offerings" of polite church-going. God is not the benign manager of a hotel of heaven, the final retirement resort for the respectable who practice private purity. He is a living God who requires even-handedness and integrity, justice and mercy, in the public affairs of the market place and the political forum.

Along with this prophetic element there is a quite un-Biblical note of immanentism in the theology of the Social Gospel. God is "within" rather than "above" history. He is the persistent impulse for good in the human heart, who inspires and assists man on his long, slow pilgrimage to the ideal society. God who is Love is not the Enemy, but the Friend, working through man, not against him, to achieve the divine purpose, the cooperative commonwealth on earth. This Kingdom comes by evolutionary growth, not by a shattering intervention from beyond. Here the Social Gospel finds the whole "Darwinian" philosophy of history more plausible than the strange eschatology (or theory of last things) of the traditional creeds, whereby God is expected to ring down a sudden curtain on the whole human drama. In keeping with most nineteenth-century scientific and social thought, the Social Gospel is confident that history is progressing toward a better order of justice and brotherhood and that to the extent that men apply Christian ideals to their public and private lives, the Kingdom will come. This philosophy of history gives to the Social Gospel its great hope and impetus for moral endeavor. What bends its bow of moral effort is the tension between the present possibility and the future ideal.

As Rauschenbusch rightly points out, the Kingdom of God ideal is the key idea of the Social Gospel, the full force of which requires the recasting of all other doctrines. The significance of Jesus Christ, for instance, lies in the fact that he is the initiator of the Kingdom on earth and provides in his moral teaching the way of its realization. The Christian church finds its worth not in itself but in its power to inspire men to work for the Kingdom; thus it is a means, one among many, toward an end larger than itself. The Kingdom ideal alters subtly and deeply the psychology of the Christian life: Confident hope and unflagging effort supplant trust and repentance as the sustaining dynamic of Christian living.

In its view of human nature, the Social Gospel also combines elements orthodox and novel. It reacts against the individualism characteristic of late Puritanism, with its view of man, like John Bunyan's pilgrim, making his lone way to the Celestial City, or economically like a Horatio Alger hero, climbing the ladder from rags to riches by his own initiative. The Social Gospel recalls its culture to the Biblical and prophetic solidaristic view of man-in-community. Men are in truth "members one of another," organically related to their fellows both in sin and salvation. Society is not a sand heap of atomistic individuals but a dense texture of organic relations, in which no single self exists except as a self-in-relation. Moreover, the solidaristic view of society includes God as a member. Here is a recovery of a Biblical and prophetic understanding of the covenant principle. By virtue of the membership of God in the community, sin against the neighbor in public policy as in private dealing is *ipso facto* a sin against God, for to tear the social fabric of brotherhood is to flout the divine will.

To this orthodox element, the Social Gospel adds something new in its theory of man, derived chiefly from the secular socialist thought of the nineteenth century—namely, the view that the cultural environment, constituted by political and economic institutions, is of high importance in determining man's inner quality. Social institutions are powerful in influencing the hearts and minds of men. They mould even moral and religious beliefs. Moreover, these social structures are not divinely fixed "orders" of life to be humbly and quietly accepted by man, as traditional Protestantism was likely to affirm. These structures are pliable and can be made over from sin to salvation by reform and legislative change.

In still another facet of its view of man, the liberal ferment shows the influence of its confident times. It looks askance at the older Calvinistic view of man's depravity and substitutes a much more optimistic view of man's spiritual condition. Man is not a worm or a "lump of perdition" but the hero of a long upward climb toward a culture in which rationality and benevolence will reign. This faith fits well the evolutionary philosophy of history. How can one strive for the ideal of the Kingdom, when "earth shall be fair, and all men glad and wise," if one believes that some fatal moral taint spoils persistently man's moral achievement? As indicated in the sources, Rauschenbusch is no sentimentalist. He takes full measure of the grip of sin on man's spirit and indeed is led in his later writings to pay his respects to the orthodox belief in "original" sin, though he treats it as socially more than "genetically" transmitted. At the same time—and in curious contradiction to his serious view of sin—he shares with the enthusiasts for the Kingdom of God ideal the faith that sin can be progressively overcome through moral striving, generation by generation.

Two further characteristics of the Social Gospel deserve mention; both are derived more from the general spirit of the nineteenth century than from Christian theology. One is the stress on the principle of continuity in the cosmos. It construes the manifold within the universe in terms of shadings and gradations rather than of jumps and chasms and dualisms, which are more typical of the Biblical world view and of much traditional theology. For the Social Gospel there is no radical discontinuity between man and nature but a genetic kinship which science is revealing and on which the scientific enterprise is based. There is likewise continuity between religion and science, the sacred and the secular, Christ and the best in human culture, the church and the world, and between God and man. In place of the older division between the damned and the saved, or between Augustine's City of Earth and the City of God, is put the gradation of a less Christian society growing more Christian on the inclined ramp of history. And the goal of history, the Kingdom, is an ideal set within time and somehow continuous with time, not "beyond history" as traditional eschatology would locate it.

Finally, the Social Gospel is so intensely preoccupied with the collective destiny of man that its interest in the individual's destiny and the question of personal immortality become quite incidental. Previous Protestant thinkers, from Luther to Kant, gave a determinative place to the "life beyond" for each man, by reference to which this life is a corridor and a preparation and always something of a "vale of tears." The writers in this liberal tradition, on the other hand, while retaining in the main the doctrine of individual immortality, are more interested in the transformation of this world than in passing through it on the way to the next. Thus the Christian ideal of man's destiny is quite thoroughly domesticated as well as socialized: Men sin corporately and are saved corporately in and for this world of time and space.

Rauschenbusch, a Prophet for America

The life of Walter Rauschenbusch, the most influential spokesman for the Social Gospel, spans the years between the Civil War and World War I. Born in Rochester, New York, of German parentage and a long line of clergymen, his early training at home and in seminary was in the pietistic tradition. For his first important charge as a young minister he was called to a small church on West 45th Street in New York City, next to a slum area known as "Hell's Kitchen." He labored here for eleven years and experienced a gradual but profound revolution in his thought as he discovered the almost total ineptness of his religious training and belief in meeting the real needs of his economically depressed parishioners. He took up with movements for social reform, especially that of Henry George, and studied the writings of the socialists both in America and abroad. He worked with the Christian Socialist movement, though he never was a member of the Socialist Party. At the age of thirty-six he returned to the Rochester Theological Seminary as professor and to a busy career of writing, lecturing, and travel in support of a wide number of social causes.

Of all social institutions, according to Rauschenbusch, the economic stands most in need of Christian redemption. Political, domestic, and educational institutions, he feels, have in large part become Christianized. But the industrial capitalism of America is under the law of Mammon. With the socialists, he subjects the capitalistic practice of his time to the most ruthless judgment, spelling out the details of its cruel power in destroying the personalities of its subjects. He lays the blame for many "sins of the flesh," like drunkenness and prostitution, at the door of economic institutions which drive men to seek degenerate escapes from drudgery. In *Christianizing the Social Order* (1912) he advances positive measures for economic reform: the unionization of labor, social legislation for health guarantees and the equalization of wealth, the democratization of industrial relations, and the extension of consumer cooperatives. He is confident that such steps will bring economic institutions under the law of Christ, into a cooperative commonwealth.

Rauschenbusch's most profound and penetrating book, *A Theology for the Social Gospel,* based on lectures given at the Yale Divinity School, was published just prior to his death in 1918. The sombre shadow of the First World War is cast over its pages.

SOURCES

From

WALTER RAUSCHENBUSCH: A THEOLOGY FOR THE SOCIAL GOSPEL[1]

The Nature of Sin

It is not easy to define sin, for sin is as elastic and complicated as life itself. Its quality, degree, and culpability vary according to the moral intelligence and maturity of the individual, according to his social freedom, and his power over others. Theologians have erred, it seems to me, by fitting their definitions to the most highly developed forms of sin and then spreading them over germinal and semi-sinful actions and conditions.

We are equipped with powerful appetites. We are often placed in difficult situations, which constitute overwhelming temptations. We are all relatively ignorant, and while we experiment with life, we go astray. Some of our instincts may become rampant and overgrown, and then trample on our inward freedom. We are gifted with high ideals, with a wonderful range of possibilities, with aspiration and longing, and also weighted with inertia and moral incapacity to achieve. We are keenly alive to the call of the senses and the pleasures of the moment, and only dimly and occasionally conscious of our own higher destiny, of the mystic value of personality in others, and of God.

This sensual equipment, this ignorance and inertia, out of which our moral delinquencies sprout, are part of our human nature. We did not order it so. Instead of increasing our guilt, our make-up seems to entitle us to the forbearing judgment of every onlooker, especially God. Yet no doubt we are involved in objective wrong and evil; we frustrate our possi-

[1] All subsequent material in this chapter is taken from Walter Rauschenbusch, *A Theology for the Social Gospel* (New York: The Macmillan Company, 1918). Copyright 1918 by The Macmillan Company. Reprinted by permission of the family of Walter Rauschenbusch.

bilities; we injure others; we disturb the divine harmonies. We are unfree, unhappy, conscious of a burden which we are unable to lift or escape.

Sin becomes guilt in the full sense in the degree in which intelligence and will enter. We have the impulse to live our life, to exercise our freedom, to express and satisfy the limitless cravings in us, and we are impatient of restraint. We know that our idleness or sensuality will cripple our higher self, yet we want what we want. We set our desires against the rights of others, and disregard the claims of mercy, of gratitude, or of parental love. Our self-love is wrought up to hot ill-will, hate, lying, slander, and malevolence. Men press their covetousness to the injury of society. They are willing to frustrate the cause of liberty and social justice in whole nations in order to hold their selfish social and economic privileges. Men who were powerful enough to do so, have left broad trails of destruction and enslavement through history in order to satisfy their selfish caprice, avarice, and thirst for glory.

Two things strike us as we thus consider the development of sin from its cotyledon leaves to its blossom and fruit. First, that the element of selfishness emerges as the character of sin matures. Second, that in the higher forms of sin it assumes the aspect of a conflict between the selfish Ego and the common good of humanity; or, expressing it in religious terms, it becomes a conflict between self and God.

The three forms of sin,—sensuousness, selfishness, and godlessness,—are ascending and expanding stages, in which we sin against our higher self, against the good of men, and against the universal good.

Theology with remarkable unanimity has discerned that sin is essentially selfishness. This is an ethical and social definition, and is proof of the unquenchable social spirit of Christianity. It is more essentially Christian than the dualistic conception of the Greek Fathers, who thought of sin as fundamentally sensuousness and materiality, and saw the chief consequence of the fall in the present reign of death rather than in the reign of selfishness.

The definition of sin as selfishness furnishes an excellent theological basis for a social conception of sin and salvation. But the social gospel can contribute a good deal to socialize and vitalize it.

Theology pictures the self-affirmation of the sinner as a sort of solitary duel of the will between him and God. We get a mental image of God sitting on his throne in glory, holy and benevolent, and the sinner down below, sullenly shaking his fist at God while he repudiates the divine will and chooses his own. Now, in actual life such titanic rebellion against the Almighty is rare. Perhaps our Puritan forefathers knew more cases than we because their theological God was accustomed to issue arbitrary decrees which invited rebellion. We do not rebel; we dodge and evade. We kneel in lowly submission and kick our duty under the bed while God is not looking.

The theological definitions of sin have too much the flavour of the monarchical institutions under the spiritual influence of which they were first formed. In an absolute monarchy the first duty is to bow to the royal will. A man may spear peasants or outrage their wives, but crossing the king is another matter. When theological definitions speak of rebellion against God as the common characteristic of all sin, it reminds one of the readiness of despotic governments to treat every offence as treason.

Sin is not a private transaction between the sinner and God. Humanity always crowds the audience-room when God holds court. We must democratize the conception of God; then the definition of sin will become more realistic.

We love and serve God when we love and serve our fellows whom he loves and in whom he lives. We rebel against God and repudiate his will when we set our profit and ambition above the welfare of our fellows and above the Kingdom of God which binds them together.

We rarely sin against God alone. The decalogue gives a simple illustration of this. Theology used to distinguish between the first and second table of the decalogue; the first enumerated the sins against God and the second the sins against men. Jesus took the Sabbath commandment off the first table and added it to the second; he said the Sabbath is not a taboo day of God, but an institution for the good of man. The command to honour our parents is also ethical. There remain the first three commandments, against polytheism, image worship, and the misuse of the holy name. The worship of various gods and the use of idols is no longer one of our dangers. The misuse of the holy name has lost much of its religious significance since sorcery and magic have moved to the back-streets. On the other hand, the commandments of the second table grow more important all the time. Science supplies the means of killing, finance the methods of stealing, the newspapers have learned how to bear false witness artistically to a globeful of people daily, and covetousness is the moral basis of our civilization.

God is not only the spiritual representative of humanity; he is identified with it. In him we live and move and have our being. In us he lives and moves, though his being transcends ours. He is the life and light in every man and the mystic bond that unites us all. He is the spiritual power behind and beneath all our aspirations and achievements. He works through humanity to realize his purposes, and our sins block and destroy the Reign of God in which he might fully reveal and realize himself. Therefore our sins against the least of our fellow-men in the last resort concern God. Therefore when we retard the progress of mankind, we retard the revelation of the glory of God. Our universe is not a despotic monarchy, with God above the starry canopy and ourselves down here; it is a spiritual commonwealth with God in the midst of us.

Sin is essentially selfishness. That definition is more in harmony with the social gospel than with any individualistic type of religion. The sinful mind, then, is the unsocial and anti-social mind. To find the climax of sin we must not linger over a man who swears, or sneers at religion, or denies the mystery of the trinity, but put our hands on social groups who have turned the patrimony of a nation into the private property of a small class, or have left the peasant labourers cowed, degraded, demoralized, and without rights in the land. When we find such in history, or in present-day life, we shall know we have struck real rebellion against God on the higher levels of sin.

This is the chief significance of the social gospel for the doctrine of sin: it revives the vision of the Kingdom of God. When men see the actual world over against the religious ideal, they become conscious of its constitutional defects and wrongs. Those who do their thinking in the light of the Kingdom of God make less of heresy and private sins. They reserve their shudders for men who keep the liquor and vice trade alive against public intelligence and law; for interests that organize powerful lobbies to defeat tenement or factory legislation, or turn factory inspection into sham; for nations that are willing to set the world at war in order to win or protect colonial areas of trade or usurious profit from loans to weaker peoples; and for private interests which are willing to push a peaceful nation into war because the stock exchange has a panic at the rumour of peace. These seem the unforgivable sins, the great demonstrations of rebellious selfishness, wherever the social gospel has revived the faith of the Kingdom of God.

Two aspects of the Kingdom of God demand special consideration in this connection: the Kingdom is the realm of love, and it is the commonwealth of labour.

Jesus Christ superimposed his own personality on the previous conception of God and made love the distinctive characteristic of God and the supreme law of human conduct. Consequently the reign of God would be the reign of love. It is not enough to think of the Kingdom as a prevalence of good will. The institutions of life must be fundamentally fraternal and co-operative if they are to train men to love their fellow-men as co-workers. Sin, being selfish, is covetous and grasping. It favours institutions and laws which permit unrestricted exploitation and accumulation. This in turn sets up antagonistic interests, increases law suits, class hostility, and wars, and so miseducates mankind that love and co-operation seem unworkable, and men are taught to put their trust in coercive control by the strong and in the sting of hunger and compulsion for the poor.

Being the realm of love, the Kingdom of God must also be the commonwealth of co-operative labour, for how can we actively love others without serving their needs by our abilities? If the Kingdom of God is a community of highly developed personalities, it must also be an organization for labour, for none can realize himself fully without labour. A divinely ordered community, therefore, would offer to all the opportunities of education and enjoyment, and expect from all their contribution of labour.

Here again we realize the nature of sin over against the religious ideal of society. Sin selfishly takes from others their opportunities for self-realization in order to increase its own opportunities abnormally; and it shirks its own labour and thereby abnormally increases the labour of others. Idleness is active selfishness; it is not only unethical, but a sin against the Kingdom of God. To lay a heavy burden of support on our fellows, usually on the weakest classes, and to do no productive labour in return, is so crude a manifestation of sinful selfishness that one would suppose only an occasional instance of such delinquency could be found, and only under medical treatment. But in fact throughout history the policy of most States has been shaped in order to make such a sinful condition easy and perpetual. Men who have been under the teachings of Christianity all their lives do not even see that parasitism is a sin. So deeply has our insight into sin been darkened by the lack of a religious ideal of social life. We shall not be doing our thinking in a Christian way until we agree that productive labour according to the ability of each is one of "the conditions of salvation."[2]

The Kingdom of Evil

We have sought to show that in the following points a modification or expansion is needed in order to give the

[2] *A Theology for the Social Gospel,* chap. vi.

social gospel an intellectual basis and a full medium of expression in theology.

1. Theological teaching on the first origin of sin ought not to obscure the active sources of sin in later generations and in present-day life, by which sin is quickened and increased. An approximation to the reticence of Jesus and the prophets about the fall of men, and to their strong emphasis on the realistic facts of contemporary sin, would increase the practical efficiency of theology.

2. Since an active sense of failure and sin is produced by contrast with the corresponding ideal of righteousness, theology, by obscuring and forgetting the Kingdom of God, has kept the Christian world out of a full realization of the social sins which frustrate the Kingdom. The social gospel needs above all a restoration of religious faith in the Reign of God in order to create an adequate sense of guilt for public sins, and it must look to theology to furnish the doctrinal basis of it.

3. The doctrine of original sin has directed attention to the biological channels for the transmission of general sinfulness from generation to generation, but has neglected and diverted attention from the transmission and perpetuation of specific evils through the channels of social tradition.

4. Theology has not given adequate attention to the social idealizations of evil, which falsify the ethical standards for the individual by the authority of his group or community, deaden the voice of the Holy Spirit to the conscience of individuals and communities, and perpetuate antiquated wrongs in society. These social idealizations are the real heretical doctrines from the point of view of the Kingdom of God.

5. New spiritual factors of the highest significance are disclosed by the realization of the super-personal forces, or composite personalities, in society. When these backslide and become combinations for evil, they add enormously to the power of sin. Theology has utilized the terminology and results of psychology to interpret the sin and regeneration of individuals. Would it stray from its field if it utilized soci-

ological terms and results in order to interpret the sin and redemption of these super-personal entities in human life?

The solidaristic spiritual conceptions which have been discussed must all be kept in mind and seen together, in order to realize the power and scope of the doctrine to which they converge: the Kingdom of Evil.

The life of humanity is infinitely interwoven, always renewing itself, yet always perpetuating what has been. The evils of one generation are caused by the wrongs of the generations that preceded, and will in turn condition the sufferings and temptations of those who come after. Our Italian immigrants are what they are because the Church and the land system of Italy have made them so. The Mexican peon is ridden by the Spanish past. Capitalistic Europe has fastened its yoke on the neck of Africa. When Negroes are hunted from a Northern city like beasts, or when a Southern city degrades the whole nation by turning the savage inhumanity of a mob into a public festivity, we are continuing to sin because our fathers created the conditions of sin by the African slave trade and by the unearned wealth they gathered from slave labour for generations.

Stupid dynasties go on reigning by right of the long time they have reigned. The laws of the ancient Roman despotism were foisted by ambitious lawyers on mediaeval communities, to which they were in no wise fitted, and once more strangled liberty, and dragged free farmers into serfdom. When once the common land of a nation, and its mines and waters, have become the private property of a privileged band, nothing short of a social earthquake can pry them from their right of collecting private taxes. Superstitions which originated in the third century are still faithfully cultivated by great churches, compressing the minds of the young with fear and cherished by the old as their most precious faith. Ideas struck out by a wrestling mind in the heat of an argument are erected by later times into proof-texts more decisive than masses of living facts. One nation arms because it fears another; the other arms more because this armament alarms it; each subsidizes a third and a fourth to aid it. Two fight;

all fight; none knows how to stop; a planet is stained red in a solidarity of hate and horror.

This is what the modern social gospel would call the Kingdom of Evil. Our theological conception of sin is but fragmentary unless we see all men in their natural groups bound together in a solidarity of all times and all places, bearing the yoke of evil and suffering. This is the explanation of the amazing regularity of social statistics. A nation registers so and so many suicides, criminal assaults, bankruptcies, and divorces per 100,000 of the population. If the proportion changes seriously, we search for the disturbing social causes, just as we search for the physical causes if the rhythm of our pulse-beat runs away from the normal. The statistics of social morality are the pulse-beat of the social organism. The apparently free and unrelated acts of individuals are also the acts of the social group. When the social group is evil, evil is over all.

A social conception of the Kingdom of Evil, such as I have tried to sketch, makes a powerful appeal to our growing sense of racial unity. It is modern and grows spontaneously out of our livest interests and ideas. Instead of appealing to conservatives, who are fond of sitting on antique furniture, it would appeal to the radicals. It would contain the political and social protest against oppression and illusion for which the belief in a Satanic kingdom stood in the times of its greatest vitality. The practical insight into the solidarity of all nations in their sin would emphasize the obligation to share with them all every element of salvation we possess, and thus strengthen the appeal for missionary and educational efforts.

The doctrine of original sin was meant to bring us all under the sense of guilt. Theology in the past has labored to show that we are in some sense partakers of Adam's guilt. But the conscience of mankind has never been convinced. Partakers in his wretchedness we might well be by our family coherence, but guilt belongs only to personality, and requires will and freedom. On the other hand an enlightened conscience can not help feeling a growing sense of responsibility and guilt for the common sins under which humanity is bound and to which we all contribute. Who of us can say that he has never by word or look contributed to the atmospheric pressure of lubricous sex stimulation which bears down on young and old, and the effect of which after the war no man can predict without sickening? Whose hand has never been stained with income for which no equivalent had been given in service? How many business men have promoted the advance of democracy in their own industrial kingdom when autocracy seemed safer and more efficient? What nation has never been drunk with a sense of its glory and importance, and which has never seized colonial possessions or developed its little imperialism when the temptation came its way? The sin of all is in each of us, and every one of us has scattered seeds of evil, the final multiplied harvest of which no man knows.[3]

The Social Gospel and Personal Salvation

We take up now the doctrine of salvation. All that has been said about sin will have to be kept in mind in discussing salvation, for the conceptions of sin and salvation are always closely correlated in every theological or religious system.

The new thing in the social gospel is the clearness and insistence with which it sets forth the necessity and the possibility of redeeming the historical life of humanity from the social wrongs which now pervade it and which act as temptations and incitements to evil and as forces of resistance to the powers of redemption. Its chief interest is concentrated on those manifestations of sin and redemption which lie beyond the individual soul. If our exposition of the superpersonal agents of sin and of the Kingdom of Evil is true, then evidently a salvation confined to the soul and its personal interests is an imperfect and only partly effective salvation.

The social gospel furnishes new tests for religious experience. We are not disposed to accept the converted souls whom the individualistic evangelism supplies, without looking them over. Some who have been saved and perhaps re-

[3] *Ibid.*, chap. ix.

consecrated a number of times are worth no more to the Kingdom of God than they were before. Some become worse through their revival experiences, more self-righteous, more opinionated, more steeped in unrealities and stupid over against the most important things, more devoted to emotions and unresponsive to real duties. We have the highest authority for the fact that men may grow worse by getting religion. Jesus says the Pharisees compassed sea and land to make a proselyte, and after they had him, he was twofold more a child of hell than his converters. It is time to overhaul our understanding of the kind of change we hope to produce by personal conversion and regeneration. The social gospel furnishes some tests and standards.

When we undertook to define the nature of sin, we accepted the old definition, that sin is selfishness and rebellion against God, but we insisted on putting humanity into the picture. The definition of sin as selfishness gets its reality and nipping force only when we see humanity as a great solidarity and God indwelling in it. In the same way the terms and definitions of salvation get more realistic significance and ethical reach when we see the internal crises of the individual in connection with the social forces that play upon him or go out from him. The form which the process of redemption takes in a given personality will be determined by the historical and social spiritual environment of the man. At any rate any religious experience in which our fellow-men have no part or thought, does not seem to be a distinctively Christian experience.

If sin is selfishness, salvation must be a change which turns a man from self to God and humanity. His sinfulness consisted in a selfish attitude, in which he was at the centre of the universe, and God and all his fellow-men were means to serve his pleasures, increase his wealth, and set off his egotisms. Complete salvation, therefore, would consist in an attitude of love in which he would freely co-ordinate his life with the life of his fellows in obedience to the loving impulses of the spirit of God, thus taking his part in a divine organism of mutual service. When a man is in a state of sin, he may be willing to harm the life and lower the self-respect of a woman for the sake of his desires; he may be willing to take some of the mental and spiritual values out of the life of a thousand families, and lower the human level of a whole mill-town in order to increase his own dividends or maintain his autocratic sense of power. If this man came under the influence of the mind of Christ, he would see men and women as children of God with divine worth and beauty, and this realization would cool his lust or covetousness. Living now in the consciousness of the pervading spiritual life of God, he would realize that all his gifts and resources are a loan of God for higher ends, and would do his work with greater simplicity of mind and brotherliness.

Of course in actual life there is no case of complete Christian transformation. It takes an awakened and regenerated mind a long time to find itself intellectually and discover what life henceforth is to mean to him, and his capacity for putting into practice what he knows he wants to do, will be something like the capacity of an untrained hand to express artistic imaginations. But in some germinal and rudimentary form salvation must turn us from a life centered on ourselves toward a life going out toward God and men. God is the all-embracing source and exponent of the common life and good of mankind. When we submit to God, we submit to the supremacy of the common good. Salvation is the voluntary socializing of the soul.

Through the experience and influence of Paul the word "faith" has gained a central place in the terminology of salvation. Its meaning fluctuates according to the dominant conception of religion. With Paul it was a comprehensive mystical symbol covering his whole inner experience of salvation and emancipation, which flooded his soul with joy and power. On the other hand wherever doctrine becomes rigid and is the pre-eminent thing in religion, "faith" means submission of the mind to the affirmations of dogma and theology, and, in particular, acceptance of the plan of salvation and trust in the vicarious atonement of Christ. Where the idea of the Church dominates religion, "faith" means mainly submission to the teaching and guidance of the Church. In popular religion it may shrivel up to something so small as putting a finger on a Scripture text and "claiming the promise."

In primitive Christianity the forward look of expectancy was characteristic of religion. The glory of the coming dawn was on the Eastern clouds. This influenced the conception of "faith." It was akin to hope, the forward gaze of the pioneers. The historical illustrations of faith in Hebrews 11 show faith launching life toward the unseen future.

This is the aspect of faith which is emphasized by the social gospel. It is not so much the endorsement of ideas formulated in the past, as expectancy and confidence in the coming salvation of God. In this respect the forward look of primitive Christianity is resumed. Faith once more means prophetic vision. It is faith to assume that this is a good world and that life is worth living. It is faith to assert the feasibility of a fairly righteous and fraternal social order. In the midst of a despotic and predatory industrial life it is faith to stake our business future on the proposition that fairness, kindness, and fraternity will work. When war inflames a nation, it is faith to believe that a peaceable disposition is a workable international policy. Amidst the disunion of Christendom it is faith to look for unity and to express unity in action. It is faith to see God at work in the world and to claim a share in his job. Faith is an energetic act of the will, affirming our fellowship with God and men, declaring our solidarity with the Kingdom of God, and repudiating selfish isolation.[4]

The Salvation of the Super-Personal Forces

In discussing the doctrine of sin we faced the fact that redemption will have to deal not only with the weakness of flesh and blood, but with the strength of principalities and powers. Beyond the feeble and short-lived individual towers the social group as a super-personal entity, dominating the

[4] *Ibid.*, chap. x.

individual, assimilating him to its moral standards, and enforcing them by the social sanctions of approval or disapproval.

In our age these super-personal social forces present more difficult problems than ever before. The scope and diversity of combination is becoming constantly greater. The strategy of the Kingdom of God is short-sighted indeed if it does not devote thought to their salvation and conversion.

The salvation of the composite personalities, like that of individuals, consists in coming under the law of Christ. A few illustrations will explain how this applies.

Two principles are contending with each other for future control in the field of industrial and commercial organization, the capitalistic and the co-operative. The effectiveness of the capitalistic method in the production of wealth is not questioned; modern civilization is evidence of it. But we are also familiar with capitalistic methods in the production of human wreckage. Its one-sided control of economic power tempts to exploitation and oppression; it directs the productive process of society primarily toward the creation of private profit rather than the service of human needs; it demands autocratic management and strengthens the autocratic principle in all social affairs; it has impressed a materialistic spirit on our whole civilization.

On the other hand organizations formed on the co-operative principle are not primarily for profit but for the satisfaction of human wants, and the aim is to distribute ownership, control, and economic benefits to a large number of co-operators.

The difference between a capitalistic organization and a co-operative comes out clearly in the distribution of voting power. Capitalistic joint-stock companies work on the plan of "one share, one vote." Therewith power is located in money. One crafty person who has a hundred shares can outvote ninety-nine righteous men who have a share apiece, and a small minority can outvote all the rest if it holds a majority of stock. Money is stronger than life, character, and personality.

Co-operatives work on the plan of "one man, one vote." A man who holds one share has as much voting power as a man with ten shares; his personality counts. If a man wants to lead and direct, he can not do it by money power; he must do it by character, sobriety, and good judgment. The small stockholders are not passive; they take part; they must be persuaded and taught. The superior ability of the capable can not outvote the rest, but has to train them. Consequently the co-operatives develop men and educate a community in helpful loyalty and comradeship. This is the advent of true democracy in economic life. Of course the co-operative principle is not a sovereign specific; the practical success of a given association depends on good judgment and the loyalty of its constituents. But the co-operatives, managed by plain men, often with little experience, have not only held their own in Europe against the picked survivors of the capitalistic competitive battle, but have forged steadily ahead into enormous financial totals, have survived and increased even during the war, and by their helpful moral influence have gone a long way to restore a country like Ireland which had long been drained and ruined by capitalism.

Here, I think, we have the difference between saved and unsaved organizations. The one class is under the law of Christ, the other under the law of mammon. The one is democratic and the other autocratic. Whenever capitalism has invaded a new country or industry, there has been a speeding up in labor and in the production of wealth, but always with a trail of human misery, discontent, bitterness, and demoralization. When co-operation has invaded a country there has been increased thrift, education, and neighborly feeling, and there has been no trail of concomitant evil and no cries of protest. The men in capitalistic business may be the best of men, far superior in ability to the average committee member of a co-operative, but the latter type of organization is the higher, and when co-operation has had as long a time to try out its methods as capitalism, the latter will rank with feudalism as an evil memory of mankind.

Super-personal forces are saved when they come under the law of Christ. A State which uses its terrible power of coercion to smite and crush offenders as a protection to the rest, is still under brutal law. A State which deals with those who have erred in the way of teaching, discipline, and restoration, has come under the law of Christ and is to that extent a saved community. "By their fruits ye shall know them." States are known by their courts and prisons and contract labor systems, or by their juvenile courts and parole systems. A change in penology may be an evidence of salvation.

A State which uses its superior power to overrun a weaker neighbor by force, or to wrest a valuable right of way from it by instigating a *coup d'état,* or uses intimidation to secure mining or railway concessions or to force a loan at usurious rates on a half-civilized State, is in mortal sin. A State which asks only for an open door and keeps its own door open in return, and which speaks as courteously to a backward State as to one with a big fleet, is to that extent a Christian community.

The salvation of the super-personal beings is by coming under the law of Christ. The fundamental step of repentance and conversion for professions and organizations is to give up monopoly power and the incomes derived from legalized extortion, and to come under the law of service, content with a fair income for honest work. The corresponding step in the case of governments and political oligarchies, both in monarchies and in capitalistic semi-democracies, is to submit to real democracy. Therewith they step out of the Kingdom of Evil into the Kingdom of God.[5]

The Kingdom of God

If theology is to offer an adequate doctrinal basis for the social gospel, it must not only make room for the doctrine of the Kingdom of God, but give it a central place and revise all

[5] *Ibid.,* chap. xi.

other doctrines so that they will articulate organically with it.

This doctrine is itself the social gospel. Without it, the idea of redeeming the social order will be but an annex to the orthodox conception of the scheme of salvation. If this doctrine gets the place which has always been its legitimate right, the practical proclamation and application of social morality will have a firm footing.

To those whose minds live in the social gospel, the Kingdom of God is a dear truth, the marrow of the gospel, just as the incarnation was to Athanasius, justification by faith alone to Luther, and the sovereignty of God to Jonathan Edwards. It was just as dear to Jesus. He too lived in it, and from it looked out on the world and the work he had to do.

Jesus always spoke of the Kingdom of God. Only two of his reported sayings contain the word "Church," and both passages are of questionable authenticity. It is safe to say that he never thought of founding the kind of institution which afterward claimed to be acting for him.

Yet immediately after his death, groups of disciples joined and consolidated by inward necessity. Each local group knew that it was part of a divinely founded fellowship mysteriously spreading through humanity, and awaiting the return of the Lord and the establishing of his Kingdom. This universal Church was loved with the same religious faith and reverence with which Jesus had loved the Kingdom of God. It was the partial and earthly realization of the divine Society, and at the Parousia the Church and the Kingdom would merge.

But the Kingdom was merely a hope, the Church a present reality. The chief interest and affection flowed toward the Church. Soon, through a combination of causes, the name and idea of "the Kingdom" began to be displaced by the name and idea of "the Church" in the preaching, literature, and theological thought of the Church. Augustine completed this process in his *De Civitate Dei.* The Kingdom of God which has, throughout human history, opposed the Kingdom of Sin, is today embodied in the Church. The millennium began when the Church was founded. This practically substituted the actual, not the ideal church for the Kingdom of God. The beloved ideal of Jesus became a vague phrase which kept intruding from the New Testament. Like Cinderella in the kitchen, it saw the other great dogmas furbished up for the ball, but no prince of theology restored it to its rightful place. The Reformation, too, brought no renascence of the doctrine of the Kingdom; it had only eschatological value, or was defined in blurred phrases borrowed from the Church. The present revival of the Kingdom idea is due to the combined influence of the historical study of the Bible and of the social gospel.

In the following brief propositions I should like to offer a few suggestions, on behalf of the social gospel, for the theological formulation of the doctrine of the Kingdom. Something like this is needed to give us "a theology for the social gospel."

1. The Kingdom of God is divine in its origin, progress and consummation. It was initiated by Jesus Christ, in whom the prophetic spirit came to its consummation, it is sustained by the Holy Spirit, and it will be brought to its fulfilment by the power of God in his own time. The passive and active resistance of the Kingdom of Evil at every stage of its advance is so great, and the human resources of the Kingdom of God so slender, that no explanation can satisfy a religious mind which does not see the power of God in its movements. The Kingdom of God, therefore, is miraculous all the way, and is the continuous revelation of the power, the righteousness, and the love of God. The establishment of a community of righteousness in mankind is just as much a saving act of God as the salvation of an individual from his natural selfishness and moral inability. The Kingdom of God, therefore, is not merely ethical, but has a rightful place in theology. This doctrine is absolutely necessary to establish that organic union between religion and morality, between theology and ethics, which is one of the characteristics of the Christian religion. When our moral actions are consciously related to the Kingdom of God they gain religious quality. Without this doctrine we shall have expositions of schemes of redemp-

tion and we shall have systems of ethics, but we shall not have a true exposition of Christianity. The first step to the reform of the Churches is the restoration of the doctrine of the Kingdom of God.

2. The Kingdom of God contains the teleology of the Christian religion. It translates theology from the static to the dynamic. It sees, not doctrines or rites to be conserved and perpetuated, but resistance to be overcome and great ends to be achieved. Since the Kingdom of God is the supreme purpose of God, we shall understand the Kingdom so far as we understand God, and we shall understand God so far as we understand his Kingdom. As long as organized sin is in the world, the Kingdom of God is characterized by conflict with evil. But if there were no evil, or after evil has been overcome, the Kingdom of God will still be the end to which God is lifting the race. It is realized not only by redemption, but also by the education of mankind and the revelation of his life within it.

3. Since God is in it, the Kingdom of God is always both present and future. Like God it is in all tenses, eternal in the midst of time. It is the energy of God realizing itself in human life. Its future lies among the mysteries of God. It invites and justifies prophecy, but all prophecy is fallible; it is valuable in so far as it grows out of action for the Kingdom and impels action. No theories about the future of the Kingdom of God are likely to be valuable or true which paralyze or postpone redemptive action on our part. To those who postpone, it is a theory and not a reality. It is for us to see the Kingdom of God as always coming, always pressing in on the present, always big with possibility, and always inviting immediate action. We walk by faith. Every human life is so placed that it can share with God in the creation of the Kingdom, or can resist and retard its progress. The Kingdom is for each of us the supreme task and the supreme gift of God. By accepting it as a task, we experience it as a gift. By labouring for it we enter into the joy and peace of the Kingdom as our divine fatherland and habitation.

4. Even before Christ, men of God saw the Kingdom of God as the great end to which all divine leadings were pointing. Every idealistic interpretation of the world, religious or philosophical, needs some such conception. Within the Christian religion the idea of the Kingdom gets its distinctive interpretation from Christ. (a) Jesus emancipated the idea of the Kingdom from previous nationalistic limitations and from the debasement of lower religious tendencies, and made it worldwide and spiritual. (b) He made the purpose of salvation essential in it. (c) He imposed his own mind, his personality, his love and holy will on the idea of the Kingdom. (d) He not only foretold it but initiated it by his life and work. As humanity more and more develops a racial consciousness in modern life, idealistic interpretations of the destiny of humanity will become more influential and important. Unless theology has a solidaristic vision higher and fuller than any other, it can not maintain the spiritual leadership of mankind, but will be outdistanced. Its business is to infuse the distinctive qualities of Jesus Christ into its teachings about the Kingdom, and this will be a fresh competitive test of his continued headship of humanity.

5. The Kingdom of God is humanity organized according to the will of God. Interpreting it through the consciousness of Jesus we may affirm these convictions about the ethical relations within the Kingdom: (a) Since Christ revealed the divine worth of life and personality, and since his salvation seeks the restoration and fulfilment of even the least, it follows that the Kingdom of God, at every stage of human development, tends toward a social order which will best guarantee to all personalities their freest and highest development. This involves the redemption of social life from the cramping influence of religious bigotry, from the repression of self-assertion in the relation of upper and lower classes, and from all forms of slavery in which human beings are treated as mere means to serve the ends of others. (b) Since love is the supreme law of Christ, the Kingdom of God implies a progressive reign of love in human affairs. We can see its advance wherever the free will of love supersedes the

use of force and legal coercion as a regulative of the social order. This involves the redemption of society from political autocracies and economic oligarchies; the substitution of redemptive for vindictive penology; the abolition of constraint through hunger as part of the industrial system; and the abolition of war as the supreme expression of hate and the completest cessation of freedom. (c) The highest expression of love is the free surrender of what is truly our own, life, property, and rights. A much lower but perhaps more decisive expression of love is the surrender of any opportunity to exploit men. No social group or organization can claim to be clearly within the Kingdom of God which drains others for its own ease, and resists the effort to abate this fundamental evil. This involves the redemption of society from private property in the natural resources of the earth, and from any condition in industry which makes monopoly profits possible. (d) The reign of love tends toward the progressive unity of mankind, but with the maintenance of individual liberty and the opportunity of nations to work out their own national peculiarities and ideals.

6. Since the Kingdom is the supreme end of God, it must be the purpose for which the Church exists. The measure in which it fulfils this purpose is also the measure of its spiritual authority and honour. The institutions of the Church, its activities, its worship, and its theology must in the long run be tested by its effectiveness in creating the Kingdom of God. For the Church to see itself apart from the Kingdom, and to find its aims in itself, is the same sin of selfish detachment as when an individual selfishly separates himself from the common good. The Church has the power to save in so far as the Kingdom of God is present in it. If the Church is not living for the Kingdom, its institutions are part of the "world." In that case it is not the power of redemption but its object. It may even become an anti-Christian power. If any form of church organization which formerly aided the Kingdom now impedes it, the reason for its existence is gone.

7. Since the Kingdom is the supreme end, all problems of personal salvation must be reconsidered from the point of view of the Kingdom. It is not sufficient to set the two aims of Christianity side by side. There must be a synthesis, and theology must explain how the two react on each other. The entire redemptive work of Christ must also be reconsidered under this orientation. Early Greek theology saw salvation chiefly as the redemption from ignorance by the revelation of God and from earthliness by the impartation of immortality. It interpreted the work of Christ accordingly, and laid stress on his incarnation and resurrection. Western theology saw salvation mainly as forgiveness of guilt and freedom from punishment. It interpreted the work of Christ accordingly, and laid stress on "the death and atonement." If the Kingdom of God was the guiding idea and chief end of Jesus—as we now know it was—we may be sure that every step in His life, including His death, was related to that aim and its realization, and when the idea of the Kingdom of God takes its due place in theology, the work of Christ will have to be interpreted afresh.

8. The Kingdom of God is not confined within the limits of the Church and its activities. It embraces the whole of human life. It is the Christian transfiguration of the social order. The Church is one social institution alongside of the family, the industrial organization of society, and the State. The Kingdom of God is in all these, and realizes itself through them all. During the Middle Ages all society was ruled and guided by the Church. Few of us would want modern life to return to such a condition. Functions which the Church used to perform, have now far outgrown its capacities. The Church is indispensable to the religious education of humanity and to the conservation of religion, but the greatest future awaits religion in the public life of humanity.[6]

[6] *Ibid.*, chap. xiii.

Further Readings

Primary Sources

Handy, Robert (ed.). *The Social Gospel in America, 1870–1920.* New York: Oxford University Press, 1966.

Rauschenbusch, Walter. *A Rauschenbusch Reader.* Compiled by Benson Landis. New York: Harper and Row, 1957.

———. *A Theology for the Social Gospel.* New York: Macmillan, 1918. (Republished Nashville: Abingdon Press, 1960.)

Secondary Sources

Hopkins, C. Howard. *The Rise of the Social Gospel in American Protestantism, 1865–1915.* New Haven: Yale University Press, 1940.

Miller, Robert. *American Protestantism and Social Issues, 1919–1939.* Chapel Hill: University of North Carolina Press, 1959.

Niebuhr, H. Richard. *The Kingdom of God in America.* Chicago and New York: Willett, Clark and Co., 1937. (Republished New York: Harper and Row, 1959.)

Sharpe, Doris. *Walter Rauschenbusch.* New York: Macmillan, 1942.

Chapter 16

THE ETHICS OF ECUMENICAL PROTESTANTISM

The Social Gospel movement described in the last chapter was no passing phase or period piece in the history of Christian ethics. In the middle decades of the twentieth century, the impetus of the Social Gospel in America, with parallel movements in England and on the continent, proved to be the main inspiration for the ecumenical movement here to be reviewed. The "ecumenical revolution," as it has been called, was and is not merely a movement of the churches of Christendom to "get together." The reunion of the churches as institutions is more a function or by-product of the recovery of a common faith and ethos by which they are brought together. Again and again, delegates to the ecumenical conferences discovered a stronger binding consensus on issues of Christian ethics than on matters of church polity or ways of worship and found that, whatever their residual differences, they could make common witness to the relevance of Christian moral norms to the problems of the twentieth-century urban culture.

To be sure, most of church life and practice at the parish level throughout this epoch continued to provide a retreat from the new besetting problems of industrial and city life. In common practice, Christian theology was taken as the supporting ideology of the middle-class "establishment," and Christian ethics was reduced to the etiquette of bourgeois proprieties or the pietistic prohibition of the sins of the flesh.

The leadership in the churches, however, the prophetic theologians who led the first ecumenical assemblies, were concerned with more significant matters. From nineteenth-century students of society like Karl Marx and Max Weber, as well as Rauschenbusch, they had learned of the tremendous impact of social institutions upon the soul of man and the quality of his life. The corporate problems of the balancing of power blocs and interests in society, of the proper distribution of income, of the conditions of work, of trade and technology, of the structures of justice and law—these are the matters requiring ethical guidance. If it be the Christian claim that God's saving word is incarnate in Christ, then it is the public life of man, as much as the private, that stands in need of this promised salvation. Indeed, there is no distinction, in the last analysis, between the private and public realms, between individual and social ethics, between "character" and "policy."

It has been said of the thought of the ecumenical leaders that it moves politically to the left and theologically to the right. It would be more accurate to say that the major ecumenical conferences represented an extension of the ethics of the Social Gospel, but with a theological foundation of premises concerning God and man and history derived rather more from the Reformation heritage than from the liberal faith of the late nineteenth century. Under the leadership of men like Nils Ehrenström of Sweden, Walter Moberly, J. H. Oldham, and William Temple of the Church of England (partisans of the Christian Socialist Movement there), and in America, John C. Bennett and Reinhold Niebuhr, a young theologian at Union Theological Seminary who had been for thirteen years in an industrial pastorate in Detroit, with many other distinguished churchmen, the Conference on Church, Community and State gathered in 1937 at Oxford. In the preparatory study volumes and in its Official Report, certain trends are clearly evident:

1. The need is urgent to discover and articulate the normative guidelines for Christian social policy relevant to the growing problem of social disorder.

2. The authority of the Bible is affirmed, not as a rulebook for particular policy decisions, or even as commending the principles of the Sermon on the Mount, in the spirit of

liberalism, but as it bears witness to the Lordship of God in Christ over men and nations.

3. "Let the Church be the Church." A high view of the authority of the Christian Church is restated. It is still the accepted sacred authority for the peoples of the West and speaks as the moral conscience of the community. When true to its Lord in worship and witness, it should command the respect and obedience in moral action of its members. At the same time, there is full acknowledgment of the tragic gap between this norm and actual practice—churchmen should repent for the complicity of the churches with the sins of the world. Their word of witness need not be any less affirmative for being contrite.

The context of Oxford was the troubled thirties, a time of widespread failure of nerve. A protracted global economic depression had produced a marked loss of confidence in capitalistic and democratic institutions. The rise of communism as an opposing ideology, openly critical of traditional Western Christianity, posed serious dilemmas for the Christian conscience. This setting explains the preoccupation of Oxford with economic issues. The other major challenge was the rising power of totalitarian governments in Italy and Germany. The threat of Nazism especially posed difficult questions for German Protestants (who for political reasons could not be present at the Conference). The impending black cloud of war, which was to break within two years, hung over the meetings. What should be the Christian response to this peril? How might fellowship in Christ be held fast across the borderlines of nations at war? How might the colliding values of national loyalties, resistance to aggression, and international peace be reconciled?

The "style" of Christian ethics in the Official Report is not an inward analysis of the motivations of Christian decision, such as one might find in an Augustine or a Kierkegaard, but the delineations of the norms for policy in the economic and political fields derived from the understanding of God's will incarnate in Christ. These norms (sometimes spoken of as "middle axioms") stand both as principles of judgment whereby existing social systems are to be critically measured and as guides for reformed Christian action. It will be plain to the student of these sources that there is much less confidence about the "Christianization" of the social order than in Rauschenbusch and his hopeful followers, and no talk about "bringing the Kingdom of God on earth." There is rather a mood of sober realism, mindful both of the distance between all of sinful man's social institutions and the Kingdom of God and of God's forgiving and renewing grace, enabling courageous Christian action, protected by the terms of its faith from either overconfidence or despair.

From Oxford to Amsterdam

The eleven years from 1937 to 1948, when the major church bodies (excepting Roman Catholic) convening at Amsterdam established officially the World Council of Churches, saw even more drastic changes in the social order. The dislocations and realignments of power with the close of World War II, the political polarization of Western Europe and America from the Soviet Union, the emergence of the new nations of Asia and Africa from colonialism, the increased rate of industrialization and mass migration from the country to the city, the technological revolution and the development of nuclear weapons, the paradox of a growing economic interdependence of the nations of the world with an increased political nationalism—all these posed in magnified form the perennial life-and-death problem of human existence in community.

At the Amsterdam Assembly in 1948, the dynamic power of secular ideologies in influencing the life-style of contemporary man was underscored. The recognition of the "non-theological" factors in social change proved a corrective to the impression, derived from an earlier age, that the main traffic of influence flows from the Christian church to the world. Quite the contrary: "the world-rulers of this present darkness" are in control—materialism, nationalism, racism.

In many subtle ways they have supplanted loyalty to Christ even in the worship and practice of the churches. The radical secularization of life renders the Christian premises of faith and ethics no longer axiomatic. Even in the so-called Christian nations, where the churches were prospering in a post-war boom of membership and affluence, authentic Christianity, it would seem, had become a minority movement, with slight impact on public policy.

In the face of all this, the Assembly reaffirmed its confident trust in the Lordship of God in Christ and the wisdom of his way for the world. Its normative ethical concept was that of "the Responsible Society." This term invokes the respect for the sacredness of persons and the moral necessity to emancipate man from the crush of the dehumanizing forces killing his spirit. The debate continued unresolved from Oxford between those who would advocate more governmental control in the economy and the advocates of laissez-faire capitalism and free enterprise. Actually, the Responsible Society is taken as a norm transcendent of either alternative of communism or capitalism. It does not provide a formula for the right mix of freedom and control but is a point of critique against the irresponsible abuse of public or private power and a mandate that power be distributed and used in ways responsible to God and neighbor.

From Amsterdam to Geneva

Amsterdam was followed by a series of ecumenical conferences such as at Evanston in 1954 and New Delhi in 1961, extending further the lines of thought projected at Oxford and Amsterdam. The most recent conference of the "Life and Work" division of the W.C.C. (the other sector being "Faith and Order") was held at Geneva in 1966. Its report, "Christians in the Technical and Social Revolutions of Our Time," reflects the catastrophic changes and the rising tide of revolutionary thought of the late 1960s. The leadership represented eighty nations and one hundred sixty-four member churches (including "observers" from Rome), a genuine meeting of East and West, since almost half were from the nations of the Third World. Laymen outnumbered theologians and brought an expertise about political and economic realities not as evident at earlier sessions.

In consequence, the word at Geneva was not so much from the church addressed to the world, pointing out the path to its salvation, as from the world to the churches, challenging their conservatism and pointing to the need of the conversion of the churches to Christianity. The dominant issues of the day, Black Power, the generation gap, the population explosion, the choice between revolutionary and evolutionary modes of social change, were vigorously debated. The revolutionary impact of radical Christianity was put in ways jarring to the decorous sensibilities of many churchmen, accustomed to gentle and settled niceties. The language was more that of the social scientist, describing the "cultural lag" between churchly traditions and the new needs of modern man, than of the theologian proclaiming the Lordship of Christ. Yet the link, however slender it appeared, between the Christian faith and the ethical aspects of economic and political policy is to be found in the category of "the human."

"The Christian understanding of the human derives from the belief that Jesus Christ is the disclosure to us of both true God and true man. In him we see most clearly what it means to say that man is made in the image of God, that in his dealing with the material world the Christian is called to express the Lordship of Christ, and to do so with a sense of his solidarity with all men." [1]

Unlike the earlier selections in this volume, the source materials below represent the text of commission reports rather than the thought of a single man (though in the Oxford Conference selection the hand of Reinhold Niebuhr can be detected). There may be some blunting of individuality in the process of expressing a consensus. The bite of pro-

[1] "Christians in the Technical and Social Revolutions of Our Time": World Conference on Church and Society. (World Council of Churches, Geneva, 1967), p. 52.

phetic witness is nonetheless to be felt. Oxford and Amsterdam may not reflect the conception of the Christian life held by the Men's Bible Class at the First Methodist Church in middle America, but this gap between normative prophecy and the average opinion of the people is more or less perennial.

The two selections are from the *Official Report of the Oxford Conference* (1937) (Section on Church, Community and State in Relation to the Economic Order) with minor deletions, and from the *Findings and Decisions of the First Assembly of the World Council of Churches,* (Amsterdam, 1948), Section III: The Church and the Disorder of Society.

SOURCES

From

THE OXFORD CONFERENCE REPORT

III. Report of the Section on Church, Community and State in Relation to the Economic Order

The Basis of the Christian Concern for the Economic Order

The Christian church approaches the problems of the social and economic order from the standpoint of her faith in the revelation of God in Christ. In the life and death of our Lord, God is revealed as a just God who condemns sin and as a merciful God who redeems sinners. The nature and will of God as thus revealed form the basis of human existence and the standard of human conduct. The chief end of man is to glorify God, to honor and love him, in work and life as in worship. This love involves the obligations to love our neighbors as ourselves, a second commandment which Jesus declared to be like unto the first.

This love of neighbor is an obligation which rests partly upon the native worth and dignity of man as made in the image of God. In all systems of morality this obligation is to a greater or less degree recognized. Christianity, however, recognizes that the image of God in man is so defaced by sin that man's native worth and dignity are largely obscured. For this reason it must be emphasized that our obligation to the neighbor springs not so much from our recognition of man's native dignity as from the Christian revelation of God's purpose to restore that dignity through the redemption that is in Christ. The obligation is therefore a duty toward God and continues to be operative even when the neighbor does not obviously demand or deserve respect. We must love our fellow men because God loves them and wills to redeem them.

The kingdom of God, as proclaimed in the gospel, is the reign of God which both has come and is coming. It is an established reality in the coming of Christ and in the presence of his Spirit in the world. It is, however, still in conflict with a sinful world which crucified its Lord, and its ultimate triumph is still to come. In so far as it has come, the will of God as revealed in Christ (that is, the commandment of love) is the ultimate standard of Christian conduct. Standards drawn from the observation of human behavior or prompted by immediate necessities are not only less complete than the commandment of love but frequently contain elements that contradict it. In so far as the kingdom of God is in conflict with the world and is therefore still to come, the Christian finds himself under the necessity of discovering the best available means of checking human sinfulness and of increasing the possibilities and opportunities of love within a sinful world.

The relative and departmental standard for all the social arrangements and institutions, all the economic structures and political systems, by which the life of man is ordered is the principle of justice. Justice, as the ideal of a harmonious relation of life to life, obviously presupposes the sinful tendency of one life to take advantage of another. This sinful tendency it seeks to check by defining the rightful place and privilege which each life must have in the harmony of the whole and by assigning the duty of each to each. Justice does not demand that the self sacrifice itself completely for the neighbor's good, but seeks to define and to maintain the good which each member of the community may rightfully claim in the harmony of the whole.

The principle of justice has both a positive and a negative significance. Negatively, principles of justice restrain evil and the evildoer. They must therefore become embodied in systems of coercion which prevent men from doing what sinful ambition, pride, lust and greed might prompt them to do. This necessary coercion is itself a root of new evils, since its exercise involves power and power tempts the possessor to its unrighteous use. Furthermore, coercion may rouse resentment among those coerced even when its purpose is a necessary social end. The use of power and coercion cannot therefore be regarded by Christians as ultimately desirable. Criticism against its abuses must be constantly maintained. On the other hand, it cannot be assumed that the practice of Christian love will ever obviate the necessity for coercive political and economic arrangements.

The laws of justice are not purely negative. They are not merely "dikes against sin." The political and economic structure of society is also the mechanical skeleton which carries the organic element in society. Forms of production and methods of cooperation may serve the cause of human brotherhood by serving and extending the principle of love beyond the sphere of purely personal relations.

The commandment of love therefore always presents possibilities for individuals beyond the requirements of economic and social institutions. There is no legal, political or economic system so bad or so good as to absolve individuals from the responsibility to transcend its requirements by acts of Christian charity. Institutional requirements necessarily prescribe only the minimum. Even in the best possible social system they can only achieve general standards in which the selfishness of the human heart is taken for granted and presupposed. But the man who is in Christ knows a higher obligation which transcends the requirements of justice—the obligation of a love which is the fulfillment of the law.

The love which is the fulfillment of the law is, however, no substitute for law, for institutions or for systems. Individual acts of charity within a given system of government or economics may mitigate its injustices and increase its justice. But they do not absolve the Christian from seeking the best possible institutional arrangement and social structure for the ordering of human life. Undue emphasis upon the higher possibilities of love in personal relations, within the limits of a given system of justice or an established social structure, may tempt Christians to allow individual acts of charity to become a screen for injustice and a substitute for justice. Christianity becomes socially futile if it does not recognize that love must will justice and that the Christian is under an obligation to secure the best possible social and economic structure, in so far as such structure is determined by human decisions.

The relation of the commandment of love to the justice of political and economic systems is twofold. It is an ideal which reaches beyond any possible achievements in the field of political relations, but it is nevertheless also a standard by which various schemes of justice may be judged. In attempting to deal with political and economic problems, the Christian must therefore be specially on his guard against two errors.

The one is to regard the realities of social justice incorporated in given systems and orders as so inferior to the law of love that the latter cannot be a principle of discrimination among them but only a principle of indiscriminate judgment upon them all. This error makes Christianity futile as a guide in all those decisions which Christians, like other people, must constantly be making in the political and economic sphere. Practically, it gives the advantage to established systems as against the challenge of new social adventures and experiments; for it tempts Christians to make no decisions at all, and such efforts to reserve decision become in practice decisions in favor of the status quo.

The other error is to identify some particular social system with the will of God or to equate it with the kingdom of God. When conservatives insist on such an identification in favor of the status quo, they impart to it a dangerous religious sanction which must drive those who challenge it into a secular revolt against religion itself. If, on the other hand, this identification is made in the interests of a new social order, it will lead to the same complacency which the critic deprecates in the old social situation. Every tendency to identify the kingdom of God with a particular social structure or economic mechanism must result in moral confusion for those who maintain the system and in disillusionment for those who suffer from its limitations. The former will regard conformity with its standards as identical with the fulfillment of the law, thus falling into the sin of pharisaism. The latter will be tempted to a cynical disavowal of the religion because it falsely gives absolute worth to partial values and achievements. Both errors are essentially heretical from the point of view of Christian faith. The one denies the reality of the kingdom of God in history; the other equates the kingdom of God with the processes of history. In the one case, the ultimate and eternal destiny of human existence, which transcends history, is made to support an attitude of indifference toward historical social issues; in the other case, the eternal destiny of human existence is denied or obscured. The law of love which is the standard of the Christian life is properly to be regarded as being at the same time a present reality and an ultimate possibility. It is not only a criterion of judgment in all the fateful decisions which men must make in history, but also an indictment against all historical achievements.

As a criterion of judgment upon the relative merits of economic arrangements and social structures, the law of love gives positive guidance in terms of justice, even though it transcends the realities of all possible social structures. The obligation to love our neighbors as ourselves places clearly under condemnation all social and economic systems which give one man undue advantage over others. It must create an uneasy conscience (for example) in all Christians who are involved in a social system which denies children, of whatever race or class, the fullest opportunity to develop whatever gifts God has given them and makes their education depend upon the fortuitous circumstance of a father's possession or lack of means to provide the necessary funds. It must challenge any social system which provides social privileges without reference to the social functions performed by individuals, or which creates luxury and pride on the one hand and want and insecurity on the other. It makes the conscience of Christians particularly uneasy in regard to the deprivation of basic security for large masses of human beings.

Points at Which the Christian Understanding of Life Is Challenged

At the beginning of this part of the report attention should be called to the potentialities for good in the economic order. Situations vary in different parts of the world but in many countries it already seems possible, through the full utilization of the resources of the new technology and through the release of human productive power, to remove the kind of poverty which is crippling to human personality. There is a sense in which poverty is a relative matter and hence in any situation would be present in some form; but we are thinking of the poverty which would be regarded in any age as denying the physical necessities of life. The abolition of such poverty now seems to depend on the human organization of economic life, rather than on factors given in nature or on what might be called the inevitable constitution of every economic order. But the possibility of economic "plenty" has this moral importance, that to an increasing extent it makes the persistence of poverty a matter for which men are morally responsible. This possibility marks off our time from the period of the New Testament and from other periods in which Christian thinking about economic life has been formulated. In the light of it the direction of Christian effort in relation to the economic order should henceforth be turned from charitable paternalism to the realization of more equal justice in the distribution of wealth. Moreover, Christians who live in the more privileged geographical areas must recognize that the securing of economic plenty and greater justice in its distribution within their respective national groups is not the whole of their duty in this connection; they cannot escape some measure of responsibility for those areas where for years to come there will doubtless be desperate economic need.

It seems to us that the moral and spiritual nature of man, according to the Christian understanding of that nature, is affronted by the assumptions and operation of the economic order of the industrialized world in four respects to which we wish to draw special attention.

(a) *The Enhancement of Acquisitiveness.* That economic order results, in the first place, in a serious danger that the finer qualities of the human spirit will be sacrificed to an overmastering preoccupation with a department of life which, though important on its own plane, ought to be strictly subordinated to other more serious aspects of life. We are warned by the New Testament that riches are a danger to their possessors, and experience would appear to confirm that diagnosis. It is not possible to serve both God and Mammon. When the necessary work of society is so organized as to make the acquisition of wealth the chief criterion of success, it encourages a feverish scramble for money, and a false respect for the victors in the struggle which is as fatal in its moral consequences as any other form of idolatry. In so far as the pursuit of monetary gain becomes the dominant factor in the lives of men, the quality of society undergoes a subtle disintegration. That such a society should be the scene of a perpetual conflict of interests, sometimes concealed, sometimes overt, between the economic groups composing them, is not surprising. Men can cooperate only in so far as they are united by allegiance to a common purpose which is recognized as superior to their sectional interests. As long as industry is organized primarily not for the service of the community but with the object of producing a purely financial result for some of its members, it cannot be recognized as properly fulfilling its social purpose.

(b) *Inequalities.* The second feature of the economic system which challenges the conscience of Christians is the existence of disparities of economic circumstance on a scale which differs from country to country, but in some is shocking, in all considerable. Not only is the product of industry distributed with an inequality so extreme (though the extent of this inequality also varies considerably from country to country) that a small minority of the population are in receipt of incomes exceeding in the aggregate those of many times their number, but—even more seriously—the latter are condemned throughout their lives to environmental evils which the former escape, and are deprived of the opportunities of fully developing their powers which are accessible, as a matter of course, to their more fortunate fellows. It is no part of the teaching of Christianity that all men are equally endowed by nature or that identical provision should be made for all, irrespective of difference of capacity and need. What Christianity does assert is that all men are children of one Father, and that, compared with that primary and overwhelming fact, the differences between the races, nationalities and classes of men, though important on their own plane, are external and trivial. Any social arrangement which outrages the dignity of man by treating some men as ends and others as means, any institution which obscures the common humanity of men by emphasizing the external accidents of birth or wealth or social position, is ipso facto anti-Christian.

One aspect of the matter deserves special emphasis. Whatever their differences on other subjects, Christians cannot be in doubt as to the primary duty of insuring that the conditions required for full personal development are enjoyed by the whole of the rising generation. In some countries that obligation receives fuller recognition than in others, but of few, if any, can it be said that equal opportunities of physical and mental growth are available for all. It is still the case, even in some of the wealthy nations of western Europe, that large numbers of children undergo grave injury to their health before they reach the age of school attendance, though the methods by which such injury can be prevented are well known; that the education given them at school is often, owing to reluctance to spend the sums required, gravely defective in quality; that many of them are plunged prematurely into full-time work in industry, where too often they are employed under conditions injurious both to their characters and to their physical well-being; and that diversities of educational provision correspond to differences of income among parents rather than of capacity among children. It often happens that these disadvantages are greatly increased where economic opportunities are denied on racial grounds. This racial discrimination is seen in various forms: a double standard of wages; the inability of members of certain races, whatever their competence may be, to rise above a certain level of responsibility in their respective callings; their exclusion in some circumstances from labor unions; and the refusal to admit members of some racial groups to occupations reserved for members of the dominant race.

(c) *Irresponsible Possession of Economic Power.* A third feature of the existing situation which is repugnant to the Christian conscience consists in the power wielded by a few individuals or groups who are not responsible to any organ of society. This gives the economic order in many countries some resemblance to a tyranny, in the classical sense of that term, where rulers are not accountable for their actions to any superior authority representing the community over whom power is exercised. At the top of this hierarchy are the leaders of the world of finance, whose decisions raise and lower the economic temperature. Below them are the controllers of certain great key industries, the conduct and policy of which vitally affect the lives of millions of human beings. Below them again are a mass of economic undertakings, large and small, the masters of which exercise power over the few hundred or few thousand persons dependent on each of them. The power which these latter wield is qualified at many points by trade unionism and by the law. On the whole, however, the action both of trade unionism and of the state has been confined hitherto to establishing and maintaining certain minimum standards. Almost the whole field of economic strategy, which in the long run determines what standards can be maintained, escapes their control.

Economic like political autocracy is attended doubtless by certain advantages. However, it is liable to produce both in individuals and in society a character and an outlook on life which it is difficult to reconcile with any relationship that can be described as Christian. It tends to create in those who wield authority, and in the agents through whom they exercise it, a dictatorial temper which springs not from any defect of character peculiar to them but from the influence upon them of the position they occupy. The effect of excessive economic power on those over whom it is exercised is equally serious. Often it makes them servile; fear of losing their jobs, and a vague belief that in the end the richer members of society always hold the whip hand, tends to destroy their spiritual virility. Often, again, it makes them bitter and cynical; they feel that force, not justice, rules their world, and they are tempted to dismiss as insincere cant words which imply a different view.

(d) *The Frustration of the Sense of Christian Vocation.* A profound conflict has arisen between the demand that the Christian should be doing the will of God in his daily work, and the actual kinds of work which Christians find themselves forced to do within the economic order. With regard to the worker and employee, there is the fact that most of them are directly conscious of working for the profit of the employer (and for the sake of their wages) and only indirectly conscious of working for any public good; while this fact may in some cases be only part of the mechanism by which the work is done for the public good, the difficulty in some degree remains. Again, there is the fact that at present many workers must produce things which are useless or shoddy or destructive. Finally, one other form of work which seems clearly to be in conflict with the Christian's vocation is salesmanship of a kind which involves deception—the deception which may be no more than insinuation and exaggeration, but which is a serious threat to the integrity of the worker.

But even more serious is the constant threat of unemployment. This produces a feeling of extreme insecurity in the minds of the masses of the people. Unemployment, especially when prolonged, tends to create in the mind of the unemployed person a sense of uselessness or even of being a nuisance, and to empty his life of any meaning. This situation cannot be met by measures of unemployment assistance, because it is the lack of significant activity which tends to destroy his human self-respect.

Christian Teaching in Relation to the Economic Order

We stated in the third section of this report the special points at which there is a conflict between the present economic order and the Christian understanding of life. In the next section we pointed out the kind of social decisions which have to be made by all Christians as citizens.

But it is not enough to say that these problems are chiefly the responsibility of Christian individuals or Christian lay groups and leave the matter there. The further question must be raised: What guidance can those who must make these decisions concerning the economic order receive from their Christian faith? That question places great responsibility upon those in the church who have the task of interpreting the meaning of Christian faith. In this work of interpretation the clergy should have a specially important contribution to make, but that contribution must be made with understanding of the experience of laymen. It is important that whenever this Christian guidance is crystallized in the reports and pronouncements of official church bodies, or of such a conference as the Oxford Conference, laymen should share with the clergy this task of formulation. These laymen should come from various economic groups. This section of the report will be an attempt to formulate this kind of guidance which it is now possible to receive from Christian faith for economic life. We are here dealing directly with what the teaching of the church as a church should be concerning the economic order.

We must begin by recognizing that there are some factors in economic life which are more clearly within the province of the church and concerning which more light can be gained from the Christian message than others, and that there are many matters of judgment in particular situations which involve chiefly expert knowledge. Recognizing, then, the importance of attempting to mark out as clearly as possible the precise areas within which the Christian can expect to receive light from the Christian faith and within which the teaching of the church as church in regard to economic life should be carried on, we proceed to suggest three such areas. In presenting these areas we are suggesting what might be the framework of the Christian message in relation to the economic order in the next decade.

(1) Christian teaching should deal with ends, in the sense of long-range goals, standards and principles in the light of which every concrete situation and every proposal for improving it must be tested. It is in the light of such ends and principles that the four characteristics of the existing economic order discussed in section two stand out as challenges to the Christian church. There are differences in theory concerning the way in which these ends are related to the Christian faith. Some would be very careful not to call these ends Christian and yet they would recognize that they are ends which Christians should seek in obedience to God.

We suggest five such ends or standards, by way of example, as applicable to the testing of any economic situation.

(a) Right fellowship between man and man being a condition of man's fellowship with God, every economic arrangement which frustrates or restricts it must be modified—and in particular such ordering of economic life as tends to divide the community into classes based upon differences of wealth and to occasion a sense of injustice among the poorer members of society. To every member of the community there must be made open a worthy means of livelihood. The possibilities of amassing private accumulations of wealth should be so limited that the scale of social values is not perverted by the fear and the envy, the insolence and the servility, which tend to accompany extreme inequality.

(b) Regardless of race or class every child and youth must have opportunities of education suitable for the full development of his particular capacities, and must be free from those adventitious handicaps in the matter of health and environment which our society loads upon large numbers of the children of the less privileged classes. In this connection, the protection of the family as a social unit should be an urgent concern of the community.

(c) Persons disabled from economic activity, whether by sickness, infirmity or age, should not be economically penalized on account of their disability, but on the contrary should be the object of particular care. Here again the safeguarding of the family is involved.

(d) Labor has intrinsic worth and dignity, since it is designed by God for man's welfare. The duty and the right of men to work should therefore alike be emphasized. In the industrial process, labor should never be considered a mere commodity. In their daily work men should be able to recognize and fulfill a Christian vocation. The workingman, whether in field or factory, is entitled to a living wage, wholesome surroundings and a recognized voice in the decisions which affect his welfare as a worker.

(e) The resources of the earth, such as the soil and mineral wealth, should be recognized as gifts of God to the whole human race and used with due and balanced consideration for the needs of the present and future generations.

The implications of even one of these standards, seriously taken, will involve drastic changes in economic life. Each one of them must be made more definite in terms of the problems which face particular communities.

Closely connected with the foregoing paragraphs is the whole question of property—so closely indeed that any action on the part of the community which affects property rights will also affect the application of the standards mentioned. This is a sphere in which Christian teaching on ends and principles in relation to economic life could have immediate results if it were translated into actual economic decisions. Christian thought has already supplied a background which is of great importance, but it has not been brought into effective relationship with the development of the institutions of property under modern economic conditions. This subject should be given close attention by any agencies for further study which may be established in the future. Meanwhile we suggest a few of the directions along which Christian thought should move.

(a) It should be reaffirmed without qualification that all human property rights are relative and contingent only, in virtue of the dependence of man upon God as the giver of all wealth and as the creator of man's capacities to develop the resources of nature. This fundamental Christian conviction must express itself both in the idea of stewardship or trusteeship and in the willingness of the Christian to examine accumulations of property in the light of their social consequences.

(b) The existing system of property rights and the existing distribution of property must be criticized in the light of the largely nonmoral processes by which they have been developed, and criticism must take account of the fact that every argument in defense of property rights which is valid for Christian thinking is also an argument for the widest possible distribution of these rights.

(c) It should further be affirmed that individual property rights must never be maintained or exercised without regard to their social consequences or without regard to the contribution which the community makes in the production of all wealth.

(d) It is very important to make clear distinction between various forms of property. The property which consists in personal possessions for use, such as the home, has behind it a clearer moral justification than property in the means of production and in land which gives the owners power over other persons. All property which represents social power stands in special need of moral scrutiny, since power to determine the lives of others is the crucial point in any scheme of justice. The question must always be asked whether this is the kind of power which can be brought under adequate social control or whether it is of the type which by its very nature escapes and evades social control. Industrial property in particular encourages the concentration of power; for it gives the owner control over both the place and the instruments of labor and thus leaves the worker powerless so far as property relations are concerned, allowing him only the organized strength of his union and his political franchise to set against the power of ownership. Property in land on a large scale may represent a similar power over those who are forced to rent it for a livelihood. There are consequently forms of feudal land ownership in Europe, in some states of America and in the Orient, which are frequent sources of social injustice. On the other hand property in land which does not extend beyond the capacity of one family to cultivate—the small freehold which determines a large part of the agriculture of the Western world—belongs to a unique category. The small freeholder may find it increasingly difficult to compete against mechanized large-scale production and to make a living without being overdriven. But on the other hand there is a special justification for this type of property, since it gives freedom to perform a social function without the interference of capricious power and without the exercise of power over others. Furthermore, there is a more organic relation between owner and property in agricultural land than in any type of industrial ownership. Small-scale property in industry and in retail trade possesses some of these same characteristics in a lesser degree. Yet there is always the danger that small-scale productive property, whether in land, industry or trade, may tempt the owner, in his competition with more powerful productive units, to exploit his own family and the other workers employed, especially since in any given case the latter may be too few to organize effectively.

(2) The message of Christianity should throw a searchlight on the actual facts of the existing situation, and in particular reveal the human consequences of present forms of economic behavior. It is this which saves statements of principles from being platitudes. The kind of critical analysis which is set forth in section two must be a part of the message of the church. Here it is important not to impute motives or to denounce individuals (except where special circumstances call for such denunciation) but to present facts in such a way that they speak for themselves to the individual conscience. What in isolation seems to be purely destructive criticism is a necessary part of the total process by which constructive change is brought about.

The most obvious human consequences of existing economic behavior are quite as much, if not more, within the province of the Christian as they are within the province of the expert in the social sciences. The clergyman in the course of pastoral work has opportunities, if he is capable of using them, of knowing what the present economic situation does to the character, the morale, the true welfare of men, women and children and to family life. The expert may have to supply statistics, but the meaning of the statistics can be known only to those who see the particular results of an economic situation in the lives of persons. As it has been said, "Love implies the ability to read statistics with compassion." Christian insight ought to enable men and women to see more deeply into the effects of an economic situation. Where there are secular agencies which have the facts, the task of the church is to aid in making those facts available to its members and especially to those who have a teaching function within the church. But there are occasions on which some agency of the church may have the task of securing the facts. This can be most helpful in controversial situations in which the church has a position of relative independence of the parties to the controversy.

It is not enough to catalogue particular cases of poverty and exploitation or to call attention to specific cases of selfish and irresponsible conduct on the part of those in power. It is the business of the church to point out where the economic institutions of our time are in themselves infected with evil. They place narrow limits on the choices of the best men who work within them. The individual employer, for example, is often greatly handicapped in paying a living wage if he must compete with less scrupulous employers. There are multitudes of high-minded Christians who as employers, businessmen and trade unionists do a great deal to develop happy relationships between employers and employees and to preserve the highest standards of personal integrity within their spheres of influence. Many of the most praiseworthy human motives—constructive service to mankind, the creation of cultural and material values, the desire to achieve conditions essential to the development of human personality—inspire their conduct. No criticisms of the present consequences of economic behavior in general should obscure the positive contribution of such men. On the other hand the presence of such conscientious Christians in places of responsibility should not create the expectation that, without changes in institutions and legal relationships, they will be able to overcome the evils set forth in section three of this report.

(3) This searchlight of the Christian message can also make clear the obstacles to economic justice in the human heart, and especially those that are present in the hearts of people within the church. It is not enough that individual Christians become good in their intentions or become changed in their conscious motives. What is needed is the kind of self-knowledge which will help Christians to understand how far their attitudes are molded by the position which they hold in the economic order. Self-knowledge is no less important than knowledge of external conditions, and more important than the knowledge of the sins of others.

Christians must come to understand how far they really do seek, in spite of all pretensions to the contrary, a world in which they and their group are on top, how far their opinions on economic issues are controlled by the interests of the group or class to which they belong, how far they are deceived by false slogans and rationalizations, how far they are callous to "evil at a distance" or to evil experienced by another national or class group than their own—evil to which they may consent, for which they may vote, or by which they may profit. Here, again, the important activity is not to denounce, but to help people to that self-knowledge which comes from the perspective of the Christian emphasis upon sin, so that they will condemn themselves.

From

The Amsterdam Assembly Report

The Church and the Disorder of Society

I. *The Disorder of Society*

The world today is experiencing a social crisis of unparalleled proportions. The deepest root of that disorder is the refusal of men to see and admit that their responsibility to God stands over and above their loyalty to any earthly community and their obedience to any worldly power. Our modern society, in which religious tradition and family life have been weakened, and which is for the most part secular in its outlook, underestimates both the depth of evil in human nature and the full heights of freedom and dignity in the children of God.

The Christian Church approaches the disorder of our society with faith in the Lordship of Jesus Christ. In Him God has established His Kingdom and its gates stand open for all who will enter. Their lives belong to God with a certainty that no disorder of society can destroy, and on them is laid the duty to seek God's Kingdom and His righteousness.

In the light of that Kingdom, with its judgment and mercy, Christians are conscious of the sins which corrupt human communities and institutions in every age, but they are also assured of the final victory over all sin and death through Christ. It is He who has bidden us pray that God's Kingdom may come and that His will may be done on earth as it is in heaven; and our obedience to that command requires that we seek in every age to overcome the specific disorders which aggravate the perennial evil in human society, and that we search out the means of securing their elimination or control.

Men are often disillusioned by finding that changes of particular systems do not bring unqualified good, but fresh evils. New temptations to greed and power arise even in systems more just than those they have replaced because sin is ever present in the human heart. Many, therefore, lapse into apathy, irresponsibility and despair. The Christian faith leaves no room for such despair, being based on the fact that the Kingdom of God is firmly established in Christ and will come by God's act despite all human failure.

Two chief factors contribute to the crisis of our age. One of these is the vast concentrations of power—which are under capitalism mainly economic and under communism both economic and political. In such conditions, social evil is manifest on the largest scale not only in the greed, pride, and cruelty of persons and groups, but also in the momentum or inertia of huge organizations of men, which diminish their ability to act as moral and accountable beings. To find ways of realizing personal responsibility for collective action in the large aggregations of power in modern society is a task which has not yet been undertaken seriously.

The second factor is that society, as a whole dominated as it is by technics, is likewise more controlled by a momentum of its own than in previous periods. While it enables men the better to use nature, it has the possibilities of destruction, both through war and through the undermining of the natural foundations of society in family, neighbourhood and craft. It has collected men into great industrial cities and has deprived many societies of those forms of association in which men can grow most fully as persons. It has accentuated the tendency in men to waste God's gift to them in the soil and in other natural resources.

On the other hand, technical developments have relieved men and women of much drudgery and poverty, and are still capable of doing more. There is a limit to what they can do in this direction. Large parts of the world, however, are far from that limit. Justice demands that the inhabitants of Asia and Africa, for instance, should have benefits of more machine production. They may learn to avoid the mechanization of life and the other dangers of an unbalanced economy which impair the social health of the older industrial peoples. Technical progress also provides channels of communication and interdependence which can be aids to fellowship, though closer contact may also produce friction.

There is no inescapable necessity for society to succumb to undirected developments of technology, and the Christian Church has an urgent responsibility today to help men to achieve fuller personal life within the technical society.

In doing so, the Churches should not forget to what extent they themselves have contributed to the very evils which they are tempted to blame wholly on the secularism of society. While they have raised up many Christians who have taken the lead in movements of reform, and while many of them have come to see in a fresh way the relevance of their faith to the problems of society, and the imperative obligations thus laid upon them, they share responsibility for the contemporary disorder. Our churches have often given religious sanction to the special privileges of dominant classes, races and political groups, and so they have been obstacles to changes necessary in the interests of social justice and political freedom. They have often concentrated on a purely spiritual or other-worldly or individualistic interpretation of their message and their responsibility. They have often failed to understand the forces which have shaped society around them, and so they have been unprepared to deal creatively with new problems as they have arisen in technical civilization; they have often neglected the effects of industrialization on agricultural communities.

II. *Economic and Political Organization*

In the industrial revolution economic activity was freed from previous social controls and outgrew its modest place in human life. It created the vast network of financial, commercial and industrial relations which we know as the capitalist order. In all parts of the world new controls have in various degrees been put upon the free play of economic forces, but there are economic necessities which no political system can afford to defy. In our days for instance, the need for stability in the value of money, for creation of capital and for incentives in production, is inescapable and world-wide. Justice, however, demands that economic activities be subordinated to social ends. It is intolerable that vast millions of people be exposed to insecurity, hunger and frustration by periodic inflation or depression.

The Church cannot resolve the debate between those who feel that the primary solution is to socialize the means of production, and those who fear that such a course will merely lead to new and inordinate combinations of political and economic power, culminating finally in an omnicompetent State. In the light of the Christian understanding of man we must, however, say to the advocates of socialization that the institution of property is not the root of the corruption of human nature. We must equally say to the defenders of existing property relations that ownership is not an unconditional right; it must, therefore, be preserved, curtailed or distributed in accordance with the requirements of justice.

On the one hand we must vindicate the supremacy of persons over purely technical considerations by subordinating all economic processes and cherished rights to the needs of the community as a whole. On the other hand, we must preserve the possibility of a satisfying life for "little men in big societies." We must prevent abuse of authority and keep open as wide a sphere as possible in which men can have direct and responsible relations with each other as persons.

Coherent and purposeful ordering of society has now become a major necessity. Here governments have responsibilities which they must not shirk. But centres of initiative in economic life must be so encouraged as to avoid placing too great a burden upon centralized judgment and decision. To achieve religious, cultural, economic, social and other ends it is of vital importance that society should have a rich variety of smaller forms of community, in local government, within industrial organizations, including trade unions, through the development of public corporations and through voluntary associations. By such means it is possible to prevent an undue centralization of power in modern, technically organized communities, and thus escape the perils of tyranny while avoiding the dangers of anarchy.

III. *The Responsible Society*

Man is created and called to be a free being, responsible to God and his neighbour. Any tendencies in State and society depriving man of the possibility of acting responsibly are a denial of God's intention for man and His work of salvation. A responsible society is one where freedom is the freedom of men who acknowledge responsibility to justice and public order, and where those who hold political authority or economic power are responsible for its exercise to God and the people whose welfare is affected by it.

Man must never be made for the State but the State for man. Man is not made for production, but production for man. For a society to be responsible under modern conditions it is required that the people have freedom to control, to criticize and to change their governments, that power be made responsible by law and tradition, and be distributed as widely as possible through the whole community. It is required that economic justice and provision of equality of opportunity be established for all the members of society.

We therefore condemn:

1. Any attempt to limit the freedom of the Church to witness to its Lord and His design for mankind and any attempt to impair the freedom of men to obey God and to act according to conscience, for those freedoms are implied in man's responsibility before God;

2. Any denial to man of an opportunity to participate in the shaping of society, for this is a duty implied in man's responsibility towards his neighbour;

3. Any attempt to prevent men from learning and spreading the truth.

IV. *Communism and Capitalism*

Christians should ask why communism in its modern totalitarian form makes so strong an appeal to great masses of people in many parts of the world. They should recognize the hand of God in the revolt of multitudes against injustice that gives communism much of its strength. They should seek to recapture for the Church the original Christian solidarity with the world's distressed people, not to curb their aspirations towards justice, but, on the contrary, to go beyond them and direct them towards the only road which does not lead to a blank wall, obedience to God's will and His justice. Christians should realize that for many, especially for many young men and women, communism seems to stand for a vision of human equality and universal brotherhood for which they were prepared by Christian influences. Christians who are beneficiaries of capitalism should try to see the world as it appears to many who know themselves excluded from its privileges and who see in communism a means of deliverance from poverty and insecurity. All should understand that the proclamation of racial equality by communists and their support of the cause of colonial peoples makes a strong appeal to the populations of Asia and Africa and to racial minorities elsewhere. It is a great human tragedy that so much that is good in the motives and aspirations of many communists and of those whose sympathies they win has been transformed into a force that engenders new forms of injustice and oppression, and that what is true in communist criticism should be used to give convincing power to untrustworthy propaganda.

Christians should recognize with contrition that many churches are involved in the forms of economic injustice and racial discrimination which have created the conditions favourable to the growth of communism, and that the atheism and the anti-religious teaching of communism are in part a reaction to the chequered record of a professedly Christian society. It is one of the most fateful facts in modern history that often the working classes, including tenant farmers, came to believe that the churches were against them or indifferent to their plight. Christians should realize that the Church has often failed to offer to its youth the appeal that can evoke a disciplined, purposeful and sacrificial response, and that in this respect communism has for many filled a moral and psychological vacuum.

The points of conflict between Christianity and the atheistic Marxian communism of our day are as follows: (1) the communist promise of what amounts to a complete redemption of man in history; (2) the belief that a particular class by virtue of its role as the bearer of a new order is free from the sins and ambiguities that Christians believe to be characteristic of all human existence; (3) the materialistic and deterministic teachings, however they may be qualified, that are incompatible with belief in God and with the Christian view of man as a person, made in God's image and responsible to Him; (4) the ruthless methods of communists in dealing with their opponents; (5) the demand of the party on its members for an exclusive and unqualified loyalty which belongs only to God, and the coercive policies of communist dictatorship in controlling every aspect of life.

The Church should seek to resist the extension of any system, that not only includes oppressive elements but fails to provide any means by which the victims of oppression may criticize or act to correct it. It is a part of the mission of the Church to raise its voice of protest wherever men are the victims of terror, wherever they are denied such fundamental human rights as the right to be secure against arbitrary arrest, and wherever governments use torture and cruel punishments to intimidate the consciences of men.

The Church should make clear that there are conflicts between Christianity and capitalism. The developments of capitalism vary from country to country and often the exploitation of the workers that was characteristic of early capitalism has been corrected in considerable measure by the influence of trade unions, social legislation and responsible management. But (1) capitalism tends to subordinate what should be the primary task of any economy—the meeting of human needs—to the economic advantages of those who have most power over its institutions. (2) It tends to produce serious inequalities. (3) It has developed a practical form of materialism in western nations in spite of their Christian background, for it has placed the greatest emphasis upon success in making money. (4) It has also kept the people of capitalist countries subject to a kind of fate which has taken the form of such social catastrophes as mass unemployment.

The Christian churches should reject the ideologies of both communism and laissez-faire capitalism, and should seek to draw men away from the false assumption that these extremes are the only alternatives. Each has made promises which it could not redeem. Communist ideology puts the emphasis upon economic justice, and promises that freedom will come automatically after the completion of the revolution. Capitalism puts the emphasis upon freedom, and promises that justice will follow as a by-product of free enterprise; that, too, is an ideology which has been proved false. It is the responsibility of Christians to seek new, creative solutions which never allow either justice or freedom to destroy the other.

V. *The Social Function of the Church*

The greatest contribution that the Church can make to the renewal of society is for it to be renewed in its own life in faith and obedience to its Lord. Such inner renewal includes a clearer grasp of the meaning of the Gospel for the whole life of men. This renewal must take place both in the larger units of the Church and in the local congregations. The influence of worshipping congregations upon the problems of society is very great when those congregations include people from many social groups. If the Church can overcome the national and social barriers which now divide it, it can help society to overcome those barriers.

This is especially clear in the case of racial distinction. It is here that the Church has failed most lamentably, where it has reflected and then by its example sanctified the racial prejudice that is rampant in the world. And yet it is here that today its guidance concerning what God wills for it is especially clear. It knows that it must call society away from prejudice based upon race or colour and from the practices of discrimination and segregation as denials of justice and human dignity, but it cannot say a convincing word to society unless it takes steps to eliminate these practices from the Christian community because they contradict all that it believes about God's love for all His children.

There are occasions on which the churches, through their councils or through such persons as they may commission to speak on their behalf, should declare directly what they see to be the will of God for the public decisions of the hour. Such guidance will often take the form of warnings against concrete forms of injustice or oppression or social idolatry. They should also point to the main objectives toward which a particular society should move.

One problem is raised by the existence in several countries of Christian political parties. The Church as such should not be identified with any political party, and it must not act as though it were itself a political party. In general, the formation of such parties is hazardous because they easily confuse Christianity with the inherent compromises of politics. They may cut Christians off from the other parties which need the leaven of Christianity, and they may consolidate all who do not share the political principles of the Christian party not only against that party but against Christianity itself. Nevertheless, it may still be desirable in some situations for Christians to organize themselves into a political party for specific objectives, so long as they do not claim that it is the only possible expression of Christian loyalty in the situation.

But the social influence of the Church must come primarily from its influence upon its members through constant teaching and preaching of Christian truth in ways that illuminate the historical conditions in which men live and the problems which they face. The Church can be most effective in society as it inspires its members to ask in a new way what their Christian responsibility is whenever they vote or discharge the duties of public office, whenever they influence public opinion, whenever they make decisions as employers or as workers or in any other vocation to which they may be called. One of the most creative developments in the contemporary Church is the practice of groups of Christians facing much the same problems in their occupations to pray and take counsel together in order to find out what they should do as Christians.

In discussing the social function of the Church, Christians should always remember the great variety of situations in which the Church lives. Nations in which professing Christians are in the majority, nations in which the Church represents only a few per cent of the population, nations in which the Church lives under a hostile and oppressive government offer very different problems for the Church. It is one of the contributions of the ecumenical experience of recent years that churches under these contrasting conditions have come not only to appreciate one another's practices, but to learn from one another's failures and achievements and sufferings.

VI. *Conclusion*

There is a great discrepancy between all that has been said here and the possibility of action in many parts of the world. Obedience to God will be possible under all external circumstances, and no one need despair when conditions restrict greatly the area of responsible action. The responsible society of which we have spoken represents, however, the goal for which the churches in all lands must work, to the glory of the one God and Father of all, and looking for the day of God and a new earth, wherein dwelleth righteousness.

Further Readings

Primary Sources

J. H. Oldham (ed.). *Foundations of Ecumenical Social Thought; the Oxford Conference Report (1937).* Introduction by Harold Lunger. Philadelphia: Fortress Press, 1966.

World Council of Churches. *Man's Disorder and God's Design: The Amsterdam Assembly Series.* New York: Harper and Row, 1948.

———. *"Christians in the Technical and Social Revolutions of Our Time,"* World Conference on Church and Society. Geneva: World Council of Churches, 1967.

Secondary Sources

Brown, Robert M. *The Ecumenical Revolution.* Garden City, N.Y.: Doubleday, 1967.

Carter, Paul. *The Decline and Revival of the Social Gospel, 1920–1940.* Ithaca: Cornell University Press, 1954.

Duff, Edward. *The Social Thought of the World Council of Churches.* New York: Association Press, 1950.

Smith, H. Shelton, Handy, Robert T., and Loetscher, Lefferts (eds.). *American Christianity: An Historical Interpretation, with Representative Documents.* Vol. 2. New York: Scribner's, 1963, Chaps. 21, 22.

Chapter 17

ECUMENICAL ETHICS IN ROMAN CATHOLICISM

Parallel to Protestant ecumenical ethics traversed in the preceding chapter is a revolution in Roman Catholicism of major ethical importance. "Revolution" and "Catholicism" are not usually linked. A common popular image of Roman Catholic ethics is that of a bastion of conservatism, a walled-in castle of archaic, medieval rules, resistant to all changes of modern culture. Catholic morality is frequently identified with a prohibition of abortion and artificial contraception. Actually, while this may be the most publicized feature of Catholic moral theory, it is one aspect only of a deep concern of the Roman church over the disorders of twentieth century life and for the relevance of Christian norms for the recovery of its true order and health.

The modern Roman Catholic theory of the good society can be traced back through a series of papal encyclicals to the letter *Rerum Novarum* of Leo XIII in 1891, who addressed himself to the grievous problems of a Europe already far into the morass of the industrial revolution. From the scholastic tradition of Natural Law, the Pope drew guiding moral norms of common justice in property rights and the rights of workers in a way that identified Catholic economic policy neither with free enterprise capitalism nor with state socialism. Subsequent encyclicals, like *Quadregesimo Anno* (1931) of Pius XI, pursued this line further.

With the papacy of John XXIII (1959–1963), brief though it was, the church experienced a new infusion of vitality through the inspiration of his charismatic leadership. The term *aggiornamento* (or "modernization") befitted his own encyclicals, such as *Mater et Magistra* (1961) and *Pacem in Terris* (1963) and the ecumenical conference, the second Vatican Council (1962–65), which he convoked into session. The movement of Vatican II toward a more democratic political structure in the church, the open cordiality of Rome to non-Catholics and to "all men of good will," the glad acceptance of scientific and technological learning, all marked a new kind of ecumenicity and a momentum which has continued into the papacy of Paul VI (1963–), though some would interpret the contemporary period as one of reaction and the tightening of lines.

Distinctive Ethical Motifs

In order to comprehend the ethics of the social encyclicals and such a document as "The Pastoral Constitution on the Church in the Modern World" from Vatican II, it may be of help to review the characteristic motifs and premises that pervade their lines.

1. The chief resource which the encyclicals bring to social policy is the doctrine of natural law. (See Chapter 7 above.) The norms for the good society are written by God into the very constitution of man, distinguished from the animal by his reason and conscience. The innate or natural bent of every man to preserve his own life, to seek the good and avoid the evil, to take care of his children, for example, is supernatural in source and universal in scope. Natural law is both innate in man as creature and objective to his actual behavior at any particular moment, in that it sets the right form of order and the true terms of community between man and man by which his empirical behavior can be judged good or bad. The principles of natural law are supplemented by revelation and divine law. Emanating as they do from a single divine source, natural law and the law of Christ must be in accord. But the natural law premise does give a basis for a universal morality valid for Christian and non-Christian alike.

That there is indeed such a reason in man and such an

objective moral order of right relations is a premise argued *from* rather than argued *to*. Many a social scientist or cultural anthropologist would challenge the authority of this claim. But the resolute position of the Church is that belief in natural law is an indispensable foundation. Remove this premise from underneath morality, and there is left only caprice and chaos, with no criterion for judging right from wrong save convenience, or the interests of the strong.

2. The doctrine of man, or anthropology, posited in Roman Catholic ethics is a lofty one. Adam is a person of dignity, endowed with reason and conscience, the "crown" of creation. The worth of persons is the ethical end of all economic and political institutions and the criterion of their reformation. Thus Pope John begins *Pacem in Terris* with a Christian declaration of the rights of man. He appeals to the conscience of man to cooperate for the common good. Personalism is the Catholic rejoinder to what the Church claims is the dehumanizing quality in secular communism, where the person is submerged in the collective. On this point, Catholic anthropology is akin to Protestant ecumenical ethics. On the other hand, there is relatively little said in the encyclicals (though more at Vatican II) about man as sinner, his proclivity *not* to cooperate with his neighbor, his willful bent to violate the moral dictates of reason and conscience, and thus the necessity of framing the rules of society to limit his sin. From such a standpoint, a critic might also question how disinterestedly man actually does reason, how minded for the common good, or how much the sin of his will twists the reasoning of his mind to justify his partiality.

3. In contrast to the dialectical way of doing Christian ethics, where policy is framed partly as compromise to adjust colliding values and interests, Roman Catholic ethical theory, following in the scholastic tradition, pushes through seemingly irreconcilable opposites into a synthesis, a both-and resolution. The moral good for society is a harmony of the parts within the whole, like the Platonic ideal of justice, where each sector seeks the common good, even to subordinate private to public interest, whether this be at the dinner

table at home or at the negotiating table settling international disputes. The important principle of subsidiarity, entrusting initiative and authority locally rather than to the larger collective, anticipates a peaceful harmony of the parts on the premise of this synthesis.

4. Roman Catholic ethics centers on the primacy of the monogamous family as the archetypal institution of western society. The nuclear family is the setting in which alone authentic personality can flower. The fabric of the public society is no stronger than the quality of its homes, for here children are schooled in discipline, in right religious faith and ethics, in the ways of stable citizenship. Against all the forces of collectivism or of a sensate materialism which tend to disintegrate the cohesive family unit, the church poses a conservative ethic: the monogamous family as a sacramental institution, an indissoluble bond of fidelity, for the procreation of children. Permissive legislation on matters of divorce, abortion, and artificial modes of contraception are practices contravening the very laws of nature and the Christian reverence for the sacredness of life.

The Church and the World

One of the most marked changes in the modern Roman church concerns its attitude toward the world. In earlier chapters (5 and 6) extended examples were given of mystical and ascetic ethics, wherein the secular world is regarded as enemy to the Christian life, to be rejected ("Christ against culture") or transcended ("Christ above culture"). The spirit of *aggiornamento* in the stance of Pope John or the clerical leaders at Vatican II is quite different: a hearty worldliness, an appeal to welcome the goodness of the natural order, the marvels of science and technology, and the promises of man's art and culture. The world beyond this life, though still assumed as man's supernal home, is given relatively slight attention. The process of the domestication of Christian ethics evident in the whole sweep of its historical development characterizes current Catholicism almost as much as Protestantism.

Instead of aloofness or an imperious "triumphalism" that would call for the church to prescribe to the world the terms of life in community, there is a call for a dialogue of equals between the church and the secular institutions. The faithful may learn from the world all the skills of mind and hand that can make life humane and beautiful. They should be ready to learn, said Vatican II, even from "those who oppress the church and harass her in manifold ways." The world can learn from the church, on its part, its vision of the human ends to which technology should be turned, and the moral order of peace and justice which the political and economic kingdoms of the earth should seek and guard. In such a spirit of dialogue, the church puts aside its imperial image and takes the form of a servant, in faithfulness to its Lord who came as servant, not to be ministered unto, but to minister.

It is interesting to note what happens to the ascetic *motif* and the rigorous commands of the gospel in this process of secularizing Christian ethics. "Do not lay up for yourselves treasures on earth . . . but lay up for yourselves treasures in heaven" is no less exacting an ethic about possessions. But in Pope John's reading of this command the basic polarity is no longer between earth and heaven but between private acquisition and the public sharing of goods. The commandment of Christ becomes an injunction to charity and peace on earth. (*Mater et Magistra,* para. 121.) Likewise, in place of the medieval dual pattern of a higher call for the "religious," the priest or monk, to practice the "counsels of perfection," and the lesser way of the secular man, there is now a call for the lay witness to Christ for all the faithful in every worldly walk of life. In tones much like Luther's doctrine of vocation, Pope John reminds the faithful that "farming is an assignment from God with a sublime purpose." Vatican II proclaimed that "in the exercise of all their earthly activities, [Christians] can thereby gather their human, domestic, professional, social, and technical enterprises into one vital synthesis with religious values, under whose supreme direction all things are harmonized unto God's glory." (Vatican II: *Church in the Modern World,* para. 43.)

It is clear from even this rapid scan of the ecumenical ethics of Protestantism and Catholicism that there is a strong family resemblance between the two, a striking convergence in Christian ethical policy. On many matters of doctrine, worship, or church authority the gaps of difference are wide, but they fade in significance by comparison to the shared ethical consensus. Without sacrificing its claim that the church of Rome carries the divine truth, its new ecumenical spirit calls for dialogue and cooperation between the faithful and "separated brethren" (no longer "heretics") in making common cause to infuse the world with the spirit of Christ.

SOURCES

From

JOHN XXIII: *Pacem in Terris*

PART I

ORDER BETWEEN MEN

Every Man Is a Person with Rights and Duties

First of all, it is necessary to speak of the order which should exist between men. Any human society, if it is to be well-ordered and productive, must lay down as a foundation this principle, namely, that every human being is a person, that is, his nature is endowed with intelligence and free will. By virtue of this, he has rights and duties of his own, flowing directly and simultaneously from his very nature, which are therefore universal, inviolable and inalienable.

If we look upon the dignity of the human person in the light of divinely revealed truth, we cannot help but esteem it far more highly. For men are redeemed by the blood of

Jesus Christ, they are by grace the children and friends of God and heirs of eternal glory.

Rights

The Right to Life and a Worthy Standard of Living

Beginning our discussion of the rights of man, we see that every man has the right to life, to bodily integrity and to the means which are necessary and suitable for the proper development of life. These are primarily food, clothing, shelter, rest, medical care and, finally, the necessary social services. Therefore, a human being also has the right to security in cases of sickness, inability to work, widowhood, old age, unemployment, or in any other case in which he is deprived of the means of subsistence through no fault of his own.

Right Pertaining to Moral and Cultural Values

By the natural law every human being has the right to respect for his person, to his good reputation, the right to freedom in searching for truth and in expressing and communicating his opinions, and in pursuit of art, within the limits laid down by the moral order and the common good. And he has the right to be informed truthfully about public events.

The natural law also gives man the right to share in the benefits of culture, and therefore the right to a basic education and to technical and professional training in keeping with the stage of educational development in the country to which he belongs. Every effort should be made to insure that persons be enabled, on the basis of merit, to go on to higher studies, so that, as far as possible, they may occupy posts and take on responsibilities in human society in accordance with their natural gifts and the skills they have acquired.

The Right to Worship God According to One's Conscience

Every human being has the right to honor God according to the dictates of an upright conscience, and therefore the right to worship God privately and publicly. For, as Lactantius so clearly taught: We were created for the purpose of showing to the God who bore us the submission we owe Him, or recognizing Him alone, and of serving Him. We are obliged and bound by this duty to God. From this religion itself receives its name. And on this point our predecessor of immortal memory, Leo XIII, declared: "This genuine, this honorable freedom of the sons of God, which most nobly protects the dignity of the human person, is greater than any violence or injustice. It has always been sought by the church, and always most dear to her. This was the freedom which the apologists claimed with intrepid constancy, which the apologists defended with their writings, and which the martyrs in such numbers consecrated with their blood."

The Right to Choose Freely One's State of Life

Human beings have the right to choose freely the state of life which they prefer, and therefore the right to set up a family, with equal rights and duties for man and woman, and also the right to follow a vocation to the priesthood or the religious life.

The family, grounded on marriage freely contracted, monogamous and indissoluble, is and must be considered the first and essential cell of human society. To it must be given every consideration of an economic, social, cultural and moral nature, which will strengthen its stability and facilitate the fulfilment of its specific mission.

Parents, however, have a prior right in the support and education of their children.

Economic Rights

Human beings have the natural right to free initiative in the economic field and the right to work.

Indissolubly linked with those rights is the right to working conditions in which physical health is not endangered, morals are safeguarded and young people's normal development is not impaired. Women have the right to working conditions in accordance with their requirements and their duties as wives and mothers.

From the dignity of the human person, there also arises the right to carry on economic activities according to the degree of responsibility of which one is capable. Furthermore—and this must be specially emphasized—there is the right to a working wage, determined according to criterions of justice and sufficient, therefore, in proportion to the available resources, to give the worker and his family a standard of living in keeping with the dignity of the human person. In this regard, our predecessor Pius XII said: "To the personal duty to work imposed by nature, there corresponds and follows the natural right of each individual to make of his work the means to provide for his own life and the lives of his children. So profoundly is the empire of nature ordained for the preservation of man."

The right to private property, even of productive goods, also derives from the nature of man. This right, as we have elsewhere declared, is a suitable means for safeguarding the dignity of the human person and for the exercise of responsibility in all fields; it strengthens and gives serenity to family life, thereby increasing the peace and prosperity of the state.

However, it is opportune to point out that there is a social duty essentially inherent in the right of private property.

The Right of Meeting and Association

From the fact that human beings are by nature social, there arises the right of assembly and association. They have also the right to give the societies of which they are members the form they consider most suitable for the aim they have in view, and to act within such societies on their own initiative and on their own responsibility in order to achieve their desired objectives.

We ourselves stated in the encyclical "Mater et Magistra" that, for the achievement of ends which individual human beings cannot attain except by association, it is necessary and indispensable to set up a great variety of such intermediate groups and societies in order to guarantee for the human person a sufficient sphere of freedom and responsibility.

The Right to Emigrate and Immigrate

Every human being has the right to freedom of movement and of residence within the confines of his own country; and, when there are just reasons for it, the right to emigrate to other countries and take up residence there. The fact that one is a citizen of a particular state does not detract in any way from his membership of the human family as a whole, nor from his citizenship of the world community.

Political Rights

The dignity of the human person involves the right to take an active part in public affairs and to contribute one's part to the common good of the citizenry. For, as our predecessor of happy memory, Pius XII, pointed out: The human individual, far from being an object and, as it were, a merely passive element in the social order, is in fact, must be and must continue to be, its subject, its foundation and its end.

The human person is also entitled to a juridical protection of his rights, a protection that should be efficacious, impartial and inspired by the true norms of justice.

As our predecessor Pius XII teaches: That perpetual privilege proper to man, by which every individual has a claim to the protection of his rights, and by which there is assigned to each a definite and particular sphere of rights, immune from all arbitrary attacks, is the logical consequence of the order of justice willed by God.

Duties

Rights and Duties Necessarily Linked in the One Person

The natural rights with which we have been dealing are, however, inseparably connected, in the very person who is their subject, with just as many respective duties; and rights as well as duties find their source, their sustenance and their inviolability in the natural law which grants or enjoins them.

For example, the right of every man to life is correlative with the duty to preserve it; his right to a decent standard of living with the duty of living it becomingly; and his right to investigate the truth freely, with the duty of seeking it and of possessing it ever more completely and profoundly.

Reciprocity of Rights and Duties Between Persons

Once this is admitted, it is also clear that in human society to one man's right there corresponds a duty in all other persons: the duty, namely, of acknowledging and respecting the right in question. For every fundamental human right draws its indestructible moral force from the natural law, which, in granting it, imposes a corresponding obligation. Those, therefore, who claim their own rights, yet altogether forget or neglect to carry out their respective duties, are people who build with one hand and destroy with the other. . . .

Social Life in Truth, Justice, Charity and Freedom

A political society is to be considered well-ordered, beneficial and in keeping with human dignity if it is grounded on truth. As the Apostle Paul exhorts us: "Away with falsehood then; let everyone speak out the truth to his neighbor; membership of the body binds us to one another." This demands that reciprocal rights and duties be sincerely recognized. Furthermore, human society will be such as we have just described it, if the citizens, guided by justice, apply themselves seriously to respecting the rights of others and discharging their own duties; if they are moved by such fervor of charity as to make their own the needs of others and share with others their own goods: if, finally, they work for a progressively closer fellowship in the world of spiritual values. Human society is realized in freedom, that is to say, in ways and means in keeping with the dignity of its citizens, who accept the responsibility of their actions, precisely because they are by nature rational beings.

Human society, venerable brothers and beloved children, ought to be regarded above all as a spiritual reality: in which men communicate knowledge to each other in the light of truth; in which they can enjoy their rights and fulfil their duties, and are inspired to strive for moral good. Society should enable men to share in and enjoy every legitimate expression of beauty, and encourage them constantly to pass on to others all that is best in themselves, while they strive to make their own the spiritual achievements of others. These are the spiritual values which continually give life and basic orientation to cultural expressions, economic and social institutions, political movements and forms, laws, and all other structures by which society is outwardly established and constantly developed.

God and the Moral Order

The order which prevails in society is by nature moral. Grounded as it is in truth, it must function according to the norms of justice, it should be inspired and perfected by mutual love, and finally it should be brought to an ever more refined and human balance in freedom.

Now an order of this kind, whose principles are universal, absolute and unchangeable, has its ultimate source in the one true God, who is personal and transcends human nature. Inasmuch as God is the first truth and the highest good, He alone is that deepest source from which human society can draw its vitality, if that society is to be well-ordered, beneficial, and in keeping with human dignity. As St. Thomas Aquinas says: "Human reason is the norm of the human will, according to which its goodness is measured, because reason derives from the eternal law which is the divine reason itself. It is evident then that the goodness of the human will depends much more on the eternal law than on human reason."

Characteristics of the Present

Our age has three distinctive characteristics. First of all, the working classes have gradually gained ground in economic and public affairs. They began by claiming their rights in the socio-economic sphere; they extended their action then to claims on the political level; and finally applied themselves to the acquisition of the benefits of a more refined culture. Today, therefore, workers all over the world refuse to be treated as if they were irrational objects without freedom, to be used at the arbitrary disposition of others. They insist that they be always regarded as men with a share in every sector of human society: in the social and economic sphere, in the fields of learning and culture, and in public life.

Secondly, it is obvious to everyone that women are now taking a part in public life. This is happening more rapidly, perhaps, in nations of Christian civilization, and, more slowly but broadly, among peoples who have inherited other traditions or cultures. Since women are becoming ever more conscious of their human dignity, they will not tolerate being treated as mere material instruments, but demand rights befitting a human person both in domestic and in public life.

Finally, the modern world, as compared with the recent past, has taken on an entirely new appearance in the field of social and political life. For since all nations have either achieved or are on the way to achieving independence, there will soon no longer exist a world divided into nations that rule others and nations that are subject to others.

Men all over the world have today—or will soon have—the rank of citizens in independent nations. No one wants to feel subject to political powers located outside his own country or ethnic group. Thus in very many human beings the inferiority complex which endured for hundreds and thousands of years is disappearing, while in others there is an attenuation and gradual fading of the corresponding superiority complex which had its roots in social-economic privileges, sex or political standing.

On the contrary, the conviction that all men are equal by reason of their natural dignity has been generally accepted. Hence racial discrimination can no longer be justified, at least doctrinally or in theory. And this is of fundamental importance and significance for the formation of human society according to those principles which we have outlined above. For, if a man becomes conscious of his rights, he must become equally aware of his duties. Thus he who possesses certain rights has likewise the duty to claim those rights as marks of his dignity, while all others have the obligation to acknowledge those rights and respect them.

When the relations of human society are expressed in terms of rights and duties, men become conscious of spiritual values, understand the meaning and significance of truth, justice, charity and freedom, and become deeply aware that they belong to this world of values. Moreover, when moved by such concerns, they are brought to a better knowledge of the true God who is personal and transcendent, and thus they make the ties that bind them to God the solid foundations and supreme criterion of their lives, both of that life which they live interiorly in the depths of their own souls and of that in which they are united to other men in society.

Part II

Relations Between Individuals and the Public Authorities

Necessity and Divine Origin of Authority

Human society can be neither well-ordered nor prosperous unless it has some people invested with legitimate authority to preserve its institutions and to devote themselves as far as is necessary to work and care for the good of all. These, however, derive their authority from God, as St. Paul teaches in the words, "Authority comes from God alone." These words of St. Paul are explained thus by St. John Chrysostom: What are you saying? Is every ruler appointed by God? I do not say that, he replies, for I am not dealing now with individual rulers, but with authority itself. What I say is that it is the divine wisdom and not mere chance that has ordained that there should be government, that some should command and others obey. Moreover, since God made men social by nature, and since no society can hold together unless some one be over all directing all to strive earnestly for the common good, every civilized community must have a ruling authority, and this authority, no less than society itself, has its source in nature, and has, consequently, God for its authority.

But authority is not to be thought of as a force lacking all control. Indeed, since it is the power to command according to right reason, authority must derive its obligatory force from the moral order, which in turn has God for its first source and final end. Wherefore our predecessor of happy memory, Pius XII, said: "That same absolute order of beings and their ends which presents man as an autonomous person, that is, as the subject of inviolable duties and rights, and as at once the basis of society and the purpose for which it exists also includes the state as necessary society invested with the authority without which it could not come into being or live. . . . And since this absolute order, as we learn from sound reason, especially from the Christian faith, can have no origin save in a personal God who is our Creator, it follows that the dignity of the state's authority is due to its sharing to some extent in the authority of God himself.

Where the civil authority uses as its only or its chief means either threats and fear of punishment or promises of rewards, it cannot effectively move men to promote the common good of all. Even if it did so move them, this would be altogether opposed to their dignity as men, endowed with reason and free will. As authority is chiefly concerned with moral force, it follows that civil authority must appeal primarily to the conscience of individual citizens, that is, to each one's duty to collaborate readily for the common good of all. Since by nature all men are equal in human dignity, it follows that no one may be coerced to perform interior acts. That is in the power of God alone, who sees and judges the hidden designs of men's hearts. Those therefore who have authority in the state may oblige men in conscience only if their authority is intrinsically related with the authority of God and shares in it.

By this principle the dignity of the citizens is protected. When, in fact, men obey their rulers, it is not all as men that they obey them, but through their obedience it is God, the provident Creator of all things, whom they reverence, since he has decreed that men's dealings with one another should be regulated by an order which he himself has established. Moreover, in showing this due reverence to God, men not only do not debase themselves but rather perfect and ennoble themselves. For to serve God is to rule.

Since the right to command is required by the moral order and has its source in God, it follows that, if civil authorities legislate for or allow anything that is contrary to that order and therefore contrary to the will of God, neither the laws made nor the authorizations granted can be binding on the consciences of the citizens, since God has more right to be obeyed than men. Otherwise, authority breaks down completely and results in shameful abuse. As St. Thomas Aquinas teaches: Human law has the true nature of law only insofar as it corresponds to right reason, and therefore is derived from the eternal law. Insofar as it falls short of right reason, a law is said to be a wicked law. And so, lacking the true nature of law, it is rather a kind of violence.

It must not be concluded, however, because authority comes from God, that therefore men have no right to choose those who are to rule the state, to decide the form of government and to determine both the way in which authority is to be exercised and its limits. It is thus clear that the doctrine which we have set forth is fully consonant with any true democratic regime.

Attainment of the Common Good

Purposes of the Public Authority

Individual citizens and intermediate groups are obliged to make their specific contributions to the common welfare.

One of the chief consequences of this is that they must bring their own interests into harmony with the needs of the community, and must dispose of their goods and their services as civil authorities have prescribed, in accord with the norms of justice, in due form and within the limits of their competence. This they must do by means of formally perfect actions, the content of which must be morally good, or at least capable of being directed towards good.

Indeed, since the whole reason for the existence of civil authorities is the realization of the common good, it is clearly necessary that, in pursuing this objective, they should respect its essential elements, and at the same time conform their laws to the needs of a given historical situation.

Assuredly, the ethnic characteristics of the various human groups are to be respected as constituent elements of the common good, but these values and characteristics by no means exhaust the content of the common good. For the common good is intimately bound up with human nature. It can never exist fully and completely unless, its intimate nature and realization being what they are, the human person is taken into account.

In the second place, the very nature of the common good requires that all members of the political community be entitled to share in it, although in different ways according to each one's tasks, merits and circumstances. For this reason, every civil authority must take pains to promote the common good of all, without preference for any single citizen or civil group. As our predecessor of immortal memory, Leo XIII, has said: The civil power must not serve the advantage of any one individual or of some few persons, inasmuch as it was established for the common good of all. Considerations of justice and equity, however, can at times demand that those involved in civil government give more attention to the less fortunate members of the community, since they are less able to defend their rights and to assert their legitimate claims.

In this context, we judge that attention should be called to the fact that the common good touches the whole man, the needs both of his body and of his soul. Hence it follows that the civil authorities must undertake to effect the common good by ways and means that are proper to them. That is, while respecting the hierarchy of values, they should promote simultaneously both the material and the spiritual welfare of the citizens.

These principles are clearly contained in the doctrine stated in our encyclical, "Mater et Magistra," where we emphasized that the common good of all embraces the sum total of those conditions of social living whereby men are enabled to achieve their own integral perfection more fully and more easily.

Men, however, composed as they are of bodies and immortal souls, can never in this mortal life succeed in satisfying all their needs or in attaining perfect happiness. Therefore, all efforts made to promote the common good, far from endangering the eternal salvation of men, ought rather to serve to promote it.

Responsibilities of the Public Authority, and Rights and Duties of Individuals

It is agreed that in our time the common good is chiefly guaranteed when personal rights and duties are maintained. The chief concern of civil authorities must therefore be to insure that these rights are acknowledged, respected, coordinated with other rights, defended and promoted, so that in this way each one may more easily carry out his duties. For to safeguard the inviolable rights of the human person, and to facilitate the fulfilment of its duties, should be the essential office of every public authority.

This means that, if any government does not acknowledge the rights of man or violates them, it not only fails its duty, but its orders completely lack juridical force.

Reconciliation and Protection of Rights and Duties of Individuals

One of the fundamental duties of civil authorities, therefore, is to coordinate social relations in such fashion that the exercise of one man's rights does not threaten others in the exercise of their own rights nor hinder them in the fulfilment of their duties. Finally, the rights of all should be effectively safeguarded and, if they have been violated, completely restored.

Duty of Promoting the Rights of Individuals

It is also demanded by the common good that civil authorities should make earnest efforts to bring about a situation in which individual citizens can easily exercise their rights and fulfil their duties as well. For experience has taught us that, unless these authorities take suitable action with regard to economic, political and cultural matters, inequalities between the citizens tend to become more and more widespread, especially in the modern world, and as a result human rights are rendered totally ineffective, and the fulfilment of duties is compromised.

It is therefore necessary that the Administration give wholehearted and careful attention to the social as well as to the economic progress of the citizens, and to the development, in keeping with the development of the productive system, of such essential services as the building of roads, transportation, communications, water supply, housing, public health, education, facilitation of the practice of religion and recreational facilities. It is necessary also that governments make efforts to see that insurance systems are made available to the citizens, so that, in case of misfortune or increased family responsibilities, no person will be without the necessary means to maintain a decent standard of living. The government should make similarly effective efforts to see that those who are able to work can find employment in keeping with their aptitudes, and that each worker receives a wage in keeping with the laws of justice and equity. It should be equally the concern of civil authorities to insure that workers be allowed their proper responsibility in the work undertaken in industrial organization, and to facilitate the establishment of intermediate groups which will make social life richer and more effective. Finally, it should be possible for all citizens to share as far as they are able in their country's cultural advantages.

Harmonious Relation Between Public Authority's Two Forms of Intervention

The common good requires that civil authorities maintain a careful balance between coordinating and protecting the rights of the citizens, on the one hand, and promoting them, on the other. It should not happen that certain individuals or social groups derive special advantage from the fact that their rights have received preferential protection. Nor should it happen that governments, in seeking to protect these rights, become obstacles to their full expression and free use. For this principle must always be retained: that state activity in the economic field, no matter what its breadth or depth may be, ought not to be exercised in such a way as to curtail an individual's freedom of personal initiative. Rather it should work to expand that freedom as much as possible by the effective protection of the essential personal rights of each and every individual.

The same principle should inspire the various steps which governments take in order to make it possible for the citizens more easily to exercise their rights and fulfil their duties in every sector of social life.

Structure and Operation of Public Authority

It is impossible to determine, once and for all, what is the most suitable form of government, or how civil authorities can most effectively fulfill their respective functions, i.e., the legislative, judicial and executive functions of the state. In determining the structure and operation of government which a state is to have, great weight has to be given to the historical background and circumstances of given political communities, circumstances which will vary at different times and in different places. We consider, however, that it is in keeping with the innate demands of human nature that the state should take a form which embodies the three-fold division of powers corresponding to the three principal functions of public authority. In that type of state, not only the official functions of government but also the mutual relations between citizens and public officials are set down according to the law, which in itself affords protection to the citizens both in the enjoyment of their rights and in the fulfillment of their duties.

If, however, this political and juridical structure is to produce the advantages which may be expected of it, public officials must strive to meet the problems which arise in a way that conforms both to the complexities of the situation and the proper exercise of their function. This requires that, in constantly changing conditions, legislators never forget the norms of morality, or constitutional provisions, or the objective requirements of the common good. Moreover, executive authorities must coordinate the activities of society with discretion, with a full knowledge of the law and after a careful consideration of circumstances, and the courts must administer justice impartially and without being influenced by favoritism or pressure. The good order of society also demands that individual citizens and intermediate organizations should be effectively protected by law whenever they have rights to be exercised or obligations to be fulfilled. This protection should be granted to citizens both in their dealings with each other and in their relations with government agencies.

Law and Conscience

It is unquestionable that a legal structure in conformity with the moral order and corresponding to the level of development of the political community is of great advantage to achievement of the common good.

And yet, social life in the modern world is so varied, complex and dynamic that even a juridical structure which has been prudently and thoughtfully established is always inadequate for the needs of society.

It is also true that the relations of the citizens with each other, of citizens and intermediate groups with public authorities, and finally of the public authorities with one another are often so complex and so sensitive that they cannot be regulated by inflexible legal provisions. Such a situation therefore demands that the civil authorities have clear ideas about the nature and extent of their official duties if they wish to maintain the existing juridical structure in its basic elements and principles, and at the same time meet the exigencies of social life, adapting their legislation to the changing social scene and solving new problems. They must be men of great equilibrium and integrity, competent and courageous enough to see at once what the situation requires and to take necessary action quickly and effectively. . . .

Further Readings

Primary Sources

Papal Encyclicals: Leo XIII: *Rerum Novarum;* Pius XI: *Quadregesimo Anno;* John XXIII: *Mater et Magistra* and *Pacem in Terris,* available in Anne Fremantle (ed.): *The Social Teachings of the Church* (New York: New American Library, 1963), and in many other editions.

Abbott, Walter M. (ed.). *The Documents of Vatican II* (New York: American Press, 1966), especially *Pastoral Constitution on the Church in the Modern World.*

Murray, John Courtney. *We Hold These Truths.* New York: Sheed and Ward, 1960.

Secondary Sources

Ford, John C., and Kelly, Gerald. *Contemporary Moral Theology,* Vol. 1. Westminster, Md.: Newman Press, 1958.

Rynne, Xavier (pseudo.). *Vatican Council II.* New York: Farrar, Straus and Giroux, 1968.

Chapter 18

CURRENT TRENDS

The trends in Christian ethics through the decades spanning midtwentieth century are difficult to trace, not only because they are so near at hand, but because of the complexity and magnitude of the revolutions in theology and culture which they reflect. No less now than in the past, Christian ethics is best understood as a mediating or "relational" discipline, finding the truth of its assertions in dialogue with cognate disciplines of human analysis and reflection. The Christian definition of the ethically good must currently pay attention to what is explored in the sciences of man, such as the psychologist's concepts of selfhood and identity, or the philosopher's analysis of moral language and of the perennial problems of knowledge and existence. The most significant disciplines cognate to Christian ethics are Christian theology, on the one side, as it deals with the root and ground of Christian moral norms, and the social sciences, on the other side, describing the dynamics of the social order in which moral decision is made. To consider the issues of theology is to ask about the ultimate "why" of Christian action. To consider the patterns of economic and political power in twentieth century culture is to ask about the limiting or permissive circumstances of Christian choice. Questions about what is possible under these circumstances must be addressed in order to find viable answers for the "how" of Christian decision in the world. How one "does" Christian ethics requires technical competence about the workings of cause-effect sequence in the affairs of man, as well as the distinctive ethical "how" of a Christian life-style. When it loses contact with social science, ethics becomes remote, abstract, and irrelevant. When it is out of touch with theology, it loses its moorings in faith and may drift into formal legalism or normless expediency.

The perennial questions of theology standing close by ethics have received major attention and drastic revision in this century. Conventional creeds, dutifully recited in the churches, rarely incite ethical action. Yet the great affirmations behind the creeds about the nature of God and Christ, of man and his destiny, of the Bible and its authority, and of the church, have been addressed by many formidable thinkers who have been "doing" theology in a manner responsible both to the classical heritage and to the searchings of contemporary man for direction and sure footing.

In their eagerness for social reform and their confidence in the potentials of man, the spokesmen for the liberal ethics of the Kingdom of God were at some points quite casual about certain traditional theological insights of the Reformation. As noted in Chapter 16, one clear trend of twentieth century theology has been the recovery of several of these Protestant motifs, themselves derived from the Pauline and Augustinian heritage. These faiths affect profoundly the tone and style of Christian ethical decision.

The Sovereignty of God

The first such doctrine has to do with the character of God's rule in history. For Walter Rauschenbusch, the Social Gospel was the permanent element in Christianity, and the doctrine of God should be altered as the dependent variable, to fit the Social Gospel. Among the most influential Protestant thinkers of the twentieth century, such theologians as Karl Barth (1886–1968), Emil Brunner (1889–1966) and Dietrich Bonhoeffer (1906–1945) affirmed the sovereignty of God as uniquely revealed in Christ as the only sure foundation of the Christian life. In the divine-human encounter the human is the dependent variable. In place of continuity between the human and the divine and the immanence of God in the natural world, Barth counterposed discontinuity between man and God and the divine transcendence. Christian ethics cannot be built on any natural reason or conscience, however refined. It rests on the incarnation of God in Christ. Barth's *Church Dogmatics* (1932–59; English translation, 1936–62), the most extensive systematic statement of the Christian faith in the modern period, spells out the Protestant convictions about the radical sovereignty of God, the divine grace overbridging in Christ the chasm between God and sinful man, the Christocentric character of the new life of the believer, and the church as the community of sinners being forgiven. The Christian life is the fruit of justification by grace through faith, to be practiced in the "orders" of family, state, and economy, with resolute confidence and courage in the face of the secular earthly kingdoms such as Barth himself challenged in the Nazi regime in Germany.

The testimony of Bonhoeffer, who was involved in a plot to assassinate Hitler and died at the hands of the Nazis, wrote from his prison cell of the need for a "worldly" Christianity and a costly discipleship, against the soothing nostrums of "cheap grace" offered by conventional churches.

Emil Brunner, a Swiss theologian, while somewhat more cordial to natural morality than was Barth, followed many parallel Protestant lines. *The Divine Imperative* (1932, English translation, 1937) was a restatement of Christian morality in terms of the Reformed tradition. The first and last affirmation of faith is to point to the continual rule of a creating and redeeming God. Because God's rule is dynamic, forever making all things new, Christian morality is not a set of rules or a list of virtues. The single ethical quality of the Christian life is *agape*. Obedient and grateful love to God must issue in service to neighbor within the orders of society. The particular form such service will take cannot be specified exactly ahead of time. In some of his concepts, Brunner anticipated the "situation ethics" school. But the major concept here to note is that the ethically good is defined as a divine imperative: it depends utterly upon the faith in the character of God's rule.

The Nature of Human Nature

Secondly, the view of human nature has undergone considerable shift and revision. The tragic events of this century, the warfares of class and nation and race, together with the probings of psychologists and novelists and dramatists into the secret soul, have brought to light the dark and passionate aspects of human nature. Man's actions reveal a creature much less rational and benevolent than that assumed by the disciples of the Enlightenment. Reinhold Niebuhr (1892–1971), in his famous *Nature and Destiny of Man* (1941, 1943), and in numerous penetrating commentaries on the crises of the times, challenged in the name of classical Christian doctrine many of the confident assumptions about man and his progress carried over from the nineteenth century. As creature, created in the image of God for a high destiny, he is also "fallen," a sinful rebel who defies the sovereignty of God, bedevilling his existence by his individual and collective egocentricity, rendering all his social relations morally ambiguous and his motives deviously mixed. To speak of Christianizing the social order by simply extending Christian good will from the private to the public sector becomes utopian and delusive, for it overlooks this dark taint in man's will. Niebuhr recognized that social policy should indeed incarnate the benevolent impulse of neighbor-love, but also it must set checks and restraints upon men's collective, colliding self-interests to keep at best a precarious, "rough justice" on earth, necessarily less than the perfect concord of heaven. This is the anthropological base for Niebuhr's "realistic" style of Christian ethics.

The inner, psychological aspect of the Christian view of man has been probed in another direction by Reinhold's brother, H. Richard Niebuhr (1894–1962), for many years professor of Christian ethics at Yale University. Especially intriguing to Richard Niebuhr were the existential, psychological roots of action, revealing man primarily as a relational, affectional, responding being, one whose actions spring out of the trusts and loyalties of his heart. With this relational premise, Niebuhr defines moral choices as man's responses to whatever he takes in trust to be supremely real and good. Thus among Christians, as spelled out in *The Responsible Self* (1963) and *Radical Monotheism and Western Culture* (1960), the ethically good is faithful, trusting action toward neighbor befitting the action of God toward man in history, as Creator, Judge, and Redeemer.

The Direction of History

The third premise of morality to undergo drastic revision is the concept of the direction and outcome of human history. In terms of St. Paul's triad of virtues, how are faith and love related to hope? The strong confidence of the Kingdom of God ethic was in progress, the faith that the movement of the human venture, however painful and slow, was on an upward inclined plane, toward the realization of the Christian society of peace and brotherhood on earth. Such a buoyant eschatology has been challenged in the twentieth century, both by historians and theologians and more tellingly by the devastating events of history themselves that have dashed this particular form of the human hope. Though the faith in progress is still sounded in political and business rhetoric, it has disappeared from theological discourse.

The search among Christian thinkers has been toward another kind of eschatology and another spring of action beyond man's fluctuations between hope and despair. From the Bible has been recovered a view of historical movement stressing the precarious character of human accomplishment, the equidistance of every moment in time from the citadel of heaven and the abyss of hell, the fateful urgency of present choice, a view of man's call under the Providence of God that can give permanent validity to his faithful decisions, and establish the work of his hands, whether they succeed or fail in the course of time. What bends the bow of moral action is a tension not between present possibility and future realization, *along* the line of time, but between God's present command and the human potential for response, *across* the line of time. By the light of this faith, history is seen by the metaphor of a fateful arena of human choices for or against the Kingdom of God, where each epoch hangs in the balance between civilization and catastrophe, order and chaos. The current revival of a "theology of hope" among certain continental theologians like Wolfhart Pannenburg and Jürgen Moltmann rests its case upon biblical eschatology, an expectation of a future kingdom promised in the Resurrection and brought by the power of God, not of a human utopia brought by the ingenuity and good will of man.

Wisdom From the World

We have noted earlier that the distinctive feature of Christian ethical theory in the modern period derives from the confluence of the revived theological insights of the Reformation with the secular thought of the nineteenth and twentieth centuries. The Social Gospel had absorbed many of the insights of Marx and other students of western society. The ecumenical thought both of Protestantism and Catholicism has been strongly infused with this environmentalism. From this point on, the Christian conception of the good life is irrevocably a social ethic. It takes full account of the impingement of the dynamic forces of social environment upon the human self as well as the potentiality of man, by the grace of his endowed freedom, to shape the character of that environment for good or ill. No longer may the Christian retreat from the world into a private purity, or, in the prospect of his heavenly destination, regard the secular world as insignificant or ephemeral.

The culture of New York City is a long way from Nazareth. In contrast to the relatively simple pattern of domestic and economic relations which was the setting of biblical ethics, the world of the twentieth century Christian is vastly more complex, where the interdependence of life with life makes each man his brother's keeper in ways unimaginable in Eden or Palestine or even medieval Europe. The geographically remote neighbor is brought near. The needs of the Vietnam peasant, the South African mine worker, and the Alaskan Indian impinge on the conscience of the American with the same urgency as the needs of the neighbor down the hall. The policies that set the terms of interracial, interclass, international relations are at the discretion of each self, in his or her daily decision as a parent, as consumer and producer, as voter and citizen. Questions about private character and public policy interpenetrate, making obsolete the old distinction between "individual" and "social" ethics.

A poignant paradox arises: the members of the family of man are now highly interdependent upon each other, daily making decisions that affect the well-being of the far neighbor as much as the near. Yet in a technological, mass society, the traffic is highly impersonal, desensitized, mechanical. Man's charity to his neighbor is formalized. The neighbor is not known in the bond of compassion; he becomes a charity case, to be "handled" by the proper agency. The task then in Christian choice becomes doubly difficult: how to infuse the impersonal policies of systems and structures with the personal and human qualities of Christian love?

Christian worldly decision becomes even more difficult and puzzling because the process of secularization has made Christianity a minority movement. To be sure, authentic Christianity has always been, in a certain sense, in the minority. Yet the avowed moral norms honored in Western Christendom have been, well into the twentieth century, those of the Hebrew-Christian faith. These premises no longer hold good. In world terms, the so-called "Christian" nations make up about one fourth of the nations around the globe. And within "Christendom," whatever may be the statistics for church membership, and whatever be the prevalence of religious rhetoric in common talk, for a world "come of age" the moral rules of the game are actually set by those who no longer accept the Christian faith as normative. If Christendom be no longer in allegiance to the mind of Christ, in faith or practice, how does the Christian operate in his minority role? How does he cope with the militant foes of Christianity? How does he relate his theocentric morality to that of the conscientious humanist who might champion the ethics of Christianity but dispense with its theology as intellectually decrepit baggage?

Contextual Ethics

It is within the bewilderment of this secularized setting that a major debate has arisen over so-called "situation" or "contextual" ethics, a debate best understood as contended between the polarities of freedom and order.

When it comes to stating how one moves from Christian norms to social policy, one group of ethicists, such as Bishop John Robinson or Joseph Fletcher (*Situation Ethics,* 1966), are struck by the irrelevance of the conventional rules, however time-honored and sacred, to the unprecedented requirements of choice. The Christian simply cannot apply biblical commands to this or that case. The Gospel economic injunctions, for example, do not fit the hard choices to be made in an industrialized, affluent society. But the alternative to legalism, they affirm, is not lawlessness. The broad mandate of the Great Commandment, the norm of love, is the absolute imperative. This has to be applied in novel ways, however, with all the risks of freedom and the discretion of prudent judgment brought to bear on the exigencies of the moment, bending principles to serve the good of persons rather than bending persons to principles, however right. The specific empirical context, with all its novelty and dense ambiguity, determines how love is to operate.

Other Christian ethicists warn of the perils of contextualism, at least in its simplified form. Thinkers like Paul Ramsey and John C. Bennett grant readily that there is need for constant flexibility and fresh applications to new occasions, but the norm of love just by itself is too slippery, too amorphous to supply clear guidance. There are derivative guideline principles which Christian ethics provides at the crossroads of choice. Moreover, say the "principled" ethicists, there are continuities between the past and the present, certain persisting dilemmas of life and traits of human nature as real as the discontinuities. No serious moral quandary is entirely unprecedented. Lest Christian love fall into sheer improvisation on the spot, the norms of historic Christian moral reflection should be brought to bear.

The discussion about contextual ethics has been called correctly a "misplaced debate" if the matter is read as an open-or-shut case between the view that empirical context alone determines what love should do, versus a legalism which would prescribe the right as a list of Christian rules carved in stone. It falsifies the debate to cast it as a choice between opposite mental ailments: the arthritis of legalism or the vertigo of relativity. Actually, there is considerable consensus underneath the points in dispute. It is granted by all that the day of closed systems of Christian ethics is past, that all attempts to define the responsibilities of the Christian life must be sensitive to the changing cultural context in order to make out proximate and relative criteria. But also, there is recognition that the ultimate context of choice derives from the theological faith. So, as before, the current debate has served to confirm our original thesis that Christian ethics moves in a double context, between the Christian faith and the empirical facts of culture, deriving its permanent answers to "why" from the former, and its relative answers to the "whats" in part from the latter.

On the Frontiers of Christian Ethics

In the latter part of the present century the following issues stand high on the agenda for study and reflection and testing in action:

(1) Shadowing the contextual ethics debate is the perennial problem of freedom versus authority. Authentic freedom, all Christian thinkers would agree, is lawful freedom, action in obedience to the ultimate authority of God. Anything less is betrayed into the license of anarchy. But the next question follows hard on: what mediate or proximate authority on earth should prevail to discriminate between

the objective will of God and the subjective conscience of the individual? Church or Councils, the Bible, Reason, Christ, the Spirit, the mystic vision, the Inner Light? There are difficulties in taking any one of these as exclusively final. The testimony of them all has never been unanimous. If the Pope in Rome seems fallible to a protestant Catholic, on some such issue as priestly celibacy or abortion, to what higher court of appeal may he in conscience have redress? If the Bible is in some sense authoritative to the Protestant's conscience, as the unique revelation of God, how is he to delineate the definitive Word among its sometimes contradictory words? Does he employ an extra-biblical authority, or is there an intrabiblical norm? As for Reason, since Freud's discernment of the subrational springs of action and Marx's detection of ideology, modern man can no longer ask: what does Reason say? He must ask rather: whose reasons? What partiality of will or class do his reasons betray? Jesus Christ alone, then? The "mind of Christ"? With Barth, many Protestants would agree on this authority as all-sufficient. But there are problems here too. Which of the several portraits of Christ in the New Testament? The Christ of St. Paul, St. John, or of the synoptic gospels? Christ the criminal or Christ the cosmic King? Or if one should accept the findings of church councils, ancient or modern, how are we to be assured that a majority vote should be more authoritative and closer to the will of God than the conscientious dissent of a minority? *Vox populi, vox dei?* Kierkegaard may be right after all: "The crowd is untruth."

The Protestant principle, as Paul Tillich reminds us, questions any finite, conditioned authority when it claims to stand in for the unconditioned will of God. In the last analysis, then, the inner voice of conscience has the final word. Yet the private moral persuasions of the lone conscience do not come out of the blue, like "the swoop of a gull." They are derived partly from and must be checked against the moral experience of the Christian *koinonia*. Christians are inclined conscientiously to read that experience differently. Yet the loner cannot be his own final court of appeal. So, the issue of freedom and authority is always open, and the best possible working provisional answers must be given by each generation of seekers and believers.

(2) A second major issue is that of determining ethical norms for Christian social policy: how to move from the absolute norm of *agape* love to proximate policies of justice in societal interaction? The attempt to translate love for the single neighbor unilaterally into justice for many neighbors multi-laterally is not a simple arithmetical process of addition. In between love and justice lie many tangled issues of preference and priority, in the balancing and weighing of competing group interests and needs, in an economy of moral scarcity, where it would seem one is always having to rob Peter to pay Paul. How to reconcile love and justice?

Students of Christian ethics have approached the love-justice problem in different ways. Some, in the liberal Protestant tradition, would still try to pursue a single ethic: justice is love extended out from good will shown to the back-fence neighbor to a "good-neighbor" foreign policy of the United States. Justice is simply love multiplied. Others would adopt the Lutheran heritage of "two kingdoms," the dualism of gospel and law, wherein the spirit of love holds good for the private sector of life, the spirit of justice for the public. Roman Catholic moral theory, as we have seen, relies on natural law as the basis for justice and order in social policy, supplemented by the gospel norm of *agape*. The school of "Christian realism" associated with the name of Reinhold Niebuhr espouses a dialectical relation of love and justice, where a "rough" justice in social policy is the necessarily partial, deflected, and ambiguous expression of pure *agape*. Though no statute law can express what sacrificial and disinterested Christian love would ask, its justice should be as sensitive and gracious as possible. In the field of politics, "the art of the possible," such realism can move in between pure love and sheer pragmatic expediency and incarnate a responsible integrity within the required compromises that are the stuff of politics in practice.

(3) The final ethical issue of major moment concerns the

use of power. Though perennial, it is posed in the modern era with an apocalyptic urgency by the developments in science and technology that have heightened immeasurably the human potential in the uses of nature for either ruin or redemption.

Power itself, whether physical, technical, intellectual, psychological, economic, or political is one of the "givens" of mortal life. In a theological world-view, it is a good aspect of the order of creation, entrusted to man in all the risks of his freedom, with no guarantee of its beneficent use. Power is highly precarious, just as readily turned to destroy as to create community.

The technology of the machine is the invention of human ingenuity to subdue the earth and release man from the drudgery of a primitive culture. This has been the redeeming, the humanizing result of technology. But in the process, man has become mastered by the machine, victimized and brutalized by its demands, his spirit trapped in the concrete jungles of his cities, huddled in terror under the dark threat of nuclear weapons. Industrialization and urbanization have disordered man's relation to his environment. His exploitation of the good earth, his only home, has produced the ecological crisis, threatening not only the quality of his life but even human existence itself. If it is not yet too late, there is urgent need for a Christian ethic of stewardship that can restore the right balance of man with nature.

Closely related is the problem of the use of economic power in the production and consumption of goods. Its distribution has proved to be much more complex than as posed at the Oxford Conference in the debate between the advocates of private vs. public ownership and control of property. The balancing of the economic interests among the various segments in the economy, the reduction in the cruel disparity between rich and poor, both within the nation and among the nations of the earth, the dialectical tension between quality of life and quantitative criteria of economic growth and health, the protection of the worth of persons from exploitation in consumer engineering—these are all matters that do not admit of solution by the sheer weight of economic facts or the technical decisions of the computer. The answers derive from the value-systems of men, or their ethical priorities in relating means to ends and material goods to spiritual good, and from their faith as to where man's authentic treasure lies.

The problem of the Christian use of power is also evident in the area of race relations, particularly on the current American scene, in black-white relations. The movement from a segregated to an integrated society has involved a major shift in the power balance of the tacit terms of community between black and white. While the ethical ends of justice and equality have been acknowledged by most parties as valid, the question of strategy for the realization of these ends has proved troublesome and divisive. Martin Luther King espoused Christian ethical norms and the strategy of non-violence to gain justice for the Negro, by appealing to the conscience of the white man to concede voluntarily a larger portion of rights to the black man. Since King's assassination, out of frustration at the failure of the white community to grant them civil and economic rights, the advocates of Black Power have pushed hard for more rapid changes, with a readiness to use violence, if need be, to get them. Instead of integration on the white man's terms, Black Power leaders are calling for a new separatism, where the black man can find his true worth by centering on black identity, establishing his own economy and culture, creating a parity of power. Others, more moderate, black and white, would hold for the realization of genuine integration, in public education, in housing, in commerce, to be achieved by the gradual pressure of law without and the appeal within to democratic and Christian principles in the soul of America.

Technological, economic, and racial versions of the problem of power merge closely with politics. Here the issues most pressing are: (1) What is the relevance, if any, of Christian ethical norms to such democratic political traditions and structures as popular sovereignty, or representative government, or the constitutional distribution of power among the various branches and sectors? (2) What inner ethos may keep dissenting freedom and consenting loyalty in creative tension with each other in the body politic and so avoid both tyranny and anarchy, or in other words, how at once to "secure these rights" for the individual and assure the common good? (3) To what extent can the constitutional structures of democracy lend themselves to revolutionary modes for social change? Where must "due process" be set aside to realize radical justice? What, if any, are the Christian guidelines for a revolutionary overturn of power that can give reasonable promise of substituting a better order for the repressive disorder it would overthrow? In the councils of the World Council of Churches, many Christian leaders, particularly those from the Third World, are making the case for a Christian revolutionary strategy, with the use of violence if needed, to redress the imbalance of economic power created and perpetuated by Western colonial powers, the so-called "Christian" nations of the earth.

The final form of the power problem, pervading all these others, is as to the ethics of military might, or physical violence. This has vexed the conscience of Christians since the beginning. There has been no unanimity as to *the* Christian way. Some have made witness to absolute pacifism, others have affirmed the necessity, with St. Augustine, of bearing the sword to secure justice. Others have waged holy war, in crusade for the cause of Christ against the Evil One.

In the contemporary world, the issue has been forced upon Christians in a new form by cultural changes and technology. Historical circumstances have brought the far neighbor near, in the interdependence of nations and peoples with each other, yet put persons at far distance from each other psychologically, in social space, by their treatment as cases of nationality or of a collective, like "the police" or "the Chinese." The weapons of modern warfare have heightened to levels unimaginable in earlier ages man's efficiency in the destruction of life. It is no longer a matter of striking one's neighbor on the cheek or bearing the sword, but of dropping the bomb. The bomb makes more and more obsolete the observance of the rules of justice in warfare. Mechanization of warfare has rendered combatants immune from a personal sense of its brutality. The young bombardier who pulls the bomb-release handle never sees or feels the anguish of death that follows his deed. So, in councils of state and conferences of Christians, there is a close searching of hearts and minds for a Christian ethic of war and peace, suitable to the exigencies of modern international relations and faithful to the will of God revealed in Christ.

To many a devout Christian it may appear that these issues of power are technical and practical matters, whose solution should be left to the experts who know the facts. Christianity, it would seem to them, has to do with faith in God, with prayer and Christ-like devotion, not with tax rates, or restrictive covenants in housing, or ABM systems. The rejoinder to this view is that close beneath the technical data of facts and figures are value questions unanswerable by accumulating more facts, but only answerable by considering and championing the values that make for the welfare of man, that make and keep human life human. These values in turn hang upon the theological questions of faith about the divine-human encounter in history, and how men in the present respond to the action of God. If it be true, even in an oblique way, that public policies are framed and changed by the inner wills of men, as well as vice versa, and that men publicly do as they inwardly pray, then the study of the bearing of Christian ethics upon contemporary culture, desperately seeking its salvation, is all to the good.

Further Readings

Barth, Karl. *Church Dogmatics.* New York: Scribner's, 1949–1962. (Vol. 2, part 2; and Vol. 3, part 4 deal with ethics.)

Bennett, John. *Christian Ethics and Social Policy.* New York: Scribner's, 1946.

———. (ed.). *Christian Social Ethics in a Changing World.* New York: Association Press, 1966.

Bonhoeffer, Dietrich. *The Cost of Discipleship.* New York: Macmillan, 1963.

BRUNNER, EMIL. *The Divine Imperative.* New York: Macmillan, 1937.

GUSTAFSON, JAMES. "Christian Ethics," in PAUL RAMSEY (ed.): *Religion* (Humanistic Scholarship in America: The Princeton Studies.) Englewood Cliffs, N. J.: Prentice-Hall, 1965.

LONG, EDWARD LEROY. *A Survey of Christian Ethics.* New York: Oxford University Press, 1967.

NIEBUHR, REINHOLD. *The Nature and Destiny of Man.* 2 vols. New York: Scribner's, 1941, 1943.

NIEBUHR, RICHARD. *Radical Monotheism and Western Culture.* New York: Harper and Row, 1961.

———. *The Responsible Self.* New York: Harper and Row, 1963.

RAMSEY, PAUL. *Deeds and Rules in Christian Ethics.* New York: Scribner's, 1967.

THOMAS, GEORGE. *Christian Ethics and Moral Philosophy.* New York: Scribner's, 1955.

INDEX